Routledge Readings on Law, Development and Legal Pluralism

Routledge Readings on Law, Development and Legal Pluralism presents some of the finest essays on social justice, environment, rights and governance. With a lucid new Introduction, it covers a vast range of issues and offers a compelling guide to understanding the harm and risk relating to biodiversity, agro-ecology, disaster and forest rights. The book covers critical themes such as ecology, families and governance and establishes the trajectory of contemporary ecology and law in South Asia. The thirteen chapters in the volume, divided into three sections, trace violence and marginality in the plurality of families and their laws in India, as well as discuss community-based just practices. With debates on development, governance and families, the book highlights the politics and practices of law making, law reform and law application. This multidisciplinary volume foregrounds the politics and plural lives of/in law by including perspectives from major authors who have contributed to the academic and/or policy discourse of the subject.

This book will be useful to students, scholars, policymakers and practitioners interested in a nuanced understanding of law, especially those studying law, marginality, kinship and indigeneity studies. It will serve as essential reading for those in law, socio-legal studies, environment studies and ecology, social exclusion studies, development studies, South Asian studies, human rights, jurisprudence and constitutional studies, gender studies, history, politics, conflict and peace studies, sociology and social anthropology. It will also appeal to legal historians and practitioners of law, environmentalists and those in public administration.

Kalpana Kannabiran, is a sociologist and legal scholar, and is Distinguished Professor at the Council for Social Development. Among her book publications are *Tools of Justice: Non-Discrimination and the Indian Constitution* (2012), *Gender Regimes and the Politics of Privacy: A Feminist Re-Reading of Puttaswamy vs. Union of India* (2021), *Law, Justice and Human Rights* *in India: Short Reflections* (2021) and the edited volumes *Violence Studies* (2016) and *Re-Presenting Feminist Methodologies: Interdisciplinary Explorations* (2017). Based in Hyderabad, India, she was formerly Professor and Director at the Council for Social Development, Southern Regional Centre, has taught at NALSAR University of Law, and is co-founder of Asmita Resource Centre for Women. She is a recipient of the VKRV Rao Prize for Social Science Research (2003) and the Amartya Sen Award for Distinguished Social Scientists (2012), both for her work in the field of law.

Routledge Readings

The *Routledge Readings* series brings together a cluster of key readings into a single volume which capture important research directions, policy suggestions, current trends and aspects of history and future trajectories in the humanities and social sciences. The volumes in the series feature the diversity of scholarship by presenting a selection of articles by experts in their fields organized around key themes in academic disciplines and professional fields, including law, politics, international relations, regional studies, sociology and development studies. These will provide a useful resource for a range of subjects in the social sciences and humanities by offering a selection of readings on a variety of issues related to theoretical and applied research. These multidisciplinary readers include important contributions to the respective disciplines, focusing on the key topics encountered by undergraduates, postgraduates and scholars in social sciences and humanities. Each reader contains a detailed general introduction and sections prepared by the volume editor to place the selections in context, illustrate relations among topics, indicate developments, and point readers towards related bibliographic material.

Key Features

- Accessible, reader-friendly volumes containing 12–15 selections on contemporary and classic themes divided into sections.
- A new comprehensive Introduction with relevant sections describing the nature and purpose of the reader while placing the readings in context designed to aid understanding.
- Topical studies that bring together expert analyses and emerging research in the discipline, combining a rich diversity of theoretical approaches and perspectives, analytical strategies, case studies, empirical data and policy suggestions.
- Comprehensive subject guides that will prove invaluable for scholars, researchers, and policymakers.

Routledge Readings on Law and Social Justice
Dispossessions, Marginalities, Rights
Edited by Kalpana Kannabiran

Routledge Readings on Law, Development and Legal Pluralism
Ecology, Families, Governance
Edited by Kalpana Kannabiran

Routledge Readings on Colonial to Contemporary Northeastern India
Customary Practices, Gender and Livelihoods
Edited by Sumi Krishna

Routledge Readings on Security and Governance in Northeastern India
Resource Conflicts, Militarisation and Development
Edited by Sumi Krishna

For more information about this series, please visit:
www.routledge.com/Routledge-Readings/book-series/RRE

Routledge Readings on Law, Development and Legal Pluralism

Ecology, Families, Governance

Edited by
Kalpana Kannabiran

Routledge
Taylor & Francis Group
LONDON AND NEW YORK

First published 2022
by Routledge
4 Park Square, Milton Park, Abingdon, Oxon OX14 4RN

and by Routledge
605 Third Avenue, New York, NY 10158

Routledge is an imprint of the Taylor & Francis Group, an informa business

British Library Cataloguing-in-Publication Data
A catalogue record for this book is available from the British Library

Library of Congress Cataloging-in-Publication Data
A catalog record has been requested for this book

ISBN: 978-1-03-226928-3 (hbk)
ISBN: 978-1-03-229013-3 (pbk)
ISBN: 978-1-00-329956-1 (ebk)

DOI: 10.4324/9781003299561

Typeset in Sabon LT Std
by Newgen Publishing UK

Contents

Contributors

Niharika Bahl is an advocate and independent law researcher based in New Delhi.

Rikil Chyrmang is Assistant Professor in Economics at the Central University of South Bihar, Gaya, Bihar.

Nandita Haksar, is a human rights lawyer and campaigner, and is author of several books and articles on aspects of nationalism and conflicts.

Kalpana Kannabiran, is a feminist sociologist, and Distinguished Professor, Council for Social Development.

Shomona Khanna is an Advocate practicing in the Supreme Court of India and the Delhi High Court, with a focus on the rights of indigenous peoples and forest-dwelling communities.

Bijayalaxmi Nanda is Professor in the Department of Political Science, Miranda House, University of Delhi, and currently the Officiating Principal of the college.

Shalu Nigam is an Advocate currently practicing in the courts in Delhi in India, and is engaged in research on law, governance, and gender issues.

Kamala Sankaran teaches at the Faculty of Law, University of Delhi.

Anjana Singh teaches in the Department of History, Nirmala College, Ranchi University, Jharkhand, and works on the linguistic, cultural, and political movements of Adivasis.

Nitin Sinha is a social historian based at Leibniz Zentrum Moderner Orient, Berlin and is currently heading the ERC consolidator project on the histories of temporal cultures in South Asia.

Deepa Sonpal is a social development researcher and educator.

T. R. Subramanya is Dean, School of Legal Studies, CMR University, Bengaluru.

Patricia Uberoi is a former Professor of Sociology, Institute of Economic Growth, Delhi.

Acknowledgements

The following chapters are reprinted with permission and reproduced from the original works. References have been added as required.

Chapter 1. 'Law, Agro-Ecology and Colonialism in Mid-Gangetic India, 1770s–1910s' by Nitin Sinha (Gunnel Cederlöf and Sanjukta Das Gupta, eds, *Subjects, Citizens and Law: Colonial and Independent India*, Copyright © 2017, Routledge, Chapter 8). Reproduced by permission of Taylor & Francis Group.

Chapter 2. 'Historical wrongs and forest rights: Nascent jurisprudence on FRA and participatory evidence making' by Shomona Khanna (Varsha Bhagat-Ganguly and Sujit Kumar, eds, *India's Scheduled Areas: Untangling Governance, Law and Politics*, Copyright © 2020, Routledge, Chapter 8). Reproduced by permission of Taylor & Francis Group.

Chapter 3. 'Feminist dimension of biodiversity challenges' by Niharika Bahl (Usha Tandon, Mohan Parasaran and Sidharth Luthra, eds, *Biodiversity: Law, Policy and Governance*, Copyright © 2018, Routledge, Chapter 11). Reproduced by permission of Taylor & Francis Group.

Chapter 4. 'An Overview of the Law Governing Hazardous Substances in the Post-Bhopal Era' by T. R. Subramanya (T. R. Subramanya, *Hazardous Substances in India and the World: Legislations, Frameworks and Management*, Copyright © 2021, Routledge, Chapter 5). Reproduced by permission of Taylor & Francis Group.

Chapter 5. 'Disability, disaster and the law: Developing a Mandate for Disability Inclusive Law Making Process for Disaster Risk Reduction' by Deepa Sonpal (Amita Singh, ed., *Disaster Law: Emerging Thresholds*, Copyright © 2018, Routledge, Chapter 15). Reproduced by permission of Taylor & Francis Group.

Chapter 6. 'Family, Work and Matrimonial Property: Implications for Women and Children' by Kamala Sankaran (Archana Parashar and Amita Dhanda, eds, *Redefining Family Law in India*, Copyright © 2009, Routledge, Chapter 10). Reproduced by permission of Taylor & Francis Group.

Chapter 7. 'Sex-selective abortion and reproductive rights: A syncretic feminist approach' by Bijayalaxmi Nanda (Bijayalaxmi Nanda and Nupur Ray, eds, *Discourse on Rights in India: Debates and Dilemmas*, Copyright © 2019, Routledge, Chapter 7). Reproduced by permission of Taylor & Francis Group.

Chapter 8. 'Adjudicating domestic violence in the courts' by Shalu Nigam (Shalu Nigam, *Women and Domestic Violence Law in India: A Quest for Justice*, Copyright © 2020, Routledge, Chapter 6). Reproduced by permission of Taylor & Francis Group.

Chapter 9. 'India' by Kalpana Kannabiran (Mehnaz Afkhami, Yakin Erturk and Ann Elizabeth Mayer, eds, *Feminist Advocacy, Family Law and Violence against Women: International Perspectives*, Copyright © 2019, Routledge, co-published with International Development Research Centre, Chapter 4). Reproduced by permission of Taylor & Francis Group.

Chapter 10. 'Saving Custom or Promoting Incest? Post-Independence Marriage Law and Dravidian Marriage Practices' by Patricia Uberoi (Archana Parashar and Amita Dhanda, eds, *Redefining Family Law in India*, Copyright © 2009, Routledge, Chapter 3). Reproduced by permission of Taylor & Francis Group.

Chapter 11. 'Conflict Resolution Systems in the Tribal Societies of Northeast India: Legal Pluralism and Indian Democracy' by Nandita Haksar (Melvil Pereira, Bitopi Dutta and Binita Kakati, eds, *Legal Pluralism and Indian Democracy: Tribal Conflict Resolution Systems in Northeast India*, Copyright © 2018, Routledge, Chapter 1). Reproduced by permission of Taylor & Francis Group.

Chapter 12. 'Forums for conflict resolution in the Jaintia tribal community over land resources' by Rikil Chyrmang (Melvil Pereira, Bitopi Dutta and Binita Kakati, eds, *Legal Pluralism and Indian Democracy: Tribal Conflict Resolution Systems in Northeast India*, Copyright © 2018, Routledge, Chapter 15). Reproduced by permission of Taylor & Francis Group.

Chapter 13. 'Pathalgadi movement and conflicting ideologies of tribal village governance' by Anjana Singh (Varsha Bhagat-Ganguly and Sujit Kumar, eds, *India's Scheduled Areas: Untangling Governance, Law and*

Politics, Copyright © 2020, Routledge, Chapter 10). Reproduced by permission of Taylor & Francis Group.

~

I thank Rimina Mohapatra for her support and advice in working through this volume and for her comments on the introduction. It has been a pleasure to work with her as always. I am grateful to the contributors for their cooperation despite very tight timelines. V.S. Elizabeth, Ruchira Goswami and Rukmini Sen reviewed the manuscript proposal at very short notice. My sincere thanks to them.

Finally, I express my sincere thanks to the production team for this project at Taylor and Francis and Newgen Knowledge Works Pvt. Ltd. for their deft and reassuring handling of this manuscript.

Introduction

The Sites and Possibilities of Interdisciplinary Law

Kalpana Kannabiran

The two volumes – *Routledge Readings on Law and Social Justice: Dispossessions, Marginalities, Rights* and *Routledge Readings on Law, Development and Legal Pluralism: Ecology, Families, Governance* – explore the possibilities for an interdisciplinary conversation on law. A vast and enduring project, given the pervasiveness and criticality of law in lives and indeed its constitutive role in societies at different levels not limited to formal law, the chapters in this collection contribute to an understanding of different dimensions of law in different locales and historical moments, and follow different analytical trajectories. The common feature (except for the article on COVID-19 in *Routledge Readings on Law and Social Justice*) is that they are all focused on the South Asian region, specifically India. Each of the chapters in these volumes speaks to a particular problem that connects law to social justice, development, and legal pluralism, helping us understand these questions from different disciplinary standpoints. In their diversity and plurality, they make for a scintillating conversation on the subject that is relevant both to a general and a specialist international, interdisciplinary readership for the insights they offer on the field of law, as well as the insights they offer on law's travels in India. The chapters in these two volumes cover conversations around the constitution, gendered precarities – in relation to gender identity, work, migration, trafficking – questions of property, dispossession and emplacement, ecologies, environment and disaster, the family as a site of rights and wrongs, and legal pluralism, which is a running thread in several chapters across both volumes. The chapters also cover different regions and social locations. Bringing them together in these two volumes and placing them in conversation with each other and with other relevant work in interconnected fields, enables us to revisit the expansive possibilities of an ethnographic and historical engagement with law, justice, and the constitution.

In the introduction, my attempt will be twofold: the first section examines how a study of law may be approached, and some of its conceptual fields. This section, common to both volumes, discusses themes that emerge in the chapters even while moving beyond them to cover, skeletally, some significant gaps. The second section, specific to each volume, contextualizes each chapter within a larger reflection in the field, and where necessary, points to recent developments. While this cannot be exhaustive for reasons of space among others, the discussion of chapters opens a window into the fields through which the chapters chart their course.

Section 1: Law, Development, and Social Justice

Representing Justice, Intersectionality, and Interpretive Communities

The Tamil feature film *Jai Bhim* (2021), coming as it did at a moment of ferment in the national discourse in India on the meanings of law – presents a rare coming-together (perhaps not the first) of cinematic and legal representation on Article 21 rights, and indeed of the meanings of 'law', triggering a wide-ranging debate on the relationship between justice, law, constitution, and legal process, that is rooted in the experience of social vulnerability and exclusion. This is the most visible and evident frame of law – arrest, torture, custodial murder, legal defence, legal exceptionalism, violence, and the travels from home to police station to courtroom to prison (and to the gallows) and eventually to theatre in an act of retelling that is popular but not fictional, factual but not documentary. There are several iterations of law in creative writing, cinema, theatre, and other traditions of performance, and the visual arts – that offer interpretations of the relationship between law and justice, or law and insurgency, or law and resistance. The figure of law takes shape through its representation by interpretive communities and interpretive modes. We may consider Mahasweta Devi's *Dopdi* [Bengali, 'Draupadi'] (1978), Vijay Tendulkar's *Shantata! Court Chalu Ahe!* [Marathi, 'Silence! The court is in session!'] (1967), Sivasagar's poetic statement before the court where he stood accused in the Parvathipuram Conspiracy Case in Andhra Pradesh in 1971, *'Kutradaru' Vangmulam* [Statement of a 'Conspirator'], and Aamir Aziz's *Sab Yaad Rakha Jayega* [Everything will be remembered] (2019) – each with its own interpretive communities and grammar and each about 'law' in its plurality – although all these instances focus on the different faces of state impunity in a constitutional democracy. Most importantly *Jai Bhim* is an invocation of B.R. Ambedkar and his constitutional labours – and also signals the large movements, 'cultural labour' (Prakash 2019), and the scholarship he inspired led by Dalits – that put the liberation from caste and untouchability at the centre of a groundbreaking vision of 'constitutional morality' in a country imprisoned by the 'public morality' of caste. It was this vision on which the decriminalization of homosexuality and queer relationships rested in the judgment of the Delhi High Court in *Naz Foundation vs. NCT Delhi* (2009), and several other cases subsequently. Interpretive intersectionality, this case demonstrates, strengthens constitutional and statutory protections against social vulnerability and marginality.

The possibilities for an exploration of law are illimitable, and ever expanding, as societies invent socialities anew, and the spaces and authorities of legal discourse shift and draw in constituencies outside the hitherto known circles of law, its professional spaces, and thereby set up new normative standards and signposts for the emergent and fluid social. This may extend for instance from reimagining the basis of belonging through human–non-human relationships spatially rooted in distinct ecologies (Govindrajan 2018); to reclaiming constitutional socialities through the assertion of non-denominational citizenship (Jayal 2019; Rodrigues 2008) and the annihilation of caste and untouchability (Geetha 2021); to the regulation of technologies and digital spaces, security discourses (in matters of surveillance of different orders, among others) (Arun 2014; Lokaneeta 2020); to a redefinition of intimacy, sexuality, family, property, and state; to the proliferation of the sites and meanings of legal pluralism; and to an assertion of the right to disobedience. Legislation, norms, processes, institutions, and interpretive communities, are all inextricably woven together in the figure of law with the debate on norm, ethics, and (permissible) force, often at the centre. It would be trite to say that the law is never absent from human sociality – it may not be visible and 'in motion', but it is a force that constitutes and mediates (inter) relationships and transactions, often only rendering itself visible at the moment of violation/rupture.

Law is political by definition, and domains of law overlap at times in harmony, and in dissonance at others. The *Telangana Eunuchs Act, 1329 F* (Act No. XVI of 1329 F [1919]), that criminalizes transgender persons through interlocking repressions by the agencies of state seamlessly from colonial to independent Telangana – still a live law suspended but not repealed – exists in contradiction to the interpretive reduction of Section 377, Indian Penal Code (IPC) that decriminalized consensual sexual conduct irrespective of gender identity or sexual preference. The reading down of Section 377 also coexists with the marital rape exception in Section 375, IPC. While intimate relationships that come within the remit of Section 377 are lawful as long as they are consensual, sexual intercourse of a husband with his adult wife in heterosexual marriage does not require the wife's consent in India.

How do we understand the boundaries of a law? What are its constituents? While the penal code is a law of crimes, each section is a law that defines a distinct crime, has distinct protocols for recognition and procedure – in which consent and *mens rea* play critical roles, and each has distinct spaces of occurrence. These distinct laws within the law may, as in the instance cited above, contradict one another, dispelling any presumption of overall coherence of the law as a single, unitary system that is monologic and monolingual in character. This is an aspect we will return to.

States of Exception, Lawfare, and Self-Determination

There could be 'good' or 'enabling' or 'protective' legislation, or 'bad' or 'harmful' or 'repressive' law as the foregoing demonstrates – but these are deeply contested descriptions contingent on the interpretive communities evaluating the effects of particular laws on particular peoples living in particular locations. The spatiotemporal and cultural effects of law are material to its reception or evaluation on a scale of ethics. The *Citizenship Amendment Act, 2019* (CAA), is a law that foregrounds the contentious debates on citizenship under the constitution and the question of *birthright*. As we witnessed with the struggles of Muslims, especially Muslim women in India in 2019, the assertion of birthright is about lived experience providing the basis for claims to citizenship – through collective assertions of disobedience if necessary. The assertion, the claim, and the disobedience are all matters of law, each of which follow different trajectories through history. V. Geetha traces the plural approaches B.R. Ambedkar adopted in asserting the illegality of untouchability and the Hindu caste order – mobilizing temple entry, moving the court on access to public water sources, demanding separate electorates, reservations, the constitutional ban on untouchability, and his announcement of his intention to move the UN on the untouchability complex in India, for instance – all of these drawing on the assertion of self-determination (Geetha 2021). On another register, his enunciation of caste predicated on women's subjugation, drew on the illegalities of sati, enforced widowhood, and the age of consent (child marriage) (Ambedkar [1917] 2002).

Not limited to national sovereignty, self-determination expresses itself in plural realms of law – plural lawscapes – yielding different questions of (il)legality: if the Dalit question is one, autonomy for scheduled areas is another, autonomy for Jammu and Kashmir (Article 370 of the Indian Constitution – abrogated in 2019) yet another. The question of autonomy and dignity in intimate relationships, and for persons with disabilities throws up further questions on the complex interplay of law, justice, and force/coercion.

Adivasi and tribal communities have reinvented ideas of sovereignty drawing on Jaipal Singh Munda's ideas, expressed through the declaration of self-rule: *maava nate maava raaj* [our land, our rule]. The centrality of justice as spatial comes through most forcefully in adivasi politics which is often thrown into crisis owing to the conflict of laws: on the one hand the network of protections deriving from Schedules V and VI of the Indian constitution: *Panchayat (Extension to Scheduled Areas) Act, 1996*, the various land transfer prohibition acts in various states that prevent transfer of land to non-tribals, and *Scheduled Tribes And Other Traditional Forest Dwellers (Recognition Of Forest Rights) Act, 2006*; and on the other the *Wildlife Protection Act, 1972* that is *interpreted* by a section of environmentalists and judicial functionaries as a human–non-human conflict, which may only be resolved by evicting forest dwellers from the forest, as we witness in ongoing litigation in the Supreme Court of India.[1]

The question of self-determination and sovereignty also leads us into the realms of international law and the writing on global justice – but importantly, the interpretation of domestic state action and corporate responsibility in terms of the standards of international law read with constitutional guarantees. Lawfare is a term that has been used to describe the use of law as a weapon of war, i.e., 'the use of law, or exploitation of aspects of a legal system, to achieve tactical or strategic advantages in the context of conflict' (Craig 2019). While war is one context in which this poses a concern, its long shadow in militarized state action in regions of internal conflict (whether or not this is officially named as 'conflict') poses an enduring challenge to human rights and constitutionalism, as we see in the case of *The Armed Forces (Special Powers) Act, 1958* in the North Eastern Region and in Kashmir. The consequences on everyday lives, the precarity specific to the interlocked contexts of militarization and militancy, and the absence of effective legal redress or political resolution are serious and well documented in the literature on human rights and civil liberties in India and internationally – not to speak of the steady legal challenge mounted by the people of these regions in the constitutional courts in the country.

Turning the gaze within, Hoffmann speaks of 'anti-corruption lawfare' in Brazil, which was represented as 'a necessary reassertion of the rule of law in the face of a political system gone entirely overboard'. What it could not mask was the conflict between a 'developmentalist and welfarist path' followed by the political system in power, and the priorities of the market and its representatives for whom these 'modes of governance [were] no longer deemed "good" enough' (Hoffmann 2021, p. 236).[2] The problem presents itself in an inversion in India where the notification of the Finance Ministry (Finance notification number S.O. 3407(E)), ostensibly to put an end to corruption, has been widely held to be unconstitutional and illegal for its manifest disregard of the provisions of the *Reserve Bank of India Act, 1934* and the *Banking Regulation Act, 1949*, in declaring restrictions on deposits and withdrawals, and discriminating between holders and non-holders of bank accounts (Wahi 2016). This manifestation of anti-corruption law (by executive fiat) takes the form of legal exceptionalism – another face of the law, that we may encounter in very many different locales in relation to arbitrary state action.

Vernacularization, Demosprudence, and Justice Claims

The terms 'Lava Jato' ('car wash' used in Brazil) and 'Notebandi' ('note ban' used in India) take us to the heart of the 'vernacularization' of law in a starkly different context, not ordinarily associated with the term. Sally Merry uses the term 'vernacularization' to refer to 'the way an idea or norm is redefined and represented in a way that is more or less compatible with the existing social world. This does not mean its meaning is changed entirely (although it may be altered), but rather to the altered mode of presentation' and describes for instance the translation of global human rights standards into local, culturally rooted discourses on human rights (Merry 2018, p. viii; see also Madhok 2021), and more generally to speak to legal pluralism (Merry 1988). V. Geetha speaks of the ways in which B.R. Ambedkar '"vernacularized" political concepts, terms of analysis and argument, and even descriptions, by bringing them within the ambit of experiences and histories which defamiliarized them and demanded their reconstitution' (Geetha 2021, p. 3) – particularly in developing a multi layered discourse on the rights of Dalits. The documentation of testimonies and evidence of the Champaran indigo peasants by Gandhi and his team of lawyers in 1917 is yet another stellar precursor to the radical edge of vernacularization (Amin et al. 2022). Speaking of Gandhi, Narendra Chapalgaonkar (2022), reflecting on the Gandhian constitution of Aundh provides us with possible pathways to think through the interweaving of constitutions within plural legal spaces.

The process of vernacularization is dynamic and dialogic, rendering 'the law' intelligible and malleable in the popular imagination. The farmer's struggle against the Farm Laws enacted in 2019 and repealed in 2021, presented an important aspect of vernacularization of law and its sites. The challenge to the state/parliament, which exercises the prerogative of enactments of law from the borders of the national capital, literally and metaphorically demonstrated the power of the enactment of the vernacular through public, cascading protest as witnessed in the unconditional repeal (also a law) of a set of unlawful laws, forced on the government by the protestors.

The farmers' movement also presents a classic case of 'demosprudence', illustrating how social movements may make legal change possible and opens out a new frame of legal pluralism:

> The texts of their stories were written with the ink of consummate courage by a mobilized community that actively represented itself. These social movement actors changed the background against which questions of legality and justice were understood. They marched. They sang. They declaimed in their unschooled voices. They changed the wind. And in the process, they transformed the "thin paper" of democracy to the "thick action" of government of, by, and for the people.
>
> (Guinier and Torres 2014, p. 2804)

The anti-CAA protests presented a different set of political possibilities of vernacularization of law in the public – plurilingual performance of the

Constitution of India, notably the Preamble – rupturing in the process the monolingual and monologic monopoly of the constitution enclosed in courts. Language, words, and speech – plurilingual practices – are constitutive of law.

Rather than see 'law' as a singular, abstract entity therefore, the discussion on illegalities of law, lawless laws, and law's violence – especially evident in, but not limited to criminal law and property – is immediately relevant to an understanding of 'the law', the abstract fading before (or deriving from) the concrete, everyday lives of law and practices of interpretation by courts (Cover 1986). Pratiksha Baxi's ethnography of rape trials illustrates this through a mapping of the ways in which 'the culture of a courtroom alters the very meaning of rape from the point of view of the woman or child' (Baxi 2014, p. xxix). From 'challenging the commonplace idea that talking about rape is indecent or immoral' to contesting the framing of the ethnographic project as 'courageous', she observes pertinently that '[t]he framing of the research as shameful or courageous … is complicit in the public secrecy of rape' (Baxi 2017, p. 183).

Ecologies of Justice and Belonging

Indeed, 'place matters' (Kapur 2022) with respect to law, generally. Digital and virtual worlds are governed by different ideas of space – their circulation 'in space' is material to their possibilities and their effects. On the ground, the railway line not only ferries passengers to destinations, but threads them along the way to places rendered legible by particular artefacts, artisanry, cuisine, vegetables, fruit, and grain – and indeed by particular ecological attributes (especially river/tributary) that connected people to their deepest prayers. Environmental degradation and the dismantling of traditional livelihoods therefore have specific implications for justice, survival with dignity, and enactments of belonging that are both material and non-material and embedded in ideas of place.

Place matters in other realms of law that have been discussed here as well – the emplacement of people, prisons, courts, habitations, and publics fuels the journeys of law from enactment through process to consequence – 'spatial justice' (Philippopoulos-Mihalopoulos 2015) is essential to a comprehension of the complex relationship between law and justice. The significance of 'place' is luminously present in debates on global justice. Möller's model for global constitutional law, for instance, does not assert that the principles must be accepted by all jurisdictions, but rather that it draws on principles enunciated across different regions that can travel across jurisdictions, and thus have a global appeal (Möller 2012, p. 15). The law is mobile. Sen's theory of justice examines the possibilities of developing a non-parochial global theory that draws on philosophical traditions across culture, region and time, forms of democracy, public reasoning, institutions, and historical-empirical evidence (Sen 2009). The argument offered by Upendra Baxi that Gandhi's practice of politics 'may be traced to a multicultural tradition of human rights that resulted decades later in the maturation of *jus cogens* of international law', which delegitimated Enlightenment legacy in unprecedented ways (Baxi 2002, p. 27), is compelling in its insurgent narration of the role of Southern anti-colonial resistance in the development of international law.

Development, ecology, environment, and disaster are critical concerns today in society and in law. This is also one of the most contested sites of law and policy (see Divan and Rosencranz 2001 for a comprehensive overview). Elaborating on the growing conflict over natural resources in the country, Anil Agarwal uses the term 'ecological refugees' to refer to the large sections of the poor displaced by dams, mines, deforestation, floods, droughts, and urban expansion, and suggests that it is the dependence on the 'Gross Nature Product' that helps ecological refugees survive adversity – natural and development-induced (Divan and Rosencranz 2001, p. 15). 'The Anthropocene' observes Upendra Baxi, 'signals the narrative of continuing anthropogenic harm manifest in common experience as global warming and climate change but signifies wider changes in the planetary system' (Baxi 2019; see also Robinson 2018). While there are disagreements on models of measurement, Baxi points out that the reality of anthropogenic harm remains uncontested and impacts adversely the 'human rights to a legitimate aspiration for green futures'. The exercise of biopower, 'sovereignty', and surveillance through authoritarian environmentalism evident in the politics of denialism, and its implications for lives, futures, and politics, Baxi urges, calls for urgent rethinking of the meanings of freedom and unfreedom under the constitution. 'Climate justice', 'climate witnesses', 'climate hearings' (Robinson 2018), and 'climate refugees' (Tokar 2019, p. 14) inaugurate new languages of law, justice, and geographies of injustice – transforming our understanding of the global in relation to local, and the place of the human in relation to the larger environment.

Radhika Govindrajan opens out to view the entanglements, dense, affective kinships, ethics, and biopower that are enacted in the everyday lives of animals – human and non-human – in intensely fraught environments. In her words, 'the "village" ... does not represent a self-contained, pristine Arcadia outside time and space' (Govindrajan 2018, p. 12). In looking at environment, ecology, forests, biodiversity, and related questions therefore, Govindrajan's work helps us grasp the importance of reckoning with the complex 'storied experiences' and histories of human and non-human persons – of doing multispecies ethnography in a way that 'extends subjectivity to nonhuman animals and approaches them as persons whose inner lives and affective states are critically shaped by the experience of life in a world they inhabit in relation to a host of others'. Importantly, for our present purposes, how is the 'we' constituted in particular cohabitational contexts, and how might this help us understand the assemblages of multispecies persons at different moments? (Govindrajan 2018, p. 20). This is a particularly compelling question if we examine anthropomorphic narrations of environmental history, for instance, despite the 'presence' of multiple species in the evidence humans have left behind – literary, textual, archaeological, architectural (see also Rangarajan and Sivaramakrishnan 2015; Morrison 2015).

At a time when we witness a surge in religious nationalism challenged by agonistic assertions of citizenship, Cederlöf and Sivaramakrishnan ask critical questions of the histories of 'entanglement of nature devotion and nationalist aspirations' that offer a site for the enactment of 'sovereignty, self-determination, and placebased collective identities' (Cederlöf and Sivaramakrishnan 2005, p. 3). They use the concept of 'ecological nationalism' to refer to 'a condition where both cosmopolitan and nativist versions of nature devotion converge and express themselves as a form of nationpride in order to become part of processes legitimizing and consolidating a nation', which 'links cultural and political aspirations with programs of nature conservation or environmental protection, while noting their expression in, and through, a rhetoric of rights that include civil, human, and intellectual property rights' (Cederlöf and Sivaramakrishnan 2005, p. 6).

The debates on the commons (Hess and Ostrom 2007, among others) and its contestations (see Bardhan and Ray 2008) guide us in our attempt to mobilize it for a radical departure in our quest for justice.

Technology, Development, and Social Justice

> Our decision must address the dialogue between technology and power. The decision will analyse the extent to which technology has reconfigured the role of the state and has the potential to reset the lines which mark off nofly zones: areas where the sanctity of the individual is inviolable. Our path will define our commitment to limited government. Technology confronts the future of freedom itself.
>
> (Justice D.Y. Chandrachud, *Aadhar* (Dissenting Judgment) 2019, para 3)

Concerns around gender, caste, community, class, region, ethnicity, citizenship status, emplacement, sovereignty, technology, among others, fuel precarity along several intersecting axes. Social justice is a term that evokes specific experiences of precarity, marginality, and dispossession – each a concern of laws (domestic and international), and the constitution, especially Part IV, the Directive Principles of State Policy (see Baxi 1969).

The COVID-19 pandemic has set in motion questions ranging from public health to technologies of care, treatment, and surveillance (not limited to medical surveillance), to carceral governance and dignity in death. Law is implicated at every stage at each level. Surveillance and the erosion of privacy are fuelled anew at each moment with renewed force.

The relationship between law and technology is critical to an understanding of social justice, indeed of citizenship itself. Recent writing deliberates on the ways in which technology serves as a medium for the enforcement of law's coercive power.[3] While the modalities of this exercise of power differ with social location and bodies, escalating along the scale from 'normal' (able bodied, heterosexual, cis-male, majoritarian) to 'different' (non binary, queer, disabled, female, minority, transgender), the gaze of 'law' merits intensive decoding. This section begins with an excerpt from the single judicial dissent on Aadhar, which suddenly catapulted the debate on technology and law to the centre of national debate, although this debate has a longer and more complex provenance. Arun Sukumar traces a history of the role of political machinations in shaping the public understanding of technology in independent India (Sukumar 2019, pp. 3–4): 'Malviya and Visvesvaraya were the intellectual progenitors of a school of thought, alive and well in India today, that argued technology would inevitably improve the citizen's way of life' and would 'lead us to progress, and eventually, God'. While the rhetorical preoccupations followed a trajectory of their own, through successive regimes, the political journeys of technological advance and failure were mixed – and inextricably connected with law, policy, the state, and statutory bodies for scientific and technological research. Digital technologies and biometrics have escalated the people–technology–state relationship to a new high.

Of the themes most relevant to the present discussion, the debate on surveillance brings together the debates around the law on Aadhar, criminal investigation, medical surveillance, and most recently the convergence of various surveillant modes during COVID-19. The question of surveillance also brings to the fore debates on the fundamental right to privacy (see Kannabiran and Ballakrishnen 2021). In relation to the law on privacy protection, India ranks among the lowest – the factors on which the ranking was arrived at included border surveillance, the lack of a comprehensive data protection bill, the country's attempts to make instant messaging platforms such as WhatsApp traceable through a digital footprint, and CCTV regulations without clear evidentiary safeguards (see Arun 2019).[4] The scholarship on Surveillance Studies and Feminist Surveillance Studies, as also Feminist Science and Technology Studies helps us grapple with the complex relationship between surveillance, gendered bodies, and law – the fact of surveillance itself connotes the marking of territory and bodies by law and their 'regulation' at the cost of privacy and personal liberty (see Smith 2015). Chinmayi Arun (2014), argues that mass surveillance signals the state's shift towards an 'unfettered large-scale monitoring of communication' even while there is a constitutional framework for the protection of individual autonomy and dignity that is purportedly operative in a democracy amidst a constitutional framework that has been lax about adequately protecting individual dignity and democracy. Viewed in relation to the framework of international human rights norms, Arun (2014, pp. 111–12) draws attention to the leap from targeted surveillance[5] to mass surveillance.

The technology–law–society–coercive state complex also figures in the Supreme Court's reference to 'forced sterilization' and 'compulsory drug trials of non-consenting men or women' as a violation of the fundamental right to privacy by infringing on the 'liberty of procreation' (*Puttaswamy* 2017, para 271). Reproductive autonomy and reproductive justice have historically been central to an understanding of technological regulation of the social. The question of reproductive justice and law is about more than exercising autonomy and choice. Aziza Ahmed's (2020) research points to the use of forensic science from the mid-1800s to attribute criminality to women whose pregnancies had resulted in still births or late miscarriages – with legal consequences visited on such women. While on the subject of reproductive autonomy and informed consent Anita Ghai and Rachana Johri speaking from a disability rights perspective (2014, p. 243) raise the pertinent point in relation to the *Pre-Conception and Pre-Natal Diagnostic Testing Act (PCPNDT Act)* that arguments on foetal selection must be 'located within discussions of hegemonies of gender, normalcy and normativity, be it male sex or absence of disability'. The terms 'stratified reproduction' (Rapp 1999, p. 311) or the 'reproductive caste system' (Roberts 2015, p. 169) describe what Roberts calls 'reproductive dystopias' – processes of 'social sorting' whereby old inequalities and hierarchies are overlaid with new ones, all deeply patriarchal (Lyon et al. 2012, p. 3) – and yet validated by law. Shoshana Zuboff's work (2019) on the perils of the new digital regime that dispenses with human consent and is a new lethal mutant form of capitalism, bears reiteration, not the least because we presume informed consent in our understanding of the power of law and resist the negation of such consent – the reason why the 'legality' of marital rape is seen by rights advocates the world over as a travesty of the constitution and of basic human rights standards.

On the restricted exploration of law and technology in India, Thayyil, reviewing writing in the field, points out that there has been an implicit equation of law and technology with Information and Communications Technologies (ICT) law and Intellectual Property Rights (IPR) law, when in fact it spreads across all branches of law, from criminal law to environment to bioethics and more (Thayyil 2015, p. 5). He argues that this reductive treatment of the field – the 'technocratic cage for imagining the law' – 'impoverishes any promise of understanding the implications of the impact of deployment of technologies in the democratisation of Indian society' (Thayyil 2015, p. 11). Yet, even a 'signature' aspect of law and technology as conceived so far, viz., IPR, is in fact a network of vast and plural regimes of ownership claims, regulatory practices, and claims of 'knowledge as property' as Rajshree Chandra (2010) and Prashant Reddy and Sumathi Chandrashekaran (2017) demonstrate. Chandra, situating IPRs within rights discourse and within larger debates about 'human rights, distributional equalities, and social justice' (Chandra 2010, p. xviii), poses fundamental questions that interrogate the basis of juridification of rights – especially in this instance, IPR, which, far from being a 'monolithic concept,' is in fact 'an umbrella term for various legal entitlements which attach to certain types of information, ideas, or other intangibles in their expressed form' (Chandra 2010, p. xvi): 'Does intellectual labour comprise property? Can rights be morally claimed for Intellectual Property?' (Chandra 2010, p. xxi). Reddy and Chandrashekaran take us through the fields of IPR ranging from pharmaceuticals, agricultural products, and internet search engines to religious symbols, gods, gurus, and yoga; from trademark and copyright to geographical indications (GI) and more – the meanderings of law in this unnavigably diverse terrain and its travels within and across borders of all orders and 'courts' of different jurisdictions. These discussions further illuminate our understanding of the lives of law and its interweaving with human claims to rights (individual and group), dignity, ownership (collective and exclusive), authorship and protection from dispossessions, abuse, blasphemy, obscenity, and theft.

The next section discusses briefly the chapters in this volume and related writing.

Section 2: Ecology, Families, Legal Pluralism

Questions of Justice: Environment, Ecology, and Disaster

Upendra Baxi (1979) encapsulates the theme of this volume by looking at the interconnections between pluralism (people's law), development, and justice. He urges us to begin with questions – development for whom, of what, through what, from whom? (Baxi 1979, p. 97). It is only if this is settled, that we may begin to contemplate on the ways in which law may be situated in this debate – not merely as a technological artifice, but as a constantly changing and evolving aspect of culture, fashioned in plural ways in a plural society (1979, p. 99). The challenge is to make a shift away from a technocratic approach to law and development and towards a 'new consciousness' that attempts 'to relate "people's" law to "state" law' (Baxi 1979, p. 102).

Mapping the formation of the environmental subject from colonial to contemporary India, Anil Agrawal proposes the concept of 'environmentality' by which he 'refers to the knowledges, politics, institutions, and subjectivities that come to be linked together with the emergence of the environment as a domain that requires regulation and protection' (Agrawal 2005, p. 216) and takes us to the heart of the conceptualization of environmental legal history – especially the embeddedness of a plurality of ideas of legalities within environmentality. The marking of territories and boundaries of villages and forests; the separation by the state of access to subsistence produce and the barricading of resources for commerce; the distribution of power between the state authority on the one hand and local elite and common villagers (forest councils for instance) on the other *in the matter of regulation*; the distinctiveness of the local councils in protocols and processes (Agrawal 2005, p. 125); all these point to the workings of legal pluralism in unexpected ways. Particularly instructive in this regard is Agrawal's observation that unlike the forest department,

> regulatory communities operate at a finer level of social interaction. They deploy a more precise set of instruments, which can be elaborated and calibrated with much greater detail. These instruments help make visible much that is hidden from the official eye of the state and transform residents' views about ecological practice.
>
> (Agrawal 2005, p. 132)

There is a wide-ranging scholarship on environment and ecology that is rich in detail and insights. It is of interest here to look for the figures of the law in this scholarship and plot its plurality (of jurisdiction, method, and purpose) for a better understanding of what we refer to as the field of environment and law, not limiting the scope of the field to boundaries inscribed by formal law alone. The boundaries of formal law too, in a sense are malleable. As Sivaramakrishnan points out, 'the social and cultural space of statemaking takes place on a common ground shaped by bureaucratic practice and popular attitudes', with innovative bureaucrats and the people invoking 'their tactical power within determinate settings offered by structural power' (Sivaramakrishnan 1999, p. 9).[6] Alongside following the trails of law in forest governance as a way of understanding environmental legal history, how might an 'amplification of non-human voices' historically contribute to a more nuanced understanding of the light and shadow plays of law – to adapt from Kathleen Morrison's account of the use of *proxy records* in environment historiography (Morrison 2015, p. 43).

Fluvial Landscapes and Fluid Lawscapes

Nitin Sinha's (Chapter 1) account of law and agro-ecology in the historical context of *diaras* in Bihar, contains several very illuminating insights for our understanding of law in practice – in relation to 'ecological fluidity', but also in relation to the land question generally. He brings together the concerns of spatial justice in fluvial landscapes, where boundaries between land and water do not lend themselves easily to bureaucratic inscription; where the relationship between codified and customary law, in an important sense, was also the ground of tension between 'statist' prerogatives and the inscrutability of 'local knowledge'; and where the interplay between rights in land, ownership, and occupancy provided the contours of claims to justice. Far from being 'an abstract institution of rule', the twists and turns of the law both in its making and in its application – its negotiations and settlements – was demonstration in the everyday of the reconciliations the state was forced to make in terms of governance and policy in specific ecological landscapes. This includes the 'siting' of the mobile 'court' in these landscapes. This then – the 'messiness' between fluid landscapes and legal standardization – serves as a metaphor of legal pluralism that we examine in a separate section.

Tribal peoples, adivasis, and forest dwellers live in different states and union territories in India and are spread across the country. Their social, cultural, religious, political, and economic conditions as well as their local knowledge distinguish them from other citizens; their customs, traditions, and livelihoods may differ to varying degrees from other citizens; as far as tribes are concerned, the criteria for the identification of tribes may include but are not restricted to: distinctive lifestyles, customs, livelihood practices, habitations and habitats, culture including language, dialect, and sacral practices. Because of their distance from communities unlike their own, such tribes and forest dwelling communities are particularly vulnerable to exploitation and stereotyping in situations of contact with the world outside theirs, although this contact may historically be frequent and routine. Their status, autonomy, rights, and entitlements are affirmed by the Constitution of India, and by special legislations, importantly the *Scheduled Tribes and Other Traditional Forest Dwellers (Recognition of Forest Rights) Act, 2006*.

Despite constitutional guarantees, protective legislation, and earmarked budgets as well as policy initiatives for over seven decades, tribal and forest peoples (hereafter ST and OTFD) in the constitutional era in India have faced chronic and escalating immiserization and have been pushed to the margins of vulnerability. This vulnerability is the cumulative consequence of centuries of historical injustice, and regimes of oppression and dispossession against STs and OTFDs. Tribal and forest communities have witnessed their habitats and homelands fragmented, their cultures disrupted and disturbed through predatory tourism, forced evictions, disruption of silvicultural practices through policies of state enclosure of forests, and their communities shattered and impoverished. Displacement from the forests and resettlement in peri-urban and urban areas turn them from collective owners of common forest resources to individual wage earners in the urban agglomerates with uncertain futures and threatened existence.

Examining the rights of forest dwelling communities and the long history of their subjugation and exploitation, Shomona Khanna (Chapter 2) examines the complex constitutional and statutory framework that guarantees right to life, liberty, freedom, and dignity to forest dwellers in India. Importantly, she draws on litigation to map the shifts in Adivasi participation in court processes and the gathering of 'evidence' to strengthen their claims in legal proceedings. The account of this process demonstrates yet again that legal pluralism may be located at several points on the continuum of legal process, with the law as it unfolds making new meaning as it winds its way to a final resolution. The journey of the law is constitutive of an understanding of justice for claimants, even while concerns of state abandonment and coercion remain.

Carolyn Finney's interrogation of the racial basis of environmentalism in the US, and her exploration of an environmental justice movement led by African Americans (Finney 2014), has resonated in India with Abhay Xaxa's powerful critique of 'Brahmanical environmentalism' (2019) evident in the Supreme Court ordering the eviction of forest dwellers en masse. Ambika Ayyadurai and Prashant Ingole (2021) argue that '[p]reservation of resources, protection of species, setting up of protected areas and campaigns for environment often do not acknowledge the role of as well as impact of these initiatives on the marginalised' in a society graded and segregated by caste. In looking at the relationship between law and environment therefore, the intersectional lens of caste, community, tribe, and gender is critical.

Feminist Environmentalism

> Can you tell me, we women being mothers, what kind of future we are giving to our children? Are we not passing on our past as their future? Have we undertaken these innumerable treks to do just that?
>
> (Santhal woman to anthropologist Narayan Banerjee, 1982. Quoted in Mazumdar 2016, p. 179)

The fraught nature of women's relationship to forests and ecology has been foregrounded by feminist environmentalists, whose work has also pointed to the plural engagements women have historically had with land and nature, that are reflected in the present in the active participation of women in the forest rights movement for instance (see Ramdas 2014).

Bina Agarwal in an early essay sets out the signposts of 'feminist environmentalism' succinctly: women's and men's relationship with nature cannot be understood apart from their material reality and their specific relationships with the environment on a daily basis. The stratified and graded distribution of access to resources, property, and graded division of labour and power (both gendered) would therefore shape the relationship with the environment and be shaped by it (Agarwal 1992, p. 126; see also Omvedt 1987 and Baviskar 1997). Maria Mies and Vandana Shiva, in delineating the field of ecofeminism, mark the 'common ground for women's liberation and the preservation of life on earth', which, in their view is to be found in the resistance of women who have suffered the harms of the development process (Mies and Shiva 2014, p. 12) – Chipko, Narmada, and other mega dams, the struggles against mining in scheduled areas, Niyamgiri, for instance. In terms of thinking about the forest, Shiva disentangles different ways of imagining and being with the forest – 'life enhancing' as we witness with forest dwellers' relationships and 'life destroying' as evident from statist approaches to the forest through the prism of commercial extraction and maximization of revenues (Shiva 2014, p. 135). Each of these questions is intimately connected to the lives of law in relation to ecology and environment. As Madhu Sarin points out in another context, resistance to exclusionary forest governance policy by the state in Uttarakhand led to women protestors being summoned to courts; questions of security in the forest importantly focused on the insecurity of women on a daily basis as they went about their chores in the presence of armed forest guards, as the Kumaon Grievances Committee set up by the administration found (Sarin 2001, p. 345). In collective efforts at self-governance, the formation of community institutions such as the lath panchayats, van samitis (informal forest committees) (Sarin 2001, p. 349), and similar locally constituted bodies point to ways in which sites of legal pluralism abound in almost every area in which formal law operates, often, but not always, as ameliorative spaces that wrest a small measure of autonomy from the state. Niharika Bahl (Chapter 3) takes a close look at feminism and biodiversity in different parts of India bringing together voices from movements with the challenges before legal regimes on environment, ecology, and biodiversity.

Bhopal Catastrophe

The Bhopal catastrophe of 1984, to use Upendra Baxi's description, takes us back to the questions raised earlier in this introduction – the intertwined lives of humans and all sentient beings, unequal before law in a system of graded privileges and rights. While the gas leak in the Union Carbide factory in Bhopal in December 1984 is widely described as a disaster, and resulted in a series of regulatory measures with respect to hazardous substances, as T.R. Subramanya (Chapter 4) discusses in this volume, it is important to dwell on the catastrophe and its afterlives, in terms of its implications for our understanding of the intersectional realities of human rights and environment. A detailed review of the cascading interdisciplinary writing on Bhopal over close to four decades, while extremely important, is outside the scope of this present chapter. Some questions however are compelling from the standpoint of environmental justice as human rights. Baxi proposes an illuminating classification of the legal action in the context of mass disasters and catastrophes into 'legalization' and 'juridicalization': legalization refers to the 'ways in which in which legislative and judicial remedies are fashioned to assure justice according to the law to the victims of "mass torts", where the numbers of people, as well as injuries they suffer, remain indeterminate'; and 'juridicalization' points to 'ways in which the communities of suffering human beings and peoples in resistance reinvent responsive law and jurisprudence towards a more emancipatory and dialogical openness of adjudicatory and legislative power' (Baxi 2010, p. 29). The possibilities of the latter are evident in the cases the victims' families and survivors brought to court. Although '[c]onventional approaches suggest that tort law remedies are private, not public, law remedies', he says, 'the Bhopal juristic innovations transcend these limits, relating tort law to human rights and environmental violations' (Baxi 2010, p. 37). Although this might not end suffering, it signals resistance and not passive acquiescence to impunity.

That the risk, harm, and suffering imposed by disasters spread unequally along a scale of vulnerability is evident from Deepa Sonpal's chapter (Chapter 5) on disaster and disability. She proposes the development of national frameworks for disaster risk reduction from a disability rights perspective.

Families in Law

The dispersion of the family in law across several sites presents rich possibilities for a renewed examination of the meanings of 'the family' in law. Brought into focus through discourses on women's rights – starting with Tarabai Shinde and the early debates on age of consent – family law has remained largely confined to the domains of inheritance and gender-based rights within families and heterosexual marriage. The family is a preconfigured space, the boundaries of which determine the circulation of concerns (of morality, the public good, custom, justice, for instance), campaigns, and litigation. This renders the actual constitution of 'the family' in the public imaginary and in law (folded together) opaque and beyond interrogation, ceaselessly reproduced in successive generations, notwithstanding seismic changes in the legalities of biology, kinship imaginaries, graded and striated socialities, plural intimacies (see Kannabiran 2017). For the present, however, we examine families in law specifically in relation to rights of women in heterosexual marriage – to property, against violence, to reproductive rights, and justice, in relation to custom. This is an old and well-worn theme, yet persistent, encrusted, and resistant to change, despite significant victories in law and campaigns for reform.

Ambedkar and Hindu Kinship

It is useful to begin with the slogan 'the personal is the political', but approach it through a different route. The chapters in this section speak to issues of property, domestic violence, the appropriation of reproduction, practices of exogamy and endogamy – predominantly with respect to Hindu society. It is exactly this constellation of concerns that B.R. Ambedkar identifies as lying at the root of the caste order, powering caste supremacy (Ambedkar [1917] 2002). He traces the conflictual development of kinship rules in Hindu society where the elaborate and exacting rules of exogamy (*sapindas* and *sagotras*) are encased in prescriptions of caste endogamy, creating a social crisis in the numerical parity of marriage partners which is then resolved through three 'uxorial practices' – sati, enforced widowhood, and child marriage. This '*superimposition of endogamy on exogamy means the creation of caste*', he famously declared (Ibid., p. 246, emphasis in original).

We live under neoliberal Hindutva. This interlocked regime oversees the consolidation of a (Hindu) nationalist state through the folding together of state and non-state actors enforcing religious and caste endogamy ('love jihad' and delegated surveillance of intimacies), forced conversions ('ghar wapsi'), and narrowly prescriptive ideologies of religious nationalism (intolerance of 'anti-nationals'), for instance. We return again to B.R. Ambedkar's wisdom and his early, prescient articulation of the deathly coils of supremacist ideologies – Hindu, caste in the case of India – in family spaces and relationships. Every one of these sites of enforcement sits deep in the belly of family law. We will return to this question of kinship he raises and its wider implications at the end of this section.

Chirashree Dasgupta, in her discussion of social reproduction also underscores the connection Ambedkar makes between kinship and caste, going on to observe that the control of women's bodies and sexuality through kinship systems ensures the appropriation of their labour and their absorption into unpaid work for social reproduction (Dasgupta 2020, p. 32). Legislative and constitutional changes in matters of property rights, she demonstrates, contributes significantly to social reproduction through the extraction of surplus value (Dasgupta 2020, p. 31; see also Jaivir Singh ([2004] 2012). Property regimes, whether with reference to zamindari abolition and land reforms, land acquisition, redistribution of land or the regulation of the commons are nested in the unit of the family, unevenly dispersed across gender lines and segregated along intersecting lines of community, caste and class. Bina Agarwal's work in mapping women's land rights is monumental (Agarwal 1994). Dasgupta's work on tax regimes looks at the legal recognition of the Hindu undivided family (HUF) as an independent, legal tax entity that benefits the wealthy propertied class of Hindus, evidently savarna – not defined as such in tax laws, but defined in the first instance in Hindu personal law through its codification in 1955–56 and subsequently imported into the *Income Tax Act, 1961* in Section 2 (Dasgupta 2013). Research on 'devadasi reform' in colonial Madras showed that on the crucial question of inheritance and ownership of property, the court decided in a series of cases that

> [i]f a woman of this community elected to marry, her rights to inheritance would be in conformity with the ordinary Hindu law and subject to the disability of the ordinary Hindu woman to take absolute estate. This would also apply to women who married and 'lapsed' into their traditional calling later, as regards property they held while they were part of the ordinary Hindu family. Where the case was one of inheritance by dasi descendants of dasis, judgments were governed by the general principle that daughters inherited 'as sons' in this community.
>
> (Kannabiran 1995, p. WS 61)

The sexual division of labour – paid and unpaid labour of women especially – were intricately interwoven with questions of inheritance and property rights for women especially in legislative and judicial debates and dialogue.

Against the palimpsest of constructions, negotiation, and bargaining on property rights on the subcontinent, Kamala Sankaran (Chapter 6) offers a comprehensive interdisciplinary review of Hindu women's property rights that extends from legislative history to contemporary jurisprudence. Drawing on the work of B. Sivaramayya, she underscores the effects of non-recognition at the institutional and societal levels to acknowledge marriage as an 'economic partnership', the resultant devaluation of domestic work as not productive, the conflation of nature and nurture that impose disproportionate burdens of reproductive labour (child bearing and child rearing) on women, and the devaluation of women's paid work. What are the concrete effects the mis-recognition of women's labour has for her rights in matrimonial property? Sankaran suggests that women's lower wages and employment levels are related to their low property holdings within the family. The connection has also been drawn elsewhere between the legality of marital rape and the appropriation of women's labour in the family (Kannabiran and Jagani, unpublished).

Violence and Women's Lifeworlds

Extending this debate on reproductive labour and the reproductive body further, Bijayalaxmi Nanda (Chapter 7) draws attention to the drastic decline in female sex ratio which is not adequately explained by neglect of female children, suggesting that there is an active prevention of female births – that combines the use of technology, fertility, and reproductive choice and autonomy. She offers a 'syncretic feminist approach' to understanding reproductive rights, specifically sex-selective abortions in India, that focuses on substantive equality, reproductive justice, and rights and consciously eschews practices in law and policy that tend towards demographic approaches, criminalization, and the focus on the rights of the unborn child. This is a complex debate that also brings in questions of disability rights that sit uneasily with articulations of women's rights (see Ghai and Johri 2014).

The issue of domestic violence has been at the centre of debate on feminist demands for legal reform in India. Beginning with Tarabai Shinde's strident challenge to the patriarchal Hindu caste order in *Stri Purusha Tulana* ([1882] 1994), to present judicial pronouncements on the ways in which women 'misuse' the statutory protections against domestic violence, the travails of women challenging violence in the family has not been adequately comprehended institutionally – either by investigating authorities or courts across jurisdictions. It remains therefore an important concern to reflect on alongside a host of new and emerging concerns. Shalu Nigam (Chapter 8) follows the journey of litigation on domestic violence through the institutions of justice, to provide an assessment of the extent to which pro-active legislation and women's rights campaigns have changed the perceptions and gains on the ground. Kalpana Kannabiran (Chapter 9) tracks attempts at reform in family law concerning violence from the late 1970s across community – from Shahnaz Sheikh and Satyarani Chadha – till the present time – Shayara Bano, to understand the ways in which women have negotiated, litigated, and invented plural legal spaces to ensure a measure of justice for victims and survivors.

An Unresolved Question

The final chapter in this section by Patricia Uberoi (Chapter 10) returns us to the questions Ambedkar raised – speaking precisely to the problem of the folding together of exogamy and endogamy in her examination of the problem of incest through a different route. She discusses the legislative and judicial prevarication and ambivalence on the matter of 'prohibited degrees' in Hindu marriage, especially in the context of South Indian marriage custom, which queered the pitch of nationalist (and judicial) declamations on the morality, and genetic risks of marriage within prohibited degrees – uncle–niece and cross cousin marriage especially. Reading Uberoi's finely tuned analysis of the unresolved problem of 'incest', in the light of Ambedkar's assertion that endogamy was the enclosure that fuelled caste, exogamous rules notwithstanding, leads us to new insights. The ambivalence on prohibited degrees was deliberate and predicated on ideologies of caste. Endogamy, therefore, even if it violated 'prohibited degrees' could be countenanced insofar as it did not disrupt the caste order, but rather reinforced it. This conclusion may be gleaned in a series of observations regarding the paucity of litigation, the disjuncture between objections and legislation, and between legislation and legitimate kinship practices that have been documented by anthropologists.

Plural Domains of Law and Governance

Legal pluralism has been a recurring theme across this volume, presenting itself in many different hues in different historical, regional, and social settings. Sally Moore provides us with a cogent description of plural legal orderings that encompasses the relations between different simultaneous spaces in the locality as well as the relation between formal state orders and proximate orders. Plural orders in her view

> can generate rules and customs and symbols internally, but that ... is also vulnerable to rules and decisions and other forces emanating from the larger world by which it is surrounded. The semi-autonomous social field has rulemaking capacities, and the means to induce or coerce compliance; but it is simultaneously set in a larger social matrix which can, and does, affect and invade it, sometimes at the invitation of persons inside it, sometimes at its own instance.
>
> (Moore 1973, p. 720)

'People's Law' and 'State Law'

In unravelling the layers of proximate legal orders in contemporary India and its relationship to state law, Peter Fitzpatrick's idea of 'integral plurality' speaks to the ways in which state law and plural proximate orders mutually constitute and are constituted by each other. What emerges therefore is an entangled order that is both proximate and distant in terms of its siting and in terms of its protocols. For Fitzpatrick '[s]tate law is integrally constituted in relation to a plurality of social forms' (Fitzpatrick 1984, p. 115), and is 'an unsettled product of relations with a plurality of social forms. As such, law's identity is constantly and inherently subject to challenge and change' (Ibid., p. 138). Yet, Merry's caveat on the place of state law is relevant especially in counter-colonial contexts where although the constitution challenges social dominance of certain groups as well as places restraints on state action:

> it is essential to see state law as fundamentally different in that it exercises the coercive power of the state and monopolizes the symbolic power associated with state authority. But, in many ways, it ideologically shapes other normative orders as well as provides an inescapable framework for their practice.
>
> (Merry 1988, p. 879)

Vernacular Laws

Various chapters in this volume speak of the plural ways in which people's approaches to law (relating to fluid land, forests, catastrophe induced suffering and harms, and family violence) were shaped by their specific experiences and in turn shaped the law even while it was set in motion. We also encounter the fraught domain of custom as a force of law, that has its beginnings in colonial jurisprudence where the Madras High Court ruled in 1868 in the case of *Collector of Madura vs. Mootoo Ramalinga Sathupathy* that custom could override the written text of law if its antiquity was proved (see Kannabiran 1995). We have it seeping into postcolonial Indian debates on the contradictions between custom and written text of law in cases especially to do with family law.

There were also ways in which formal (state) law was rendered intelligible in formal domains through acts of translation of experience into claims, as Sylvia Vatuk's ethnographic research in courtroom settings reveal. Family law regimes are rendered infinitely more complex through plural approaches to formal law and the existence of plural forums adjudicating on codified and uncodified aspects of law. Speaking of formal law for instance, the distinction between the law as written and the law as practiced is revealed to us in the widely divergent strategies in the use of formal law to secure protections for women in different locales (Vatuk 2017). The formal setting is a choice among several available options – and often may not be the preferred option. Nitin Sinha (Chapter 1) points us towards other acts of translation of state law to people's law, in the course of laying claim to legal possession of land with particular agro-ecological attributes. It is the 'concrete particulars' in which legal pluralism resides (to borrow from Delaney 2003) that render law legible.

Sally Merry's elaboration of the process of 'vernacularization' (2018) is particularly instructive in that it helps us step out of monolinguality, into plurilingual expressions of law – in terms of languages spoken, written, lived, and in terms of the ways in which fields of justice are conceptualized. Marc Galanter (1981) revisits the plural ways in which law figures in people's lives, and suggests importantly, that rather than adopt an approach of 'legal centralism' that privileges the formal processes of state law and a centripetal ordering of all matters to do with law in a society, we view lawscapes as centrifugal orderings that address disputes and questions of the 'access to justice' substantively, but do not necessarily emanate from the formal justice system. Pointing out the plural engagements even with state law, in terms of bargaining, settlement, and other forms of dispute resolution that take place outside of the court in order to resolve a dispute being heard in a court, he offers the possibility that even formal courts are not effective in shutting out the social in adjudication and resolution. The alien figure of formal law, as Pratiksha Baxi points out, becomes proximate, familiar, and malleable in its meanderings among the intensely social. She suggests that we may discern the plural ways of state law. There are for instance, 'the different forms of legalities and illegalities that are constitutive of state law simultaneously' (Baxi 2008, p. 82) – notably compromise and the offer of a perpetrator of rape to marry the victim.

Raising the question of what actually is signified by the term 'law', Galanter looks at various 'regulatory spaces' in social settings as in fact engaged actively in deliberating on the law in the everyday. Importantly, he observes,

> courts resolve only a small fraction of all disputes that are brought to their attention. These are only a small fraction of the disputes that might conceivably be brought to court and an even smaller fraction of the whole universe of disputes.
>
> (Galanter 1981, p. 3)

His observation that participants can often devise better solutions to their problems (Ibid., p. 4), is borne out by Upendra Baxi's account of the Rangpur Panchayat in Gujarat (Baxi 1979), and the accounts we have from Vatuk (2017). Since '[l]aw is more capacious as a system of cultural and symbolic meanings than as a set of operative controls', Galanter argues, '[t]he social effects they produce by communication must be far more important than the direct effects of the relatively few decisions they render' (Galanter 1981, p. 13). This may influence the ways in which proximate orderings or proximate law get (re)structured.[7] But also, since these proximate spaces are 'not barren of normative ordering', central to an effort to map the domains of legal pluralism and its methods, is also to unpack the ways in which the legal messaging from formal domains layers or complicates local/'vernacular' orderings (Merry 2018).

Women, Custom, and Resistance

There are several different contexts within which legal pluralism manifests itself in contemporary India. Some of these expressions are deeply problematic in that they reinforce violent coercion by dominant groups on subaltern groups (Dalit, Adivasi, Muslim, especially), or patriarchal dominance through non-consensual decisions on marriage and cohabitation within groups (Dhagamwar 2005), or community reactions to marriage of choice (see Chowdhry 2007). There are other expressions of pluralism that translate constitutional goals and visions into local actions and understandings around the law. The struggle of Koya women in West Godavari district to force the implementation of the *Land Transfer Regulation Act of 1970* that prevented sale of land in scheduled areas to non-tribal people, involved a translation of state law into lived experience and the use of collectively crafted methods of resistance against the coercive state acting against its own laws in the service of dominance (Kannabiran 2002, pp. 384–88). The process of securing forest rights, challenging the interpretation of the Supreme Court by Adivasi collectives across the country, described by Shomona Khanna in Chapter 2 in this volume speaks to contexts of integral plurality that Fitzpatrick outlines.

Testimonios of the Ambedkarite women are rich in detail on the ways in which the Ambedkarite movement, generally, and Dalit women in the movement, in particular, evolved norms around individual, familial, and collective conduct and relations, using Ambedkarite philosophy as a guide, removed as they were from effective, formal spaces of law and justice (see Rege 2006). The proximity was established through the dynamic adoption of the ideals of the constitution on radical equality in everyday lives and work. From the standpoint of legal pluralism however, this is a little explored area. The case of Bhanwari Devi forces a conversation on the disjunctures between the spaces of formal law and local spaces of proximate law. After a judgment in a trial court that was violative of her human dignity in every respect, Bhanwari decided to return to her village, Bhateri and call a jati panchayat, as a way of recovering her sense of dignity and personhood. In 1995, the Bhateri panchayat, which consisted of five villages, with elected members who were scheduled caste, scheduled tribe, and brahmin honoured her, calling her the 'mukhiya sadasya' (chief guest) (Kannabiran 2012, pp. 398–400).

The #MeToo movement is a stunning articulation of the plurality of law and sensibilities of justice that may yield insights for a better understanding of the complex fields of legal pluralism. In Catharine McKinnnon's words,

> #MeToo is cultural, driven principally by forces other than litigation, and is surpassing the law in changing norms and providing relief for human rights violations that the law did not – in some ways in current form could not, although law is embedded in culture and can and will change with it.
>
> (McKinnon 2020, p. 5)

Autonomy and Self Governance

Within this larger discourse on legal pluralism in diverse settings, this section presents three chapters on legal pluralism, that speak to some of the concerns outlined above. Nandita Haksar (Chapter 11) argues, importantly, that 'legal pluralism is embedded in the Constitution of India in the form of the Fifth and Sixth Schedules'. Speaking in the context of conflict in the North Eastern Region, she identifies six sites of actual/potential conflict and explores the ways in which a serious consideration of legal pluralism in this region could pave the way for political pluralism, a celebration of cultural diversity, and create pathways for autonomy and democratic self-governance among tribal societies. Rikil Chyrmang (Chapter 12) deepens this exploration by looking at forums for conflict resolution on questions of land among three principal tribes in Meghalaya – the Khasis, Garos, and Jaintias – through specific cases, tracing the ways in which traditional village courts (with a significant participation of women) were able to resolve long-standing disputes and conflict over land. Adivasi societies, as observed earlier, have honed methods of absorbing constitutional guarantees into claims made in plural law-ways. Anjana Singh (Chapter 13) details the experience of the Pathalgadi movement in Jharkhand which broke new ground in the Adivasi assertion of justice. Through the installation of stone inscriptions containing key provisions of the Constitution of India on village boundaries, the Adivasi Mahasabha enunciated an idea of 'development' distinct from statist rhetoric, and asserted the autonomy of Schedule V areas under the Constitution.

In taking possession of the Constitution, and using it to thwart a repressive state, this account of legal pluralism is rich with possibilities for a radical understanding of the constitution and its cascading into different realms of struggle – indeed the possibilities for an insurgent, people's constitutionalism, which I have elsewhere elaborated in terms of the constitution-as-commons (Kannabiran 2022).

Conclusion

The chapters in this volume explore issues of ecology, forests, disaster and its impact on persons with disabilities; families – in relation to property, kinship and violence; and legal pluralism which focuses on Schedule V and Schedule VI areas within a framework of autonomy and self-governance. The diversity in approaches and the intersecting questions asked – implicitly or explicitly – are the strengths of the volume. The chapters deliberate on difficult issues and attempt to address them in all their complexity.

Routledge Readings on Law, Development and Legal Pluralism does not aim to be encyclopedic or exhaustive of the meaning, sites, and fields of law, nor does it aim to cover specific fields in their entirety. There is a limitation to this selection: since this volume consists of chapters that have been curated from other collections and monographs published by Routledge – there are several areas that may be unrepresented or underrepresented. The chapters are distributed between theoretical, historical, and empirical research on various dimensions of development, ecologies, family studies, and legal pluralism. There are also chapters that have focussed on opening out a single legislation. While most chapters were published in the last decade, the inclusion of chapters has been guided by representativeness – spatially, socially, and thematically, to the best extent possible. There are therefore a few chapters that were published over a decade ago on the family for instance, or very recently, on concerns such as on disaster laws. Impossible as it is to present an all-encompassing selection of chapters on law, our attempt here is to contribute to an interdisciplinary conversation on the plural lives of law, and the plural meanings of justice. The contemporaneity of concerns reflected here enable critical engagements especially by scholars and practitioners interested in South Asia and in the lives of law.

Cases Cited

Justice K.S. Puttaswamy (Retd.) (I) v. Union of India (2017) 10 SCC 1 [Puttaswamy].
Justice K.S. Puttaswamy (Retd.) (II) v. Union of India (2019) 1 SCC 1 [Aadhar].
Naz Foundation vs. Government of NCT of Delhi and Ors. 2009 (111) DRJ 1 (DB).
The Collector of Madhura v/s Mottoo Ramalinga Sathupathy. Decided On, 29 February 1868. Privy Council.
Wildlife First and Others vs. Ministry of Environment and Forests, Writ Petition (Civil) 109/ 2008.

Notes

1 On 13 February 2019 the Supreme Court ordered all States to evict forest dwellers whose claims under the Forest Rights Act (FRA) had been rejected. This order, after large-scale protests across the country, was stayed and further information has been sought from the States. *Wildlife First and Others vs. Ministry of Environment and Forests,* Writ Petition (Civil) 109/ 2008.

2 See also Zanin et al. (2022) for a cogent mapping of 'lawfare' using the Brazilian example.
3 This discussion draws substantially from Chapter 6 of Kannabiran and Ballakrishnen 2021.
4 www.comparitech.com/blog/vpn-privacy/surveillance-states/ Comparitech, 15 October 2019. For an analysis report on the implications of these security safeguards, especially in the context of data sharing between WhatsApp and the Indian government and its resultant disinformation and incitement to violence, see Arun (2019).
5 Targeted surveillance currently stays weighted against the degree of proposed intrusion and the anticipated violence of a particular investigation, para 7, *Report of the Special Rapporteur on the Promotion and Protection of Human Rights and Fundamental Freedoms while Countering Terrorism*, UN General Assembly (23 September 2014). (Report of Special Rapporteur 2014).
6 I have elsewhere described this process of engaging with law and the constitution in the everyday to combat discrimination, untouchability and structural violence as 'insurgent administration'. See Kannabiran (2012).
7 Galanter uses the term 'indigenous ordering' and 'indigenous law' (Galanter 1981). I prefer the term 'proximate law' or 'proximate ordering' to describe the off-court spaces that deliberate on law, justice, and disputes.

References

Agarwal, Bina. 1992. 'The Gender and Environment Debate: Lessons from India'. *Feminist Studies*, 18 (1) Spring, 1992, pp. 119–158.

Agarwal, Bina. 1994. *A Field of One's Own: Gender and Land Rights in South Asia*. Cambridge: Cambridge University Press.

Agrawal, Anil. 2005. *Environmentality: Technologies of Government and the Making of Subjects*. Durham and London: Duke University Press.

Ahmed, Aziza. 2020. 'Floating Lungs: Forensic Science in Self-Induced Abortion Proceedings'. Boston University Law Review, 100, p. 1111.

Ambedkar, B.R. [1917] 2002. 'Castes in India'. In Rodrigues, Valerian, ed. *The Essential Writings of B.R. Ambedkar*. New Delhi: Oxford University Press, pp. 239–262.

Arun, Chinmayi. 2014. 'Thin Safeguards and Mass Surveillance in India'. *National Law School of India Review* 26 (2014), p. 105.

Arun, Chinmayi. 2019. 'On WhatsApp, Rumours, Lynchings, and the Indian Government'. *Economic & Political Weekly*, 54 (6), pp. 30–35.

Ayyadurai, Ambika and Ingole, Prashant. 2021. 'Invisibility of caste in environmental studies'. *Indian Express*, 29 November. https://indianexpress.com/article/opinion/columns/invisibility-of-caste-in-environmental-studies-7644987/ Accessed on 25 December 2021.

Bardhan, Pranab and Ray, Isha. 2008. *The Contested Commons: Conversations between Economists and Anthropologists*. New Delhi: Oxford University Press.

Baviskar, Amita. 1997. 'Ecology and Development in India: A Field and its Future'. *Sociological Bulletin*, 46 (2) September, pp. 193–207.

Baxi, Pratiksha. 2008. 'Feminist Contributions to a Sociology of Law: A Review'. *Economic and Political Weekly*, 43 (43), October 25, pp. 79–85.

Baxi, Pratiksha. 2014. *Public Secrets of Law: Rape Trials in India*. New Delhi: Oxford University Press.

Baxi, Pratiksha. 2017. 'Impractical Topics, Practical Fields: Notes on Researching Sexual Violence in India'. In Kannabiran, Kalpana and Swaminathan, Padmini, eds. *Re-Presenting Feminist Methodologies: Interdisciplinary Explorations*. New Delhi: Routledge, pp. 179–199.

Baxi, Upendra. 1969. 'Directive Principles and Sociology of Indian Law: A Reply to Dr. Jagat Narain'. *Journal of the Indian Law Institute*, 11 (3), July–September, pp. 245–272.

Baxi, Upendra. 1979. 'People's Law, Development, Justice'. *Verfassung und Recht in Übersee / Law and Politics in Africa, Asia and Latin America*, 12 (2), pp. 97–114.

Baxi, Upendra. 2002. *The Future of Human Rights*. New Delhi: Oxford University Press.

Baxi, Upendra. 2010. 'Writing about Impunity and Environment: The "silver jubilee" of the Bhopal catastrophe'. *Journal of Human Rights and the Environment*, 1 (1), January 2010, pp. 23–44.

Baxi, Upendra. 2019. 'The Future of Dissent in the Anthropocene'. Rabi Ray Memorial Lecture. Mainstream, Vol LVII No 15, New Delhi, March 30. http://mainstreamweekly.net/article8604.html Accessed on 5 January 2022.

Cederlöf, Gunnel and Sivaramakrishnan, K. 2005. *Ecological Nationalisms: Nature, Livelihoods and Identities in South Asia*. New Delhi: Permanent Black.

Chandra, Rajshree. 2010. *Knowledge As Property: Issues in the Moral Grounding of Intellectual Property Rights*. New Delhi: Oxford University Press.

Chapalgaonkar, Narendra. 2022. 'The Gandhian Conception of the Constitution'. In Kannabiran, Kalpana, ed. *Routledge Readings on Law and Social Justice: Dispossessions, Marginalities, Rights*. Oxon & New York: Routledge, pp. 73–89.

Chowdhry, Prem. 2007. *Contentious Marriages, Eloping Couples: Gender, Caste and Patriarchy in Northern India*, New Delhi: Oxford University Press.

Cover, Robert. 1986. 'Violence and the Word'. *Yale Law Journal*, 95, p. 1601.

Craig, Martin. 2019. 'What Are the Limits on Lawfare?' *OpinioJuris*, 5 May. http://opiniojuris.org/2019/05/05/what-are-the-limits-on-lawfare/ Accessed on 4 January 2022.

Dasgupta, Chirashree. 2013. 'The Tenacity of the Hindu Undivided Family: Gender, Religion and Tax Concessions'. *Economic and Political Weekly*. October 5, XLVIII (40), pp. 73–75.

Dasgupta, Chirashree. 2020. 'Social Reproduction, Constitutional Provisions and Capital Accumulation in Post-Independent India'. *Economic and Political Weekly*, LV (20), pp. 30–36.

Delaney, David. 2003. *Law and Nature*. Cambridge: Cambridge University Press. Ebook.

Dhagamwar, Vasudha. 2005. '" The Shoe Fitted Me and I Wore It...": Women and Traditional Justice Systems in India'. In Kannabiran, Kalpana, ed. *The Violence of Normal Times: Essays on Women's Lived Realities*. New Delhi: Women Unlimited in association with Kali for Women, pp. 46–66.

Divan, Shyam and Rosencranz, Armin. 2001. *Environmental Law and Policy in India: Cases, Materials and Statutes*. New Delhi: Oxford University Press.

Finney, Carolyn. 2014. *Black Faces, White Spaces: Reimagining the Relationship of African Americans to the Great Outdoors*, Chapel Hill: The University of North Carolina Press.

Fitzpatrick, Peter. 1984. 'Law and Societies'. *Osgoode Hall Law Journal*, 22, p. 115.

Galanter, Marc. 1981. 'Justice in many Rooms: Courts, Private Ordering, and Indigenous Law'. *The Journal of Legal Pluralism and Unofficial Law*, 13 (19), pp. 1–47, DOI: 10.1080/07329113.1981.10756257.

Geetha, V. 2021. *Bhimrao Ramji Ambedkar and the Question of Socialism in India*. Switzerland: Palgrave Macmillan.

Ghai, Anita and Rachana Johri. 2014. 'Prenatal Diagnosis: Where Do We Draw the Line?' In Kannabiran, Kalpana, ed. *Women and Law: Critical Feminist Perspectives*. New Delhi: Sage, pp. 240–263.

Govindrajan, Radhika. 2018. *Animal Intimacies: Interspecies Relatedness in India's Central Himalayas*. Chicago and London: University of Chicago Press.

Guinier, Lani and Torres, Gerald. 2014. 'Changing the Wind: Notes Toward a Demosprudence of Law and Social Movements'. *Yale Law Journal*, 123, pp. 2740–2804.

Hess, Charlotte, and Ostrom, Elinor. 2007. 'Introduction: An Overview of the Knowledge Commons'. In Hess, Charlotte and Ostrom, Elinor, eds. *Understanding Knowledge as a Commons: From Theory to Practice*. Cambridge, MA and London: MIT Press, p. 10.

Hoffmann, Florian. 2021. 'Before the Law: (Anti-)Corruption and the Politics of Anti-politics in Contemporary Brazil'. In Kannabiran, Kalpana, Hollstein, Bettina, and Hoffmann, Florian, eds. *Discourses on Corruption: Interdisciplinary and Intercultural Perspectives*. New Delhi: Sage/Spectrum, pp. 215–242.

Jayal, Neeraja G. 2019. 'Faith-based citizenship'. *The India Forum*. www.theindiaforum.in/article/faith-criterion-citizenship Accessed on 1 November 2021.

Kannabiran, Kalpana. 1995. 'Judiciary, Social Reform and Debate on "Religious Prostitution" in Colonial India'. *Economic and Political Weekly*, 30 (43), October 28, pp. WS59–WS69.

Kannabiran, Kalpana. 2002. 'Defining Citizenship: Issues in Women's Leadership in Andhra Pradesh'. In Tambiah, Yasmin, ed. *Women and Governance in South Asia: Re-Imagining the State*. Colombo: International Centre for Ethnic Studies, pp. 364–384.

Kannabiran, Kalpana. 2012. *Tools of Justice: Non-Discrimination and the Indian Constitution*. New Delhi: Routledge.

Kannabiran, Kalpana. 2017. 'To Bounce Like a Ball that has Been Hit': Feminist Reflections on the Family'. In Kannabiran, Kalpana and Swaminathan, Padmini, eds. *Re-Presenting Feminist Methodologies: Interdisciplinary Explorations*. New Delhi: Routledge, pp. 49–73.

Kannabiran, Kalpana. 2022. 'Constitution-as-Commons, Spatial Justice, and Estrangements in Adivasi India: The Continuing Legacy of Three Legal Cases.' In Linkenbach, Antje and Verma, Vidhu. eds. *State Law and Adivasis: Shifting Terrains of Exclusion*. New Delhi: Sage, pp. 129–152.

Kannabiran, Kalpana and Ballakrishnen, Swethaa. 2021. *Gender Regimes and the Politics of Privacy: A Feminist Re-Reading of Puttaswamy vs. Union of India*. New Delhi: Zubaan.

Kannabiran, Kalpana and Jagani, Devi. *Gendered Bodies and Worlds of Labour: ReConceptualizing Dignity after Puttaswamy vs. Union of India*. Unpublished.

Kapur, Anu. 2022. 'Geographical Indications: Place Matters'. In Kannabiran, Kalpana, ed. *Routledge Readings on Social Justice: Dispossessions, Marginalities, Rights* . New Delhi: Routledge, pp.364–380.

Lokaneeta, Jinee. 2020. *The Truth Machines: Policing, Violence, and Scientific Interrogations in India*. Hyderabad: Orient BlackSwan.

Lyon, David, Haggerty, Kevin D. and Ball, Kirstie. 2012. 'Introducing Surveillance Studies'. In Ball, Kirstie, Haggerty, Kevin D. and Lyon, David, eds. *Routledge Handbook of Surveillance Studies*. London & New York: Routledge, pp. 1–11.

Madhok, Sumi. 2021. *Vernacular Rights Cultures: The Politics of Origins, Human Rights, and Gendered Struggles for Justice*. Cambridge University Press.

Mazumdar, Indrani. 2016. 'Unfree Mobility; Adivasi Women's Migration'. In Radhakrishna, Meena, ed. *First Citizens: Studies on Adivasis, Tribals and Indigenous Peoples in India*. New Delhi: Oxford University Press, pp. 178–206.

McKinnon, Catharine A. 2020.'Global #MeToo'. In Noel, Ann M. and Oppenheimer, David B., eds. *The Global #MeToo Movement*. Washington DC: Full Court Press, pp. 1–15.

Merry, Sally Engle. 1988. 'Legal Pluralism'. *Law & Society Review*, 22 (5), pp. 869–896.

Merry, Sally Engle. 2018. 'Preface'. In Destrooper, Tine and Merry, Sally Engle, eds. *Human Rights Transformation in Practice*. Philadelphia: University of Pennsylvania Press, pp. vii–ix.

Mies, Maria and Shiva, Vandana. [1993] 2014. *Ecofeminism* (With a Foreword by Ariel Salleh). London and New York, Zed Books.

Möller, Kai. 2012. *The Global Model of Constitutional Rights*. Oxford: Oxford University Press.

Moore, Sally Falk. 1973. 'Law and Social Change: The Semi-Autonomous Social Field as an Appropriate Subject of Study'. *Law & Society Review*, 7, p. 719.

Morrison, Kathleen D. 2015.'Conceiving Ecology and Stopping the Clock: Narratives of Balance, Loss, and Degradation'. In Rangarajan, Mahesh and Sivaramakrishnan, K., eds. *Shifting Ground: People, Animals and Mobility in India's Environmental History*. Oxford Scholarship, pp. 40–64. Online. DOI: 10.1093/acprof:oso/9780198098959.001.0001.

Omvedt, Gail. 1987. 'India's Green Movements'. *Race and Class*, XXVIII (4), pp. 29–38.

Philippopoulos-Mihalopoulos, Andreas. 2015. *Spatial Justice: Body, Lawscape, Atmosphere*. Oxon: Routledge.

Ramdas, Sagari. 2014. 'Women, Forestspaces and the Law: Transgressing the Boundaries'. In Kannabiran, Kalpana, ed. *Women and Law: Critical Feminist Perspectives*, New Delhi: Sage, pp. 59–85.

Rangarajan, Mahesh and Sivaramakrishnan, K. 2015. *Shifting Ground: People, Animals and Mobility in India's Environmental History*. Oxford Scholarship Online. DOI: 10.1093/acprof:oso/9780198098959.001.0001.

Rapp, Rayna. 1999. *Testing Women, Testing the Fetus: The Social Impact of Amniocentesis in America*. New York and London: Routledge.

Reddy, Prashant T. and Chandrashekaran, Sumathi. 2017. *Create, Copy, Disrupt: India's Intellectual Property Dilemmas*. New Delhi: Oxford University Press.

Rege, Sharmila. 2006. *Writing Caste/Writing Gender: Reading Dalit Women's Testimonios*. New Delhi: Zubaan.

Roberts, Dorothy E. 2015. 'Race, Gender and Genetic Technologies: A New Reproductive Dystopia?' In Dubrofsky, Rachel E. and Magnet, Shoshanna Amielle, eds. *Feminist Surveillance Studies*. Durham & London: Duke University Press, pp. 169–187.

Robinson, Mary. 2018. *Climate Justice: Hope, Resilience and the Fight for a Sustainable Future*. London: Bloomsbury.
Rodrigues, Valerian. 2008. 'Citizenship and the Indian Constitution'. In Bhargava, Rajeev, ed. *Politics and Ethics of the Indian Constitution*. New Delhi: Oxford University Press, pp. 164–188.
Sarin, Madhu. 2001. 'Empowerment and Disempowerment of Forest Women in Uttarakhand, India'. *Gender Technology and Development*, 5, p. 341
Sen, Amartya. 2009. *The Idea of Justice*. London: Allen Lane.
Shinde, Tarabai, [1882] 1994. 'A Comparison between Women and Men: An Essay to Show Who's Really Wicked and Immoral, Women or Men?' In O'Hanlon, Rosalind, ed. *A Comparison between Women and Men: Tarabai Shinde and the Critique of Gender Relations in Colonial India*. New Delhi: Oxford University Press, pp. 73–134.
Shiva, Vandana. 2014. *The Vandana Shiva Reader* (with a Foreword by Wendell Berry). Lexington: The University of Kentucky Press.
Singh, Jaivir. [2004] 2012. (Un)Constituting Property: The Destruction of the 'Right to Property' in India. 'Working Paper Series, Centre for the Study of Law and Governance, Jawaharlal Nehru University, New Delhi', August 2004 [2012 Reprint] CSLG/WP/05.
Sivaramakrishnan, K. 1999. *Modern Forests: Statemaking and Environmental Change in Colonial Eastern India*. Stanford, CA: Stanford University Press.
Smith, Andrea. 2015. 'Not-Seeing: State Surveillance, Settler Colonialism, and Gender Violence'. In Dubrofsky, Rachel E. and Magnet, Shoshanna Amielle, eds. *Feminist Surveillance Studies*. Durham & London: Duke University Press, pp. 21–38.
Sukumar, Arun Mohan. 2019. *Midnight's Machines: A Political History of Technology in India*. New Delhi: Penguin/Viking.
Thayyil, Naveen. 2015. 'Claiming the Social: Beyond "Law as Technology"'. *SocioLegal Review*, 11 (2), pp. 1–21.
Tokar, Brian. 2019. 'On the Evolution and Continuing Development of the Climate Justice Movement'. In Jafry, Tahseen, ed. *Routledge Handbook of Climate Justice*. Oxon and New York: Routledge, pp. 13–25.
Vatuk, Sylvia. 2017. *Marriage and its Discontents: Women, Islam and the Law in India*. New Delhi: Women Unlimited.
Wahi, Namita. 2016. 'Is the Current Demonetisation Legal?' Centre for Policy Research, 6 December. https://cprindia.org/news/5692 Accessed on 4 January 2022.
Xaxa, Abhay F. 2019. 'Brahminical environmentalism the reason behind attack on FRA'. 5 March. https://twocircles.net/2019mar05/429810.html Accessed on 25 December 2021.
Zanin, Cristiano, Martins, Valeska and Valim. Rafael. 2022. *Lawfare: Waging War through Law*. Oxon & New York: Routledge
Zuboff, Shoshana. 2019. *The Age of Surveillance Capitalism: The Fight for a Human Future at the New Frontier of Power*. London: Profile Books.

PART I

Questions of Justice

Environment, Ecology, and Disaster

1 Law, Agro-Ecology and Colonialism in Mid-Gangetic India, 1770s–1910s

Nitin Sinha

This chapter looks at fluvial landscape of northern and eastern India – variously called *diaras* or *churs* – to understand the process of colonial legal interventions, and how such interventions shaped the meanings of land and rights in this landscape. By doing so, it addresses two core conceptual questions of this volume: first, how do codified laws and regulations converse with legal practices, and how together they shape the parameters of rights and subjecthood; and second, what role does space and spatial practices play in the relationship between law and subjecthood?

According to informed estimates, *diaras* comprised about 10 to 15 per cent of the total land in different riverine districts of Bihar. The chapter looks at two interrelated aspects: one, a series of riparian laws and regulations to understand the nature of the colonial state's legal intervention; and two, the rights of *raiyats* cultivating these lands. The concluding section offers a set of broader reflections on how to understand the history of *diara* lands that were/are marked by ecological fluidity. In other words, when looked through the triangulated prism of land, law and rights, the chapter attempts to answer the question of a typicality or anomaly of *diara* lands.

Usually, courtrooms serve as an appropriate site for understanding legal aspects of claim making and dispute settlement. In our case, the 'nature' itself was no less important. On-the-spot surveys and measurement, with tents and writing desks of officials pitched in the middle of the fields, tell us that agrarian fields were as much the site of formation of legal injunctions as *thanas* (police outposts) and *kachahris* (courtrooms) were. This will also be true for other types of agrarian landscapes. In the case of *diaras*, measurement acquired a specific significance, as we will see in the text that follows.

To some surprise, the archives of *diara* settlements (in Bihar, which the author is best familiar with and empirically draws upon) are largely silent on the issue of *raiyati* (related to actual cultivators) rights. If historical choices cast any bearing on archive formation, the story of fluvial landscape

DOI: 10.4324/9781003299561-1

as understood through processes of agrarian control and expansion could be its best example; the immediate fallout of the choice of settling lands with *zamindars* (landlords) and other agrarian intermediaries in Bihar reflects in a relative absence of *raiyats* in the records.[1]

A quick comparison with eastern Bengal lays bare the role of ecology and state policies that regionally were variegated. In the fluvial eastern Bengal where the land was directly settled with *raiyats*, the hold of intermediaries was less prominent; as Sumit Sarkar has summarised, 'A zone of relatively stable and undifferentiated peasant agriculture, with a modicum of prosperity' emerged.[2] This was distinct from the cases in western and northern Bengal, where lands were leased by absentee landlords to *jotedars* and *latdars* who in turn would employ sharecroppers and labourers.[3]

Rich alluvial land and cultivation of cash crop (jute) alone, however, do not explain the prosperity or stability of peasant agriculture in eastern Bengal.[4] These two factors were also present in the case of mid-Gangetic fluvial set-up. They were also present in the region of north Bihar Kosi *diaras*, where rather than undifferentiated peasantry, a new class of landless labourers emerged (Hill 1990: 14). The fundamental reason of differentiation, it seems, arose because the *chur* lands of the Bengal delta were already outside the purview of the Permanent Settlement (PS) implemented in 1793, and hence in the wake of the criticism of the PS, they were settled directly with the cultivators. The active policy of the government to directly engage with cultivators led to the weakening of the intermediaries.[5] One of the paradoxical implications that emerge from this comparison is that in the frontier zone of the Sunderbans the weak colonial state committed to the idea of agrarian expansion and revenue maximisation dealt directly with the *raiyats*, and hence went deeper into the agrarian structure; in the mid-Gangetic Bihar where the state had a relatively firmer footing, it cut a deal with landed class and intermediaries. The invisibility of actual cultivators (for which I am using the word *raiyat*) in the archives is an outcome of ecological settings and state policies. The 'everydayness' of fluvial shifts together with the state's preference for landed elites rendered *raiyats* invisible.

This, of course, is not true for landholding elites. Their disputes on the question of propriety are well reflected in the archives (Bhargava 2007: 183–208; Sinha 2014: 209–237). From time to time concerns regarding *raiyats* also surfaced. True to the spirit of the PS, the riparian laws were not blind to the existence of *raiyats*. The PS had envisioned the enactment of such regulations in future that would be necessary for the 'protection and welfare of the dependent talookdars, ryots, and other cultivators of the soil'.[6] However, subsequent to the PS, the pro-*zamindar* inclination meant that the state suspended the rights of the actual cultivators to the custody of 'customs' that needed to be determined through a private relationship between them and *zamindars*. Nonetheless, these very same immemorially established usages now refracted through legal frameworks meant two things: first, the state did not go deeper into agrarian relations to legally define the relationship between *zamindars* and *raiyats*; and second, precisely, because it did not do so, it legalised the 'private' arrangement between them.[7]

To give one example of law 'privatising' the custom, we need to look at the 1833 Circular Order related to alluvial settlement. In the case of land increment to a subordinate tenure due to alluviation, its holder was entitled to the increment 'provided he pay [*sic*] an increase of rent [to his superior] according to his engagements, or the established usage that obtains in respect of alluvion where it has taken place'. Further, the undertenant's increment would be assessed by his superior 'at such rate as is fair and proper, and conformable to the conditions of his lease or Talook, and to local custom' (Peters 1838, no. CLXXVII: 287). The privatisation of this arrangement is evident from the unambiguous wording in the order that for revenue and its share of rent, the government (represented by the Collector) will deal only with superiors (maliks, *zamindars*). *Diara* lands had become the source of speculative farming for revenue and profit both for local state authorities and for *zamindars*.[8] In such a scenario, perhaps, the mix of relationship between law and custom on the one hand and the everydayness of fluvial landscape on the other created conditions for *raiyats*' greater exploitation.[9]

One last point on the relationship between *diaras* and wastelands before turning to the practice of measurement and riparian laws is that the authors of an ethnographic study of *char* lands of the Damodar River have suggested that these lands were part of reclaimed or cleared lands (*baze zameen*) exempt from tax (Lahiri-Dutt and Samanta 2013: 62). In early 19th-century accounts, there are clear evidences that *raiyats* paid relatively lesser rent on cultivating the 'waste'. According to official wisdom, wilful cultivation of the waste was a strategy to minimise rent payment, which therefore needed to be 'strictly prohibited'.[10] For instance, in the southern parts of Shahabad district, tenants undertook the cultivation of waste on the payment of low cash rent (Hubbock [1918] 1928: 64). In the mid-Gangetic case, the classificatory categories used by contemporary officials suggest that *diaras* or *churs* were not conceptually part of the waste;[11] hence, the logic of lesser rent does not apply by default to *diara raiyats*. For instance, in the northern part of the same Shahabad district, which was prone to annual overflow of the Ganga, rents were high (Hubbock 1918: 13).

Seasonality, measurement and law

Bernardo A. Michael has recently argued that revenue surveys helped the company state to construct a compact sense of 'territory' out of the precolonial intermixed and dispersed units of revenue (Michael 2007: 78–95). The role of surveys and measurements in state-making is, of course, crucial and much explored. So far surveying the agrarian field is concerned, which is a lesser-worked area, I intend to go beyond his claim; I wish to argue and demonstrate here that measurement led towards the formation of some form of putative agrarian subjecthood in the juridical sense of the term. Measurement was not only an act that aimed to objectively draw boundaries and prepare the list of fields with their measured area but was also part of the process of record preparation that facilitated proprietorial claims and counterclaims.

I find useful insights from David Ludden's account in thinking about measurement as a point at which 'managerial empiricism' (to borrow his term) intersects with the agrarian field (Ludden 1999: 7). Agrarian space is one which is appropriated by political and social formations, and hence the structures and practices of those appropriations could possibly be one of the gateways to write the social history of law and subjecthood. Simultaneously, we also need to move beyond the conventional frameworks of writing this history only through essentialised social groups such as landlords, *raiyats* and a range of intermediaries, a point forcefully made by Neeladri Bhattacharya (1983: 121–170) and K. Sivaramakrishnan (1999b). These are indeed important and find a place in this chapter as well. The agrarian-ecological spaces were, however, constituted not only of specific groups but also of processes by which they were made part of the political and social formations (ranging from state initiatives such as mapping to ritual propitiation to land, gods and beasts). Concentrating on the processes (and their failures) can provide glimpses into forms of resistance as well as dynamism of agrarian space and social world.[12]

On the role of seasonality in agriculture and in the making of agrarian practices and spaces, each with their own specific dynamism, Ludden writes:

> The regularity of seasonal rhythms – which define the calendar of human activities in each farm setting – allows investment to occur in one season with the hope and probabilistic expectation that dividends will accrue in the next. The cyclical quality of seasons thus encourages thinking about the future and the past, together, and calculations of past yield for making future-oriented decisions.[13]

In *diara*-prone agricultural landscape, seasonality played an extremely important role. Annual shift or inundation led to alluviation or diluviation of the whole land or its parts.[14] Further, it was seasonality combined with the force of water that resulted in graded quality of the land – from *doras* (a mix of clay and sandy soil yielding two crops a year) to *parti* (very sandy infertile land). The amount of revenue, the willingness of the maliks to either enter into the arrangement or let the land in lease, the rate of the lease and the private custom-based negotiations between holders and cultivators all depended on this seasonality. The future investment relied as much on the calculation of future gain as on the unpredictability of the loss. It was one important reason why maliks sometimes offered more than the assessed revenue and sometimes completely denied to enter into any agreement. The 'everydayness' of this landform was therefore negotiated through a range of mechanisms. For the state the interplay of revenue and rights remained the final goal of a set of negotiations; for maliks, securing their own gains was crucial. The cultivators also devised ways to minimise their loss.[15]

I must clarify that in the non-literal sense of the word, the term 'everyday' is used here to refer to a recurring feature of shifts in the rivers or in their streams, leading to appearance, disappearance and reappearance of lands. If we appreciate how deeply the annual farming activities are interconnected with each other, yearly shifts in the position of cultivated or cultivable land would appear an everyday phenomenon. There are various official attestations to these 'continual' and 'yearly' shifts. To give one example from the person who had physically invested a lot of time in knowing this landscape, the Deputy Collector H.C. Hamilton had said: 'This district of Monghyr being on the banks of the Ganges is surrounded by immense tracts of Dearah land which shift with the course of the River more or less every year'.[16]

Rent, revenue and resources were dependent on seasonality. The rainy seasons, often between June and September, almost at an annual basis inundated riverine villages. The first step towards negotiating with the change was by knowing the extent of the change. Not unsurprisingly then, winter tours of officials and subordinate staff of the revenue department usually took place for the next six to seven months (September to March) to know, fix and settle this altered landscape. Seasonality once again played a role in the rhythm of this bureaucratic work: Europeans touring the field avoided extreme heat between April/May and June/July.[17] The second reason was related to decisions made on the basis of agricultural cycles. Measurements took place between September and March because no crops stood on the fields.[18] Maliks or leaseholders preferred to attain the lease during this lean period so that they knew their responsibility and could start the new cycle by leaving the land ploughed and allowing it to be well saturated by rains and inundations.[19]

Although apparent, the meaning of measuring the land was not restricted to its purely quantifiable attribute. The measured units of land served as a map to define social relationships (that often took recourse to judicial apparatus). Measurement created a record of lands, rates and crops on the one hand and a record of rights on the other; while the first helped the state in assessing the revenue which it ought to demand, the second, the state thought, would create a social order and a juridical basis to restore that order, when needed.[20] Once again, taking clue from Ludden's study in which he has argued that 'ideas moving among farmers create territories of knowledge' (Ludden 1999: 38), one could argue that special landscapes such as *diaras* would require and give rise to specialised knowledge. Measurement was thus also an act to tap into this specialised knowledge, which, for instance, involved chatting with older people about the history of erosion and accruement.[21] It was as much an exercise in imposing 'statist' knowledge as in accessing 'local' knowledge. All this was, however, very idealistic and normative. The capacity of the state machinery was limited (and as we will see divided); and the social and ecological conditions posited problems at various stages.

Differences existed among officials and institutions on the subject of measurement. The disagreements were not on the question of whether it was required; there was unanimity on that. But the issue was its timing – when were the tracts to be surveyed, that is at which stage of the season and settlement would measurement become the most appropriate. Nisbet, the Commissioner of Bhagalpur under whom Wells and Hamilton worked, believed that the property was valueless till the time the river receded or it 'remit[ed] its direct attack'. In this period, measurement was 'useless'.[22] Only when the river had stopped its 'direct' attack, measurement could be undertaken, and a permanent settlement be expected.[23] Hamilton echoed Nisbet's views; nevertheless, he favoured first having maliks agreeing to the settlement in perpetuity before starting the survey work.[24] Hamilton was well aware of maliks' intransigency in entering into any agreement when they felt *diaras* would shrink in size leading to loss. Clearly, these officials differed, but both contextualised their choices using ecological reasoning and presented a course that would least burden the state. Wells, the officer posted at the rank between Nisbet and Hamilton, had the following to say:

> The more I see of the continual change that these villages on the banks of the River are relegated to the more I am impressed with the advantage that would accrue to Govt & to the Landholders from an establishment of a European surveyor in these parts to measure yearly the losses sustained on one side & the accretions on the other side of the Ganges.[25]

The European style for him meant deploying the contemporary method of trigonometrical survey by taking such points which the river would not wash away. From the correspondences of these two officers (Wells and Hamilton), it becomes clear that they had benefited from using maps prepared by Captain Tanner who had surveyed this area in the 1820s. However, the Board of Revenue, the apex body in the field, stopped Tanner's surveys in 1833, and hence, we get repeated requests made by these lower-level officials to re-establish the survey work. Following Wells, Hamilton made various pleas to the board, in one of which he said: 'Appointment of a Revenue Surveyor to note the changes of the Churs & Dearahs and to ascertain the particulars of lands which become Gungshikust & ...&' was 'most assuredly highly desirable'.[26] The massive resumption drive between the 1820s and the 1840s that drained the revenue and judicial infrastructure of the colonial state was in itself not the problem; in fact, it became the cause for pressing 'the importance of an honest survey' on which 'all other parts' of settlement rested.

The board and the government were in complete agreement on having an exhaustive survey of those *diaras* and other types of lands that post-PS had come under the resumption drive.[27] They argued that the 'precise ascertainment of the identity, and limits, and boundary marks of the land in dispute' would actually simplify judicial investigations. But they countered the view that measurement needed to follow settlement; measurement, on contrary, was made the precondition. Still, Well's proposal for yearly surveys was turned down; the board instead asked to rely on the services of 'respectable *ameens*'. The revenue surveys did start in different districts of Bihar between the late 1830s and 1840s, but they did not prove to be very helpful in settling *diara* lands.[28] The reasons were also financial. Extensive and annual *diara* surveys in this period were not seen economically viable. Even for revenue surveys, an inexpensive system of survey and record preparation was devised (Michael 2007: 85).

It is important here to point out that if seen through the ideology and practice of measuring agrarian land, there is a connection between the mainland agrarian history and what would appear to be an anomalous zone of *diaras*. For both types, the state was overly depending on measurement. This is a move away from the ethos of the PS. The PS was not done on the basis of field measurement but on crop estimation.[29] In the 1820s, the criticism of the PS was at its peak. There was some disconnect between different layers of bureaucratic thinking as reflected in a variety of sources. Normative legal pieces (the 1825 Regulation and two subsequent clarifications, Circular Orders of 1833 and 1838) on *diara* lands did not make any *direct* reference to measurement, but as seen earlier, the officials on the ground very much favoured survey and measurement. The 1825 Regulation definitely did not invoke any idea of measurement. This regulation betrays a unique fusion of Orientalist thinking with Utilitarian values. The preamble of the regulation claimed that in India laws and customs have had established rules to deal with fluvial cases, but they were *not known*. The way to know them was to go back to traditions. Hindu and Muslim law officers were asked to furnish reports on this matter. However, in cases where customs and established usages were unclear, the regulation advocated the courts of justice to follow the 'general principles of equity and justice'.[30] In late 19th-century Punjab, as Neeladri Bhattacharya has shown, the post-Utilitarian phase of going back to customs was not based on going back to ancient texts but practices.[31] In the case of the 1825 Regulation, it is not clear whether the Hindu and Muslim law officers sampled cases or based their reports simply on texts. The phrase 'established local usage' does suggest that here too the emphasis was on knowing the practices.

The other two orders also did not explicitly mention measurement, but *jumma* and assessment were obviously made in settling these lands. The timing of the debates that ensued between different officials and the board on the question of measurement as outlined earlier corresponds with the passage of these two orders (1830s). This was also the period when village-based revenue surveys and production of maps had started. My understanding is that by this period, precisely because of the resumption drive and the growing critique of the PS, measurement, at least idealistically, became the central tool of assessment and settlement of lands. The specific nature of the shifting landscape in fact strengthened rather than mitigated the faith in measurement. Mapping the fluvial landscape seemed tougher, but persistent policy directions show that the state thought it was achievable. Maps emerged as the central tool to understand this landscape and also to regulate claims over it.

The 1841 Circular Order modified the previous order of 1838 on the issue of proprietorial rights in the increment area, bringing survey and measurement into sharper relief. According to the 1838 Circular, the alluvial accretion was part of the parent estate and the assessment of revenue on the increment would be an increase in the total *jumma* of the estate. If the maliks refused to enter into agreement, the alluvial increment would be put on a lease for a period not exceeding ten years but still would be considered an integral part of the original mahal (Jones 1851, no. CCCCLIX: 54). The 1841 Circular made it necessary to take local conditions of each alluvial formation into consideration before deciding on the number of years of temporary lease or even permanent settlement. More important, should the maliks refuse to let increment become part of the parent estate, the alluvial increment would be settled as a distinct mahal but the boundary lines between the distinct *diara* and already-settled estates had to be delineated on the map and recorded with the settlement papers 'to prevent the occurrence of future doubt or dispute'.[32] Subsequently, Act IX of 1847 paid the utmost importance to measurement and mapping. The government retained the right to direct surveys and the preparation of new maps 'from time to time whenever ten years from the approval of any such survey shall have expired … to ascertain the changes that may have taken place since the date of the last previous survey'.[33] New maps also ideally formed the basis of re-adjusting the *jumma* in cases of lands both being washed away and newly added.[34]

Collectively, officials working at different levels looked upon survey and measurement instrumentally, something that would create not only well-defined boundaries that because of being mapped would become self-referential in ascertaining areas and claims over them but also one that would create an archive of those self-referential points in the landscape. In other words, it would ensure the right to property which could be upheld in the court of law in the future. It will do so by making the occupant proprietors aware of their property and its boundaries.[35] This in turn attempted one way of defining agrarian subjecthood.

However, delineation of land and land-based rights was a clumsy process. A significant number of acts, regulations and orders passed on the basic question of who owned the alluvial land and how to settle such lands within a short period of almost 30 years (starting 1825) show that the process of settlement was far from clear. On several occasions the government categorically pointed out discrepancies or confusion prevalent in settling *diara* lands.[36] The broader changes, of course, are visible, the most important being the central role of survey and measurement. But given the nature of constant shift and expenses involved in the surveys, we can hardly be sure if measurement indeed was universally and widely followed. What indeed appears to have been taking grounds was the process of putative formation of juridical agro-ecological subjecthood based on the idea of proprietorship (aided by measurement). I call it putative because the role of customary practices and practices that ought to be based on equity and justice were entangled. Custom was understood and recorded in the fields and offices, and upheld in the court of law. And as we will see in the following pages, they were also redefined and sometimes 'violated'. In this mix, the formation of the agrarian subjecthood was taking place at the intersection of state's mechanisms to enlarge the revenue net, to stabilise its claims, to delineate the boundaries and to give the landholding groups some sense of proprietorial rights and awareness – a sense that could be affirmed, if required, through law.

The *putativeness* of the formation also manifests once we move away from the normative and instrumental understanding of measurement and see it 'in action'. We then realise the historical messiness which accompanied it. Prior to producing 'data', the act meant negotiating with the social set-up. Measurement was as much an interface between technology and agrarian field as an encounter between colonial bureaucratic choices and practical possible actions permissible through social and ecological setup. It involved more than one visit to the land, most probably with some equipment and documents; equipment helped in knowing the current area and preparing a future record, while documents helped in providing a past genealogy and general understanding. However, often it would happen that decisions by superior officials remained pending because junior officials took away the documents on their tours. Carts would then be hired to bring documents back to the mofussil office 'for the purpose of testing the measurement'.[37]

The knowledge of this landscape was attempted to be gathered by entering into a ritualised stock-taking interview in the village (usually with the elderly) to know the history of the shifts in river courses, the possible future shifts, the quantity of the possible yield and so on. The white sahibs exercised power and authority in conducting 'on-the-spot inquiry' and determining a 'general view of the locality', which we can safely assume was just about 'general'. The 'on-the-spot work' was done by native subordinates. *Mohurrirs* did the measurement work under the supervision of *ameens* or *tehsildars* who prepared the details. There was a great degree of dependence on native staff, but they were also seen as conniving and conspiring elements with vested agrarian interests. Their conduct was assessed with great suspicion.[38] In fact, this conundrum percolated down to the lowest level of native staff. For his tour, Hamilton spent Rs 7 for four brass badges for the *peadahs* (peons) to carry the emblem of state authority.[39] Probably, it was prompted by an earlier incident in which villagers denied entry to them to collect the revenue.[40]

The interesting link between measurement, colonial ideology, suspicion towards native staff and letting landowners understand the bases of their proprietorial claims is discernible in Wells's statement:

> When once the true area of a Village is ascertained with the aggregate of cultivated & waste & mapped in the style of a European Surveyor, it is next to impossible for any subordinate native establishment to mislead you [?] much in the remainder of the work. The Village too being laid down trigonometrically & fixed points taken that are not liable to be cut away by the River the maliks can have their own again when the course of the river recedes.[41]

The regulations, as we have argued earlier, had attempted to legalise the private arrangements based on 'usages and customs', but on-the-spot inquiries and revision of subordinates' reports provided opportunities to redefine both law and custom. In the assessment of Rahatpur, *ameen*'s calculation had included 'Butta', supposedly a Mughal *abwab*, under which landholders received some money from the *raiyats*. Wells omitted this column from the *ameen*'s report saying the *abwab* was just another means 'to give a foundation for the illegal & uncertain exactions of the Malliks on the Ryots'.[42] Here we see a zealous state official redefining 'custom' with the twin intentions of breaking up the alleged nexus between *ameens* and maliks, and providing some security to the *raiyats*. On other occasions, we see in Hamilton an official who insisted on overriding the legal framework of the settlements. According to the *kabooleat* (deed) recognised during the PS, the government was obliged to remit revenues in cases when lands turned *gangashikasht* (diluvated) or *baloobund* (sandy, infertile). Hamilton nonetheless insisted that maliks ought to bear the loss arising due to diluviation. On another occasion we find Hamilton directing his junior to reduce the customary *malikana* from 10 to 5 per cent.[43]

'Principle of equity': rights and occupancy

It is a matter of widespread consensus that the interventionist nature of colonial state started manifesting in the second half of the 19th century, which Sarkar elegantly characterises as a progressive enhancement in 'ability to enforce' and not necessarily a change in the outlook of ruling groups (Sarkar 2014: 82). The quest for securing 'tenants' rights' was a feature of various legal interventions made in this period. Starting with the Rent Act of 1859, the state laid down the criteria for the security of tenure of 'occupancy tenants' giving them the protection from arbitrary rent increase by maliks (Swamy 2010: 9. Also see Robb 1997: 81). This, however, did not happen. The act 'was only a half-measure which did not serve the interests of either the landlords or the tenantry' (Sen Gupta 1974: 33, footnote 18). The 1885 Tenancy Act plugged in some of the loopholes though not very successfully, one important measure related to the 12-year continuous occupancy in the same plot.[44]

This section chronologically carries the story forward by looking at the interplay of some of the themes we have explored earlier, primarily of measurement, law and custom. The central focus is on understanding *raiyati* conditions, once again in association with the mainland agrarian history as well as specific to *diaras*.

Before the rent and tenancy acts, tenancy in Bengal and Bihar was embedded in social and political relationships governed through the zamindari system. The early 19th-century feature of the state to not go deep into the agrarian system (what we have described as legalising the privatisation of relationship between *zamindars* and *raiyats*) meant that the *raiyat* remained a social category tied with maliks not only in economic but in socio-political sense as well.[45] In the second half of the 19th century, the state's shift from its overt concern about revenue to that of the rights of tenants meant that legal interventions recast the category of *raiyat*. Tenancies that were socially embedded were now tried to be extracted into legal frameworks and categories. Some existing accounts will let us believe that there was an absolute shift in the colonial policy towards *raiyats* (tenants) in the second half of the 19th century. This, of course, is an oversimplification of the historical complexity. In spite of intending to be pro-*raiyat*, the state never could antagonise *zamindars*. In 1875, for instance, the Bengal government denied the prevalence of any adequate grounds for adoption of special measures to protect *raiyats*.[46]

The 1885 Tenancy Act also evoked responses which were vague and mixed. Similar to what the nationalists had tried to do a little later, that is to downplay the differences between landholders and cultivators, the colonial state also tried to sell its policies as benefiting one and all. Stuart Bayley, the late governor of Bihar, thought that the post-1885 survey and settlement process would

> define the holdings and rents of each ryot, [it would] place in the landlord's hands means which very few now have of proving without difficulty what they are entitled to claim, and [it would] give the ryots the power of resisting illegal and improper claims.[47]

The administration was aware of the uneasiness which the act would cause to the *zamindars*, and so it tried to sell it to them by arguing that the exactness of knowledge embedded in record of rights would help them to know who their *raiyats* were and with what rights, and where their lands lay with what rents. Conversely, in cases where the state found it difficult to access the knowledge, as it did during the survey and settlement operations in Monghyr, both sections – landlords and *raiyats* – became untrustworthy. It was argued that 'raiyats' statements as to the rent payable were not to be believed, while the landlords were generally unwilling to produce their books of accounts' (Murphy 1914: 7).

In this backdrop of broader contour of agrarian change and colonial policies, for *diara* lands we can broadly identify three phases of active engagement by the state. The first was between the 1820s and 1840s, in which the revenue surveys followed resumption. The acknowledgement of scientific value of survey went hand in hand with the reliance on customary practices. Revenue surveys yielded maps which helped the state in assessment and settlement of land. The riparian regulations and orders from this time also show the same ideological bent in adopting surveys for settling *diara* lands and in the growing reliance on maps. The primary thrust was to know who held the land and how to fix the revenue. In other words, tenancy rights were not directly on the agenda. Also, unlike the PS which was 'estate' based (crops in the estate and not its area), the revenue surveys used the village as the unit of survey and mapping.

It would be interesting to once again have a closer look at the first riparian law of colonial India (1825 Regulation), which used both languages of the customs indicating an agrarian world inhabited by *zamindar–raiyat* social relationship and that of tenurial rights. The only place where the regulation accepted the role of an under-tenant needs to be quoted in full:

> Nor, if annexed to a subordinate tenure [the alluvial increment] held under a superior landholder, shall the under-tenant, whether a khudkast raiyat, holding a maurasi istimrari tenure at a fixed rate of rent per bigha, or any other description of under-tenant liable by his engagements or by established usage, to an increase of rent for the land annexed to his tenure by alluvion, be considered exempt from the payment of any increase of rent to which he may be justly liable.[48]

The 1858 Act, which provisioned that alluvial increment could also be settled as a separate estate with a separate *jumma* (on refusal of the maliks), also provisioned that such an arrangement would not disturb the rights of under-tenants as described in the 1825 Regulation. The act said,

> It shall be duty of all officers making settlements of such land, whether the land be settled separately or incorporated with the original estate, to ascertain and record all such rights according to the rules prescribed in Regulation VII of 1822, and determine whether any and what additional rent shall be payable in respect of the alluvial land by the person or persons entitled to any under-tenure in the original estate.[49]

A close reading of these two legal pieces suggests that the state was more concerned with securing the payment of additional rent to maliks and that the existing tenurial system of *raiyats* should not interfere with that. Even a *maurasi istimrari* tenure holder (a hereditary holding, or a farm or lease granted in perpetuity by government or a *zamindar* at a stipulated rent, and exempt from *abwabs*) (Wilson 1855: 221) was not exempt from the increase in rent. The difference between these two nonetheless was that the earlier *justly liable* increase of rent based on custom and established usage was now to be determined by the settling officer.

There always existed officials like Wells and Hamilton who used their tours and measurement and survey operations to act on the spot in favour of *raiyats*. We have noted earlier how Wells curtailed the levy of one *abwab*. In another settlement for *diara* Seetulpore, he reduced the rate of some of the *pottahs* (deeds) granted to the *raiyats* from Rs 3 and 8 annas to Rs 2 per *beegah*. Besides, he lowered the rate of all the *pottahs* by 2 annas because he considered them to be very high.[50] For two of the *diara*-prone *mauzas* of pargana Pharkiya in Monghyr, where Wells had given land to a majority of *raiyats* on *pottahs*, Hamilton argued that any measurement would bring 'considerable injury' to the *raiyats* and by extension such a loss would eventually fall on the government.[51] In all probability, these were *khas* and not zamindari *diaras* (that is *diaras* of which the property rights were either vested in or managed by the state). In zamindari *diaras*, such interference by the state to ascertain *raiyati* rights would have been a lot tougher and in fact undesirable. The offside remark by Hamilton on measurement is significant – it shows how partial the state could get in using it when it threatened to affect its rent.[52]

The 1825 Regulation referred to *khudkasht* (settled occupancy) and other secured and better-off *raiyats*. Subsequent decisions on cases involving this regulation brought out the implication of such references more clearly. The regulation did envisage that the tenant had the right to continue in the occupation of the increment area provided he paid the increased rent; decisions were passed, which made a distinction between the kinds of tenants mentioned. In one case, it was declared that the regulation did not mention tenant from year to year, while in another it was claimed no law of the country allowed the right of accretion to the *raiyat*.[53] The picture which emerges is that the better-off tenantry with some security was a marginal feature in *diara* lands. We can get an idea of this if we look at variable uses of land and resources, akin to the current historiographical sophistication that rightly urges us not to regard fields and pastures, cultivated land and forest as strictly secluded zones. More research is required in areas such as the role of family labour, family size, farm size, plot location and other related matters, but some references at hand support this historiographical position. Pargana Pharkiya in Monghyr, which lay north to the Ganga, had a good extent of *diara* lands. Being the low-lying tract, the pargana was inundated in the rainy seasons but also afforded excellent pasturage in the drier seasons. This resulted in a localised seasonal migration in search of better pastures. More direct agricultural seasonal migration also took place; after the rains, cultivators in large numbers from the adjoining districts of Bhagalpur, Darbhanga and Muzaffarpur came to Pharkiya with their cattle to till the lands at a low rate and left for their homes after the harvest of the rabi crops.[54]

In all the five *mauzas* of Nundlalpore *talooqa*, *nukuddy* rate existed (i.e. cash rent), which indicates that either the land was of high productive quality or maliks were reluctant to enter into *batai* (the crop division form of rent payment) or both.[55] Ecological fluidity played a role in deciding cash rent, which in the whole of the talooqa was of 32 types ranging from 4 annas to Rs 2 per *beegah*. The *raiyats* in the whole of the *talooqa* were of *pykasht* (migratory occupancy) nature and belonged to 'all castes and descriptions'.[56] This fluidity made migration an integral feature of how *raiyats* negotiated with this landscape. Writing about Monghyr, O'Malley says: 'Migration from village to village is rare, except along the banks of the Ganges and its affluents [*sic*], where the frequent shiftings of the river beds necessitate the movement of the villagers' (O'Malley [1926] 2007: 56). Therefore, in the first phase while we notice the construction and implementation of various legal codifications which gradually prioritised survey and measurement (the elements denoting fixity), the actual ground reality of *diara* lands comprised seasonal mobility.

The second phase extended from the 1860s to the 1880s, with a major intensive focus in the beginning of the 1860s. The Gangetic *diara* surveys were instituted in the 1860s in different districts of Bihar, subsequent to which the settlement of revenue for areas that had changed was done under the provisions of the Act IX of 1847.[57] A considerable amount of time and money was spent. Nisbet must have felt vindicated as the survey was done of the river beds. New maps were made, and new assessments were based on comparing these maps with those produced during the revenue surveys (Murphy 1912: 23, 1914: 19; Sen 1915: 1). Like revenue surveys, this one also had the village as the unit of mapping. They showed topographical details with village boundaries. This shows that regardless of the imperfect nature of mapping during both surveys, maps did become the bases for assessing revenue and fixing proprietorial rights in the future.[58]

Once again, the clarity which the state had intended to achieve was missing, and we are thrown back to not lose sight of historical complexity amid bureaucratic proclamations about standardisation. This existed at many levels. Administratively, it was subsequently pointed out that records and maps were not kept properly. They were also not revised (Sen 1915: 1). Conceptually, it was argued that showing village boundaries on maps was inadequate because rather than the village, 'estate' was the unit on which the PS was based. Therefore, many a time two estates existed or shared boundaries in the same village. In Shahabad district, where three survey maps existed (one from revenue and two from *diara* surveys), the problem confounded even further (Hubbock [1918] 1928: 28–29, 35). In each of them the village boundaries differed; some villages had completely disappeared and were replaced by new and differently bounded villages.[59] This was the third type of difficulty. The ecology of the land was fluid, and the mechanisms to 'fix' it were grounded in the principles of fixity. In an extremely eloquent way, the Shahabad settlement officer gave it a conceptual dressing: he asked the law to be amended to secure *geographical* stability even if the *physical* stability was wanting (Hubbock [1918] 1928: 28, emphasis mine). The idea behind using the village as the unit was based on the principle of possession. Therefore, the 1881–83 survey in Shahabad did alter the village boundaries shown in maps from the previous survey but only according to possession. Ecological fluidity rendered possessions also impermanent, so the fourth level of difficulty was in the financial capacity of the state to do almost annual measurements and map corrections. It was emphatically argued, 'In diara lands, a map six years old is often no better clue to actual possession than a map sixty years old. Possession alters every year' (Murphy 1912: 27).

In the settlement records of *diara* lands from the 1860s to the 1870s, we see five classifications that, based on who cultivated the lands, defined the forms of occupancy:

1 By proprietors
2 By cultivators having a right of possession at fixed rates
3 By cultivators with a right of occupancy
4 By other cultivators
5 Cultivable, not cultivated land occupied by

In the earlier-prescribed format of information collection, in a majority of cases *diara* lands were marked as cultivated by 'other cultivators' (category 4), signifying that they were either of *pykasht* nature or of other under-tenurial status that largely depended on seasonal migration. *Raiyats* did dwell on *diara* lands, but diluviation rendered them mobile; they made a comeback claim once the lands had reformed as it happened in the case of Jaffernugger Salempore estate.[60] From the size of 4,397 *beegahs* it shrunk to a little more than 7 *beegahs*, which was all occupied by the dwelling houses of the *raiyats*. In 1866, the remaining land was also washed away, and so the estate was bought by the state and put under the charge of *surburakar* (a native subordinate revenue official). The land started re-forming in November 1867, which was reported by Jhontee Singh. The land, about 40 *beegahs*, was then settled with him and others for Rs 45 for one year. For 1868–69, the increased land area (311 *beegahs*) was settled again with them for Rs 253. The first settlement was a *bhaoli* one, that is based on crop production (the half of it); the second was *nukuddy* at a differential rate of Rs 1 for 40 *beegahs* and 12 annas for the remaining. Once again, the preference for cash or produce rent shows how the state or the maliks calculated their profits exposing the nexus between ecology and revenue/rent. For the next five years the *surburakar* recommended the settlement with the same lessees for rent rising up from Rs 310 to Rs 485. However, as the area kept on increasing, the higher lease offers kept pouring in. In 1869–70, it was put up for auction and given to James Daniel McGiveron, who offered the rental of Rs 3,232 per annum. The settlement papers do not explain this huge 'discrepancy' or 'rise' in assessment apart from the fact that the *surburakar* was accused of being either inefficient or dishonest.

The interesting fact is not the inexplicable ten times hike but the petition of Jhontee Singh and others, who were the former cultivators (and not the intermediary leaseholders) and were the first to report on the re-formation of land. Seemingly, being the former cultivators (who claimed to possess specialised knowledge by knowing the history and boundaries of the estate very well), they were chosen for two 1-year settlements (from 1867 to 1869), but subsequent to realising that the area was gradually increasing, the state thought it prudent to auction the estate. The result was that the actual cultivators lost the chance to compete with higher bidders. Their petition to possess the right to have the first rejection was dismissed. The state argued that technically auction was open to all parties, which went against the argument the board had given some 30 years ago, clarifying that the existing holders had the right to first rejection. And this was precisely the catch here: Jhontee Singh and others were just 'cultivators' and not leaseholders. The Collector pointed out that they were only 'tenants-at-will' and not settlement holders and so 'have no right to settlement'. The legal vocabulary permeated the bureaucratic practice as the words 'ryots' and 'cultivators' on two different occasions in the text were struck off and replaced by tenants-at-will. This was in spite of the categorical nature of 'the current rules [that] enjoin[ed] that pending regular settlement of an estate awaiting re-settlement, the Collector shall review the existing lease from year to year with the prior settlement holder, if he be willing to engage on such terms'.[61] Clearly, the existing cultivators were first legally 'downgraded' into the category of tenants-at-will, and then the case was made against them.

Further, the petitioners' charge of settling the land with McGiveron without any measurement and preparation of *khasra* (record) was not disputed by the Collector; the later only noticed that the 'summary settlement' was made because the season of local enquiry had already passed. Similarly, on the allegation that the settlement was done without taking any security, the Collector defended his act by saying that McGiveron was a 'respectable man' and his depositing Rs 600 in cash was 'sufficient'. The petitioners also invoked the logic of outsider-stranger, suggesting that McGiveron or his servants were unacquainted with the landscape and therefore their management could lead to loss. Working within the legal framework of dispute resolution, the general tone of the petition was first to point out the discrepancies in the practice of settlement and second to convince the state of the losses it might suffer. Nowhere could one read the tone of assertion of 'rights'.[62] From the reply to the last point, it becomes clear that McGiveron was not a 'stranger'; he had several other farms on lease and had convinced the authorities by making no losses on them.

The petitioner's reference to *khasra* even for *diara* lands does signify that technically the record of rights for the fluvial landscape was not non-existent. The migratory *pykasht* nature of cultivation, the preponderance of cultivators defined as 'other cultivators' or 'tenants-at-will' and the summary nature of settlement nonetheless leave little doubt that in only few cases *diara* cultivators legally fought to gain fixed rent or occupancy *raiyat* status.[63] One such case surprisingly involved the same McGiveron and the *raiyats* of Kootloopur *diara*.[64] It will be unnecessary to reproduce the long case history in its full complexity, but significant for our purposes is to know that *raiyats* fought a legal battle against McGiveron's attempt to enhance the rent, and the district court and High Court upheld them as occupancy *raiyats*. The case also brings out the ambiguous relationship between 'white' administrators and private Europeans because McGiveron's attempt to increase the rent was based on the claim that he was verbally assured by the Collector that *raiyats* on this *diara* had no rights and that they could be ejected at will.[65] While presenting his case, McGiveron asserted that most of the *raiyats* were well-to-do, but by a way of general admittance the new Collector accepted that the system of farming *diaras* on lease put tenantry in a very disastrous position.[66] Posing a legal challenge to an established private European through the hierarchies of district and high courts reasonably means that some of the *raiyats* were definitely well-to-do. Some of them owned cattle as McGiveron accused them of destroying the crop by letting loose their cattle.

However, the legal and administrative debate on this case also shows that the issue of rights and 'fair rent' was complex, more so because of ecological reasons. This *diara* had not existed during the PS. It arose from the bed of the river in 1836, and therefore the administration claimed that *raiyats* could not have held *maurusi* rights (hereditary).[67] However, if they claimed to be 'occupancy *raiyats*', they could only do so by claiming it to hold on 'fair and equitable rates'. This was the line of argument which the High Court also followed, meaning that even for occupancy *raiyats* the rent could have been enhanced had it been proven that adjacent *diaras*/estates paid the higher rent. McGiveron enhancement suits were based on this claim, but the district judge found it unacceptable. On appeal, the High Court declined to interfere with the finding of the fact by a judge. The denial of enhancement meant denial of eviction and hence the confirmation of occupancy status.

The aforementioned case shows that *raiyats* could at times manage to claim their rights through law but based on other settlement papers in which the classificatory schema often downgraded cultivators as 'others' meant that usually the actual cultivators were getting excluded by the law.[68] Cadastral survey and preparation of record of rights became the backbone of the fresh stint of land survey and settlement programme that followed in the wake of the 1885 Tenancy Act. This is the third phase of colonial engagement with *diara* lands under the rubric of broader agrarian changes. The act had two sets of concerns regarding *diara* lands as for other landforms as well, but with significant differences. One dealt with the issue of rights and rents, another with record preparation. The act clearly lay down that even on *diara* lands the way to gain right to occupancy was through 12 years of continuous holding but of the *same* land (and not any land in the village). In essence, the *diara raiyats* were now legally confirmed neither to be settled nor occupancy *raiyats* for the first 12 years; they were practically tenants-at-will as they were earlier. The 1885 Act only made their wilful eviction further difficult.[69]

As far as provisions of Chapter X of the act dealing with record preparation were concerned, as early as in 1892 doubts crept up on including *diara* lands within the ambit of this part of the act which required first traverse and then cadastral survey, followed by preparation of record of rights. The latter was a prolonged multilayered process. It started with the issue of notices for attestation and settlement of fair rents, the latter requiring each individual's rent to be calculated, proposed and settled and, in case of opposition and dispute, to be further inquired into and resolved. This was followed by draft publication and then, after resolution of disputes, by final publication. The rent collection was allowed only from the commencement of the next agricultural year when the final publication was made. The obvious problem in the case of *diaras* was that all these processes could hardly be completed in one winter season. The postponement of operations meant fresh surveys as the quantity of land would have changed.[70] Creation of accurate maps from time to time also became an impending factor (Sen 1915: 2–3).

Some work on survey and settlement had started in north Bihar, but it was during the attestation in 1895 that acute problems surfaced. Some villages were found missing, while others of course had newly formed. The readjustment in fields and alterations in area also meant that old *raiyats* had disappeared and new arrived. On further deliberations, the government finally took a decision to keep *diara* lands outside the ambit of the Tenancy Act. No record of right under the tenancy act had to be prepared until *zamindars* and *raiyats* expressed their desire to do so and covered the expenses.[71] A separate *diara* survey operation was commissioned in 1907 which covered 3,195 square miles in the districts of Saran, Shahabad, Patna, Monghyr, Bhagalpur and Santhal Parganas. The main thrust of the survey was on preparing maps but most important in making 'geography' fixed by putting 834 pillars in a length of 272 miles in these districts. These maps showed the shifts in the river in the historical sense by showing differences between three sets of survey maps: revenue (1830s–40s), *diara* (1860s–80s) and the latest one (1900s–10s). In addition, they showed the 'marks of permanence' that were erected along the banks (Sen 1915: 1, 14).

Conclusions

In 1990, some of the villagers from the surrounding *diara* areas captured around 52 *beegahs* of land in Gangaldai, a village situated at some three kilometres from Kahalgaon town in Bhagalpur district. In the next two years some 628 houses were built by these migrating villagers on this land, which was jointly owned by the government and local businessmen. Clarifying his intention to not leave this possession, 70-year-old Bajrangi Das, who moved in there with his family, recounted:

> I have lost count of the many times I have been displaced in my life due to land erosion. We have no land; we have to live on sharecropping and farm labour. No matter what happens – police or army assaults or firing – we will not move from here.[72]

This is a big temporal leap from the beginning of the 20th century to 1990, but the tenor and tone of the plight does suggest a palpable historical continuity. Some recent surveys and project findings also claim that *diara* land inhabitants are poor, marred by poverty (Panda, n.d.). The use of new technology (GPS remote sensing) in tracking the rapidly changing land cover and land use of *diara* lands is highly illuminating to the sketch of the past we have presented here (Kumar *et al.* 2008: 22–28).

This chapter has looked at two interrelated processes of land settlement and rights creation. Lahiri-Dutt and Samanta have proposed to treat *chars* as 'unique', 'fluid', hybrid', 'specific' and, not least, 'environmental borderlands'.[73] In other words, a case for anomaly has been made in this study. In general, I am in agreement with treating this landscape as unique or hybrid as long as it simply means that the stable categories of land and water, as they also claim, do not help us in understanding the social and administrative history of *diara* lands. I also concur with the view, as shown in this chapter also through a close study of measurement, that colonialism was obsessed with 'land'-based thinking. Beyond that, nonetheless, my understanding of colonial intervention varies from the current studies.

In the works of Lahiri-Dutt and Samanta, D'Souza and Hill, the colonial state appears to have a well-defined and clear ideological will, possessing a robust bureaucratic apparatus to implement what it wanted to. There is hardly any doubt that the colonial state's agrarian policy was heavily determined by the ideas of well-demarcated individual property, and yet one needs to bear in mind that the ecological fluidity of *diara* lands made the bedrock of that property – the *value* – itself a flexible entity (remember Nisbet). The state wanted to settle *diaras* in the same way as it did other lands – here, the anomalous status of *diaras* in bureaucratic thinking ceases to exist. In fact, the intensity of survey and mapping shows that the application of 'general' principles was thought to be the only remedy.

However, the historical reality of constant shifts and disputes, which sucked in the state's apparatus, points towards what David Mosse has elegantly described as the 'contingent world of messiness and practices'. It is this world which is, in his view, the point of origin of universal concepts such as law, science and property (Mosse 2006: 61–90).

Law was not an abstract institution of rule. Its formation, change, adaptation and failure all signified a process of the state's coming to terms with this agro-ecological landscape. Legal flexibility does not necessarily only flow from the inherent nature of it being processual; it is also a function and a result of conscious policy making, governance practices and social and ecological conditions. And herein lays the specificity of *diara* lands: even in the application of general principle of survey and measurement, this ecological belt required a constant, almost real-time mapping of changes which was beyond the capacity of the state. If the capacity of the state to impose legal frameworks proves the robustness of the state, then the history of Gangetic fluvial landscape literally puts the state on the shaky and shifting grounds of a long series of legal meddling (albeit with the intention of providing clarity).

This historical messiness serves to explain the *context* of legal standardisations (both attempted and achieved) and hence *does not* suggest that law in itself was ineffective. The legal categorisation of subjecthood did become the premise of exclusion and inclusion.[74] It ensured rights to certain sections of the subject and simultaneously deprived others. Once again, the atypicality of *diara* lands emerging out of, say, the preponderance of migratory *raiyati* situation worked *within* the general principles of laws and rights based on occupancy. The ecological peculiarity contributed to the complexity of this relationship between law and rights. This complexity was not solved by the special *diara* surveys with which we have ended our narrative. It continued all throughout the 20th century, and the state kept on making or amending laws. In spite of appearing anomalous (as was retrospectively upheld by the law by keeping *diaras* outside of the 1885 Act), the history of *diara* lands represents the general march of the colonial state towards getting more intrusive into the agrarian social set-up. In a nutshell, the 'mainstream/anomaly' binary can prove counterproductive if our aim is to understand the interaction and interrelationship between standardising bureaucratic practices and historical complexities, as presented in this study, through ecological fluidity.

Notes

1 This observation on the absence of *raiyats* in records should not be equated with a claim made in a recent study that the colonial (and postcolonial) state policies turned *char* lands invisible. Lahiri-Dutt and Samanta (2013: 77).

2 Sarkar (2014: 137). Sarkar does not mention the recent work of Iftekhar Iqbal, which gives a detailed account of this process. Iqbal (2010: chapter 2).

3 There is though a similarity between northern and eastern Bengal, both of which are exemplified by atypicality to the Permanent Settlement (PS). Cultivation in northern Bengal was also based on reclamation of uncultivable land. See Bandyopadhyaya (1977: A111–A126).

4 As pointed out by Iqbal. Iqbal also strongly supports the thesis of relatively undifferentiated peasantry in eastern Bengal, but his account also gives a picture of subtle changes happening to the category of 'intermediaries'. The earlier *hawaldars* and *jotedars* were getting displaced by indigo planters as leaseholders and the *bhadralok* were becoming the 'new *raiyat*' (legally) who in practice were rentier intermediaries. Iqbal (2010).

5 This, however, was a gradual process, taking roots from post-mid-19th century. For a damning exposé of the 'wretched' condition of *raiyats* in the period before that, see 'Extract of Report from Commissioner in Soonderbuns to Sudder Board of Revenue Dated 10 September 1832', Monghyr Collectors' Letters Received, year 1832–35, Bihar State Archives (MCLR, BSA).

6 Government of India: Department of Revenue, Agriculture and Commerce, Land Revenue and Settlements, July 1875, prodgs. 10 and 11, National Archives of India (NAI). The Bengal PS had no intention to sweep away customary or traditional rights of agricultural tenants. Washbrook (1981: 656).

7 A point well made in the current scholarship on labour and law in South Asian history. See Joshi (2008: 439–454). This approach is different from Washbrook's position in which the law until the 1850s was characterised as inefficient and unable to penetrate into social structures after a point. Washbrook (1981).

8 Yearly bidding of land (even in non-*diara* cases) on lease must not be taken as a colonial novelty devised to increase the exploitation. In diverse regions of pre-colonial South Asia, a variety of arrangements were in practice. In Berar in central India, for instance, the land was let out to the highest bidder (either to the village headman or to the stranger-contractor) who had the right to extract as much rent as possible. Satya (1998: 57).

9 I have purposely kept the observation speculative. Before arriving at any definite view, we will need to know the pre-colonial history of Gangetic *diaras*, which to my knowledge is unfortunately not available in the existing secondary literature. Hill in his study of north Bihar concludes that colonial intervention created a new class of landless labourers (Hill 1990: 14). On the contrary, Iqbal argues that in eastern Bengal state intervention led to better conditions of *raiyats* (Iqbal 2010).

10 Martin (1838, 2: 230). Vinay Gidwani's imaginative reading of the waste is broadly acceptable, in the sense, that like other ideas such as 'improvement', the waste also symbolised a justification of colonial rule. Embedded in the invocation of the waste, Gidwani argues, was the reference not only to ecological waste that deprived the state of its revenue but also social waste that discursively inferiorised India/Bengal. One wonders what alternative reading or linguistic spin this approach would yield for words such as 'rich' and 'fertile', which were also profusely used to describe the land. Will that mean colonial administrators

'appreciated' India? In Gidwani's understanding probably not; it would still mean the same, arguing that since land was fertile, it needed colonial rule for its further improvement (Gidwani 1992: PE39–PE46).

11 Unlike forests, which were so in south-west Bengal. Sivaramakrishnan (1999a: 6–7).

12 This set of ideas is triggered by Ludden's discussion (1999: 18).

13 Ibid., 20.

14 This in turn happened because of the concentration of precipitation over much of the Indian subcontinent in a short period between June and September, leading to large seasonal variations in the level of different water bodies. Gopal and Sah (1995: 39–48).

15 Risk minimisation is the key aspect as was argued by D'Souza (2011) in his presentation 'Nature as Calamity: The Emergence of Flood Control in Colonial India'.

16 Hamilton in the letter dated 17 March 1835, Monghyr Collector Khasmahal Correspondence, year 1835, BSA (MCKC, BSA).

17 In the case of Bhownundpore *diara*, the setting-in of hot season prohibited the Deputy Collector from undertaking the tour to test the measurement done by ameens. This, in turn, happened because of delayed appointment of ameens in January instead of September when the work ideally should have started. Commissioner's Order dated 16 July 1869, Monghyr Collector Settlement Letter Received, year 1867–71, BSA (MCSLR, BSA).

18 This claim of Hamilton is incorrect. In certain parganas of Monghyr, where he travelled in 1835, *rabi* (winter) crops were important. The doras quality of land found in *diaras* yielded inferior rabi crops. Also, O'Malley mentions that being the most fertile lands, *diaras* produced 'fine *bhadoi* crops [sown in June and harvested in August or September] before the river rises and good *rabi* crops in the cold weather'. O'Malley ([1926] 2007: 99, 89–90). Large outturns of rabi crops from small cost of production were also reported from *diaras* of the Shahabad district that lay between River Ganga and the East Indian Railway Line. Hubbock (1918: 2). What, therefore, seems plausible is that Hamilton concentrated on *bhadoi* crops which were harvested in September and *aghani* crops (winter crops) that were sown in May and reaped in November but overlooked rabi crops which were sown in November and harvested in spring. See Ram (1997: 18).

19 Hamilton's letter dated 14 April 1835, year 1835, MCKC, BSA.

20 Baden-Powell summed up the role of measurement in the most explicit way: according to him the settlement must start with

> a complete *survey* of the land, involving a preliminary *demarcation* of the necessary *boundary lines*; because without that, neither can there be an exact account of the culturable land, and the extent of each kind of soil which requires a different rate of assessment; nor can there be any correct record of the rights of all parties, landlord, co-sharer, subproprietor, occupancy-tenant, or whatever they are, in case the system requires a record of rights.

The other two factors why surveys were essential were, first, to have a correct list of the revenue payers and their holdings and, second, to ascertain the valuation of the land and revenue rates. Baden-Powell ([1907] 1978: 147–148) (emphasis original).

21 In the Ruhutpoor case, a diara in the district of Monghyr, Wells's understanding of the perpetual erosion was based on what 'people' said, which cautioned him

that maliks could resort to the diluviation remission. Wells's letter dated 12 May 1834, year 1834–36, MCSLR, BSA.

22 Nisbet's letter dated 17 February 1836, year 1834–36, MCSLR, BSA.

23 In his words,

> A Permanent Settlement of Villages situated as those are said to be – actually undergoing dilapidation from the assault of the River – is neither attainable nor does it seem expedient, the utmost that can be done . . . is to make the best and most feasible arrangement each year or for such protected period as they are likely to continue without any great determination of their Ruqba. Ibid.

24 Hamilton's letter dated 22 February 1836, year 1834–36, MCSLR, BSA.

25 Well's letter dated 12 May 1834, Ibid.

26 Hamilton's letter dated 7 November 1835, Ibid.

27 'Extract from the Address of the Sudder Board to Government', 29 March 1836, Peters (1838, CCI: 535–555).

28 In Monghyr the survey was carried between 1838 and 1847; in Bhagalpur between 1846 and 1850. In Shahabad it was between 1844 and 1846. Murphy (1912: 21, 1914: 19) and Hubbock (1918: 27). On their inadequacy, see the next section of this chapter.

29 I find it rather intriguing to see Lahiri-Dutt and Samanta (2013: 61) arguing that the PS led to surveys and then anachronistically referring to James Rennell, whose surveys conducted in the 1760s and the 1770s were not necessarily related to agrarian lands.

30 'The Bengal Alluvion and Diluvion Regulation: Regulation XI, 26 May 1825', in Mitra (1934: 185, 188).

31 Bhattacharya (1996: 24). I find Bhattacharya's comparison between Bengal and Punjab showing that the knowledge production in the former was based on texts while in the latter on customary practices overstretched. Indeed, he succinctly draws out the complexity involved in the claim of custom as the basis of colonial knowledge; his comparison, nonetheless, is between the non-comparable zones of action. Similar to the Punjab *agrarian* sphere, the fluvial agro-ecological zone of Bihar and Bengal also witnessed a practice-based understanding of custom, and indeed the interplay between custom and law in this region was as complex as it were in other regions.

32 Jones (1851, no. DLXXIII: 144–145). The provisions of this circular were enacted as 'Bengal Alluvial Land Settlement Act: Act XXXI of 1858', in Mitra (1934: 215–216).

33 'The Bengal Alluvion and Diluvion Act: Act IX of 1847', Mitra (1934: 213–214).

34 Mitra (1934: 214). Any abatement of revenue in cases of diluviation had to be ascertained by inspecting new maps produced under the provisions of the 1847 Act. See Department of Secretariat of the Governor General, branch public, file no. 14/101/41-GG(B), 1941, NAI.

35 'Extract from the Address of the Sudder Board to Government'.

36 In the 1838 Order, the board took note that 'no uniform course of procedure has hitherto been followed by Settling Officers'. Twenty years later, the tone remained the same in the preamble of the 1858 Act.

37 Monghyr Collector Miscellaneous Letter Issued, year 1850–57: 18, BSA (MCMLI, BSA).

38 Once again, bureaucratic divide is noticeable: Hamilton greatly relied on one *tehsildar* Omras Singh whom he described as a 'very old servant of the Government' and 'a man of respectable connections'. Hamilton's letter dated 2

September 1835, year 1835, MCKC, BSA. The board, however, felt that it was this 'class of people' who benefited the most from the chaotic conditions of the revenue department by intentionally keeping the situation so. The board, in fact, was stuck between rhetoric and practicality. Ideally, it would have dispensed with native subordinates, but practically it accepted to rely on 'respectable' persons – a classic conundrum of colonial power and its limitation.

39 Hamilton's letter dated 16 April 1835, year 1835, MCKC, BSA.

40 Hamilton's letter dated 29 September 1833, vol. year 1835, MCKC, BSA. Such an untrustworthy relationship with measurement was a feature of both 'peasant' and 'tribal' societies. The Bhils complained that a sahib 'looked at a forest through a durbin (telescope) and grabbed it'. Sarkar (2014: 100, footnote 39).

41 Wells's letter dated 12 May 1834, year 1834–36, MCSLR, BSA.

42 Ibid.

43 Any wilful or ignorant tampering with the rate of *malikana* can also be reflective of a dense legal web that officials were required to work with. Although speculative, it might be the case that full or partial refusal to grant customary *malikana* flowed from Regulation VII of 1822 meant for the Ceded and Conquered Territories (together with Cuttack and some other principalities) in which the *malikana* was fixed at not less than 5 per cent and not more than 10 per cent. 'Regulation VII of 1822' in Papers Relating to East India Affairs: Viz. Regulations . . . in the Year 1822', *Parliamentary Papers*, 1824: 15. For the basis of this speculation, see below: 21.

44 Sen Gupta (1974: 10, footnote 18). The 1885 Act brought about a significant change by changing the site of occupation from the *same* land for 12 years to occupying any land in the same village for 12 years. For the problems the village-based arrangement posed for *diara* lands, see the discussion on pp. 27–8. Bengal Tenancy Act, Finucane, pp. 252–253.

45 One of the best empirical works demonstrating this is of McLane (1977: 19–36).

46 Government of India: Department of Revenue, Agriculture and Commerce, Land Revenue and Settlements, July 1875, Proceedings. 10 and 11, NAI. Richard Temple, the Lieutenant Governor of Bengal, thought it undesirable and unnecessary to interfere in matters between *zamindars* and cultivators. Ideologically, the case was made against the paternalist school of administration followed elsewhere in India; in Bengal, they argued, 'the more the people are left to manage their own affairs the better'. Government of India: Department of Revenue, Agriculture and Commerce, Land Revenue and Settlements, September 1875, Proceedings. 14 and 15, NAI. Even, the pro-tenant Bengali intelligentsia did not cut very deep into the privileges of *zamindars*. Sen Gupta (1974: 30–31).

47 Government of India: Revenue and Agricultural Department, Revenue Branch, February 1892, A prodgs. 12 to 16: 2, NAI. Not surprisingly then some administrators also saw the Bengal and Bihar Tenancy Act as a natural corollary to the Permanent Settlement.

48 'The Bengal Alluvion and Diluvion Regulation: Regulation XI, 26 May 1825': 187.

49 'The Bengal Alluvion and Diluvion Act: Act IX of 1847': 216.

50 Hamilton's letter dated 21 May 1835, year 1835, MCKC, BSA.

51 Ibid.

52 From *khas diaras* the state tried to raise money in every possible way. From Bindah *diara*, a very big size in Monghyr, Hamilton proposed to collect Rs 150 per annum as levy on buffaloes and other cattle grazing. Hamilton's letter 29

September 1835, year 1835, MCKC, BSA. The practice of keeping cattle on *diara* land or using *diara* fodder is still prevalent in Monghyr district. *Report of Survey Conducted on Developing Strategies to Increase Production and Enhance Market Linkage of Milk*, n.d.

53 Bengal Tenancy Act, Finucane, pp. 113–114.

54 O'Malley ([1926] 2007: 56). This was called 'dohata' cultivation. This seems to be the characteristic of fluvial landscape as cultivators from Bhagalpur also migrated to Kosi region in western Purnea with their cattle. Chakravarti (1986: 1848).

55 Writing for Shahabad, Francis Buchanan-Hamilton had observed in the early 19th century that cash rent was paid for lands near the Ganga and for fields that were carefully watered near the villages. Hubbock ([1918] 1928: 24).

56 Hamilton's letter dated 25 March 1835, year 1835, MCKC, BSA.

57 In Monghyr and Bhagalpur districts, the survey took place in 1865–66; in Shahabad two surveys took place – one in 1863–64 and two in 1881–83.

58 On the imperfection of these maps, see Hubbock ([1918] 1928: 27).

59 The Bhagalpur settlement officer pointed out the same problem: the revenue and *diara* survey maps seldom matched. Murphy (1912: 27).

60 'Report on the Settlement of Estate Juffurnugger Salempore', year 1867–71, MCSLR, BSA.

61 'Report on the Settlement of Estate Juffurnugger Salempore', year 1871–73, MCSLR, BSA.

62 Petition in the letter to the Commissioner of Bhagalpur dated 1 June 1869, year 1867–71, MCSLR, BSA.

63 The ways of ascertaining the productivity of soil were quite subjective, more so in the case of summary settlements, which is attested by remarks like 'splendid crops' and 'splendid soil' made by the visiting officials during their on-the-spot enquiries.

64 Government of India: Department of Revenue, Agriculture and Commerce, Land Revenue and Settlement, October 1873, prodgs. Nos. 28 and 29, NAI.

65 This itself became a bone of contention. An inquiry was instituted if Mr Palmer, the Collector had given such an assurance. Palmer claimed he had not. The investigating officer, Mr Lockwood, who was also the new Collector of Monghyr, however, was convinced that 'instead of taking Mr Palmer's memory, the nature of the case itself demonstrates the fact very clearly that the Collector assumed that Mr McGiveron would be able to enhance the ryots' rent'. Ibid.

66 Similar observations were made earlier also. In one case of a *khas diara* accumulating arrears of more than Rs 6,000, Hamilton observed that as long as it was managed *khas* it had no arrears; once given on lease, it did. He blamed the thikadar of primarily concerned with maximising his revenue.

67 In another case, the whole of Rahatpur *diara* was occupied by three types of occupants: proprietors (321 *beegahs* with the rate of rent at Rs 293), Dahee cultivators (130 and 231, respectively) and Patnee cultivators (125 and 168, respectively). Wells had remarked, 'No cultivators can strictly be called Moreusee in this village because the land is Deora [diara] and lately formed and therefore the present generation has first possession of it.' Patnee 'in effect consisted in giving a permanent managing lease for a part of the estate' in lieu of a rental. Baden-Powell, *Administration of Land Revenue*: 131. For maurusi, Baden-Powell makes it clear that they 'do not represent any contract tenancy, but merely a grade of interest which has gradually fallen, in the course of generations, to an

indefinite subordinate position under a superior'. Ibid.: 129. The meaning of the term 'Dahee' is unclear. If it means dohata, then migratory nature is again evident.

68 Also see Chakravarti (1986).

69 Bengal Tenancy Act, pp. 252–253. On the other hand, the act allowed the landlords to enhance the rent provided it could be proven that the productive powers of the alluvial land held by the *raiyat* had increased due to fluvial action. The court was asked to be 'fair and equitable'. BTA, 70.

70 Government of Bengal: 'Settlement of Diara Lands in North Bihar', file no. 24-S/6 of 1896 and 24-S/4 of 1897, Revenue Department (Land), BSA.

71 Some divergence in local practices seems to have appeared. The government ordered to settle diara lands of the temporarily settled areas under existing regulations, but in Bhagalpur district record of rights were prepared for the government-owned *diaras*. However, the zamindari *diaras* which amounted to 390 square miles (out of the total area of 4,158 square miles) stood outside of the purview of the act. Murphy (1912: 26).

72 Mukul, 'Bihar's Land Liberation Struggles', *EPW*, 1992, 27 (34): 1780.

73 In line with recent changes in wetlands study which revises the earlier position from treating them as 'transitional habitats' to 'distinct ecosystems'. Gopal and Sah (1995: 39).

74 There is a strand of argument which says that legal categories were no more than myths, which did not affect the ground reality much. The force of these categories is mistakenly sought in their power to 'create' something new; what they instead do is to rearrange, sometimes quite significantly, the existing reality. The *bhadralok* of Bengal, the tenure holders of Purnea and the maliks of Bihar all were jostling to get classified as *raiyats*. This was their legal way to stop rights accruing to under-*raiyats*. See a perceptive essay on law and agrarian society by Robb (2007, chapter 1).

References

Baden-Powell, B.H. [1907] 1978. *Administration of Land Revenue and Tenure in British India*, rev. ed. New Delhi: Ess Ess Publications.

Bandyopadhyaya, Nripendra. 1977. 'Causes of Sharp Increase in Agricultural Labourers, 1961–1971: A Case Study of Social-Existence Forms of Labour in North Bengal', *EPW*, 12 (53): A111–A126.

Bhargava, Meena. 2007. 'Changing River Courses in North India: Calamities, Bounties, Strategies – Sixteenth to Early Nineteenth Centuries', *The Medieval History Journal*, 10 (1 and 2): 183–208.

Bhattacharya, Neeladri. 1983. 'The Logic of Tenancy Cultivation: Central and South-East Punjab, 1870–1935', *IESHR*, 20 (2): 121–170.

Bhattacharya, Neeladri. 1996. 'Remaking Custom: The Discourse and Practice of Colonial Codification', in Romila Thapar, S. Gopal and R. Champakalakshmi (eds), *Tradition, Dissent and Ideology: Essays in Honour of Romila Thapar*, pp. 20–51. New Delhi: Oxford University Press.

Chakravarti, Anand. 1986. 'The Unfinished Struggle of Santhal Bataidars in Purnea District, 1938–42', *Economic and Political Weekly*, 21 (43) October 25: 1897–1909.

D'Souza, Rohan. 2011. 'Nature as Calamity: The Emergence of Flood Control in Colonial India', presentation at the conference on 'The Transculturality of

Historical Disasters: Governance and the Materialisation of Glocalisation', New Delhi, 3–5 March.

Gidwani, Vinay Krishin. 1992. '"Waste" and the Permanent Settlement in Bengal', *EPW*, 27 (4): PE39–PE46.

Gopal, B. and M. Sah. 1995. 'Inventory and Classification of Wetlands in India', *Vegetatio*, 118 (1 and 2): 39–48.

Hill, Christopher V. 1990. 'Water and Power: Riparian Legislation and Agrarian Control in Colonial Bengal', *Environmental History Review*, 14 (4): 1–20.

Hubbock, J.A. [1918] 1928. *Final Report on the Survey and Settlement Operations in the District of Shahabad, 1907–1916*. Patna: Government Printing, Bihar and Orissa.

Iqbal, Iftekar. 2010. *The Bengal Delta: Ecology, State and Social Change, 1840–1943*. Basingstoke: Palgrave Macmillan.

Jones (1851, no. DLXXIII: 144–145). The provisions of this circular were enacted as 'Bengal Alluvial Land Settlement Act: Act XXXI of 1858', in Mitra (1934: 215–216).

Joshi, Chitra. 2008. 'History of Indian Labour: Predicaments and Possibilities', *History Compass*, 6 (2): 439–454.

Kumar, Gopal, *et al.* 2008. 'Land Use Land Cover Change in Active Flood Plain Using Satellite Remote Sensing', *Journal of Agricultural Physics*, 8: . 22–28.

Lahiri-Dutt, Kuntala and Gopa Samanta. 2013. *Dancing with the River: People and Life on the Chars of South Asia*. New Haven, CT; London: Yale University Press.

Ludden, David. 1999. *An Agrarian History of South Asia*. Cambridge: Cambridge University Press.

Martin, Montogemory. 1838. *The History, Antiquities, Topography, and Statistics of Eastern India*, Vol. 2. London: W.H. Allen and Co.

McLane, John R. 1977. 'Revenue Farming and the Zamindari System in Eighteenth-Century Bengal', in Robert Eric Frykenberg (ed.), *Land Tenure and Peasant in South Asia*, pp. 19–36. New Delhi: Manohar Publishers.

Michael, Bernardo A. 2007. 'Making Territory Visible: The Revenue Surveys of Colonial South Asia', *Imago Mundi*, 59 (1): 78–95.

Mitra, B.B. (ed.). 1934. *The Laws of Land and Water in Bengal and Bihar, with the Case-Law Thereon*. Calcutta: Eastern Law House.

Mosse, David. 2006. 'Rule and Representation: Transformations in the Governance of the Water Commons in British South India', *Journal of Asian Studies*, 65 (1): 61–90.

Mukul. 1992. 'Bihar's Land Liberation Struggles', *Economic and Political Weekly*, 27(34), August 22: 1780–1781.

Murphy, P.W. 1912. *Final Report on the Survey and Settlement Operations in Bhagalpur District, 1902–1910*. Calcutta: Bengal Secretariat Book Depot.

Murphy, P.W. 1914. *Final Report on the Survey and Settlement Operations in the District of Monghyr (South), 1905–1912*. Ranchi: Bihar and Orissa Secretariat Printing Office.

O'Malley, L.S.S. [1926] 2007. *Bihar and Orissa District Gazetteers: Monghyr*, rev. ed. New Delhi: Logos Press.

Peters, William. 1838. *Circular Orders of the Sudder Board of Revenue at the Presidency of Fort William*. Calcutta: Baptist Mission Press.

Ram, Bindeshwar. 1997. *Land and Society in India: Agrarian Relations in Colonial North Bihar*. New Delhi: Orient Longman.

Robb, Peter. 1997. *Ancient Rights and Future Comforts: Bihar, the Bengal Tenancy Act of 1885, and British Rule in India*. Richmond, Surrey: Curzon.

Robb, Peter. 2007. *Peasants, Political Economy, and Law*. New Delhi: Oxford University Press.

Sarkar, Sumit. 2014. *Modern Times: India 1880s–1950s*. New Delhi: Permanent Black.

Satya, Laxman D. 1998. 'Colonial Encroachment and Popular Resistance: Land Survey and Settlement Operations in Berar (Central India), 1861–1877', *Agricultural History*, 72 (1): 55–76.

Sen, Babu Rajani Kanta. 1915. *Report on the Special Ganges Diara Survey, 1908–1915*. Patna: Government Printing, Bihar and Orissa.

Sen Gupta, Kalyan Kumar. 1974. 'Bengali Intelligentsia and the Politics of Rent, 1873–1885', *Social Scientist*, 3 (2): 27–34.

Sinha, Nitin. 2014. 'Fluvial Landscape and the State: Property and the Gangetic Diaras in Colonial India, 1790s–1890s', *Environment and History*, 20 (2): 209–237.

Sivaramakrishnan, K. 1999a. 'Transition Zones: Changing Landscapes and Local Authority in South-West Bengal, 1880s–1920s', *IESHR*, 36: 1–34.

Sivaramakrishnan, K. 1999b. *Modern Forests: Statemaking and Environmental Change in Colonial Eastern India*. Stanford, CA: Stanford University Press.

Washbrook, David A. 1981. 'Law, State and Agrarian Society in Colonial India', *Modern Asian Studies*, 15 (3): 649–721.

Wilson, H.H. 1855. *A Glossary of Judicial and Revenue Terms*. London: W.H. Allen.

Internet sources

Panda, B.C. n.d. 'Monitoring of the Diara Lands of Eastern India with Respect to Vegetation, Wasteland, Soil Erosion and Inundation Through Remote Sensing Techniques', www.moef.nic.in/downloads/public-information/ Eco-System-Summaries.pdf (accessed on 28 March 2015).

Swamy, Anand V. 2010. 'Land and Law in Colonial India', http://web.williams.edu/Economics/wp/SwamyLandAndLawInColonialIndia.pdf (accessed on 13 March 2015).

2 Historical Wrongs and Forest Rights

Nascent Jurisprudence on FRA and Participatory Evidence Making

Shomona Khanna

Introduction

That forests in India have for centuries been the abode of indigenous and forest-dwelling communities who have evolved methods of conservation, coexistence, and complex patterns of livelihood, is a well-documented fact. That the British colonial state, through a devious mix of legislation, centralised governance, coercion, and complicity established an architecture of forest laws across much of the country, taking over vast tracts of forests to provide timber and other raw material for its industrial machine, is also well known. The pre-existing rights and usages of forest dwelling communities remained unrecognised for a greater part, most of them continuing in blissful ignorance with life as usual until harsh contact with the colonial administration, for one reason or other, brought the *fait accompli* to their knowledge, often too late. Post-independence, one would have expected this clearly unjust legal regimen to shift. Far from it. The forest laws and administration thereof became even more stringent and centralised, while the existence of forest-dwelling communities in these forests became a 'problem' which needed to be solved through 'eviction' of 'encroachments.'

Recent studies point to the clear juxtaposition of the most dense forests in the country with the Scheduled Areas where Adivasi populations are concentrated. It is also well established that the Scheduled Tribes and other semi-tribal populations[1] outside the Scheduled Areas are found in close proximity to forest lands. Hence, the structures of forest governance and the recognition of forest rights of such populations is of integral importance to an understanding of how the law impacts the lives of Adivasi and forest-dwelling communities, both inside and outside the Scheduled Areas.

The present chapter[2] explores the legal remedies under colonial and post-independence forest laws available to such forest-dwelling communities,

DOI: 10.4324/9781003299561-2

and their inadequacy in challenging the assault on traditional rights on such a massive scale. It examines how the approach to forest governance has seen a paradigm shift with the enactment of the Scheduled Tribes and Other Traditional Forest Dwellers (Recognition of Forest Rights) Act, 2006 (henceforth 'Forest Rights Act' or 'FRA'), with special attention to the procedures and processes established for the purpose of its implementation under the Scheduled Tribes and Other Traditional Forest Dwellers (Recognition of Forest Rights) Rules, 2008 (henceforth 'Forest Rights Rules').

In particular, the chapter examines the nature of evidence and evidentiary rules which the FRA seeks to rely upon, the complexities arising out of operationalisation of such evidentiary rules in a system of forest administration based on colonial legal architectures, and the compounding of such complexity by the digital revolution. Through this examination, the chapter seeks to demonstrate the dramatic shift in the processes and procedures for recognition of forest rights by making such processes relevant and accessible to the Adivasi and forest-dwelling communities, resulting in a sea change in the administration of justice itself.

Forest laws in India: a snapshot

The unambiguous objective for declaration of forest lands, and the establishment of Forest Departments to administer these forests, was to ensure regular supply of timber for expansion of industrialisation both in England and India.

The Forest Act of 1865 (Act No. VII of 1865), the first forest legislation in India, provided that the notification by the Governor General of India of 'government forests' on 'land covered with trees, brushwood or jungle ... shall not abridge or affect any existing rights of individuals and communities' (Section 2). It proceeded to proscribe all manner of such rights, including cultivation, extraction, use of grass and minor forest produce, grazing of cattle, use of water bodies, and so on. The focus of the statute was on the preservation and management of timber. While infringement of the prohibitions under the law invited search, seizure, and arrest, there was no statutory remedy for persons whose rights had been wrongfully proscribed. Clearly, such remedies were to be exercised in the domain of civil law *outside* of this statute.

This statute was replaced by the Indian Forest Act, 1878, providing the framework for the Indian Forest Act, 1927, which remains in force today. The 1878 Act was a more complex and comprehensive law, creating different categories of forests based upon their usefulness and productivity for the colonial state (reserve forests, protected forests, village forests, and private forests), and establishing its proprietary right over such forests. The declaration of Reserve Forests (RF), over lands which were the most valuable to the state in terms of timber and therefore inviting the most stringent controls, involved a three-step process as under:

1 Issue of a *notification of intention* to declare a certain area as RF, giving its geographical boundaries.
2 A *Forest Settlement Officer* (FSO), specially appointed for the purpose, to receive, examine, and decide claims submitted by persons having pre-existing rights in the said area. Having arrived at a conclusion regarding the nature of such rights, the FSO could either exclude the area on which such rights are claimed from the RF, or acquire these rights under the Land Acquisition Act, 1894, or award compensation. Under the 1878 statute, the FSO could also allow certain rights (such as grazing, easement, right of way, etc.) to continue to the extent recorded (Sections 13, 14, 15), but this power has been significantly curtailed under the 1927 Act.
3 *Final notification* of the RF by the local government, specifying the boundary marks and limits of the forest. This notification was issued only after the statutory period for appeal had expired. After the final notification was issued, any rights inside such RF which had not been specifically permitted, stood 'extinguished' (Section 9).

During this enquiry, the FSO determined 'the existence of any rights … so far as the same may be ascertainable from the records of Government and the evidence of any persons likely to be acquainted with the same'(Section 7). Towards this end, the officer was also vested with the powers of a civil court and the power to enter upon any land himself or through an authorised officer, for demarcating the land and making a map. In practice, however, the affected communities were expected to proactively seek out the FSO, rather than the other way around.

The declaration of Protected Forests (PF) was simpler. Although the law provided that 'no such notification shall be made unless the nature and extent of the rights of Government and private persons in or over the forest land or wasteland have been enquired into and recorded' it also allowed the local government to declare a PF without undertaking a settlement process, as long as existing rights of individuals and communities are not abridged. However, it was also provided that every such record shall be presumed to be correct until the contrary is proved (Section 28). Again, the burden was on the forest dwellers to assert their rights and challenge such presumptions.

Violations of proscribed activities in such forests were defined as 'forest offences,' inviting harsh punishments, including imprisonment, seizure of property, and monetary penalties. Scrutiny of the oppressive nature of the criminal law provisions under this law, and the existing 1927 Act, must await another opportunity. Suffice to say that the severity of these provisions violates a number of basic principles of criminal jurisprudence, including due process and presumption of innocence.

This same architecture of forest law has been adopted under the Indian Forest Act, 1927, and in the various state forest laws which emerged after independence. The three-step settlement process has also been adopted under the Wildlife Protection Act, 1972, for the declaration of National Parks and Wildlife Sanctuaries.

It is now an accepted fact that these high-minded provisions for 'settlement of pre-existing rights' were followed in the breach, barring a few exceptions such as in Uttarakhand,[3] Himachal Pradesh,[4] and Jharkhand.[5] Vast swathes of forests in the Central Indian tribal belts remained unsurveyed, with the terminology 'undemarcated protected forests' even entering official parlance. Indeed, the state legislatures of Orissa and Madhya Pradesh brought amendments to the central legislation permitting the declaration of 'deemed forests' where, by definition, no procedure for settlement or recognition of rights was necessary.[6] The initial optimism generated in the early 1990s by the government scheme of Joint Forest Management (JFM) quickly unravelled after it became clear that the state forest departments had no intention of including forest-dwelling communities in the process of decision-making, and were only interested in the subsidised labour they could provide (Lele 2014).

From time to time, forest dwellers found themselves punished by forest officials for going about their normal lives, but these practices did not result in any systematic displacement or dislocation, even becoming normalised over the years. The forest guard's visit to the village to feast on poultry and indigenous liquor has become part of the folklore and literature emerging from these regions,[7] while the periodic descent of such visits into torture and rape of the forest dwellers has also been well documented (CSD 2003). However, when these very forest lands were required for large development projects or mining, the presence of traditional forest dwellers in these lands became more than a mere inconvenience. Tribals and forest dwellers who had been living in these lands for centuries suddenly found that their traditional rights had been 'extinguished' decades ago; labelled as 'encroachers' on government property, these forest dwellers were unceremoniously and often violently evicted to make room for the temples of modern India.

Courting justice: coming up empty

In one such scenario, forest dwellers in 433 villages within Dudhi and Robertsganj tehsils of Mirzapur district, Uttar Pradesh suddenly found themselves on the wrong side of the law as a result of a proposed NTPC[8] project. Several letter petitions were filed in the Indian Supreme Court by the Banwasi Seva Ashram, stating that the rights of Adivasis in the forests have not been settled, including their long-standing cultivations in and around their villages, as well as their customary and traditional rights to forest produce.

The litigation has a long and chequered history, but it is useful to examine the detailed directions passed by the Supreme Court in 1986,[9] which proceeded within the existing legislative architecture under the Indian Forest Act, 1927. The approach of the otherwise well-meaning Supreme Court greatly restricted the nature of relief that it was capable of providing to the forest dwellers.

For one thing, the court categorically excluded from its protective orders those forest dwellers in forests where the final notification of the RF had been issued (under Section 20 of the 1927 Act), stating 'it is open to the claimants to establish their rights, if any, in any other appropriate proceeding. We express no opinion about the maintainability of such claims' (Ibid. at para 10(1)). Under the extant law there was simply no remedy at all, given that the 1927 Act 'extinguishes' rights of those who have not filed claims/ objections/appeals within the statutory period. Indeed, to expect forest dwellers, who have been unable to file claims before the FSO, to approach civil courts with suits under the Civil Procedure Code, was nothing short of cruelty. The inability of the Adivasi and forest-dwelling communities to even comprehend, leave alone navigate, the adversarial dispute resolution mechanisms entrenched in the colonial justice system remained unacknowledged, and hence unaddressed.

Be that as it may, detailed directions were issued by the Supreme Court regarding forest dwellers in forest lands where only the notification of intention (under Section 4) had been issued, including the following:

- Extension of time for filing of claims before the FSO (which had long expired under the statute).
- Wide publicity to be given, including through beat of drums, to the process and also to the geographical area involved, and also its demarcation on the ground with pillars/stone piles/markings on trees.
- Protection from dispossession of anyone until the process is complete.
- All decisions on claims taken by the FSO would be scrutinised as appeals, whether an appeal is filed or not.
- Appointment of five additional District Judges, who would be located in the five relevant locations to attend to appeals.
- Once the claim is approved, a title deed to be given to the claimant.

- Oversight of the process by a court-appointed high-powered committee.[10]

These directions demonstrated the court's obdurate, and quite misplaced, faith in the existing administrative structures as well as in the judiciary itself. Indeed, the court made no observation or direction regarding the nature of evidence which could be produced in support of claims, only making a concession towards the vulnerability of the forest dwellers within this system by directing that free legal aid will be provided by the state legal services authority.[11]

Even while these directions were being put into place, and while the writ petition was still pending, the NTPC started work on the proposed power project. Instead of acknowledging that these actions constitute an encroachment upon the rights of the forest dwellers bordering on contempt of court, the Court proceeded to make a compromise in the 'interest of the nation' as electricity is considered inevitable for national development – and exempted the forest land required by NTPC from the 'ban on dispossession.'[12] As a safeguard, it was merely required that dispossession will be done in the presence of the committee, and records would be maintained of the nature of rights exercised by the person dispossessed, for future reference.

This approach is a reflection of the failure of the Court to understand the symbiotic relationship of forest-dwelling communities to their lands. It is also contrary to the principle of 'free prior informed consent,' which forms part of numerous international agreements to which India is a party, such as the United Nations Declaration on the Rights of Indigenous Peoples (2007).

Information is not readily available on what happened to the settlement process in this particular case thereafter. However, the directions issued in this judgment clearly provided no encouragement to other Adivasi and forest-dwelling communities, who may have considered approaching the courts for the protection of their historical and traditional rights over the forest lands. The benevolent approach of the court towards 'laches' could not supplant the burden on forest dwellers to establish their claims for forest rights and their territorial domains through serpentine processes under the existing forest laws. As a result, in spite of the laborious efforts of the Supreme Court to establish these mechanisms for the benefit of the petitioners before it, the judgment did not create a judicial precedent sufficiently persuasive for the millions of other similarly placed forest dwellers to approach the justice system. Nor did it reduce the mistrust in the justice system borne out of decades of lived experience.

Early shifts in forest policy towards forest governance

The National Forest Policy 1988,[13] replacing the forest policy of 1952, marked the first shift in state policy towards Adivasis and forest dwellers. It acknowledged that these communities share a 'symbiotic relationship' with the forests, including their traditional and customary livelihood practices.[14] In 1989, Dr B.D. Sharma, Commissioner for Scheduled Tribes and Scheduled Castes, presented his report to the President of India,[15] wherein he documented the myriad atrocities being committed against Adivasi and forest-dwelling communities across India as a result of the forest law regime. The report described the complete failure to settle rights during forest reservation in colonial and post-colonial India, and how the state governments have ignored the 'constitutional provisions for protection of tribal people as also their human rights.' It drew attention to the criminalisation of entire communities in the tribal areas, calling it the darkest blot on the liberal tradition of our country. The report also provided a detailed framework for the resolution of this historical wrong through a complete overhaul of the forest governance mechanisms in the country's forests and a paradigm shift in the mechanisms for the settlement of pre-existing forest rights, which would be participatory, transparent, accountable, and also accessible.

The central government, in an effort to address the concerns of forest-dwelling communities in a holistic manner, responded with a set of central circulars which have commonly come to be known as the '1990 guidelines.'[16] These guidelines made several important advancements towards the democratization of forest governance, establishing the groundwork for the Forest Rights Act which came almost three decades later, including the following:

1. Enabling the state governments to re-open the process of settlement of rights, the first circular paved the way for hundreds of thousands of forest dwellers who were otherwise barred by myriad legal barriers under the 1878 and 1927 statutes, such as statutory limitation, the doctrine of laches, the legal extinguishment of their rights, and so on.[17]
2. Instead of relying upon the process delineated in the Indian Forest Act, as the Supreme Court had done in the *Banwasi Seva Ashram* case, the guidelines proposed a new mechanism for settlement of rights involving the Gram Sabhas as well as a multi-department committee at the local level.
3. New forms of evidence in support of claims were permitted, including 'preliminary offence reports'[18] recording forest offences under the extant forest laws.

Although these guidelines, in providing for participatory rights settlement mechanisms, marked progress in the right direction, they also paradoxically reflected a patronising approach of a benevolent state towards uplift of oppressed classes. The guidelines repeatedly describe forest dwellers as 'encroachers,' and the settlement of their legal rights as the 'regularisation of encroachments.' With use of such negative terminology at the outset, the initiative soon floundered in bureaucratic quagmires, such as the complete domination of the decision-making process by the state Forest Departments. Even where the state governments overcame these barriers to arrive at decisions to recognise rights, these decisions needed approval of the central government under the Forest Conservation Act, 1980, and were stymied by unconscionable demands for payments of 'compensatory afforestation,' and later 'net present value.' Despite the enthusiasm with which these guidelines were welcomed by social movements as a shift towards democratising forest governance, the rights recognition process under the 1990 guidelines made very little progress (*Pradip Prabhu and Ors. vs. State of Maharashtra and Ors.* 1995).[19]

With the judgments and orders passed by the Indian Supreme Court in the *Godavarman case*,[20] the process came to a complete standstill. Indeed, directions of the Supreme Court came to be misrepresented by the Union government as eviction orders in 2002, leading to violent eviction drives in many parts of the country, until social movements managed to get the evictions stopped (Khanna 2014). However, the grant of formal titles, as had been proposed by the Commissioner for SCs and STs in 1989, could not be resumed.

The Forest Rights Act

Much has been written about the processes and ideations which culminated in the enactment of the Forest Rights Act in 2006 (Sarin 2014). Since the Act came into force, and until February 2019, about 1.88 million individual forest rights and 76,126 community rights extending over approximately 12.74 million acres of forest land have been granted (MoTA 2019). While many of these forest rights have been recognised in Scheduled Areas, it is important to state that the beneficial impact has been experienced by large numbers of Adivasi and non-Adivasi forest dwellers living outside of Scheduled Areas as well.

These results are unprecedented across the world, even while many estimates indicate that the rights recognition process is far from achieving its full potential (Rights and Resources Initiative 2015).[21] How did this happen? To fully understand the nature of this legislation, it is important to highlight some of its most critical features:

1 Enacted by the Union Parliament, with carefully crafted *non-obstante* clauses preceding the rights-vesting provision, the FRA is a 'special' legislation containing within it the necessary force of authority to invert the complex web of extant forest laws, both at the central and the state level. The statute, accordingly, has enabled the near total replacement of condescending terminology such as 'encroachers,' with the more accurate description of forest dwellers as 'right holders.' This reflection of the statutory paradigm shift in everyday perception of the relationship between forest dwellers and the forests has had far-reaching consequences.

2 A detailed Preamble foregrounds the foundational principles of the statute, which includes the acknowledgement that the forest dwellers in this country have suffered 'historical injustice,' that such forest dwellers are 'part of the forest ecosystem' and their relationship with the forest is necessary for the survival and preservation of the forests, while ensuring their traditional livelihoods.

3 The benefits of the statute are not restricted to the Scheduled Areas or to the Scheduled Tribes, in acknowledgement of the reality that there are significant Adivasi populations outside of the constitutionally designated Scheduled Areas. Other non-tribal and semi-tribal communities which have become integrated into the Adivasi culture, economy, and society through decades of integration as forest dwellers are also sought to be included. The governance framework grounded in constitutional and statutory provisions, which till now was restricted in geographical application exclusively to Scheduled Areas, is sought to be extended more realistically outside these areas to other Adivasi and forest-dwelling communities as well.[22]

4 The statute lists a variety of 'forest rights' which include the right to cultivation and habitation (often referred to as *individual rights*) as well as rights to minor forest produce, usufructuary rights, and rights to fishing, grazing, and so on (described as *community rights*). At the heart of the legislation is the right to protect, preserve, conserve, and manage the 'community forest resource' (CFR), for both livelihood and conservation, with the Gram Sabha actively spearheading this process.

5 A three-tier mechanism for decision-making is created, which is a judicious mix of community involvement and administrative oversight. As a first step, claims for forest rights are processed by the Gram Sabha at the village/hamlet level, and based upon inputs received from its Forest Rights Committee, the Gram Sabha passes resolutions. The definition of Gram Sabha as applicable to the Scheduled Areas under PESA, being the Gram Sabha at the hamlet level, is extended for the purpose of this Act to all areas where forest rights are to be recognised, thus extending

the benefit of a governance model which was restricted to Scheduled Areas to other areas inhabited by tribals and forest dwellers. In the second stage, the resolutions of the Gram Sabha which are recommendatory in nature, are forwarded to a multi-department committee at the subdivision level, where they are consolidated. Finally, these are forwarded to the District Level Committee, which takes a final decision.

Both the SDLC and the DLC have officers from state revenue, forest and tribal departments, as well as members from the Panchayats at the sub-division and district level, respectively, thus ensuring that they are not dominated by any one stakeholder. Representation of women at all levels is another important requirement.

6 Finally, the statute and the rules framed under it provide a completely different approach to the evidentiary requirements for the recognition of forest rights through this three-tier process. These provisions will be examined in further detail in a later section.

Given its core characteristics described here, the Forest Rights Act is an unnatural fit with the existing forest law regime. In very fundamental ways, this statute displaces state monopoly on the governance of forest lands, over forest resources, their conservation and use for livelihood, and even over decision-making regarding who is eligible to thus displace it. Predictably, the law has been met with much hostility in the last fourteen years since its implementation commenced, often from surprising loci.[23] Efforts to subvert the law in multiple mires of bureaucratic interpretation have also been unrelenting. However, through a combination of factors, which it is perhaps too early to fairly assess, the implementation of this law has continued to gain ground. As demonstrated by the analysis in the next section, the basic paradigm shift which this law embodies has resulted in a wealth of innovative approaches at the state level under the watchful eye of the central government through the nodal ministry.[24]

Innovations in evidence and evidence gathering under the Forest Rights Act

As the examination of the *Banwasi Seva Ashram* case demonstrates, while procedures for recognition and/or settlement of forest rights exist under the 1927 Act, these are unmistakably located within the mainstream paradigm of justice and its administration. This applies equally to the administrative processes undertaken by the FSO, and also the legal principles which permeate these processes. The 1927 Act placed an inordinate burden on forest dwellers to activate their rights or lose them forever, and it drew strict boundaries of limitation on the right to activate the redressal mechanism. Failure to activate such processes within the tight time frames provided under the law attracted onerous consequences. Those few who managed to approach the redressal mechanism found themselves further crushed under burden of proof standards drawn from the mainstream justice system, with a heavy reliance upon written documentation and records. The dice were loaded from the start against the Adivasis and forest dwellers within such an administrative and justice delivery mechanism.

In contrast to the Indian Forest Act of 1927, the principles and procedures under the Forest Rights Act and Rules surmount the restrictive parameters with regard to both procedures for determination of rights, as well as the evidence which may be relied upon to substantiate claims. While it may be difficult to describe the many departures made by the FRA from the dominant administration of justice approach, it would be useful to consider one such element in some detail, namely, the requirements relating to evidence in support of forest rights claims.

Types of evidence

The FRA consciously enables the claimants to produce diverse forms of evidence in support of their claims, taking into account the fact that forest-dwelling communities are primarily rural, and many of them have not transitioned to modern systems of written record-keeping, relying heavily on customary traditions based on trust. It also acknowledges the historical processes through which even the records which may existed have been destroyed, damaged, or lost in over a century of oppressive forest management regimes.

A detailed list of such evidence is provided in Rule 13 of the Forest Rights Rules, and can be divided into the following categories:

- *Written/documentary evidence* such as a variety of government records like 'Gazetteers, Census, survey and settlement reports, maps, satellite imagery, working plans, management plans, micro-plans, forest enquiry reports, other forest records, record of rights by whatever name called, pattas or leases, reports of committees and commissions constituted by the Government, Government orders, notifications, circulars, resolutions.'
- *Physical evidence* which could include 'house, huts and permanent improvements made to land including levelling, bunds, check dams and the like,' which can be easily examined for age.
- *Oral evidence* is also permissible, including 'statement of elders other than claimants, reduced in writing.'

In support of a forest rights claim, a claimant is required to produce any two pieces of evidence from the aforesaid list. This requirement applies equally to forest lands in Scheduled and non-Scheduled Areas, and also equally to

Adivasi and non-Adivasi claimants, so long as they have established the preliminary requirement for their eligibility as 'forest-dwelling communities.'

Process of examining evidence

It is apparent that the procedure for determination of forest rights, in its effort to bring justice to the doorstep of those who have suffered a 'historical injustice,' makes a departure from the existing adversarial systems of administration of justice in general, and from the colonial forest law architecture in particular. The Gram Sabha at the hamlet level[25] as a community (through the Forest Rights Committee or 'FRC') takes responsibility for the receipt of claim forms, their examination and on-site verification. The preparation of maps in support of the claims before it, and also as a method to verify such claims, is an important part of the FRC's functions. Indeed, where community claims are concerned, the FRC takes the lead in the preparation of the claim form itself.

Under the FRA, the state administrative machinery is duty bound to proactively assist the process, attend the on-site verification conducted by the FRC,[26] and support the filing of claims by providing maps and records in advance to the FRC, especially where rights of pastoralists and particularly vulnerable tribal groups (PVTGs) are concerned. In some states, the district administration has made the fullest possible use of this space and has prepared 'tool kits' for each Gram Sabha in the area, which include cadastral and other maps, forest and revenue records, gazetteer reports, census reports, and so on. These tool kits are handed over to the FRCs along with detailed instructions on how to go about filing their claims, with hands-on support for such processes.

Use of satellite imagery: the case of Gujarat

The FRA displaces a variety of entrenched interests, while re-arranging power hierarchies inside forests, and it has been met with different kinds of efforts to subvert it. In early 2009, monitoring data coming out of Gujarat revealed disturbing trends – approximately 90 percent of the claims filed had been rejected by the sub-division and district level committees, even after being approved by the Gram Sabhas. Such *en masse* rejection of claims was a cause for concern, since the post-recognition provisions relating to forest governance could not be accessed by the forest-dwelling communities.

Further examination revealed that the Gujarat government had issued a series of circulars imposing strict rules of evidence and burden of proof on the rights recognition process under the FRA, thereby perverting the object of the law. The circulars not only sought to restrict the eligibility of claims to those in possession on or before 30 October 1980[27] (as opposed to the date provided under the Forest Rights Act, which is 13 December 2005), but also required that every claim be supported by satellite imagery. At that time, the state government had made little or no provision to assist the claimants in accessing a technology which remains, even today, remote and expensive. It also insisted that such satellite images be sourced only from a specified source.[28]

The BISAG, which had been given the task of preparing 'maps' from the satellite imageries, juxtaposed the village map over the concerned satellite imageries of 2005, and earmarked as 'common plots' the areas where they found cultivation in that year. On the basis of these images, two-dimensional 'maps' were printed out for the purpose of rights recognition. Quite apart from the obvious fallacy of treating satellite imagery printouts as 'maps,' no effort at connecting these 'maps' with the actual ground reality was being made, yet these were being treated as gospel truth for the purpose of accepting or rejecting claims under the FRA. It seems incredible today that the state government adopted such an unreliable method for verification of claims.

Several rights-based organisations, who had been working for many decades with Adivasi communities to help them assert their governance rights over their traditional forest lands, brought the matter before the Gujarat High Court by way of writ petitions. They argued that the state government was actively subverting the implementation of the FRA through these circulars, which were therefore *ultra vires*.

In a detailed judgment,[29] the court examined the objectives and purpose of the FRA with regard to correcting historical injustice against forest dwellers, thereby providing a comprehensive and participatory method for the recognition of rights which is geared towards meeting such objective. It took note of provisions under the Forest Rights Rules,[30] which categorically state that 'satellite imagery and other uses of technology may supplement other form of evidence and shall not be treated as a replacement' (at paragraph 36–37). Nor can the state insist upon any particular form of evidence in support of claims, being bound by law to accept the various kinds of evidence in the inclusive list in Rule 13 (supra). The court directed the state government to re-open all the rejected claims in the state and examine them afresh in light of its decision.

Recent developments in GIS technology and role of the nodal ministry MoTA

Meanwhile, taking their cue from the proactive approach of the FRA, local organisations in Gujarat had developed their own methods for using spatial technology. Satellite imageries were obtained from the National Remote

Sensing Centre, Hyderabad. Thereafter, the physical survey of the land claimed was carried out using hand-held GPS-PDA devices, triangulating the coordinates of the corners of the lands. These images were then superimposed over the satellite imageries with an outline of the land claimed. This ground-truthing exercise produced highly reliable geo-referenced maps. Verification by the FRC on the ground would easily address anomalies which a desk-based exercise can never do.[31]

The judgment in the *ARCH Vahini* case (supra) came to be widely known across the country, and the use of stand-alone satellite images for the verification of forest rights claims has been all but abandoned. Even so, different states have come up with different technological innovations based on satellite imageries and invested considerable time and money into rolling out the use of these technologies.

The use of satellite imagery continues to require close scrutiny and monitoring. Recent evidence shows that notwithstanding the clear position of law that satellite imagery can be only a supplementary form of evidence, several states are rapidly moving towards use of satellite footage, often disregarding the validity and accuracy of other forms of documentary evidence.[32]

Concerns were being raised, both within the administration, as also by civil society organisations, that these technological innovations may yet again become a pretext for exclusion of eligible forest dwellers. Distrust of these technologies among social movements created another layer of resistance to their extensive use. It is no small task to undo the adversarial mindset of the colonial forest regime, where each individual claimant must establish his/her lawful right separately and on separate pieces of evidence before a benevolent bureaucrat.

In an attempt to challenge this mindset, the nodal ministry of the Union government, the Ministry of Tribal Affairs (MoTA), issued detailed guidelines[33] in July 2015, regarding the use of geo-referencing for assessment of potential areas, and re-examination of rejected claims under the Forest Rights Act. The statutory requirement for the district administration to play a pro-active role by providing forest and revenue maps to the Gram Sabhas and FRCs was reiterated.[34] Thus the states were encouraged to prepare Geographic Information System (GIS) maps for each village, containing spatial information of physiographic features of that village, area of the forest land, and other relevant information, and make such maps available to the FRCs. The guidelines emphasised the requirement for the ground-truthing of these images, suggesting involvement of local youth or even the FRC itself after providing necessary training and GPS/android devices.[35]

Interestingly, the guidelines stress the importance of using such technologies in both the identification of potential forest areas for rights recognition as well as for the recognition of Community Forest Resource (CFR) rights. They also reiterate that the use of satellite technology must be supplementary in nature and cannot replace other forms of evidence submitted in support of a claim. In conflating the need to address the large number of rejected claims with the use of available GIS maps through modern technologies, the central government sent out a clear message that technology must be used to support the process of forest rights recognition, not subvert it.

The 2015 guidelines issued by MoTA, by re-affirming the proactive and people-centric governance approach of the FRA, provides the enabling environment for development of new technological innovations for forest-dwelling communities to realise their forest rights in spatial terms. Recognising the need to engage with technological advances, several civil society organisations have made concerted efforts to pioneer a more user-friendly interface amongst the forest-dwelling communities themselves.

Civil society organisations and grassroots NGOs in Gujarat have emerged as the pioneers of geo-referenced mapping in support of claims under the FRA, and the use of hand-held GPS/PDA devices for ground-truthing satellite imageries. Another collaborative pilot in Odisha[36] seeks to address the disconnect of GIS technology from the communities by building an android GIS application for the development of maps primarily for mapping CFR rights, an area of rights recognition under the FRA which is lagging behind. A unique alliance has emerged between the District Administration, local NGOs, community leaders and youth, and software developers.[37]

The GIS application, which can be used readily on an android mobile phone or tablet, has been piloted in four remote villages in Mayurbanj district which are primarily inhabited by Adivasis. Bridging the technology divide, this mapping tool has a number of empowering features, such as its ability to integrate with background maps, interfaces such as adding photos/ text/voice recordings at landmarks, real-time validation and comparison with boundaries mapped by neighbouring villages, and so on. After the physical mapping process in the field is complete, the maps can be reviewed readily by village elders without the need to be physically present at the time of mapping.[38]

Transcending the exclusionary potential of such technology, the preparation of these spatial maps has become an opportunity for communities to coalesce and re-assert the traditional boundaries of their customary homelands. At the same time, it allows them to learn new technological skills which help re-knit community ties fragmented through decades of disuse, and also provides an opportunity to reconnect with their traditional role as stewards of the forest and its resources.

Other categories of evidence being used under the FRA

The use of GIS and spatial technology by Adivasi and forest-dwelling communities to advance their forest rights certainly debunks the stereotypical notion of the 'noble savage' which, unfortunately, permeates the attitudes of the state and its functionaries. At the same time, Rule 13 of the Forest Rights Rules has provided the legislative foundation for self-assessment of claims by Gram Sabhas based upon atypical evidentiary sources, which include physical evidence such as trees, structures, and wells, and oral evidence such as statements of village elders drawing upon their memories, ancient folklore, and customary practices. Cultural and spiritual practices have provided another vital source of 'evidence' outside the narrow framework confining the administrative machinery till now.

The bureaucracy has often found these innovations difficult to comprehend. To cite just one example, sometime in 2017 the Government of Karnataka approached the nodal ministry MoTA for a clarification regarding the types of physical evidence which may be presented by 'other traditional forest dwellers' to establish their dependence on forests for three generations.[39] The specific query of the state government was whether the physical evidence itself, such as a dwelling, should be 75 years old, and what method for determination of the age of such physical evidence can be used. In the ensuing discussions, the possible use of carbon-dating was proposed, only to be vehemently rejected by the central ministry. Eventually, a detailed clarification in this regard had to be issued, drawing attention to the open-ended nature of Rule 13, and to the fact that the Gram Sabha reaches a determination based upon an actual physical verification on-site.[40]

Conclusion

Before concluding the discussion on the use of evidence in recognition of forest rights in India, it would be useful to examine the landmark judgment of the Indian Supreme Court in the *Niyamgiri* case.[41] This decision came after a long and tortuous journey, which we must remit for examination another day. It is useful, however, to contrast the approach adopted by the court in this matter, with how the same court approached the *Banwasi Seva Ashram* case several decades earlier. In this case also, the customary lands of the tribal forest dwellers had been declared as government reserve forests many years before and the lands were now required for a large industrial enterprise (namely, mining of bauxite to provide raw material for an aluminium factory established nearby).

The project had obtained necessary permissions, such as a mining lease, environmental clearance and stage-1 forest clearance. Decisions of the Supreme Court itself, dating as far back as 2009, also expressed approval for grant of final forest clearance to the project. However, when the central government decided not to grant a final forest clearance on the ground that there were pre-existing rights under Forest Rights Act in the area, the matter came once again before the same court.

In the *Niyamgiri* case, the number of claims for individual forest rights were very few, and those relating to the land in question had been granted titles over equivalent alternate sites. With regard to community rights, only six claims were received of which three claims were settled by granting an alternate site, and three remained pending. Under the previous legal regime relating to forests, the court could have taken a technical approach and refused to interfere, or at best permitted some leniency with regard to laches, as was done in the *Banwasi Seva Ashram* case. Indeed, the state government and the holder of the mining lease[42] had urged the court to do just that, pressing that the legal issues arising be scrutinised on the basis of the colonial forest law architecture alone. If the court had agreed, the Dongaria Kondhs, a primitive tribal group having a population of around 8,000, would most certainly have failed to establish their rights.

The court examined the historical processes which have resulted in widespread disenfranchisement of forest-dwelling communities, and how the FRA seeks to correct this historical wrong, through substantive provisions as well as procedures for vesting and recognition of forest rights. The integral relationship between the FRA and the Panchayats (Extension to Scheduled Areas) Act, 1996 (or PESA), was also explicated by the court. It further observed:

> Many of the STs and other TFDs are totally unaware of their rights. They also experience lot of difficulties in obtaining effective access to justice because of their distinct culture and limited contact with mainstream society. Many a times, they do not have the financial resources to engage in any legal actions against development projects undertaken in their abode or the forest in which they stay. *They have a vital role to play in the environmental management and development because of their knowledge and traditional practices. State has got a duty to recognize and duly support their identity, culture and interest so that they can effectively participate in achieving sustainable development.*[43]
>
> (Author's emphasis)

The *Niyamgiri* judgment is permeated with an acknowledgement of the people-centric approach of the FRA towards governance and administration of justice. Stepping out from the narrow confines of legalism, the court linked the community rights under FRA to fundamental constitutional rights, such as freedom of religion and culture under Articles 25 and 26 of the Constitution. It reiterated the need to ensure that forest-dwelling communities are actively involved in decision-making regarding development initiatives which involve their customary forest resources, an approach the colonial era architecture of forest laws had completely erased. The Court concluded that it is the Gram Sabhas which must 'actively consider' and make a decision regarding whether they have religious rights over the Niyam Raja hilltop, and whether the proposed mining area would detrimentally impact their religious right to worship on the hilltop.

While issuing directions to ensure that these Gram Sabha meetings are held in a free and fair manner, the judgment required the attendance of a judicial officer of the rank of District Judge; such an officer would play no judicial or decision-making role on the substantive issues involved, attending only 'as an observer.' Apart from the three decades separating these directions from those issued in the *Banwasi Seva Ashram* case, they also represent a tectonic shift in the paradigm of forest rights recognition and governance in India.

This important shift in what was received wisdom till recently, represents an evolving jurisprudence around indigenous peoples' rights in India, and is reflected in subsequent judgments emerging from other courts. Judicial officers have seized upon *Niyamgiri*'s expansive approach in order to address egregious violations of environmental and forest protection legislations, where a hyper-technical and legalistic approach would most certainly have failed.[44] The examination of these jurisprudential advances must wait for another day. Equally important is the permeation of the principles espoused in *Niyamgiri* in the everyday discourse and negotiation of space – taking place between forest-dwelling communities and the local administration at ground level.

It is also remarkable that these changes are visible not only in the Scheduled Areas, but the constitutional mandate regarding Adivasi homelands has overflowed beyond such geographical exclusivity to Adivasis and forest dwellers outside such areas, who have hitherto been at a disadvantage by reason of their spatial location. By capturing the people-centric approach of the constitutional and statutory protections inside Scheduled Areas and taking them forward into a people-centric governance model for all Adivasis and forest dwellers in the country, the Forest Rights Act has provided an important framework for the undoing of historical injustice meted out to forest dwellers by a colonial dispensation.

Notes

1 It is important to note that the Scheduling of Tribes in India, under Article 342 of the Constitution of India, is a work in progress, and that there are numerous communities which have not been granted Scheduled Tribe status for a variety of reasons. The ILO Convention Concerning Indigenous and Tribal Populations (ILO Convention No. 107) to which India is a party, applies equally to 'indigenous and other tribal and semi-tribal populations,' and for this reason tribal communities which are in the process of being granted ST status would also fall under the protection of international law relating to indigenous populations.

2 An earlier version of this chapter was presented at the 4th International LASSnet Conference 'Thinking with Evidence: Seeking Certainty, Making Truth' held at New Delhi, 10–12 December, 2016. The author acknowledges the valuable research inputs provided by Ms Gayatri Raghunandan, Advocate.

3 The colonial government notified the Van Panchayat Rules of 1931 under the 'village forests' provision of the Indian Forest Act, 1927 (Section 28), providing the framework for creation and demarcation of forests governed by village communities in Kumaon and Garhwal in present day Uttarakhand.

4 The mountain regions of Himachal Pradesh, then a part of undivided Punjab, saw very detailed forest settlements in the early years of the 20th century, which recorded rights continue to form the backbone of a highly complex forest-dependent citizenry till today.

5 The Santhal Parganas Tenancy Act, 1949, and the Chota Nagpur Tenancy Act, 1908, along with the recognition of the Wilkinson's Rules, have ensured a high degree of engagement of local tribal communities in the management of forests in present-day Jharkhand.

6 Section 81 of the Orissa Forest Act, 1972, makes provision for declaration of any forest land or waste land in the merged territories which had been administered as a reserve forest under the erstwhile ruler as a 'deemed reserve forest', in which case the settlement procedure can be done away with. It further provides that those forests which were recognised as 'khasra forests, village forests or protected forests' under the merged territories, shall be 'deemed protected forests.' The requirement to undertake any exercise for settlement/enquiry/recording of rights is done away with. Existing rights continue at the will of the government till they are altered, again at the will of the government.

7 See, for instance, Hansda Sowvendra Shekhar (2017) *The Adivasi Will Not Dance*, Delhi: Speaking Tiger.

8 National Thermal Power Corporation is a government owned company.

9 *Banwasi Seva Ashram vs. State of U.P. & Ors.* (1986) 4 SCC 753, (1987) 3 SCC 304.

10 This committee included well-known social activist, the late Dr. Vasudha Dhagamwar, and also a nominee of the Banwasi Seva Ashram.

11 The Legal Service Authorities Act, 1986 provides that free legal assistance and representation will be provided to the poor and marginalized, mentioning the Scheduled Tribes specifically.

12 The Court, in an attempt to balance the requirements of development while upholding the traditional rights of forest dwellers, held that

> Indisputably, forests are a much wanted national asset. On account of the depletion thereof ecology has been disturbed; climate has undergone a major change and rains have become scanty. These have long-term adverse effects on national economy as also

on the living process. At the same time, we cannot lose sight of the fact that for industrial growth as also for provision of improved living facilities there is great demand in this country for energy such as electricity. In fact, for quite some time the entire country in general and specific parts thereof, in particular, have suffered a tremendous setback in industrial activity for want of energy. A scheme to generate electricity, therefore, is equally of national importance and cannot be deferred at paragraph 10.

13 Available at https://asbb.gov.in//Downloads/National%20Forest%20Policy.pdf (accessed on 27 April, 2022).

14 The National Forest Policy 1988 contains numerous provisions recording the importance of tribal and forest dwelling communities to the survival of forests, including:

> **4.6 Tribal People and Forests**
> Having regard to the symbiotic relationship between the tribal people and forests, a primary task of all agencies responsible for forest management, including the forest development corporations should be to associate the tribal people closely in the protection, regeneration and development of forests as well as to provide gainful employment to people living in and around the forest.

15 29th Report of the Commissioner for Scheduled Castes and Scheduled Tribes, by the late Dr B.D. Sharma who was appointed under Article 338 of the Constitution of India.

16 For our purposes, the following four guidelines are relevant (Sharma 2003):

1. Encroachments on Forest Land – a Review thereof and measures for confinement (No.13–1/90/-FP (I)):This order provides for regularisation of encroachments predating the Forest Conservation Act, 1980, that is, those prior to 25 October 1980.
2. Review of Disputed Claims over Forest Land arising out of Forest Settlement (No.13–1/90/-FP (2)): This order provides for settlement of disputed claims over reserve forests where the Settlement of Rights has been faulty or has not been done.
3. Disputes regarding pattas/leases/grants involving forest lands (No.13–1/ 90/-FP (3): This order relates to pattas/leases/grants of forest land which could not be renewed or have become 'illegal' due to the enactment of the 1980 Act.
4. Conversion of Forest Villages into Revenue Villages and Settlement of other Old Habitations(No.13–1/90/-FP): This order relates to the settlement of old habitations and dwelling sites, as well as de-reservation of forestland for conversion of forest villages into revenue villages.

Two other guidelines were also issued in the same batch, one relating to payment of wages to forest workers, and the other regarding compensation for loss of life due to predation by wild animals.

17 Under Section 6 of the 1927 Act, a claim for settlement of rights must be filed before the FSO within three months of the proclamation of intention. If such claim is not filed, Section 9 states that the rights 'shall be extinguished,' unless a satisfactory application explaining the delay is made before the final notification under Section 20 is issued, or alternately an appeal is filed under Section 17 within three months. The reality is that in vast swathes of forest lands, neither were any initial claims filed, nor were appeals filed, nor even any challenges filed before the High Courts in exercise of their writ jurisdiction, and the statutory limitations have been crossed not in months or years, but in decades.

18 Preliminary Offence Reports or PORs are similar to First Information Reports (FIRs) registered under the Criminal Procedure Code.

19 For a detailed examination of the administrative and legislative advancements made during this period, and their eventual failure, see *Unbroken History of*

Broken Promises: Indian State and the Tribal People, by Dr B.D. Sharma, Sahyog Pustak Kuteer, 2010.

20 *T.N. Godavarman Thirumalpad vs. Union of India & Ors.* Writ Petition (Civil) No. 202 of 1995, Supreme Court of India, pending.

21 This study estimates that India has the potential to recognise 40 million hectares (about 100 million acres) of 'customarily-held forest land' through the formal legal recognition under the Forest Rights Act. Since this estimate is based on already existing government records, it is very likely that the actual potential area for such rights recognition is much higher.

22 An important example of such spillover of Scheduled Area principles to non-Scheduled Areas is the definition of 'Gram Sabha' and 'village' under the Forest Rights Act, which is based upon the definition contained in the Panchayats (Extension to Scheduled Areas) Act, 1997 (PESA). Drawing upon the PESA approach to governance, FRA defines the village at the smallest unit of habitation, which could be a hamlet, tola, pada, or revenue village, and the Gram Sabha as the body of all adult members of the village. This is a significant departure from several state panchayati raj legislations. It is also integral to the functioning of the FRA, since the Gram Sabha is at the heart of the democratic governance mechanisms the statute seeks to establish.

23 The earliest opposition to the Forest Rights Act came from associations of retired forest officials, who filed writ petitions in different high courts across the country challenging its constitutional validity. The initial vehemence of these challenges dissipated over the years. Surprisingly, the most hostile opposition to the Forest Rights Act has come from wildlife conservation groups, who have continued to argue with great conviction, both inside and outside the courtroom, that the statute needs to be struck down in the interest of conservation of the forests and wildlife. Since these matters are *sub judice*, they are not being discussed in any detail in the present chapter.

24 Section 11 of FRA states that the nodal ministry dealing with the implementation of the Act at the central government is the Ministry of Tribal Affairs.

25 The proper identification of Gram Sabhas is central to the effective implementation of the Forest Rights Act. As stated earlier, the definition of Gram Sabha is drawn from PESA, previously applicable only to the Scheduled Areas.

26 Rule 12 A of the Forest Rights Rules.

27 The date of 30 October 1980 as the cut-off for rights recognition first found mention in the 1990 Guidelines, becoming written in stone over years of discourse within the administration and also in the Courts. The date is traceable to the Forest Conservation Act, 1980, which was brought into force on 30 October 1980. Needless to say, it has no relevance under the Forest Rights Act, which makes no mention of it, and also exempts the recognition of forest rights from the operation of the 1980 Act.

28 The approved source for satellite imagery in support of claims under the Forest Rights Act was stated to be the Bhaskaracharya Institute for Space Applications and Geo-Informatics (BISAG), Gujarat.

29 *Action Research in Community Health & Development (ARCH) & Ors. vs. State of Gujarat & Ors.* Judgment dt.3.5.2013 in Writ Petition (PIL) No. 100 of 2011. 2013 SCC OnLine Guj 2583.

30 One such provisions is Rule 12-A(11) of the Forest Rights Rules, which states:

12A. Process of Recognition of Rights:
XXX

(11) The Sub-Divisional Level Committee or the District Level Committee shall consider the evidence specified in rule 13 while deciding the claims and shall not insist upon any particular form of documentary evidence for consideration of a claim.

31 A ground-truthing exercise, for instance, would be able to determine whether lands which are otherwise showing up 'green' in satellite images are actually under self-cultivation within the larger definition contained in Rule 12-A (8) of the Forest Rights Rules, which states:

12A. Process of Recognition of Rights:
XXX
(8) The land rights for self-cultivation recognised under clause (a) of subsection (1) of section 3 shall be, within the specified limit, including the forest lands used for allied activities ancillary to cultivation, such as, for keeping cattle, for winnowing and other post-harvest activities, rotational fallows, tree crops and storage of produce.
Explanation: 1. Fine receipts, encroacher lists, primary offence reports, forest settlement reports, and similar documentation by whatever name called, arisen during prior official exercise, or the lack thereof, shall not be the sole basis for rejection of any claim.
2. The satellite imagery and other uses of technology may supplement other form of evidence and shall not be treated as a replacement.

32 In Maharashtra, for instance, the stated rationale behind adoption of satellite technology was described by one study as under:

The use of GPS technology assists in improving the traditional process of land measurement and helps responsible authorities to make **objective verifiable decisions** in allocating land rights under the FRA. This technology is also providing information to make plane table survey of forest land plots more cost effective and less laborious.

(Goswami 2016)

The reliance on satellite images to make 'objective verifiable decisions' regarding forest rights militates against the law at multiple levels, and could potentially defeat its historical purpose entirely.

33 Circular dated 27 July 2015 bearing F. No. 23011/18/2015-FRA issued by the Ministry of Tribal Affairs, Government of India to the Chief Secretaries of All States, available at https://tribal.nic.in/FRA/declarationsClarifications/3Guidelinesforgeo-referencing.pdf (accessed on 22 May 2018).

34 Rule 6 of the Forest Rights Rules, while delineating the Functions of the Sub-Divisional Level Committee, states '(b) provide forest and revenue maps and electoral rolls to the Gram Sabha or the Forest Rights Committee.'

35 The July 2015 Guideline issued by MoTA also stated that training support on how to use these technologies can be obtained from BISAG, Gujarat, National Resource Centre Tribal Research Institute, Odisha, the BHUVAN portal of Department of Space, and other State Remote Sensing Agencies.

36 Chaudhury, Pranab, *et al. Community Mapping through An Android OS based mobile GIS application: An attempt towards Inclusive, Transparent & Participatory mapping of Community Forest Rights in India*, unpublished paper presented at 2016 World Bank Conference on Land and Poverty, Washington DC, March 2016, at page 4.

37 The various collaborators in this pilot are *Vasundhara* (Odisha), *Centre for Land Governance* (NRMC) (Delhi), *Rights and Resources Initiative* (Washington DC), and a GIS start up *Geolysis*.

38 The simple and easy to use Android App is supported by a web portal, to which the information collected is transmitted through the server network. Although

the App is still in its testing stage, the initial results are positive, with several villages having actually submitted claims for CFR rights based on the maps generated through this innovation.

39 Section 2(o) of the Forest Rights Act requires that OTFDs establish primary residence and dependence on forests for at least three generations or 75 years.

40 Clarification dated 7 March 2017 bearing F. No. 23011/02/2013-FRA issued by the Ministry of Tribal Affairs, Government of India to the Secretary, Social Welfare Department, Karnataka government. Available at https://tribal.nic.in/FRA/declarationsClarifications/OTFDClarificationtoGovtofKarnataka.pdf (accessed on April 27, 2022).

41 *Orissa Mining Corporation vs. Ministry of Environment and Forests & Ors.* (2013) 6 SCC 476.

42 It is important to clarify that the mining lease had been granted to Orissa Mining Corporation, a state-owned mining company, and that the actual mining of bauxite was to be done by the UK-based multinational corporation Vedanta Resources through its Indian subsidiary, Sterlite Industries Pvt. Ltd.

43 Ibid. at para 47.

44 See, for instance, *Paryawaran Sanrakshan Sangarsh Samiti Lippa vs. Union of India & Ors.* Judgment dt. 4.5.2016 in Appeal No. 28 of 2013, National Green Tribunal. The *Niyamgiri* judgment has also been relied upon in the *ARCH Vahini* judgment (supra) of the Gujarat High Court which specifically relates to evidence and the meaning of Rule 13 of the Forest Rights Rules.

References

Action Research in Community Health & Development (ARCH) & Ors. vs. State of Gujarat & Ors. Judgment dt.3.5.2013 in Writ Petition (PIL) No. 100 of 2011. 2013 SCC OnLine Guj 2583.

Banwasi Seva Ashram vs. State of U.P. & Ors. (1986) 4 SCC 753, (1987) 3 SCC 304.

Campaign for Survival and Dignity (CSD). 2003. 'Endangered Symbiosis: Evictions and India's Forest Communities.' *Report of the Jan Sunwai Public Hearing*, July 19–20. New Delhi: Delhi Forum and The Other Media.

Chaudhury, P.R., Rao, G.V., Kumar, K., Deo, B. and Dash, T. 2016. 'Community Mapping Through an Android OS Based Mobile GIS Application: An Attempt Towards Inclusive, Transparent & Participatory Mapping of Community Forest Rights in India.' Paper presented at *2016 World Bank Conference on Land and Poverty*, Washington, DC.

Goswami, B. 2016. *Geo-informatics for Forest Rights: Harnessing Technology for Better livelihood Support and Access to Forest Rights* (20 November 2016). Available at: https://oneworld.net.in/wp-content/uploads/Harnessing-technology-for-better-livelihood-support-and-access-to-forest-rights.pdf (accessed on April 27, 2022)

Hansda, S.S. 2017. *The Adivasi Will Not Dance*. New Delhi: Speaking Tiger.

Khanna, S. 2014. 'Boundaries of Forest Land: The Godavarman Case and Beyond.' In S. Lele and A. Menon (Eds.), *Democratizing Forest Governance in India* (pp. 225–260). New Delhi: Oxford University Press.

Lele, S. 2014. 'What Is Wrong With Joint Forest Management.' In S. Lele and A. Menon (Eds.), *Democratizing Forest Governance in India* (pp. 25–62). New Delhi: Oxford University Press.

Lele, S. and Menon, A. (Eds.). 2014. *Democratizing Forest Governance in India*. New Delhi: Oxford University Press.

Ministry of Tribal Affairs (MoTA). 2019. 'Status Report on Implementation of the Scheduled Tribes and Other Traditional Forest Dwellers (Recognition of Forest Rights) Act, 2006 [for the period ending 28.2.2019].' *M/o Tribal Affairs of India, I.D. No.23011/3/2016-FRA dated 28.5.2019*. Available at: https://tribal.nic.in/FRA/data/MPRFeb2019.pdf (accessed on 11 June 2019).

Orissa Mining Corporation vs. Ministry of Environment and Forests & Ors. (2013) 6 SCC 476.

Paryawaran Sanrakshan Sangarsh Samiti Lippa vs. Union of India & Ors. Judgment dt. 4.5.2016 in Appeal No. 28 of 2013, National Green Tribunal.

Pradip Prabhu and Ors. vs. State of Maharashtra and Ors. 1995 Supp (3) SCC 450.

Rights and Resources Initiative. 2015. *Potential for Recognition of Community Forest Resource Rights Under India's Forest Rights Act: A Preliminary Assessment.* Washington, DC: Rights and Resources Initiative.

Sarin, M. 2014. 'Undoing Historical Injustice: Reclaiming Citizenship Rights and Democratic Forest Governance Through the Forest Rights Act.' In S. Lele and A. Menon (Eds.), *Democratizing Forest Governance in India* (pp. 100–146). New Delhi: Oxford University Press.

Sharma, Dr. B.D. 1989. *29th Report of the Commissioner for Scheduled Castes and Scheduled Tribes*. Commissioner for Scheduled Castes and Scheduled Tribes under Article 338 of the Constitution of India.

Sharma, Dr. B.D. 2003. *Forest Lands: Tribals Struggle for Survival*. New Delhi: Sahyog Pustak Kuteer.

Sharma, Dr. B.D. 2010. *Unbroken History of Broken Promises: Indian State and the Tribal People*. New Delhi: Sahyog Pustak Kuteer.

T.N. Godavarman Thirumalpad vs. Union of India & Ors. Writ Petition (Civil) No. 202 of 1995, Supreme Court of India, pending.

United Nations Declaration on Rights of Indigenous Peoples, Resolution adopted by the United Nations General Assembly on 13 September 2007, 61/295; available at https://www.un.org/development/desa/indigenouspeoples/declaration-on-the- rights-of-indigenous-peoples.html (accessed on April 27, 2022).

3 Feminist Dimension of Biodiversity Challenges

Niharika Bahl

Women and nature are intrinsically linked. Folklore and legends across the world are replete with references testifying to the same.[1] Nature, abundance and fertility have been regarded as feminine notions in almost all cultures and beliefs.[2] Ancient Indian texts regard the primordial lifegiving energy as *sakti* – female; earth itself is referred to as *aditi*; and *prithvi* – female goddess who is a nurturing mother, in whose womb seeds are germinated and who, in her infinite generosity, provides food and sustains all the flora and fauna.[3] All goddesses manifest as primal relational powers of nature, connecting all elements of life in a single biotic web.[4] The synergy between women and nature is underscored always.[5]

India is blessed with a rich treasure trove of natural resources. Embracing three major biological realms – Indo-Malayan, Eurasian and Afro-tropical – India is adorned with 10 bio-geographic zones and 26 biotic provinces.[6] With only 2.4% of the earth's land area, India accounts for 7–8% of the recorded species of the world, which includes millions of races, subspecies and local variants of species, and the ecological processes and cycles that link organisms into population, communities and all different ecosystems.[7] Demographically, it is the second largest populated country in the world[8] and a majority of its population directly depends on biological resources for livelihood.[9]

Despite this natural bounty, India is faced with a burgeoning food crisis. Its rich biodiversity is getting steadily eroded, endangering the lives of all dependent upon it, particularly women. According to the 2013 Global Hunger Index (GHI), India ranks 63rd out of the 78 hungriest countries, significantly worse than neighbouring Sri Lanka (43rd), Nepal (49th), Pakistan (57th) and Bangladesh (58th).[10] The United Nations Food and Agricultural Organization believes that 17% of Indians are too undernourished to lead a productive life. In fact, one-quarter of the world's undernourished people live in India, more than in all of Sub-Saharan Africa.[11]

DOI: 10.4324/9781003299561-3

The present chapter seeks to examine the challenges to biodiversity in India from a gendered feminist perspective of the rights and interests of woman food producers. It is divided into two parts. The first part examines the dependence of women upon the surrounding environment and discusses the integral role played by women in managing and sustaining biodiversity in India and the impact of its erosion on them. The second part analyses the framework of laws for protecting the country's natural wealth, ranging from the Constitution of India 1950, to the Biodiversity Act 2002, to the Forest Rights Act, 2006, and investigates whether the same protects the rights of the women food producers and whether it can be leveraged by women to safeguard their rights to grow, gather food, feed and sustain their households, and apply their conservation practices.

I. Women and biodiversity: a gendered difference

> *May this Earth, replete with seas, rivers and water sources, excellent food grain from agriculture, prolific and abundant living creatures, bestow upon us munificent nutrition.*
>
> Prithvi Sukta, Atharva Veda [12.1.1 to 12.1.63]

There is a lineal narrative which predominantly prevails in academic literature about women's relationship with biodiversity. It postulates a near complete dependence of women on its surrounding environment to fulfil the household needs of fuel, food and fodder which would not hold true in an urban landscape. Further, it promotes a homogenous view of women's interests, ignoring the distinctions on account of geographical location, culture and economic and social class. This is turn leads to a monolithic view of women's role as naturally inherent conservationists. Yes, rural women have a greater dependency than men on the environment. But the difference is not merely of degree, it is also qualitative. It arises on account of the gendered division of labour and limited access and control over resources. So, while men's dependency on forests is for the occasional need for timber, women's is for daily provisions of fodder and firewood, which makes their dependency not only higher but more immediate and persistent.[12]

Again, women are primarily responsible for the task of food gathering. Forests and other surrounding natural vegetation serve as supplements to daily subsistence diets and cushions during periods of scarcity. This too leads to a gendered distinction of priorities. Men prefer plant species that provide timber while women prioritize fruit bearing, fodder and firewood species. In a similar vein, there is gendered acquisition of traditional knowledge. Women are not the sole repositories of indigenous knowledge, but the wider range of products that women gather leads to gender differences of traditional know-how. Food gathering requires deep knowledge of the nutritional and medicinal properties of plants which is practiced and maintained by women in most rural communities.[13]

At the same time, though there may be commonalities of the gendered division of labour and vulnerabilities, in reality, there is a great deal of heterogeneity in women's interests and complexity in their relationship with the environment on account of class, ethnicity, region and economic capacity. For instance, while household work, child rearing and elder care largely fall within the domain of women's work, even within this domain, some women, due to their better economic standing, might not have to do the work themselves because some could afford helpers. Agarwal also points out that conflicts of interest amongst women can also be easily prevalent. Thus, while the requirement of firewood is felt by all rural women, it would be more acutely felt by women from landless households and less so by those from landed households, as they would be able to obtain firewood from their lands; therefore, landless women would be more resistant to strict forest closure rules.[14]

The foregoing discussion indicates women's response and interaction with biodiversity is intrinsically linked to the gendered access to and control over resources and the sexual division of labour. Adopting a contextual approach instead of a monolithic one is more helpful in building a better understanding of women's relationship with the environment and in developing an effective strategy to mobilize the same.

A. Women as food producers

It is in the performance of their gendered duties that rural women have over time built a vast repository of traditional knowledge, of agrarian and conservation practices. According to M. S. Swaminathan, the famous agricultural scientist, some historians believe that it was woman who first domesticated crop plants and thereby initiated the art and science of farming. While men went out hunting in search of food, women started gathering seeds from the native flora and began cultivating those of interest from the point of view of food, feed, fodder, fibre and fuel.[15]

India boasts of a rich crop diversity and agriculture forms the mainstay of the Indian economy with half of its workforce engaged in it.[16]

Unrecognized and unacknowledged, women constitute a substantial part of the agrarian workforce in India. According to the 2011 Census, there are nearly 100 million women engaged in the agricultural sector as farmers and labourers.[17] Beyond these economic figures, women perform many roles. They are simultaneously farmers, herders, forest gatherers, drawers of water, food processors, market vendors, soil conservationists and caretakers of the natural environment – functions which may not necessarily be accounted for as an 'economic productive' activity but which are integral to their existence, household food security and nutrition, and for environmental protection.[18]

A critical aspect of agrarian diversity is seed selection. Women in most rural communities in India have traditionally been the guardians of the seed.[19] Seeds, a symbol of the cycle of birth, life and death, are a part of India's cultural heritage. The practice of seed saving has been the cornerstone of Indian farming traditions that made agriculture, itself, a way of life in the country. And it is women who select the seeds which set into motion the entire agrarian cycle. They identify the valuable genes and traits in these crops and have maintained them over generations through a highly sophisticated system of crossing and selection. Selection is done on the basis of traits as diverse as disease resistance, high salt tolerance, and resistance to water logging; and traits such as drought tolerance as well as cooking time, taste, digestibility, milling and husking characteristics, like how much grain breaks during milling operations, are recognized and maintained.

Women are in the true sense owners of this complex seed technology and know-how.[20] It is due to their key role that India has displayed such vast crop diversity in its cereals, pulses, vegetables and fruits. Nearly 166 food/crop species and 320 wild relatives of crops have originated here. One species of rice (*Oryza sativa*) has been diversified into at least 50,000 (and perhaps up to 200,000!) distinct varieties while one species of mango (*Mangifera indica*) has yielded over 1,000 varieties, ranging from the size of a peanut to a muskmelon.[21] Studies have shown that in the proportionately small geographical areas of North East India, there is as much diversity of rice as in all of Asia. Amongst the *Garo* tribe in Meghalaya, some women are aware of over 300 indigenous varieties of rice.[22] Alongside food production, food gathering is also done. Surrounding natural vegetation is collected and utilized as food, fodder, medicine and building material.

In lean seasons or of crop failure, women are able to identify and gather 'hidden harvest' – wild fruit, tubers, roots and leaves which grow on common lands or in between crops as important sources of food supply.[23] Take, for instance, the case of 'bathua', a green leafy plant which grows as a weed in the wheat fields. When women weed the wheat field, they harvest the bathua as a rich source of nutrition for their families.[24] In a survey in Andhra Pradesh, village women identified 79 species of uncultivated leafy greens that they gathered for food, in addition to roots, tubers and fruits.[25] This wealth of 'traditional knowledge' of women has been applied and modified over the ages to maintain their household's food security and health. Thus, it is a continuing stream and it reflects an innate understanding of the contribution made by each and every living thing in maintaining the fragile ecological balance.

Women farmers, however, are a marginalized group. They have limited access to resources – financial and educational – and they lack secure land rights and have limited decision-making ability within their households and within the community of cultivators.[26] Agrarian land reforms in the country have left women in the sidelines. In spite of the progressive changes in the succession laws, ground reality indicates a dismal picture. The total number of female farmers in the country has declined 14% from 41.9 million in 2001 to 36 million in 2011.[27] In the same period, there has been an increase of 24% in the number of female agricultural labourers, from 49.5 million in 2001 to 61.6 million in 2011.[28] Tribal women in the country stand even more marginalized owing to the inherent disadvantaged status of their communities.[29]

A closer look highlights the starkness of the ground reality. A study of women's agricultural ownership in Gujarat covering 10 districts, 15 tehsils and 23 villages revealed that 4,188 men (81%) as against 561 women (11.81%) owned land.[30] Of the 403 cases of women ownership for which data could be collected, 193 women (47.89%) owned land following widowhood and 167 (41.43%) owned land to avail of some government benefit, escape the land ceiling or avoid payment of a tax or bribe to the revenue official.[31] In 18 (0.04%) cases, women obtained land from their parents who had no male heirs. And in 10 cases, women from tribal and Muslim communities received land on account of their husband marrying a second time.[32] Women not only owned less land than the male members of the household, but also land of inferior, low productive quality.[33]

B. *Shrinking biodiversity, shrinking lives*

> *In daily life, on Earth, whether we are sitting, standing, or in motion, may our activity be such as would never cause injury or grief.*
>
> Prithvi Sukta, Atharva Veda [12.1.1 to 12.1.63]

India's biodiversity is, however, rapidly decreasing. Rampant growth of human population and human activity has led to widespread destruction of forests and other natural habitats. Global warming and climate change have endangered many species of plants and animals. At least 10% of India's recorded wild flora and possibly more of its wild fauna are on the list of threatened species, and many are on the brink of obliteration. Of the wild fauna, 80 species of mammals, 47 of birds, 15 of reptiles, 3 of amphibians and a large number of moths, butterflies and beetles are endangered. Out of 19 species of primates, 12 are endangered. The cheetah (*Acinonyx jubatus*) and the pinkheaded duck (*Rhodonessa caryophyllacea*) are among species that have become extinct.[34]

With regard to cultivated plants, too, India's diversity is eroding. This process began with the so-called 'green revolution' which displaced the indigenous seeds with those of high-yielding varieties requiring heavy use of fertilizers, pesticides and irrigation facilities.[35] Native seeds saved and selected by women were declared to be primitive and inferior despite their suitability to climatic conditions and high nutritional content. Increasing use of pesticides and herbicides has further damaged biodiversity. Further, monocultures of uniform crop cultivation again eroded crop diversity.[36] And this process continues unabated. According to the UN Food and Agriculture Organization, the planet has lost 75% of its food crop diversity in the twentieth century as farmers shifted from genetically diverse traditional food crops to high-yielding monocultures.[37]

A further threat which has loomed on the horizon is that of Genetically Modified (GM) crops. GM crops are of two variants – herbicide tolerance (HT) and insect resistance (IR). In the case of the former, a gene that makes the crop immune to a particular chemical herbicide is inserted into the plant which enables farmers to spray the herbicide without damage to crops. IR, on the other hand, involves insertion of a gene that enables the plant to produce chemicals that kill certain pests which feed on it.[38] Though no clear verdict has been made on the biosafety of GM crops, it is feared that GM crops will have an adverse impact on human health and on the surrounding biodiversity.[39] The majority of the members of the European Union have refused to permit its cultivation.[40] Multi-National Corporations (MNCs) are heavily pushing the same. In India, BT cotton is the one that has been permitted to be commercially cultivated due to claims of high insect resistance, but the results have not been satisfactory. High cost of BT cotton seeds which have not been wholly pest resistant and the heavy dependence on irrigation have led to crop failures and escalated farmer debt and distress. Thus, Vidharba, Maharashtra, where BT cotton has been grown, continues to be labelled as the farmer suicide belt of the country.[41]

All this has had far-reaching consequences on the nation's food security. From growing crops for sustenance, post-GATT (General Agreement on Tariffs and Trade) and WTO (World Trade Organization), Indian farmers have been thrown into the global market of demand– supply. Dumping of agricultural produce from subsidized countries led to a steep fall in agricultural prices and pushed them further into debt, acerbated by rising costs of production, seeds and pesticides, etc.[42] P. Sainath explains,

> it cost Rs 2500 for a typical (non-organic) farmer to cultivate one acre of cotton in Vidharbha in 1991. Today it can cost upwards of Rs 13,000. Seed (then local) could be had for nine rupees a kilogram – if you didn't produce it yourself. By 2005, a 450-gram bag of (Monsanto's) Bt. cotton seed was selling for between Rs 1650 and Rs 1800. But in

> 2006, cotton was fetching the farmer the same per quintal as it did in 1994 though input costs had quadrupled. In Wyanad, Kerala, a farmer raising an acre of paddy could have done it for Rs 8,000. Many, lured by marketing, urged by government, shifted to vanilla – which in 2003 cost Rs 1.45 lakh an acre to grow. The risks multiplied, the costs multiplied – income did not.[43]

Thus, one scholar concludes that 'the underlying cause of the global food crisis is a corporate-dominated, fossil fuel-dependent model of agricultural production that is ecologically unsustainable and economically unjust'.[44] From a state of food self-sufficiency, we have moved to that of hunger and starvation deaths. According to the UN Food and Agriculture Organization's report, India is home to 194.6 million undernourished people, the highest in the world.[45] This translates into 15% of its population.[46]

The cumulative impact of all this on women food growers and gatherers has been devastating and has been largely unnoticed. When one thinks of farmers' suicides, one rarely thinks in terms of women farmers. However, suicides by women farmers do occur but are not recorded as such because the land is not in their names or reported as dowry death or accident.[47] Thus, in 2013 only 126 suicides by women farmers in Maharashtra were recorded by the National Crime Records Bureau against 3,020 by male farmers.[48] Further, when male farmers die, they leave behind a crushing debt for their widows. Farm widows struggle to manage their household, feed their children and pay the debts to the extent of doing more labour than a convict sentenced to rigorous imprisonment and eating even less than the prison quota of food for the convicts![49] The impact has been not just economic in terms of poverty and indebtedness, it has translated into 'a social crisis'.[50] More and more women are forced to shoulder the responsibility of their households in the wake of farmer suicides and male migration, without land, without assets – which have gone toward paying the farm debt – and thus they stand more vulnerable to exploitation. They are increasingly pushed into trafficking and there is a rising tide of violence against women.[51] In a public hearing in 2005 conducted by the National Commission for Women on the impact of the WTO on women in agriculture, in the Bundelkhand region, which has seen a spate of farmers' suicides, women spoke about the increase in domestic violence and dowry-related ill-treatment. The rise in dowry crimes was also reported by tribal and Scheduled Caste women in West Bengal, where earlier the custom of bride price prevailed.[52]

C. *Feminist voices*

Feminists' views on women's role as conservationists draw on different conceptual frameworks. The most prominent feminist strand is that of

Ecofeminism. Ecofeminists, notably Vandana Shiva and Maria Mies, perceive a common thread linking the exploitation of nature and women. They believe that the worldview that causes environmental degradation and injustice is the same worldview that causes a culture of male domination, exploitation and inequality for women.[53] The destruction of nature becomes the destruction of women's sources for sustenance for themselves and their families. That is the reason why women are found at the heart of every environmental struggle. The most celebrated instance is that of the *Chipko* movement in the 1970s when women in the Garhwal region hugged trees to prevent them from being felled by contractors licensed by the State.[54] This resistance was effective in restraining tree felling locally and it captured worldwide attention.

According to Shiva and Mies, commercial agriculture displaces women as the primary seed keeper and devalues her productive role. Trade liberalization and the Trade-Related Intellectual Property Rights (TRIPS) Agreement have adversely affected women's autonomy and control over her knowledge of seed and biodiversity by transferring the same to global corporations. As globalization shifts agriculture to capital-intensive, chemical-intensive systems, women bear disproportionate costs of both displacement and health hazards. Furthermore, as their livelihoods and productive roles are displaced, and their status is devalued, women become more disempowered, triggering further violence against them. Thus, they write,

> we see the devastation of the earth and her beings by the corporate warriors, as feminist concerns. It is the same masculinist mentality which would deny us our right to our own bodies and our own sexuality, and which depends on multiple systems of dominance and state power to have its way.[55]

The process works both ways as devaluation of women's role and status leads to further erosion of biodiversity.[56] As a counterpoint to this, there is feminist environmentalism advocated by economist Bina Agarwal, who questions the belief that women are identified with nature.[57] According to Agarwal, women, particularly rural women, are likely to be affected adversely in quite specific ways by environmental degradation. At the same time, in the course of their everyday interactions with nature, they acquire a special knowledge of species varieties and the processes of natural regeneration. They could thus be seen as both victims of the destruction of nature and as repositories of knowledge about nature, in ways distinct from the men of their class. The former aspect would provide the gendered impulse for their resistance and response to environmental destruction. The latter would condition their perceptions and choices of what should be done.[58]

Agarwal writes that

> feminist environmentalism recognizes that both women and men would have an interest in forest conservation and regeneration, but their interests would stem from *different* (and at times *conflicting*) concerns, rooted in their respective responsibilities, and the nature and intensity of their dependence on these resources.[59]

As environmental activist Anil Agarwal pointed out, while men are more interested and engaged with the cash economy, women continue to deal with the non-monetized, biomass-based subsistence economy of the household. Even within the same household, one can find cases of men supplying tonnes of bamboo to paper mills, etc. and thus destroying nature to earn cash, even though it could create greater hardships for the women in collecting daily fuel, fodder, roots, tubers, etc.[60] Further, with increasing male migration to urban areas and cash economies, the importance of women's traditional knowledge has grown as women have not only retained but added to their indigenous knowledge.[61]

Both approaches underscore the higher and more continuous nature of women's dependency upon the natural environment. This moulds women's attitude and outlook towards biodiversity management in terms of their traditional knowledge in the utilization of forests and other natural resources but also with regard to conservation. Compulsions of economic distress and class disparity would also come into play. The challenge, however, lies in enabling women, as critical stakeholders, to participate in the management and conservation of biodiversity resources and safeguard their interests.

II. International legal framework: limited recognition, limited role for women

> *O Earth, in the villages, forest, assemblies, committees and other places on Earth, may what we express always be in accord with you.*
>
> Prithvi Sukta, Atharva Veda [12.1.1 to 12.1.63]

Law makers and policy planners have paid scarce recognition to women's vital role in biodiversity conservation – internationally and at the domestic level. The primary international instrument, i.e. the Convention on Biological Diversity, 1992, contains only a bland recognition of women's role and the need to have participation of women at all levels of policy-making and implementation for biological diversity conservation.[62] There are no concrete steps outlined to achieve this participation. In most other instruments, even this recognition is also missing. Overall, the international legal framework regarding biodiversity reflects a lack of cohesion, a need rather of balancing the conservation imperatives without compromising the regime of intellectual property rights set up under the TRIPS agreement.

The International Union of the Protection of New Plant Varieties[63] (UPOV), an intergovernmental organization established under the International Convention for the Protection of New Varieties of Plants, 1961, promotes the property rights of plant breeders through the *sui generis* form of intellectual property protection.[64] The International Treaty on Plant Genetic Resources for Food and Agriculture, 2001, which India has ratified and which came into force in 2004, is an attempt to keep in free circulation the listed agricultural genetic resources which are crucial for food security, thereby providing for their conservation and sustainable use.[65] It creates a Multilateral System (MLS) that provides for facilitated access to a negotiated list of plant genetic resources and for the fair and equitable sharing of the benefits arising from their use.[66] The treaty has been hailed as protecting the interests of farmers by permitting free access to certain germplasm.[67] However, it allows patenting of genetic material received through the MLS if it has been modified in any way,[68] and this lack of a clear ban on patents or any other Intellectual Property Rights (IPRs) on crops for food and fodder is troublesome to farmers. While lauding the farmer's contribution to biodiversity, the treaty includes no recognition of the property rights of farmers – merely a grant of permission to save, exchange and sell farm seeds.[69] Further, there is no mention of the concerns or interests of women engaged in agrarian practices or in seed conservation.

In addition, the Nagoya Protocol on Access to Genetic Resources and the Fair and Equitable Sharing of Benefits, 2010 also came into force in 2014.[70] This Protocol to the Convention on Biological Diversity again seeks to facilitate access to genetic biodiversity resources with mechanisms for equitable sharing of benefits, but the onus for the establishment of the same is upon the respective party States. The Nagoya Protocol requires parties to take into consideration indigenous and local communities' customary laws, community protocols and procedures, as applicable, with respect to traditional knowledge associated with genetic resources.[71] Parties are also mandated to support the development of community protocols, model contractual clauses for sharing of benefits of traditional knowledge by indigenous and local communities, *including women*,[72] and to take measures to enhance the capacity of women of indigenous and local communities.[73] The Nagoya Protocol marks a step forward in at least acknowledging the necessity of the involvement of women in key decision-making pertaining to access to biodiversity.

III. Domestic legal framework: more access, less conservation of biodiversity

At the national level too, there is no gendered understanding in the framework of laws on food production and biodiversity conservation. The Constitution of India recognizes the principle of gender equality.[74] It also makes the right to life and personal liberty a fundamental right.[75] The scope of this right has been amplified by the courts to include privacy, legal aid, shelter and livelihood. However, this has not helped in checking the tide of deforestation and displacement of people from land and livelihoods.[76]

With respect to biodiversity specifically, the domestic statutory regime mirrors the same fragmented approach as found on the international plane. This is due to the fact that it has come about in compliance with India's international obligations. The foremost legislation in this regard is the Biological Diversity Act, 2002, enacted ostensibly for the sustainable use and conservation of biological resources and for the equitable sharing of the benefits arising out of the use of these resources and associated knowledge.[77] For these purposes, it establishes a three-tier structure with the National Biodiversity Authority (NBA), State Biodiversity Boards (SBBs) as well as Biodiversity Management Committees (BMCs) at the local level.[78] The main thrust of the Act, however, appears to be to regulate access to India's biodiversity and traditional knowledge for which it outlines clear procedures.[79] Conservation measures are confined to advising government and collating and publishing data on various aspects of biodiversity,[80] including documentation of traditional knowledge through the preparation of People's Biodiversity Registers by the BMCs.[81] In essence, the Act is more permissive than restrictive in its approach.

Women's participation in the process is through the mandatory one-third membership in the BMC.[82] This type of female participation is hemmed with all the obstacles that come with gender power-sharing in a patriarchal society, which raises questions about meaningful participation in any decision-making process. At present, there are 37,769 BMCs across all states and Union Territories in India,[83] and even these are not fully functional.[84] BMCs have also faced stiff opposition in certain states from the local government bodies who are unhappy about sharing power with them.[85] The low relevance of the BMCs in the working of the Act becomes apparent when even without all the BMCs operating properly, the NBA has executed, as of 2012, 100 Access and benefit-sharing (ABS) agreements[86] – though, under the Act, the NBA and SBBs are required to consult the BMCs while taking any decision relating to the use of biological resources and associated resources occurring within their territorial jurisdiction.[87]

The real challenge, according to activists and analysts, lies in ensuring that 'the monetary collections from these 100 agreements going into the

National Biodiversity Fund translate into real "benefits" for at least 100 local communities in India'.[88] Though there are a few reported success stories of favourable benefit sharing from the states of Andhra Pradesh and Madhya Pradesh,[89] conservation really seems to have taken a backseat under the Biodiversity Act, 2002. There is no clear roadmap on conservation ahead – no clear allocation of roles and responsibilities. The NBA too has earned a scathing criticism from the CAG for its dismal performance in this regard.[90]

The success of any conservation strategy depends upon community involvement, which is absent under the Act. The money from the Local Biodiversity Fund is to be spent on conservation and promotion of biodiversity in local areas in a manner 'as prescribed by State Government'.[91] Local participation, especially of women, at this stage would be greatly effective as it would enable employment of their strategies of conservation of biodiversity, which allow them to make sustainable use of natural resources and ensure their household's food security. Efforts are on by local women to utilize the provisions of the Act without reference to BMCs. A shining example is provided by the village women from the Zaheerabad region of the Medak district in Andhra Pradesh. These women have been practicing biodiversity conservation for generations with the use of intercropping, crop rotation practices, crop protection practices and maintaining community seed banks as well as passing the culture and practices to the next generation of women who come to the villages as daughters-in-law. They celebrate a festival of handing over seed pots to the next generation, symbolizing the handing over of the custody of the seed wealth to the next generation. Farmers in this area cultivate more than 85 types of crops, pulses, oil seeds, vegetables and medicinal plants by preserving over 80 seed varieties. In April 2010, through the intervention of a local NGO – Deccan Development Society – the farming community sent a proposal for protecting more than 50,000 acres of biodiverse farmland. This was approved by the SBB and after a considerable wait, the State government notified the area as a Bio Heritage Site (BHS) under Section 37 of the Biological Diversity Act.[92] The Medak story serves as a successful case study of women farmers successfully using the Biological Diversity Act to preserve their agrarian heritage without the BMC mechanism.

Of greater significance to women's agrarian rights is the Protection of Plant Variety and Farmers' Rights Act, 2001[93] (PPVFR). This was enacted in compliance with India's obligations under the TRIPS treaty, which required members to either opt for an Intellectual Property Rights model for plant variety protection or to develop a *sui generis* model.[94] The Act establishes plant breeders' and farmers' rights. The inclusion of farmers' rights came about as a result of a concerted campaign by farmers' advocacy groups. The

Act places farmers at the same level as plant breeders and provides that they receive the same kind of protection as plant breeders. Farmers, therefore, can also apply to have a plant variety registered which will entitle them to exclusive right to produce, sell, market, distribute, import or export the variety.[95] The actual process is tedious, not free from expense and involves a lot of paperwork which is difficult for illiterate farmers to comprehend. Conservation of genetic resources of land races and their improvement entitles farmers to be rewarded from the Gene Fund set up.[96] Further, a farmer shall be entitled 'to save, use, sow, resow, exchange, share or sell his farm produce including seed of a variety protected under this Act in the same manner as he was entitled before the coming into force of this Act'.[97] This right, dubbed 'farmers' privilege', is more in the nature of exemption than a right.[98]

Critics attack the fundamental premise of importing the concept of IPRs into agriculture. Traditional farming practices in India and the related knowledge has not been the private property of anyone.[99] The Act would only ensure to the benefit of richer farmers and corporate entities who would seek to stake claims on what is otherwise collective knowledge. This would further commercialize agriculture and marginalize women and small farmers. The rising spate of farmers' suicides is a pointer to the same. In the offing is a proposed Seeds Bill to regulate the sale and quality of seeds. It also contains provisions on the registration of GM seeds, which is a matter of controversy. At present, it has been put on hold.[100]

The Scheduled Tribes and other Traditional Forest Dwellers (Recognition of Forest Rights) Act, 2006[101] or Forest Rights Act (FRA) also has bearings on women's role in ensuring food sustenance and conserving biodiversity. The Forest Rights Act of 2006 seeks to make a shift in the conservation from purely state management of forests to a more participatory–community-oriented approach through involvement of *gram sabhas* and a Forest Rights Committee (FRC) at the local level, and by vesting of community rights in the forest dwellers since they are 'integral to the very survival and sustainability of the forest ecosystem'.[102] These include cultivation rights;[103] community land rights;[104] right to reclaim any disputed land;[105] right to convert to titles leases or grants of forest lands issued by local authorities or state government;[106] rights of settlement and conservation of all forest villages;[107] user rights like collection and usage of minor forest produce[108] and to use traditional seasonal resources, such as pastures and water bodies;[109] right of access to biodiversity; and the community right to intellectual property and traditional knowledge related to biodiversity and cultural diversity.[110]

Field studies indicate a lack of awareness amongst the forest communities about the Act. Community rights and conservation provisions seem largely to be ignored in practice.[111] A study conducted amongst the tribal *bhil* women in Banswara, Rajasthan, reveals gendered discrimination against women in the implementation of the FRA.[112] The majority of the tribal women interviewed including those who were members of the *gram panchayat* and the FRC, were unaware of the nature of the rights under the Act. An overwhelming majority also reported that their access to forests and forest produce had decreased after the passage of the Act due to the restrictions imposed by the FRC, which was more interested in selling the forest produce then in self-consumption. *Bhil* women also reported a loss of decision-making authority. Prior to the coming of the Act, there was a tradition of collective forest management by both men and women. Now women's participation has become limited to the token reserved membership in the FRC and *gram panchayat* as women are prevented from ever exceeding their reserved quota. Focus is on individual property rights and not on the collective community rights. Therefore, tribal women are dependent on extra-legal or illegal means to access forest resources for subsistence. This problem has major consequences on the future of tribal communities due to their heavy dependence on the forest as a common pool resource that is now converted into private property. The study concluded that recognizing women's traditional collective access to forest land and its resources may empower women in decision-making authority, change institutional rules, and contribute to women's socio-economic and political empowerment.[113]

Similar stories emerge from other parts of India. A study conducted across three districts in Andhra Pradesh, namely Adilabad, Srikakulam and Vizianagaram district, discloses the haste with which the state government 'fast tracked' the establishment and organization of gram sabhas and FRCs within a span of a month.[114] The emphasis, as seen in other parts of the country as well, is on individual claims and not on community rights. In Vizianagaram district, only 0.02% of the original community claims were accepted.[115] The non-recognition of community rights over common lands and forests where women were accustomed to collecting food and fodder and growing vegetables and other crops, directly and adversely impacts on women's access to sources of sustenance. With regard to individual claims, the final amount of land approved to women holders was a mere fraction of the amount claimed; this is a pointer to the inherent patriarchy ingrained in state mechanisms. Even on the individual land titles, government had undertaken to heavily promote and push monocultures of plantation farming. Thus, according to the analyst, the Adivasi women, who are being 'granted' these private titles, are left with the 'free choice' of deciding between mangoes and cashew nuts.[116] In the process, the women are becoming wage labourers, carrying out the government's programmes of plantation rather than exercising their traditional knowledge to nurture forests and gain rightful livelihoods. This completely destroys the spirit of the legislation which emphasized customary traditions and indigenous livelihoods.

The above discussion indicates that the current legal regime fails to appreciate the critical role played by women in food subsistence and managing biodiversity. Women's involvement is limited to token representation without allowing for actual decision-making. Legal illiteracy, skewed gender equations and limited access to resources makes it virtually impossible for them to avail any legal redress, even where provision is there. The existing legal framework does not secure or promote women's right to grow or gather food and feed and sustain their households, as it is directed towards facilitating commercialization of agrarian and other natural resources. The problem, which is not endemic to India but prevalent worldwide, is according to a scholar, that 'the commodification of biodiversity has caused a shift in the ownership of genetic resources from communal to private. Biodiversity knowledge and resources are alienated from the original custodians and donors and become the monopoly of private industry'.[117]

Thus, India has lost its food sovereignty and is in the throes of a deepening agrarian crisis. It may be argued that recourse may be had through the constitutional guarantees of right to life and liberty, since lives of women food producers and their families are endangered but the approach of the 'globalized Indian Supreme Court', as dubbed by Prof. Baxi, since the 1990s has, barring a few stray instances, been to endorse the wave of economic liberalization reforms for the 'development of the country'.[118] Of particular significance in recent times has been the Supreme Court ruling, impelled by the starvation deaths in the country, that fulfilment of the basic necessity of food is an integral part of the right to life.[119] Thereafter, the National Food Security Act, 2013[120] was enacted. The Act seeks to guarantee entitlement to minimum food grains to people below the poverty line and to streamline the existing Public Distribution System. The thrust of both the Supreme Court orders and the Act, as well as of other food security programmes[121] implemented in the country, has been on food distribution and not on food production or on the shrinking sources of sustenance. This strategy has come under criticism.[122] The focus, according to an analyst, should be on increasing food production in a sustainable manner.[123] And the core of this problem lies in tackling 'the fundamental question of common property resources and the right of access to them'.[124]

IV. Conclusion

Women and nature share a symbiotic relationship. A shrinkage of biodiversity entails a shrinkage of their rights to sustenance, and an erosion of women's status and decision-making ability adversely impacts the environment. The present scenario of commercialization of agriculture and plant resources has marginalized women and depleted food and other biological reserves, endangering the health of our future generation as well as of our planet. To rectify the same requires us to throw the biodiversity resources back into the community and to restore their guardianship and management to those who know how to utilize the same in a sustainable manner. Critically, it requires a change in outlook. Noted legal thinker Dhavan, in an insightful article on the environmental protection regime in India,[125] has written 'Indian law has always been more concerned with property rights than the environment, the exploitation of natural resources than their conservation, and the ruthless appropriation of natural spoils than with evolving a common understanding of the totality of the inheritance of nature'.

Even more fundamentally, women's voices therefore have to be not only heard but also counted. Law makers and policy planners have to ensure that women are not simply 'added' to the conservation programme, but rather, that biodiversity itself is defined in broader, more inclusive and fluid terms incorporating diverse gendered experiences of different groups. More importantly, one has to address the issue of gender differentiated access and control of resources, which in turn would lead to genuine women empowerment and decision-making. This is not a question of mere inclusion but of dismantling patriarchal institutions and biases, a recognition of the fact that women have a right to a dignified livelihood and sustenance, not as a measure of protection or welfare, but as a matter of right.

Notes

1 For instance, the Greek legend of Demeter and Persephone. F. Guirand (ed.), *New Larousse Encyclopaedia of Mythology*, New York: Prometheus Press, 1960; see also P. Mary Vidya Porselvi, *Nature, Culture and Gender: Re-reading the Folktale*, New York: Routledge, 2016.

2 The primary deity of fertility being female in numerous mythologies, for example *Gefjun* in Nordic mythology and *Sara Mama* in Inca mythology. See Guirand (ed.), *Encyclopaedia of Mythology*.

3 *Prithvi Sukta*, (Hymn to the Earth) Atharva Veda [12.1.1 to 12.1.63].

4 In Vedic texts, the female deities include Usha – Goddess of dawn and Prithvi – Goddess of terrestrial earth. Rivers are invariably female goddesses – Ganga, Yamuna, Cauvery. See D. R. Kinsley, *Hindu Goddesses: Visions of the Divine Feminine in Hindu Religious Tradition*, Berkeley: University of California Press, 1988.

5 Ibid.

6 K. Venkatraman, 'India's Biodiversity Act, 2002 and its Role in Conservation', *Tropical Ecology*, 2009, 50(1): 23–30, 24.

7 Venkatraman, 'India's Biodiversity Act, 2002'; National Biodiversity Authority, *Factsheet 2011*, http://nbaindia.org/uploaded/pdf/Fact%20 Sheets.pdf (accessed on 10 September 2016).

8 Statistics Times, 'Population of India,' http://statisticstimes.com/population/pop ulation-of-india.php (accessed on 10 September 2016).

9 National Biodiversity Authority, 'Defining and Explaining ABS Terminology' 2013, http://nbaindia.org/uploaded/pdf/ABS_Terminology.pdf (accessed on 10 September 2016).
10 International Food Policy Research Institute, *Global Hunger Index-The Challenge of Hunger*, 2013, www.ifpri.org/publication/2013-global-hunger-index-challenge-hunger-building-resilience-achieve-food-and- nutrition (accessed on 20 January 2016).
11 A. K. Biswas and C. Tortajada, 'India's Homemade Food Crisis', *Project-Syndicate*, August 8, 2014, www.project-syndicate.org/commentary/ asit-k—biswas-and-cecilia-tortajada-attribute-shortages-and-under nourishment-to-widespread -wastage-of-output#OZSbeTjY6j7dlt6J.99 (accessed on 20 January 2016).
12 B. Agarwal, *Gender and Green Governance-The Political Economy of Women's Presence Within and Beyond Community Forestry*, New Delhi: Oxford University Press, 2010, p. 32.
13 Zweifel, 'The Gendered Nature of Biodiversity Conservation', *NWSA Journal*, Autumn 1997, 9(3) (Women, Ecology, and the Environment): 107–123; see also M. S. Swaminathan (ed.), *Gender Dimensions in Biodiversity Management*, New Delhi: Konark, 1998.
14 Agarwal, *Gender and Green Governance*, p. 22.
15 National Commission for Women (NCW), *Impact of WTO on Women in Agriculture*, New Delhi: National Commission for Women, 2005, p. 9, http://ncw.nic.in/pdfreports/impact%20of%20wto%20women%20in% 20agriculture.pdf (accessed on 4 January 2016).
16 'World Bank Data', 2013, http://data.worldbank.org/indicator/SL.AGR EMPL.ZS?locations=IN (accessed on 10 September 2016).
17 K. Lahariya and A. S. Sethi, 'India's Quiet Women Farmers Slip into Crisis', *Business Standard*, March 10, 2015, www.business-standard.com/article/economy-policy/india-s-quiet-women-farmers-slip-into-crisis-115031000415_1.html (accessed on 4 January 2016).
18 V. Shiva, 'Women's Indigenous Knowledge and Biodiversity Conservation', *India International Centre Quarterly*, Spring-Summer 1992, 19(1/2) (Indigenous Vision: Peoples of India Attitudes to the Environment): 205–214.
19 Shiva, 'Women's Indigenous Knowledge'; see also R. Chitnis, 'Seeds and Their Keepers Are Key to Preserving India's Food Diversity', *Earth Island Journal*, June 30, 2011, www.earthisland.org/journal/index.php/elist/eListRead/seeds_and_their_keepers_are_key_to_preserving_indias_food_ diversity (accessed on 6 January 2016).
20 I. Barpujari, 'A Gendered Perspective of Indigenous Knowledge', Briefing Paper 4, July 2005', New Delhi: Gene Campaign, 2005, http://genecam paign.org/ (accessed on 20 January 2016).
21 A. Kothari, 'Agro-Biodiversity: The Future of India's Agriculture', Maharashtra Council of Agricultural Education &Research (MCAER) 1999, p. 3, http://dev.mtnforum.org/sites/default/files/publication/files/47.pdf (accessed on 4 January 2016).
22 S. Krishna, 'The Gendered Price of Rice in North-Eastern India', *Economic and Political Weekly*, June 18–24, 2005, 40(25): 2555–2562.
23 Zweifel, 'The Gendered Nature of Biodiversity Conservation'; see also Chitnis, 'Seeds and Their Keepers'.
24 NCW, *Impact of WTO on Women*, p. 51.
25 Agarwal, *Gender and Green Governance*, p. 33.

26 Ibid.
27 Lahariya and Sethi, 'India's Quiet Women Farmers Slip into Crisis'.
28 Ibid.
29 According to the UNDP India Report (2007) on Human Poverty and SociallyDisadvantaged Groups in India, the Human Development Index (HDI) at all India levels for Scheduled Tribes (ST) is estimated to be 0.270, which is lower than the HDI for Scheduled Castes (SC) and non-SC/ST for the period 1980–2000, while the Human Poverty Index (HPI) for STs is estimated at 47.79, which was higher than others for the period 1990–2000, www.undp.org/content/dam/india/docs/human_poverty_socially_dis advantaged_groups_india.pdf (accessed on 15 September 2016).
30 M. Velayudhan, 'Women's Land Rights in South Asia: Struggles and Diverse Contexts', *Economic and Political Weekly*, October 31–November 6, 2009, 44(44): 74–79.
31 Velayudhan, 'Women's Land Rights in South Asia'.
32 Ibid.
33 Ibid.
34 The Wildlife (Protection) Act, 1972 (Act No. 53 of 1972) Schedule I; S, Balaji, 'Biodiversity Challenges Ahead', *The Hindu*, May 27, 2010, www.thehindu.com/opinion/lead/biodiversity-challenges-ahead/article439099.ece (accessed on 6 January 2016).
35 B. Newman, 'A Bitter Harvest: Farmer Suicide and the Unforeseen Social, Environmental and Economic Impacts of the Green Revolution in Punjab India', Food First – Institute for Food and Development Policy, Development Report No. 15, January 2007: 13–14, https://foodfirst.org/wp-content/uploads/2013/12/DR15-A-Bitter-Harvest.pdf (accessed on 15 September 2016).
36 C. G. González, 'Introduction: The Global Politics of Food', *The University of Miami Inter-American Law Review*, Fall 2011, 43(1) (LatCrit South-North Exchange: The Global Politics of Food: Sustainability and Subordination): 77–87 at 81.
37 Ibid.
38 K. Kuruganti, 'Transgenic Crops: A Questionable Option?' *Seminar*, March 2009: 595, www.india-seminar.com/semframe.html (accessed on 6 January 2016).
39 Ibid.
40 A. Nelsen, 'Half of Europe Opts Out of New GM Crop Scheme', *The Guardian*, Brussels, October 1, 2015, www.theguardian.com/environment/2015/oct/01/half-of-europe-opts-out-of-new-gm-crop-scheme (accessed on 20 January 2016).
41 A. Malone, 'The GM Genocide: Thousands of Indian Farmers are Committing Suicide After Using Genetically Modified Crops', *Daily Mail*, November 3, 2008, www.dailymail.co.uk/news/article-1082559/The-GM-genocide-Thousands-Indian-farmers-committing-suicide-using-genetically-modified-crops.html#ixzz3u053EBiF (accessed on 20 January 2016).
42 NCW, *Impact of WTO on Women*.
43 P. Sainath, 'Ways of Seeing', *Seminar*, 5 March 2009, www.india-seminar.com/semframe.html (accessed on 6 January 2016).
44 González, 'The Global Politics of Food', p. 77.
45 'India Tops World Hunger List with 194 Million People', *The Hindu*, May 29, 2015, www.thehindu.com/news/national/india-is-home-to-194-million-hungry-people-un/article7255937.ece (accessed on 20 January 2016).
46 Biswas and Tortajada, 'India's Homemade Food Crisis'.

47 P. Kakodar, 'Records May Not Show, But Women Farmers Dying Too', *The Times of India*, May 17, 2015, http://timesofindia.indiatimes.com/ india/Records-may-not-show-but-women-farmers-dying-too/articleshow/47314082.cms (accessed on 12 September 2016).
48 Ibid.
49 P. Sainath, 'Farmer's Diet Worse than a Convict's', February 13, 2015, https://ruralindiaonline.org/articles/farmers-diet-worse-than-a-convicts/ (accessed on 12 September 2016).
50 NCW, *Impact of WTO on Women*, p. ii.
51 Ibid., p. 110.
52 Ibid., pp. 184 and 155.
53 R. Brinker, 'Dr. Vandana Shiva and Feminist Theory', *Women–Justice– Ecology*, July 4, 2009, https://womenjusticeecology.wordpress.com/2009/ 07/04/dr-vandana-shiva-and-feminist-theory/ (accessed on 4 January 2016).
54 S. Jain, 'Standing Up for Trees-Women's Role in Chipko Movement' Unasylva-Women in Forestry', 1984/4, 36(146), www.fao.org/docrep/r0465e/r0465e03.htm (accessed on 2 October 2016).
55 Maria Mies and Vandana Shiva, Ecofeminism Halifax: Fernwood Publications, 1993, p. 14
56 Brinker, 'Shiva and Feminist Theory'.
57 Agarwal, *Gender and Green Governance*, p. 41.
58 Bina Agarwal, 'The Gender and Environment Debate: Lessons from India', *Feminist Studies*, Spring, 1992, 18(1): 119–158.
59 Agarwal, *Gender and Green Governance*, p. 42.
60 Barpujari, 'A Gendered Perspective of Indigenous Knowledge'.
61 Zweifel, 'The Gendered Nature of Biodiversity Conservation'.
62 The Convention on Biological Diversity 1992, Preamble.
63 www.upov.int/portal/index.html.en (accessed on 15 September 2016); India is not yet a member but seeks to be a member.
64 International Convention for the Protection of New Varieties of Plants, 1961, as revised in 1972, 1978 and 1991, adopted in the Diplomatic Conference in Paris on 2 December 1961 and came into force on 10 August 1968 being ratified by the states of the United Kingdom, the Netherlands and Germany, Articles 6–12.
65 International Treaty on Plant Genetic Resources for Food and Agriculture, 2001, adopted at the FAO conference on 3 November 2001 and came into force on 29 June 2004 after deposit of the required fortieth instrument of ratification, Preamble.
66 International Treaty on Plant Genetic Resources for Food and Agriculture, 2001, Articles 10–13.
67 Grain and Kalpavriksh, 'The International Treaty on Plant Genetic Resources: A Challenge for Asia', April 19, 2002, www.grain.org/article/entries/41-a-challenge-for-asia-the-international-treaty-on-plant- genetic-resources (accessed on 15 September 2016).
68 International Treaty on Plant Genetic Resources for Food and Agriculture, Article 12.3.
69 International Treaty on Plant Genetic Resources for Food and Agriculture, Article 9.3.
70 www.cbd.int/abs/doc/protocol/nagoya-protocol-en.pdf (accessed on 15 September 2016); India is a party to the Protocol.

71 Nagoya Protocol on Access to Genetic Resources and the Fair and Equitable Sharing of Benefits (hereinafter Nagoya Protocol), adopted on 29 October 2010 at Nagoya, came into force on the 12 October 2014 after deposit of the required fiftieth instrument of ratification, Article 12(1).
72 Nagoya Protocol, Article 12(3).
73 Nagoya Protocol, Article 22(5) (j).
74 The Constitution of India 1950, Article 14.
75 The Constitution of India 1950, Article 21.
76 See *Narmada Bachao Andolan* v. *Union of India* (2000) 10 SCC 664; *N.D. Jayal* v. *Union of India* (2004) 9 SCC 362.
77 The Biological Diversity Act (hereinafter The BD Act), 2002, (Act 18 of 2003), Preamble.
78 The BD Act, Sections 8, 22 and 41.
79 The BD Act, Sections 3–7 and Sections 19–21.
80 The BD Act, Section 41(1) read with BD Rules 2004, Rule 22.
81 BD Rules 2004, Rule 22(6).
82 BD Rules 2004, Rule 22(2).
83 As of 2 September 2015 as per the NBA website, http://nbaindia.org/con tent/20/35//bmc.html (accessed on 21 January 2016).
84 K. Kohli and S. Bhutani, 'Ten years of the Biological Diversity Act', *Economic and Political Weekly*, September 29, 2012, 47(39): 15–18.
85 K. Kohli and S. Bhutani, 'BMC: Lost in Numbers', *Economic and Political Weekly*, April 19, 2014, 49(16): 18–20.
86 Kohli and Bhutani, 'Ten years of the Biological Diversity Act'.
87 The BD Act, Section 41(2).
88 Kohli and Bhutani, 'Ten years of the Biological Diversity Act'.
89 Kohli and Bhutani, 'BMC: Lost in Numbers'.
90 L. Jishnu, 'Biodiversity-India's Other Scandal', *Down to Earth*, 15 January 2011,www.downtoearth.org.in/blog/biodiversityindias-other—scandal-2795 (accessed on 21 January 2016).
91 The BD Act, Section 44(1).
92 R. Awadhani, '39 Villages Fight for BHS Status', *The Hindu*, September 27, 2012, www.thehindu.com/todays-paper/tp-national/tp-andhrapradesh/39-villages-fight-for-bhs-status/article3941154.ece (accessed on 21 January 2016).
93 The Protection of Plant Variety and Farmers' Rights Act, 2001, Act 53 of 2001 (hereinafter the Plant Variety Act).
94 The Agreement on Trade-Related Aspects of Intellectual Property Rights 1994 (TRIPS), adopted on 15 April 1994 at Marrakesh and came into force on 1 January 1995, Article 27.3b.
95 The Plant Variety Act, Sections 26 and 28.
96 The Plant Variety Act, Section 39(iii).
97 The Plant Variety Act, Section 39(iv).
98 S. Bhutani and K. Kohli, 'Protection of Plant Variety and Farmers' Rights Act, 2001 - Just Leave the Seed Alone', *Business Line*, 12 March 2004, www.thehindubusinessline.com/2004/03/12/stories/200403120010 0900.htm (accessed on 21 January 2016).
99 Bhutani and Kohli, 'Just Leave the Seed Alone'.
100 'Land Law Not The Only Rollback, Seeds Bill Put on Hold over GM Clause', *Indian Express*, September 3, 2015, http://indianexpress.com/

article/india/india-others/land-law-not-the-only-rollback-seeds-bill-put-on-hold-over-gm-clause/ (accessed on 21 January 2016).

101 The Scheduled Tribes and other Traditional Forest Dwellers (Recognition of Forest Rights) Act, 2006, Act 2 of 2007 (hereinafter the Recognition of Forest Rights Act).

102 The Recognition of Forest Rights Act, Preamble.

103 The Recognition of Forest Rights Act, Section 3(1) (a).

104 The Recognition of Forest Rights Act, Section 3(1) (b).

105 The Recognition of Forest Rights Act, Section 3(1) (f).

106 The Recognition of Forest Rights Act, Section 3(1) (g).

107 The Recognition of Forest Rights Act, Section 3(1) (h).

108 The Recognition of Forest Rights Act, Section 3(1) (c).

109 The Recognition of Forest Rights Act.

110 The Recognition of Forest Rights Act, Section 3(1) (k).

111 J. Sathyapalan, 'Implementation of the Forest Rights Act in the Western Ghats Region of Kerala', *Economic and Political Weekly*, July 24–30, 2010, 45(30): 65–73.

112 P. Bose, 'Forest Tenure Reform: Exclusion of Tribal Women's Rights in Semi-Arid Rajasthan, India', *The International Forestry Review*, 2011, 13(2): 220–232.

113 Ibid.

114 S. R. Ramdas, 'Women, Forest Spaces and the Law: Transgressing the Boundaries', *Economic and Political Weekly*, October 31–November 6, 2009, 44(44): 65–73.

115 Ibid.

116 Ibid.

117 Zweifel, 'The Gendered Nature of Biodiversity Conservation'.

118 U. Baxi, 'Access to Justice in a Globalized Economy: Some Reflections', Keynote address at the Golden Jubilee Celebration of Indian Law Institute, New Delhi, 2006, http://sites.google.com/site/lawcentreone/juris workshop (accessed on 21 January 2016); See also *Balco Employees Union* v. *Union of India* (2002) 2 SCC 333.

119 WP(c) 196 of 2001, *PUCL* v. *UOI*, Important orders in this Petition include *PUCL (PDS matter)* v. *Union of India* (2013) 2 SCC 688; (2013) 14 SCC 368.

120 The National Food Security Act 2013, Act No. 20 of 2013.

121 Public Distribution Scheme, Annapurna Yojna, Mid-day meal Programme, Antyodaya Anna Yojana.

122 See S. Sahai, 'Need for a Different Food Security Law', *Seminar*, June 2012, 634, www.india-seminar.com/semframe.html (accessed on 6 February 2016).

123 Ibid.

124 Ibid.

125 R. Dhavan, 'Wealth of Nations', *Seminar*, August 2000, 492, www.india-seminar.com/semframe.html (accessed on 6 January 2016).

4 An Overview of the Law Governing Hazardous Substances in the Post-Bhopal Era

T. R. Subramanya

'An Overview of the Law Governing Hazardous Substances in the Post-Bhopal Era' by T. R. Subramanya (T. R. Subramanya, *Hazardous Substances in India and the World: Legislations, Frameworks and Management*, Copyright © 2021, Routledge, Chapter 5). Reproduced by permission of Taylor & Francis Group.

Part 1

The Planning Commission's approach to environment-related problems

A report by the Planning Commission of India highlighted that the environment must not be considered as just another sector of national development. It should form a crucial guiding dimension for plans and programs in each sector.[1] In February 1972, a National Committee on Environmental Planning and Coordination (NCEPC) was established by the Government of India in the Department of Science and Technology. The NCEPC was an apex advisory body in all matters relating to environmental protection and improvement. The committee consisted of 14 members drawn from various disciplines concerned with environmental management.[2] Most of the non-official members were specialists. The committee was to plan and coordinate while the responsibility for execution remained with the various ministries and agencies of the government.

The Draft Fifth Plan (1974–1979) stressed that the NCEPC should be closely associated with all major industrial decisions so that environmental goals are fully taken into account. The Sixth Five Year Plan (1980–1985) document included a separate chapter on "Environment and Development" emphasizing sound environmental and ecological principles in land use, agriculture, forestry, wildlife, water, air, marine environment, minerals, fisheries, renewable resources, energy and human settlements. Further, the chapter provided a plethora of information on environmental concerns to administrators and resource managers, formulating and implementing programs, and laid down an institutional structure for environmental management in the central and state governments.[3]

In the Ninth Five Year Plan (1997–2002), it was noted that there was a signifcant increase in the generation of domestic, urban and industrial

DOI: 10.4324/9781003299561-4

wastes in the last few decades due to rapid population growth and industrialization. It is further noted that

> Although a major part of the waste generated is non-hazardous, substantial quantities of hazardous waste is also generated. The growth of chemical industries has resulted in the extensive use of chemicals, which release huge quantities of wastes into the environment in the form of solids, liquids and gases. A substantial amount of these wastes are potentially hazardous to the environment. The leaching of hazardous wastes at the dumping sites is a common feature. This results in the contamination of surface and groundwater supply and is a potential risk to human health. Effective control of hazardous wastes is of paramount importance for the maintenance of health, environmental protection and natural resource management.[4]

The creation of the Department of Environment in 1980 and the integrated Ministry of Environment and Forests, at the centre in 1985, by the government to serve as the focal point in the administrative structure of the central government for planning, promotion and coordination of environmental and forestry programs was a major development. The ministry's main activities include conservation and survey of fora, fauna, forests and wildlife, prevention and control of pollution, afforestation and regeneration of degraded areas and overall protection of the environment.

In 2006, the government also formulated the National Environment Policy. It was touted as a response to the national commitment to a clean environment, mandated in the Constitution in Articles 48A and 51A (g), strengthened by judicial interpretation of Article 21. It is recognized that maintaining a healthy environment is not the state's responsibility alone, but also that of every citizen.[5]

The Environment (Protection) (EP) Act, 1986

This Act[6] was passed to protect and improve the environment as also to prevent hazards to human beings and other living creatures, plants and property.[7] Section 2 (e) of the Act defines "hazardous substance" as any substance or preparation which, by reason of its chemical or physio-chemical properties or handling, is liable to cause harm to human beings, other living creatures, plants, microorganism, property or the environment."

The central government is empowered to lay down procedures and safeguards for the handling of hazardous substances.[8] Measures taken under Section 3 (2) may include the following matters:

1 Planning and execution of a nationwide program for the prevention, control and abatement of environmental pollution.[9]

2 Laying down standards for the quality of the environment in its various aspects.[10]
3 Laying down standards for emission or discharge of environmental pollutants from various sources.[11]
4 Restriction of areas in which any industrial operations, or processes or class of industries, operations or processes shall not be carried out or shall be carried out subject to certain safeguards.[12]
5 Laying down procedures and safeguards for the prevention of accidents that may cause environmental pollution and remedial measures for such accidents.[13]
6 Examination of such manufacturing processes, materials and substances which are likely to cause environmental pollution.[14]
7 Carrying out and sponsoring investigations and research relating to problems of environmental pollution.[15]
8 Inspection of any premises, plant, equipment, machinery, manufacturing or other processes, materials or substances and giving, by order, of such directions to such authorities, officers or persons as it may consider necessary for the prevention, control and abatement of environmental pollution.[16]
9 Establishment or recognition of environmental laboratories and institutes to carry out the functions entrusted to such environmental laboratories and institutes;[17] and on any other matter which the central government deems it necessary for securing the effective implementation of the provisions of this act.

The government, while exercising these powers, may make rules on all or any of the matters discussed in the list by a notifcation in the *Offcial Gazette*.[18] The government's power stretches even further to make rules on the processing, treatment, package, storage, transportation, use, collection, destruction, conversion, offering for sale and transfer of such substances.[19] The exhaustive power of the government, as we have seen, extends to the control and regulation of the manufacturers of hazardous substances and the inspection of any such premises, plant, equipment or machinery manufacturing the substances.[20] In addition, the government may make rules to provide:

1 The maximum allowable limits of concentration of various environmental pollutants for different substances.[21]
2 The procedures and safeguards for the handling of hazardous substances.[22]
3 The prohibition and restrictions on the handling of hazardous substances in different areas.[23]

4 The prohibition and restrictions on the location of industries and the carrying out of the processes and operations in different areas.[24]
5 The procedures and safeguards for the prevention of accidents that may cause environmental pollution and for the providing for remedial measures for such accidents.[25]

Under Section 7 (2) of the Act, no industry, operation or process is allowed to discharge environmental pollutants in excess of the permissible limits.

All persons handling hazardous substances must follow rules, procedures and safeguards prescribed by the government.[26] For the purpose of enforcing the provisions of the Environment Protection Act, an officer of the central government[27] is given the right to enter, at all reasonable times and with the necessary assistance, any such premises to determine whether, and to what extent, the provisions of the Act are being complied with or to perform the functions entrusted by the Central Government.[28]

While exercising such powers the officer can take samples of air, water, soil or other substance from any factory premises or from any other place for the purpose of analysis.[29] Such samples must be referred to the government analysts[30] working in environmental laboratories.[31]

A duty is imposed on the person carrying out any industry operation, or process of handling hazardous substances, to assist the person engaged by the central government in implementing the rules and regulations of this Act.[32] A person who fails to cooperate with the government, or wilfully delays in helping the officer in-charge, is guilty of offense.[33] Under Section 15 of the EP Act, each failure of compliance or contravention is punishable with a term of imprisonment up to five years or with a fine of up to one lakh rupees or with both.[34] For each act of failure to comply, happening after the conviction for such failure or contravention, an additional fine of 5,000 rupees per day is prescribed. Additionally, if such failure or contravention continues beyond a period of one year after conviction, the offender is liable to imprisonment for a term that may extend to seven years.[35]

All acts carried in good faith by an officer of the government in pursuance of the purposes and objects of this act are protected and no suit, prosecution and other legal proceedings can be brought against the government or the officer who acted on its behalf.[36]

In order to facilitate the objectives aimed under this legislation the central government, under Section 25 of the Act, is given the power to make rules on the following matters, namely:

1 The standards in excess of which environmental pollutants must not be discharged or emitted under Section 7.[37]
2 The procedures and guidelines to handle hazardous substances.[38]

3 The manner in which samples of air, water, soil or other substance must be taken for analysis.[39]

The central government passed the Environment (Protection) Rules (1986)[40] to effectively enforce the provisions of the EP Act.[41] These rules have laid down extensive provisions governing items such as prohibition and restriction on the location of industries and the carrying out of processes and operations in different areas,[42] procedures for taking samples and submitting for analysis,[43] serving notices[44] and the form of laboratory report thereon,[45] functions of environmental laboratories,[46] qualifications of government analysts,[47] manner of giving notice[48] and prohibition and restriction on handling of hazardous substances in different areas.[49]

In order to consider ways for the effective implementation of the Environment Protection Act, a meeting of experts was convened by the Consumer Education and Research Centre (CERC) and the Indian Law Institute, New Delhi, in 1986.[50] The meeting of experts felt the need to have comprehensive legislation on hazardous waste disposal as soon as possible and recommended to the government so accordingly.[51]

Transportation of dangerous/hazardous substances by road—Order of the Transport Commissioner, Maharashtra State

In order to control and regulate the transportation of dangerous/hazardous substances by road, a model legislation was passed by Maharashtra State in 1986.[52] As per the government order, "hazardous chemical" will mean any material which may pose an unreasonable risk to human health or the safety of property. This will include gases, compressed liquefied dissolved under pressure, inflammable liquids, inflammable solids, oxidizing substances, organic peroxides, poisonous (toxic) and infectious substances, corrosive substances, dangerous substances, radioactive substances and explosives. Every public or private carrier handling such hazardous chemicals, before transporting them, should satisfy the following conditions:[53]

1 Fixing of special labels or notices on packages or on vehicles, bearing emblems as specified by the transport commissioner.
2 The correct technical names of the chemical should invariably be displayed on packages or vehicles carrying hazardous chemicals.
3 The drivers of all road vehicles carrying hazardous chemicals must carry with them "instruction in writing" relating to each dangerous substance or to each class of dangerous substance whether carried in packed form (i.e. in tins, drums, etc.) or in bulk road vehicles. The instructions including first aid treatment, and advice for dealing with fire, accident, spillage or leakage must be written in English, Hindi and

Marathi and in the languages of the State of transit and destination. These instructions in writing should be obtained from the firm/chemical company which load hazardous chemicals for transportation.[54]

4 A summary of these instructions in writing should be carried by the driver in his cabin. Under the Rules, these instructions are known as "Transport Emergency Card." This card should be provided to the driver by the party or supplier of the chemical company loading the chemical.

5 In addition to the above safeguards, special signs or plates denoting that dangerous goods are being conveyed should be displayed on the vehicle so as to identify the substance and also reveal its hazardous properties and indicate the necessary action to be taken in emergencies.

In another order issued in the same year, the Maharashtra Government[55] clarified a few of the provisions contained in the earlier order. Under the new order,[56] the carriers of dangerous chemicals—while displaying the correct technical names of the chemicals on packages or vehicles—should also give the name by which those dangerous goods are referred to in the third revised edition of the United Nations Committee of Experts on the Transport of Dangerous Goods. Furthermore, the label to be affixed on a vehicle carrying this information should not be less than 250 mm square and should be marked on the vehicle in such a position that it does not obscure any markings. The carrier of the chemical waste, in addition, should affix another label not less than 50 mm in height carrying the name and telephone number of the emergency services to be contacted in the event of an accident or fire and also the name and telephone number of consignor of the dangerous goods or another person from whom expert information and advice may be obtained concerning the measures that should be taken in the event of an emergency, involving dangerous goods. All labels put either on the vehicle or on the bulk container should be weatherproof.[57]

The Government of India's rules and regulations

The order of the Government of Maharashtra has been in force in the State of Maharashtra since 1986 without central legislation on this subject until 1989. The Government of India, realizing the urgent need to promote the objective and purpose envisaged in the EP Act (1986) outlined rules and regulations in 1989 under Section 3 (1) of the EP Act[58] for the regulation of carriers of dangerous or hazardous goods.

All carriers (vehicles) of dangerous and hazardous goods, in addition to complying with any law for the time in force in relation to any category of dangerous or hazardous goods brought under the new order,[59] must display a distinct mark of the class label[60] on every package containing dangerous or hazardous goods. The "class label" must be displayed on the vehicle and be positioned at an angle of 45 degrees to the vertical and its size shall not be of less than 25 mm square.[61] The class label must be made of water-proof material and be displayed both in the front and in the rear side of the vehicle in a conspicuous manner.

The consigner intending to transport any dangerous or hazardous goods must supply to the owner carrying the goods, full and accurate information so as to make him aware of the risks created by such goods to the health or safety of any person.[62] Under Rule 132, the carrier of dangerous or hazardous goods, before undertaking the transportation of such goods, should satisfy himself of the accuracy of the information given by the consigner and then pass it on to the driver. The driver must keep this information in the cabin of the vehicle while transporting the goods. Moreover, during the course of transportation, he should act with due diligence so as to prevent the goods from fire, explosion or escape. Similarly, when the carriage is not in motion the driver should park the vehicle in a place which is safe from fire, explosion and any other risk. He should keep a watch over the goods either himself or with the help of a competent person above the age of eighteen years. Under Rule 134, the carriage used for transporting any dangerous or hazardous goods shall be legibly and conspicuously marked with emergency information containing the correct technical name of the dangerous or hazardous goods, the name and telephone number of emergency services to be contacted in the event of fire or any other accident, and the name and telephone number of the consigner of the dangerous or hazardous goods or the address of the person from whom expert information and advice can be obtained concerning the measures that should be taken in the event of an emergency involving such goods. In case of accident, the driver transporting any hazardous or dangerous goods in a carriage must report the incident to the nearest police station. The 1989 order also gives a long list of the names of hazardous and toxic chemicals.[63]

Hazardous and Other Wastes (Management and Transboundary Movement) Rules, 2016

The central government, in exercise of the powers conferred under Sections 6, 8 and 25 of the EP Act (1986) passed the Hazardous and Other Wastes (Management and Transboundary Movement) Rules in 2016.[64]

Unlike its predecessors, these rules distinguish between hazardous and other wastes.[65] Other wastes include tyre waste, paper waste, metal scrap, used electronic items, etc. and are recognized as a resource for recycling and reuse.[66] These will supplement the industrial processes and reduce the load on the virgin resources of the country.

The Hazardous Other Wastes (Management and Transboundary Movement) Rules apply to designated categories of waste, such as cyanide waste and wastes from dyes, that are enumerated in the schedule to the rules. Radioactive wastes, covered under the Atomic Energy Act of 1962, and waste discharged from ships, covered under the Merchant Shipping Act of 1958, are explicitly excluded from the Hazardous Wastes Rules, 1989. Likewise, the rules do not apply to wastewater and exhaust gases regulated under the Water Act and Air Act.[67]

Rule 4 of the Hazardous and Other Wastes Rules, 2016, makes the occupier responsible for the management of hazardous wastes by various steps such as (1) prevention; (2) minimization; (3) reuse; (4) recycling; (5) recovery, utilization including co-processing; (6) safe disposal. An obligation is placed upon the occupier for safe and environmentally sound management of hazardous and other wastes. The hazardous waste generated in the establishment of the occupier shall be sent or sold to an authorized actual user or shall be disposed of in an authorized facility, transported from an occupier's establishment to an authorized actual user or an authorized disposal facility in accordance to provisions of the Rules and after sharing such information to the operator of a treatment, storage and disposal facility, regarding the safe storage and disposal of wastes. It shall be the duty of the occupier to take steps to contain contaminants, prevent accidents and limit the consequences on human beings and the environment and provide persons working on the site with appropriate training, equipment and the information necessary to ensure safety.

The Department of Industry, or the agency duly authorized by the respective state governments, have been entrusted the responsibility of earmarking or allocating of industrial space or shed, for recycling, preprocessing and other utilization of hazardous or other waste, in existing and upcoming industrial estates, parks or clusters.[68] The Labor Department or an agency duly authorized by the respective state government has been given the responsibility of recognizing and registering workers involved in recycling, pre-processing and other utilization activities, assist the formation of groups of such workers for setting up such facilities, undertake industrial skill development of these workers and annually monitor and ensure safety and health of these workers.[69] The state government may prepare an integrated plan for effective implementation of these provisions and submit an annual report to the Ministry of Environment, Forest and Climate Change of the Central Government.[70]

Every occupier of the facility engaged in handling, generation, collection, storage, packaging, transportation, use, treatment, processing, recycling, recovery, pre-processing, co-processing, utilization, offering for sale, transfer or disposal of hazardous and other wastes shall be required to make an application to State Pollution Control Board to obtain an authorization within a period of 60 days from the date of publication of these Rules.[71] The application for authorization has to be accompanied by copies of consent to establish and operate granted under the Water (Prevention and Control of Pollution) Act 1974 and the Air (Prevention and Control of Pollution) Act (1981) and in case of renewal of authorization, it should further contain a self-certified compliance report with regard to effluent, emission standards and the conditions specified in the authorization for hazardous and other wastes. An application for renewal of authorization may be made three months before the expiry of authorization.

A person who is authorized under the Hazardous Waste (Management, Handling and Transboundary Movement) Rules, 2008, before the commencement of these Rules, shall not be required to make an application for authorization till the authorization expires. The same applies for any person engaged in recycling or reprocessing of hazardous waste[72] and having registration under the 2008 Rules.

Before granting an authorization form, the State Pollution Control Board must be satisfied after conducting the necessary inquiries about the existence of appropriate facilities for collection, storage, packaging, transportation, treatment, processing, use, destruction, recycling, recovery, pre-processing, co-processing, utilization, offering for sale, transfer or disposal of hazardous and other waste, and that the technical capabilities and equipment is in conformity with the standard operating procedure or other guidelines specified by the Central Pollution Control Board from time-to-time and through site inspection.[73] The authorization is granted within a period of 120 days, which shall be valid for a period of five years subject to certain prescribed conditions.[74] For commonly recyclable hazardous waste,[75] the guidelines already prepared by the Central Pollution Control Board must be followed. In the case of an application for renewal of authorization, before granting such authorization, the State Pollution Control Board may satisfy itself that there has been no violation of the conditions specified in the previously given authorization and same shall be recorded in the inspection report.[76]

The authorization granted by the State Pollution Control Board shall be accompanied by a copy of the field inspection report signed by the board indicating the adequacy of facilities for collection, storage, packaging, transportation, treatment, processing, use, destruction, recycling, recovery, pre-processing, co-processing, utilization, offering for sale, transfer or disposal of the hazardous and other wastes and compliance to the guidelines or standard operating procedures specified by the Central Pollution Control Board from time to time.[77]

The State Pollution Control Board may refuse to grant an authorization under these rules. The reasons for the same must be recorded and the concerned applicant should be given a reasonable opportunity for a hearing before a refusal in such a case.[78]

The user has to maintain records of hazardous and other wastes purchased in a passbook issued by the State Pollution Control Board along with the authorization.[79] Handing over of the wastes to the actual user shall only be carried out after making the entry into such passbook.[80] An occupier is required shall maintain a record of hazardous and other wastes managed by him and submit an annual return containing the details before 30 of June following the financial year to which the return pertains to the State Pollution Control Board.[81] A register containing particulars of the conditions specified for management of hazardous and other wastes has to be maintained by the State Pollution Control Board and it shall be open for inspection during office hours.

Rule 7 empowers the State Pollution Control Board, Power to suspend or cancel an authorization. The State Pollution Control Board has the power to suspend and cancel an authorization, for failure to comply with the provisions, after providing a reasonable opportunity of being heard to the occupier and after recording reasons for such cancellation in writing. It may also give suitable directions for safe storage and handling after such cancellation or suspension. The period of suspension shall be determined in the public interest.

As per Rule 8, the occupiers may store the hazardous and other wastes for a maximum period of ninety days and along with maintaining a record of sale, transfer, storage, recycling, recovery, pre-processing, co-processing and utilization of such wastes. These records must be made available for inspection. The 90 day period may be extended in certain cases.[82]

The utilization of hazardous and other wastes as a resource or after pre-processing either for co-processing or for any other use within the premises of the generator or outside it, shall be carried out only after obtaining authorization from the State Pollution Control Board on the basis of standard operating procedures or guidelines provided by the Central Pollution Control Board.[83] If standard operating procedures or guidelines are not available for specific utilization, approval has to be sought from Central Pollution Control Board which will be granted on the basis of trial runs and thereafter, standard operating procedures or guidelines have to be prepared by Central Pollution Control Board.[84] If the trial run has been conducted for particular waste with respect to particular utilization and compliance to the environmental standards has already been demonstrated, authorization may be granted by the State Pollution Control Board without the need of a separate trial run by Central Pollution Control Board. Trial runs are not required for co-processing of waste in cement plants for which guidelines by the Central Pollution Control Board are already available.[85]

Rule 10 states that the Ministry of Environment, Forest and Climate Change or the Central Pollution Control Board may issue guidelines or standard operating procedures for environmentally sound management of hazardous and other wastes.

Chapter III has been inserted to deal with the export and import of hazardous wastes. Under Rule 11, The Ministry of Environment, Forest and Climate Change has been designated to be the nodal Ministry to deal with the transboundary movement of hazardous and other wastes. The import of hazardous and other wastes from any country to India for disposal is prohibited.[86] The import of hazardous and other wastes from any country will be permitted only for recycling, recovery, reuse and utilization including co-processing.[87] The import of hazardous waste in may be allowed to actual users with the prior informed consent of the exporting country and the permission of the Ministry of Environment, Forest and Climate Change.[88] Hazardous and other wastes which are prohibited for import,[89] as per the Rules, shall in no way be imported.[90] The import of "other wastes" (which require prior informed consent)[91] may be allowed to actual users with the permission of the Ministry of Environment, Forest and Climate Change.[92] On the other hand, the import of those "other wastes" which do not require consent[93] will be allowed as per procedure given in Rule 13. Hazardous and other wastes[94] from India shall be exported with the permission of the Ministry of Environment, Forest and Climate Change.[95] Applications shall be considered on the basis of prior informed consent of the importing country. The import and export of hazardous and other wastes not specified, but exhibiting certain hazardous characteristics outlined shall require prior written permission of the Ministry of Environment, Forest and Climate Change before it is imported to or exported from India.[96]

Rule 13 lays down the procedure for the import of hazardous and other wastes. Persons intending to import or transit for transboundary movement of hazardous and other wastes shall apply along with the required documents, to the Ministry of Environment, Forest and Climate Change for the proposed import along with the prior informed consent of the exporting country, if necessary. A copy of the application shall also be sent to the concerned State Pollution Control Board for information for receipt of acknowledgment. The acknowledgment then must be submitted to the Ministry of Environment, Forest and Climate Change along with the application.[97] In case of the import of other wastes that do not require permission, the necessary information such as details as importer or exporter along with certain additional documents has to be submitted to the customs authorities.[98]

In the case of import of any used electrical and electronic assemblies or spares or part or component or consumables under the E-Waste (Management and Handling) Rules, 2011, as amended from time to time, the importer needs to obtain extended responsibility authorization as producer.[99] Before clearing the consignment of wastes listed, the custom authorities shall verify the documents.[100]

On receipt of the complete application, the Ministry of Environment, Forest and Climate Change shall examine the application and after considering the comments and observations, received from the State Pollution Control Boards, may grant the permission for import within a period of 60 days subject to the condition that the importer has (1) the environmentally sound facilities; (2) adequate arrangements for treatment and disposal of wastes generated; (3) a valid authorization and consents from the State Pollution Control Board; (4) prior informed consent from the exporting country where necessary.[101] The Ministry of Environment, Forest and Climate Change must forward a copy of the permission to the concerned port and customs authorities, Central Pollution Control Board and the concerned State Pollution Control Board for ensuring compliance in all concerned areas.[102] The importer of the hazardous and other wastes shall maintain records of the hazardous and other waste imported by him in Form 3 and the record so maintained shall be made available for inspection.[103] The importer of the hazardous and other wastes also has to file an annual return to the State Pollution Control Board on or before 30 June following the financial year to which that return relates.[104]

Samples of hazardous and other wastes being imported for testing or research and development purposes up to 1000 gm or 1000 ml are exempt attaining permission for import under these rules.[105] The port and customs authorities shall ensure that shipment is accompanied by the movement document and the test report of analysis of the waste consignment from a laboratory accredited or recognized by the exporting country. In case of any doubt, the customs may verify the analysis.[106]

Rule 14 deals with the procedure for export of hazardous and other wastes from India. For export of waste, an application along with insurance cover has to be submitted to the Ministry of Environment, Forest and Climate Change together with the prior informed consent in writing from the importing country in respect of wastes where consent is necessary.[107] After receiving an application, the Ministry of Environment, Forest and Climate Change may give permission for the proposed export within a period of 60 days from the date of submission of the complete application and may impose such conditions as it considers necessary.[108] A copy of the permission granted shall also be forwarded by the Ministry to the State Pollution Control Board of the state where the waste is generated and the

Pollution Control Board of the state where the port of export is located as well as the concerned port and customs authorities for ensuring compliance of the conditions of the export permission.[109] The exporter has to ensure that a consignment is not shipped before obtaining prior informed consent from the importing country.[110] It also has to ensure that the shipment is accompanied with a movement document.[111] The exporter of the hazardous and other wastes shall maintain the records of the waste and such record shall be made available for inspection.[112]

The export and import of hazardous or other wastes from and into India, respectively shall be deemed illegal, if (1) it is without permission of the central government in accordance with these rules; or (2) permission has been obtained through falsification, misrepresentation or fraud; or (3) it does not conform to the shipping details provided in the movement documents; or (4) it results in deliberate disposal (i.e., dumping) of hazardous or other waste in contravention of the Basel Convention and of general principles of international or domestic law.[113] In the case of illegal import of hazardous or other waste, the importer shall re-export the waste in question at his own cost within a period of 90 days from the date of its arrival into India and its implementation will be ensured by the concerned port and custom authority. Disposal of such waste by the port and custom authorities shall be done in accordance with these rules with the permission of the Pollution Control Board of the respective state.[114] If the importer is not traceable then the waste can either be sold by the customs authority to any user with authorization under these rules from the relevant State Pollution Control Board or can be sent for authorized treatment, storage and disposal facility.[115]

Chapter IV is concerned with the treatment, storage and disposal facility for hazardous and other wastes. Rule 16 (1) states that the state government, occupier, operator of a facility or any association of occupiers shall individually or jointly or severally be responsible for identification of sites for establishing the facility for treatment, storage and disposal of hazardous and other waste in the state. As per Rule 16 (2), the operator of a common facility or occupier of a captive facility shall design and set up the treatment, storage and disposal facility as per technical guidelines issued by the Central Pollution Control Board along with obtaining approval from the State Pollution Control Board for design and layout in this regard. The State Pollution Control Board shall monitor the building and operation of the common or captive treatment, storage and disposal facility, regularly.[116] The operator of a common facility or occupier of a captive facility shall be responsible for safe and environmentally sound operation of the facility and its closure and post-closure phase, as per guidelines or standard operating procedures issued by the Central Pollution Control Board.[117] Records of hazardous and other wastes handled by him also have to be maintained[118] and an annual return has to be filed to the State Pollution Control Board on or before the 30 of June following the financial year to which that return relates.[119]

Chapter V consists of provisions pertaining to the packaging, labeling, and transport of hazardous and other wastes. Rule 17 (1) states that any occupier handling hazardous or other wastes and any operator of treatment, storage and disposal facilities must ensure that the hazardous and other wastes are packaged in a manner suitable for safe handling, storage and transport as per the guidelines issued by the Central Pollution Control Board. The labeling must be done in the prescribed form[120] and should be of non-washable material, weatherproof and easily visible.[121]

Rule 18 (1) states that the transport of hazardous and other waste must be in accordance with the provisions of these Rules along with those made by the central government under the Motor Vehicles Act, 1988 and the guidelines issued by the Central Pollution Control Board. As per Rule 18 (2), the occupier has to provide the transporter with all relevant information regarding the hazardous nature of the wastes and measures to be taken in case of an emergency. They must label the hazardous and other wastes containers. In case of transportation of hazardous and other waste for final disposal to a facility existing in a state other than the state where the waste is generated, the sender shall obtain a "No Objection Certificate" from the State Pollution Control Board of both states.[122] In the case of transportation of hazardous and other waste for recycling or utilization including co-processing, the sender shall notify both relevant State Pollution Control Boards before handing over the waste to the transporter.[123] In the case of transit of hazardous and other waste for recycling, utilization including co-processing or disposal through a state other than the places of origin and destination, the sender shall give prior intimation to the concerned State Pollution Control Board of the concerned states of transit before handing over the wastes to the transporter.[124] The responsibility of the safe transportation is on the party arranging the transport with the necessary authorization from the concerned State Pollution Control Board, whether that party be the sender or the receiver. This responsibility should be clearly indicated in the manifest.[125] The authorization for transport should be obtained either by the sender or the receiver on whose behalf the transport is being arranged.[126]

Rule 19 (1) states that the sender of the waste must prepare seven copies of a document comprising of a color code as indicated in the Rules and all seven copies must be signed by the sender. Under Rule 19 (2), the sender shall forward a copy to the State Pollution Control Board and, in the case that the hazardous or other wastes are likely to be transported through any transit state, the sender shall notify the State Pollution Control Boards of transit states of the movement of the waste. Procedures regarding the sending and receiving of copies have to be carried out in accordance with the Rules.

Rule 20 states that the occupier handling hazardous or other wastes and operator of the disposal facility must maintain records of such operations and send annual returns to the State Pollution Control Board. The board, based on the annual returns received from the occupiers and the operators of the facilities for disposal of hazardous and other wastes, has to prepare an annual inventory of the waste generated, waste recycled, recovered, utilized including co-processed; waste re-exported and waste disposed and submit to the Central Pollution Control Board by 30 of September every year. The State Pollution Control Board shall also prepare an inventory of hazardous waste generators, actual users and common and captive disposal facilities and submit the information to Central Pollution Control Board every two years.

The Central Pollution Control Board must prepare a consolidated review report on the management of hazardous and other wastes. This review has to be forwarded to the Ministry of Environment, Forest and Climate Change, along with its recommendations, before 30 of December every year.

Rule 22 states that in case of an accident which occurs at the facility handling hazardous or other wastes or during transportation, the occupier, operator or the transporter shall immediately notify the State Pollution Control Board, by telephone or email, of the accident and subsequently send a report.

Rule 23 lays down the liability of the occupier of the facilities. The occupier, importer or exporter and operator of the disposal facility shall be liable for all damages caused to the environment or third party due to improper handling and management of hazardous and other waste. The occupier and operator of the disposal facility shall also be liable to pay financial penalties as levied for any violation of the provisions under these rules by the State Pollution Control Board with the prior approval of the Central Pollution Control Board.

Rule 24 contains provisions on appeal. Any person aggrieved by an order of suspension or cancellation or refusal of authorization or its renewal passed by the State Pollution Control Board may, within a period of 30 days from the date on which the order is communicated to him, prefer an appeal in to the Appellate Authority i.e. the Environment Secretary of the State. The appellate authority may entertain the appeal after expiry of the said period of 30 days if sufficient cause exists. Every appeal filed under this rule shall be disposed of within a period of 60 days from the date of its filing.

Manufacture, Storage and Import of Hazardous Chemicals Rules, 1989

The Government of India, in exercise of the powers conferred on it by Sections 6, 8 and 25 of the Environment (Protection) Act, 1986, made Rules on manufacture, storage and import of hazardous chemicals. These Rules were amended in 2000 and the Manufacture, Storage and Import of Hazardous Chemical (Amendment) Rules were passed thereafter.

Rule 3 lays down duties of the Chief Controller of Imports and Exports. According to the rule, he is responsible for:

1 Enforcing the directions issued and procedures made in respect of isolated storage of hazardous chemicals; and
2 Enforcing the directions issued and procedures made on import of hazardous chemicals.

An occupier who has control of an industrial activity, under Rule 4 (2), must provide evidence to show that he has (a) identifed the major accident hazards; (b) taken adequate steps to prevent such major accidents and to limit their consequences to persons and the environment; and (c) to provide to the persons working on the site with the information, training and equipment including antidotes necessary to ensure their safety.

In the event of an accident on a site or in a pipeline, the occupier of such site must inform the concerned authorities of the accident and furnish a report relating the accident. On receiving the information the concerned authority must undertake a full analysis of the accident and send this information through the appropriate channel to the Ministry of Environment and Forests. At an industrial site in which a quantity of hazardous chemical[127] is present the occupier (manufacturer) of such site cannot undertake any industrial activity unless he submits a written report of the industrial activity to the concerned authorities at least three months before commencing such activities.[128] If after making the application to the authority the occupier intends to involve more additional hazardous chemicals in the industrial site, or intends to increase or decrease the quantity of a hazardous chemical which affects the particulars submitted in the earlier report, he must make a subsequent report to the concerned authority.[129]

Rule 10 places an obligation on the occupier of an Industrial site to prepare safety reports and safety audit reports[130] on the industrial activity carried on in the site and send it 90 days before the commencement of such activity to the concerned authority. The three-month time limit is applicable to all site occupiers carrying their activities prior to the commencement of the Rules.[131]

When a report is made to the relevant authority, no modification of the industrial activity which could materially affect the safety report is permitted,[132] unless the occupier makes another report mentioning the modification he intends to make before its adoption, to the concerned authority. The occupier of an industrial site fulfilling the above obligations narrated in Rules 10 and 11 can carry on the industrial activity for three years. Once the three-year period of the last submission of such report expires, they must make a further report which must have due regard to the new technical knowledge which has affected the particulars of the previous report relating to safety and hazard assessments. The report prepared in accordance with the above developments must be submitted to the concerned authority within 30 days or within such time agreed by the concerned authority.[133] Rule 12 of the 1989 Rules confers power on the concerned authority to ask for any additional information by serving a notice on the occupier. In the event of receiving such a notice from the concerned authority, the occupier must send the required information to the authority within the time-frame specified in the notice or within such extended time specified subsequently.[134]

Under Rule 13, the occupier must prepare and keep an up-to-date onsite emergency plan detailing how major accidents will be dealt with on the site where industrial activity is carried on. This emergency plan prepared by the occupier must include the name of the person who is responsible for safety on the site and the names of those who are authorized to take action in accordance with the plan in case of an emergency. Any modification made in the industrial activity must be taken into account by the occupier and every person affected by the plan must be informed of the modified provisions. In the case of a new industrial activity, the emergency plan must be prepared prior to its commencement. In the case of existing industrial activity, it must be prepared within 90 days from the date of coming into operation of the Rules.

The concerned authority[135] having gained access to the necessary information is duty bound to prepare and keep an up-to-date and adequate offsite emergency plan detailing how emergencies relating to a possible major accident on the site will be dealt with. While preparing such a plan, the authority must consult the occupier and any other persons which they deem necessary.[136] The occupier of a site, when consulted, must provide information relating to the industrial activity under his control to the concerned authority.[137] Similarly, the concerned authority must also provide the necessary information from the off-site emergency plan to the occupier. In the case of a new industrial activity such emergency plan must be prepared before the commencement of its activity and in other cases within six months from the date of the commencement of these rules.[138]

Under Rule 15 (1), the occupier of a site conducting industrial activity must take steps to inform persons outside the site either himself or through

District Emergency Authority about (a) the nature of the major accident hazard; and (b) the safety measures and the "do's and don'ts" to be adopted in the event of such major accident.

Sub-clause 2 of Rule 15 places an obligation on the occupier to take steps under the sub-rule (1) to inform persons about the nature and effect of the industrial activity prior to its commencement. All new industrial activities established after the commencement of the chemicals rules must do so within 90 days from its commencement.

An occupier who has control of an industrial activity[139] must arrange to obtain or develop information in the form of a safety data sheet pertaining to the chemicals' identity.[140] The occupier, while obtaining or developing a safety data sheet in respect of a hazardous chemical handled, must take all precautions to ensure that the information collected to make a hazard determination is recorded accurately and with all the available scientific evidence. Any additional information which is significant regarding the hazards of a chemical collected later must be added to the material safety data sheet as soon as practicable.[141] The safety data sheet prepared on these lines must be accessible upon request for reference to the needy. Furthermore, every container of a hazardous chemical must be clearly labeled or marked. This is mainly to identify (1) the contents of the container; (2) the name and address of the manufacturer or importer of the hazardous chemical; (3) the physical, chemical and toxicological data.[142]

A person importing hazardous chemicals into India must provide either at the time of import or within 30 days from the date of import to the concerned authorities[143] information pertaining to (i) the name and address of the person receiving the consignment in India; (ii) the port of entry in India; (iii) mode of transport from the exporting country to India; (iv) the quantity of chemicals being imported; and (v) complete product safety information.[144] On examination of the information provided by the importer the concerned authority, if it is satisfied that the chemical being imported is likely to cause major accident, may direct the importer to take appropriate steps including the stoppage of such imports.[145] The port authority must also be simultaneously informed by the concerned authority to take the necessary steps for the safe handling and storage of hazardous chemicals while off-loading the consignment in the port premises.[146] The importer, under Rule 18 (5), must maintain the records of the hazardous chemicals imported,[147] and these records must be kept open to inspection by the concerned authority of the state, or the Ministry of Environment and Forests or an officer appointed by it.

Furthermore, the importer or the person working on his behalf while transporting the hazardous chemicals from one port of entry to the ultimate destination must adhere to, and act according to the provisions of the Motor Vehicle Rules 1989, framed under the provisions of the Motor Vehicles Act, 1988.[148]

The import rules discussed here are also applicable to the import of toxic chemicals, flammable chemicals, explosives and the 434 chemicals listed in column two of part two of Schedule 1.[149]

The concerned authority is empowered to serve a notice to any person if in its opinion the person has contravened provisions of the rules under discussion, and it can request him to remedy the contravention within a time frame specified by the concerned authority.[150] In addition, the central government, in order to carry out the rules effectively, can make changes in the schedules at any time by way of notification in the official gazette.[151]

Rules for the manufacture, use, import, export and storage of hazardous microorganisms or genetically engineered organisms or cells, 1989

The central government, in exercise of the powers conferred on it by Sections 6, 8 and 25 of the Environment (Protection) Act, 1986, adopted Rules for the Manufacture, Use, Import, Export and Storage of Hazardous Microorganisms or Genetically Engineered Organisms or Cells in 1989,[152] with a view to protecting the environment, nature and health in connection with the application of gene-technology and micro-organisms. The Recombinant DNA Advisory Committee (RADC), under Rule 4, is empowered to review developments in biotechnology[153] at national and international levels and to recommend suitable and appropriate safety regulations for India in recombinant DNA research, use and applications from time to time.[154] The Review Committee on Genetic Manipulation[155] (RCGM) monitors the safety-related aspects in respect of ongoing research projects and activities involving genetically engineered organisms/hazardous microorganisms.[156]

As part of its function, the RCGM must bring out manuals of guidelines specifying the procedure for regulatory process with respect to activities involving genetically engineered organisms in research, use and applications including industry to ensure environmental safety. All on-going projects involving high risk category and controlled field experiments must be reviewed to ensure that adequate precautions and containment conditions are followed as per the guidelines. In addition, the Review Committee on Genetic Manipulation is to lay down procedures restricting or prohibiting production, sale, importation and use of such genetically engineered organism of cells.

Rule 4 (3) puts an obligation on an occupier or any person including research institutions handling microorganisms or genetically engineered organisms to constitute committee known as the Institutional Biosafety Committee (IBSC). This committee must comprise the Head of the Institution, scientists engaged in DNA work, a medical expert and a nominee of the Department of Biotechnology. The occupier or any person including research institutions handling micro-organisms/genetically engineered organisms must prepare an up-to-date on-site emergency plan according to the manuals/guidelines of the RCGM with the assistance of the Institutional Biosafety Committee. The copies of manuals/guidelines so prepared must be made available to the district Level Committee or State Biotechnology Coordination committee and the Genetic Engineering Approval Committee.

Similarly, the Genetic Engineering Approval Committee (GEAC)[157] functions as a body under the Department of Environment, Forest and Wildlife and oversees the approval of activities involving large-scale use of hazardous microorganisms and recombinants in research and industrial production from the environmental angle. The committee has been given the power and responsibility for the approval of proposals relating to the release of genetically engineered organisms and products into the environment including experimental field trials. It can take punitive action.[158]

For effective enforcement of the Rules at the state and district levels in India, the State Biotechnology Coordination Committee (SBCC)[159] and the District Level Biotechnology Committee (DLBC)[160] have been established. The SBCC has the power to inspect, investigate and take punitive action in the case of violations of statutory provisions. Moreover, it must periodically review the safety and control measures in the various industries which handle genetically engineered organisms or hazardous microorganisms. In the same vein, the District Level Committee monitors the safety regulations in installations engaged in the use of genetically modified organisms/hazardous microorganisms and its application in the environment.[161] The DLC, or any person authorized by it, must visit the installation engaged in activity involving genetically engineered organisms and/or hazardous microorganisms, formulate an information chart and identify the hazards and risks associated with each of these installations. Using this information, it must coordinate activities with a view to meeting any emergency. Furthermore, it must also prepare an offsite emergency plan. The DLC must regularly submit reports of its activities to the SBCC.

Under Rule 7, a person can import, export, transport manufacture, use or sell any hazardous micro-organisms/genetically engineered organisms/substances only with the prior approval of the Genetic Engineering Approval Committee. The use of pathogenic micro-organism or any genetically engineered organisms or cell will be allowed only for the purpose of research in laboratories inside laboratory areas notified by the Ministry of Environment and Forests.[162] The GEAC must give directions to the occupier to determine or take measures concerning the discharge of micro-organisms or genetically engineered organisms from the laboratories and other areas. This includes laying down measures to prevent such discharges.[163] In addition, any person operating or using genetically engineered organisms/micro-organisms for scale-up or pilot operations should obtain a license from the GEAC.

The production of genetically engineered organisms or cells or micro-organisms can commence only with the consent of the GEAC. In addition, permission from the GEAC is required not only for the discharge of genetically engineered organisms from these places of production into the environment but also for the development and testing experiments carried on in such place. Rule 9 prohibits the deliberate or unintentional release of genetically engineered organisms /hazardous micro-organisms[164] into the environment.

Sections 10 and 11 are very important from the point of our investigation for the simple reason that, under Section 10, substances and products, which contain genetically engineered organisms or cells or micro-organisms must not be produced, sold, imported or used except with the approval of GEAC. Similarly, under Section 11, the approval of the GEAC is necessary for production, importing or selling of food stuffs, ingredients in food stuffs and additives including processing aids containing or consisting of genetically engineered organisms. The person who applies for approval[165] must submit the necessary information to the GEAC and make its examinations as per the specific directions issued by the GEAC at such laboratories. Further, he must also make available an onsite emergency plan to GEAC before obtaining approval.[166] In case the GEAC itself makes the examination, the expenses incurred for such examination may be borne by the person on whose behalf it was done.

While granting approval under Rules 8–11 the GEAC must lay down the terms and conditions as to the control to be exercised by the applicant and as to the submission of information to the State Biotechnology Coordination Committee for to the District Committee. All approvals granted by the GEAC are valid up to a specified period not exceeding 4years and renewable for 2 years at a time.[167] The GEAC is empowered to revoke such approval in the following situations: (a) if there is any new information as to the harmful effects of the genetically engineered organisms or cells; (b) if the genetically engineered organisms or cells cause such damage to the environment, nature or health as it could not be envisaged when the approval was given; or (c) non-compliance of any condition stipulated by GEAC.[168]

The GEAC may supervise the implementation of the above terms and conditions[169] through the State Biotechnology Co-ordination Committee (SBCC) or the State Pollution Control boards or District Pollution Control Boards or through any authorized persons.[170]

In the event of a failure to comply with the order issued by the GEAC the District Level Committee (DLC) or State Biotechnology Coordination Committee is empowered to take the necessary measures at the expense of the person responsible for the damage.[171] The SBCC or DLC, under Rule 15(2), may take the necessary steps without issuing any notice or service order on the party responsible for such act, to prevent any immediate damage to the environment, nature or health. The expenses incurred in situations of this kind must be payable by the person responsible for such damage.[172]

The SBCC or DLC is given the power to take samples for a more detailed examination of organisms and cells.[173] Further, these two committees can ask for assistance from any other Government authority to carry out their instructions.[174]

Under Rules 7–11, a person while carrying on his activities, in the event of any interruption of operations or accidents that may lead to discharges of genetically engineered organisms or cells which is harmful to the environment, nature or health, must immediately notify to the DLC or SBCC and the state medical officer.[175]

Rule 17 (1) puts an obligation on the DLC to prepare an off-site emergency plan detailing how emergencies relating to a possible major accident at a site will be dealt with, and the DLC in preparing this plan must consult the occupier of the site and other persons connected with it. In this endeavor the occupier of the site must provide the necessary information relating to the handling of hazardous micro-organisms or genetically engineered organisms which is under his control, to the DLC. Correspondingly, the DLC must also provide the occupier with the necessary information from the offsite emergency plan which relates to his duties under Rule 16.[176]

For the purpose of carrying out supervision, the SBCC, the GEAC, the DLC or any person authorized by these committees can at any time be admitted to any public as well as to private premises and localities.[177]

The occupier of such premises must allow supervision/inspection of the premise by these authorities. Moreover, the person carrying out activities under Rules 7–11 at the request of DLC, SBCC or GEAC must submit the essential information concerning financial conditions and accounts.[178] Under Rule 18 (3), the expenses incurred by the authorities in connection with approvals, examinations, supervision and control in part or in whole may be fixed by the GEAC.

The aggrieved party, within 30 days from the communication of the decision by the GEAC or SBCC, may prefer to appeal to an authority appointed by the Ministry of Environment and Forests.[179] The Ministry of Environment and forests can exempt[180] an occupier handling a particular micro-organism/ genetically engineered organism from Rules 7–11.

Part 2

Factories (Amendment) Act, 1987

A study on the legal control of hazardous substances is incomplete without analyzing the 1987 Amended Provisions of the Factories Act of 1947 relating to hazardous processes. The incident at Bhopal prompted the central government to amend the Factories Act of 1948[181] with the aim of correcting its inadequacies in order to protect the workers and to control environmental pollution.

Since the 1987 amendment, there has been substantial modernization and innovation in the industrial field. These developments introduced in the amendments place an obligation on several chemical industries to provide and adopt safeguards against the use and handling of hazardous substances by the occupiers of factories and for the laying down of emergency standards and measures. The 1987 amendment established procedures for siting to ensure that hazardous and polluting industries are not set up in areas where they can cause adverse effects on the general public. Provision had also been made in the Amendment Act for the workers' participation in safety management.[182]

The present discussion is confined to the new sections introduced in the 1987 amendments dealing with hazardous processes.

Under Section 2 (cb), "hazardous process" means any process or activity in relation to an industry specified in the First Schedule[183] where, unless special care is taken, raw materials used therein or the intermediate or the finished products, by-products, wastes or effluents thereof would: (1) cause material impairment to the health of the persons engaged in connection therewith, or (2) result in the pollution of the general environment.

As per Section 7A (1), it is the duty of every occupier to ensure the health, safety and welfare of all workers while they are at work in the factory. This duty extends to:

1 The provision and maintenance of plant and systems of work in the factory that are safe, and without risks to health.
2 The arrangements in the factory for ensuring safety and absence of risks to health in connection with the use, handling storage and transport of articles and substances.
3 The provision of such information, instruction, training and supervision that are necessary to ensure the health and safety of all workers at work.
4 The maintenance of all places of work in the factory should be in condition and safe without risks to health and provision for maintenance of such means of access, so that such places are safe and without risks.

5 The provision, maintenance or monitoring of such working environment in the factory for the workers that is safe, without risks to health and adequate as regards facilities and arrangements for their welfare at work.[184]

In addition, the occupier in special cases should revise a written statement of his general policy with respect to the health and safety of the workers and the organization and arrangements for the time being for carrying out that policy. Such revision made by the occupier must be brought to the attention of all workers.[185]

The other duties are mentioned in Section 7B. Under this provision, every person who designs, manufactures, imports or supplies any article for use in any factory must:

1 Ensure that the article is designed and constructed so as to be safe and without risks to the health of the workers when properly used.
2 Carry out or arrange for any tests and examinations that may be considered necessary for the effective implementation of clause (a).
3 Take steps to ensure that adequate information will be available:
    a In connection with the use of the article in any factory.
    b About the use for which it is designed and tested; and
    c About any conditions necessary to ensure that the article, when put to such use, will be safe and without risks to the health of the workers.

Where an article is manufactured outside India, it is obligatory for the importer to see: (a) that the article conforms to the same standards as if it was manufactured in India or (b) if the standards adopted in the country outside for the manufacture of such article are above the standards adopted in India, that the article conforms to such standards.

Under Section 36 (1), no person shall be required or allowed to enter any chamber, tank, vat, pit, pipe, flue or other confined space in any factory in which any gas, fume, vapor or dust is likely to be present to such an extent as to involve risk to persons being overcome, unless they are provided with a manhole of adequate size or other effective means of exit. Hence, workers or others can enter such places only when practical measures have been taken to remove any gas, fume, vapor or dust to bring their levels within the permissible limits. But before permitting such an entry, the following two conditions must be satisfied:

1 A certificate in writing must have been given by a competent person, based on a test carried out by himself, that claims the space is reasonably free from dangerous gas, fume, vapor or dust.

a. The person must be wearing suitable breathing apparatus and a belt which is securely attached to a rope, the free end of which is held by a person outside the confined space. Section 38 (1) of the Factories Amendment Act of 1987, imposes an obligation on every factory to take all measures to prevent the outbreak of fire and its spread both internally and externally and to provide and maintain:

   (a) Safe means of escape for all persons in the event of a fire, and
   (b) The necessary equipment and facilities for extinguishing fire. Furthermore, effective measures must also be taken to ensure that in every factory all workers are familiar with the means of escape in case of fire and are adequately trained in the routine to be followed in such cases.[186]

The state government, in order to consider applications for grant of permission for the initial location of a factory involving hazardous processes or for the expansion of any such factory, may appoint a Site Appraisal Committee.[187] This committee consists of experts on the subject from the center and the state and experts from other related subjects.[188]

The Site Appraisal Committee (SAC) must examine the application for the establishment of a factory involving hazardous processes and make its recommendations to the state within 90 days of the receipt of the application.[189] The SAC has the power to call for any information from the applicant for the establishment or expansion of a factory involving a hazardous process.[190] The state government must co-opt a representative nominated by the central government as a member of the SAC in cases where any process relates to a factory owned or controlled by the central government or to a corporation or a company owned or controlled by the central government.[191]

Under Section 41 B (l), the occupier of every factory involving a hazardous process must disclose all information[192] regarding dangers, including health hazards and the measures to overcome such hazards arising from the exposure to, or handling of, the materials or substances in the manufacture, transportation, storage and other processes, to the workers employed in the factory, the chief inspector, the local authority within whose jurisdiction the factory is situated and the general public in the vicinity. Moreover, every occupier at the time of registering the factory involving a hazardous process must lay down a detailed policy with respect to the health and safety of the workers employed there. This fact must be brought to the knowledge of the chief inspector and the local authority. Any change made in such policy at such intervals must also be brought to the knowledge of the chief inspector and the local authority.[193]

It is the duty of every occupier to draw up an onsite emergency plan and detailed disaster control measures for his factory, with the approval of the chief inspector. Such a plan must be brought to the attention of workers employed therein and to the general public living in the vicinity of the factory so as to enable them to adopt the safety measures in the event of an accident taking place.[194] In addition, every occupier of a factory involving a hazardous process must inform the chief inspector of the nature and details of the process involved as prescribed by this act.[195] Any failure to comply with the provision will lead to a penalty and the cancellation of a license issued[196] under this act.[197] Furthermore, the occupier of a factory involving a hazardous process must outline measures for the handling, usage, transportation and storage of hazardous substances inside the factory premises and the disposal of such substances outside the factory premises and publicize them among workers and the general public living in the vicinity. The measures undertaken must also have the approval of the chief inspector.[198]

The occupier of a factory involving in any hazardous process is obliged to maintain accurate and up-to-date health and medical records of the workers in the factory who are exposed to chemical, toxic or any other harmful substances which are manufactured, stored, handled or transported. The workers must be given access to these records.[199] While appointing workers to handle these substances, the occupier must appoint persons who possess qualifications and experience in handling hazardous substances, and they must be competent to supervise such handling within the factory.[200] Equally important is the duty of an occupier to arrange for medical examination of every worker under the following circumstances:

1 Before such worker is assigned to a job involving the handling of, or working with, a hazardous substance; and
2 While continuing in such job, and after he has ceased to work in such job, at intervals not exceeding twelve months.[201]

Under the provisions of Section 41 D (l) the central government is empowered to appoint an inquiry committee in the event of the occurrence of an extraordinary situation involving a factory engaged in a hazardous process, to inquire into the standards of health and safety observed in the factory with a view to identifying the causes of any failure or neglect in the adoption of the measures or standards prescribed for the health and safety of the workers employed in the factory or the general public affected or likely to be affected, due to such failure or neglect and to prevent the recurrence of such extraordinary situations in future in the factory or elsewhere.[202] The inquiry committee must consist of a chairman and two other members and their tenure of office and the terms of reference will be determined by the central government, taking into consideration the requirements of the situation.[203] The recommendations of the committee must be advisory in nature.[204] The central government may direct the Director-General of Factory Advice Service and Labor Institutes, or any other institution specialized in matters relating to standards of safety in hazardous processes, to lay down emergency standards for the enforcement of suitable standards in respect of such hazardous processes only when it is satisfied that no standards of safety exist in respect of a hazardous process or a class of hazardous processes, or the existing standards are inadequate.[205] The emergency standards laid down can be enforced immediately.[206]

The second schedule makes mention of the permissible levels of certain chemical substances in a work environment. Hence, every occupier of a factory involving a hazardous process must adhere to the schedule and must not exceed the limits laid down in the schedule.[207] The central government may make suitable changes in the schedule (in the form of a notification in the *Official Gazette*) to give effect to any scientific proof obtained from specialized institutions or experts.[208]

Another important provision added to the Factories Act is Section 41 G. Under this provision, the occupier of every factory where a hazardous process takes place or hazardous substances are used or handled must set up a safety committee consisting of an equal number of representatives of workers and management to promote cooperation between the workers and the management in maintaining proper safety and health at work and periodically to review the measures taken. However, the state government may exempt the occupier of any factory or class of factories from setting up such committee by an order in writing.[209]

In the event of a reasonable apprehension of imminent danger to their lives or health due to an accident, workers may bring this fact to the notice of the occupier, agent or manager who is in charge of the factory or the process concerned. They can do this either directly, or through their representatives in the safety committee, and also to the notice of the inspector. The occupier, agent, manager or the person in charge of the factory/process, in such situations, is legally bound to take immediate remedial action in respect to imminent danger. He should also prepare a report of the action taken and send it to the nearest inspector.[210]

The duty to inform the nearest inspector is obligatory even in cases where the occupier, agent, manager or person in charge of the factory/process does not believe there is any immediate danger as apprehended by the workers. In such cases, the decision taken by the inspector is final.[211]

If the owner or occupier has contravened the provisions relating to information required to be given under Section 41 F, failed to perform his duties under Section 41 C or failed to take remedial measures to prevent imminent danger under Section 41 E, he would be punishable with imprisonment that may extend to seven years and with a fine up to two lakh rupees. If the failure or contravention is a continuing one, an additional fine of 5,000 rupees may be imposed for every day of the failure or contravention. If such a failure or contravention continues for more than one year after the date of conviction, the offender may be punished with imprisonment, which may extend to as much as ten years. Moreover, as we have seen, if the information required under Section 41 B is not given by an occupier of a factory, his license for operating the factory may be canceled as an additional penalty.

The Public Liability Insurance Act (PLIA) 1991

This legislation[212] was passed with a view to providing immediate relief to the persons affected by accidents occurring while handling any hazardous substance.[213] Under its provisions, all hazardous chemical industries must compulsorily insure themselves and give immediate relief to all affected parties.[214] The legislative history of the Act indicates that the growth of hazardous industries, processes and operations in India has been accompanied by the growing risk of accidents that may lead to death and injury to human beings and other living beings and damage to private land/public properties. Hence, the government felt it needed to provide for mandatory public liability insurance for handling hazardous substances to provide minimum relief to victims.[215]

The Act seeks to mandate compulsory insurance to provide immediate relief to the victims of an accident caused while handling any hazardous substance. In the light of the decision of the Supreme Court, in light of the principles gained from the Oleum Gas Leak Case and the Bhopal disaster, the Act was passed to consolidate the law in relation to an enterprise's liability while handling any hazardous substance. The Act's primary goal is to protect members of economically weaker sections of society who cannot afford prolonged litigation in a court of law.[216] The Act has been envisaged to provide immediate compensation in terms of an industrial accident to a victim of a hazardous substance. However, one aspect which it fails to touch upon is the principle of "accident prevention" or its "deterrence effect."

The object of the Act clarifies that it is applicable only to accidents or incidents which result from the handling of hazardous substances. The term "accident" has been defined in the Act as an accident that involves a fortuitous, sudden or unintentional occurrence while handling any hazardous substance resulting in continuous, intermittent or repeated exposure to death, of or injury to any person or damage to any property.[217] As per the wording, this definition fails to provide any remedy to the affected where even a minuscule level of exposure results in after effects.[218] Moreover, the term "accident" does not include accidents taking place due to radioactivity.[219] Since nuclear power in India is controlled and regulated by governmental bodies,[220] it can be inferred that the Act has consciously decided to exempt the government of liability in the event of any accidents involving radioactive elements.

Hazardous substances

The term "hazardous substance" refers to any substance or preparation which has been defined as hazardous substance under the Environment (Protection) Act, 1986.[221] Furthermore, the hazardous substance, as defined under the 1986 Act is deemed hazardous as per the Act only if it exceeds the quantity as notified by the central government.[222] Thus, if any form of accident occurs which causes death, injuries to people or damages to a person's property, as a result of a substance that is hazardous but is not covered under central government's notification, then the affected has no remedy under this Act.[223]

Understanding the difficulty with this interpretation of "hazardous substance," the Indian courts have taken an equitable route. One of the first instances of this interpretation came in the case of *UP State Electricity Board and ANR. v District Magistrate and ORS.*, where the court had to decide whether "electricity" fell under the definition of "hazardous substances" as given under the Act.[224] The court identified the need for giving a wide interpretation to the definition in question as the Act was a beneficial piece of legislation. In pursuance of that, the court went on to hold that the definition included all the substances which were defined as "hazardous" under the Environment (Protection) Act, 1986 and if any such substances were also notified by the central government under Section 2 (d) of the Act, then it was to be deemed as hazardous if it exceeded the quantity specified in the notifcation.[225] With this, the court went on to interpret "electricity" as a "hazardous substance" for the purpose of the Environmental (Protection) Act, 1986.[226] As a result of this, electricity was deemed to be a form of "hazardous substance" under the Act as well. This equitable proposition of law has been followed by several other judicial decisions.[227] Likewise, the term "handling" has included activities such as manufacturing, processing, treatment, packaging, storing, transporting by vehicle, use, collection, destruction, conversion, offering for sale and transfer of such hazardous substances.[228] It is interesting to note that the act of transportation has been restricted to transportation by way of vehicles.[229] The Act has defined the term "vehicle" as any mode of surface transport other than railways.[230] This leads to the inevitable conclusion that other modes of transport such as air, water and railways have been excluded from the purview of the Act.[231] As a natural result of this, the Act again falls short of fulfilling its objective of being a piece of welfare legislation.

Owner's liability

Section 3 of the Act mandates that in the event of any death or injury to any person (excluding workmen) or damage to any property arising out of an accident, the owner shall be liable to provide relief as specified in the schedule for the death, injury or damage.[232] Sub-section (2) of Section 3 further provides that, in the event of such an accident, the claimant shall not be required to plead and establish that the death, injury or damage, in respect of which the claim has been made, was due to the wrongful act, neglect or default of any person.[233]

It is interesting to note that the Act has clearly excluded "workmen" from being compensated, as they can be compensated under the ordinary labor laws which are not as stringent as the Act in terms of the no-fault liability rule.[234] This defeats the purpose of the Act on two fronts. First, it makes a needless distinction between "workmen" and other people who are affected. This forces the affected workmen to claim under the Workmen's Compensation Act, 1923, which in turn offers certain defenses to the employer.[235] This classification is at odds with the 1986 Act's objective of providing immediate compensation to affected victims through the rule of no-fault liability. Second, the definition of "workmen" has been borrowed from the Workmen's Compensation Act, 1923.[236] After evaluating the definition of "workmen," one can deduce that a person is deemed to be a workman by virtue of his employment in the industry. He does not cease to become a "workman" when he is not working during the subsistence of his employment contract. This leads to an absurd situation where a workman, even if he is affected by the accident outside his working hours, still won't be eligible for any compensation under the Act. He will always be required to make a claim through the Workmen's Compensation Act for any remedy. Therefore, the Act has made an unnecessary distinction resulting in depriving the industry's "workmen" of the benefits of the legislation.

Moreover, the Act mandates compensatory relief as is specified in the schedule for any death, injury or damage arising out of the accident.[237] The schedule provides a relief of 25,000 rupees per person for fatal accidents, along with a reimbursement of medical expenses incurred up to a limit of 12,500 rupees.[238] Further, in the case of permanent disability, a total relief of 25,000 rupees has been mandated by the Act.[239] The Act also provides for relief in the event of loss of wages due to temporary partial disability. A fixed monthly relief, not exceeding 1,000 rupees per month for a period not extending more than three months, is to be provided to the victim in cases where the victim has been hospitalized for a period exceeding three days and is above the age of 16.[240] This wording of the provision is problematic on two fronts. First, the amount of relief is meager in today's times and has not been adjusted as per the current inflation level. On top of that, it seems absurd that a victim or their legal representatives would have to make an application to claim for relief to the collector[241] and then undergo a proceeding, lasting three months, for such a paltry amount.[242] Second, the Act, while deciding upon the victim's eligibility for compensation in the event of loss of wages, has unnecessarily mandated the condition of being hospitalized for more than three days. This dilution of the provision again leaves a large number of people in the dark who could not work even though they were medically treated within three. Therefore, this detail needs to be done away with.

Insurance structure

The Act mandates that every owner shall take out, before he starts handling any hazardous substance, one or more insurance policies to meet any potential liability arising out of any accident which takes place.[243] Further, the insurance policy so taken shall be for an amount less than the amount paid for undertaking the handling of the hazardous substance or an amount not exceeding 50 crores rupees.[244] The liability of the insurer is also restricted to the amount specified in the contract of insurance in the insurance policy.[245] The Act then makes an exception to the mandate of this section, where a central government can, by notification, exempt an "owner" which can be the central government, state government, any corporation owned or controlled by the central government or a state government and any local authority.[246] This raises some concern, as the interests of the government have been placed on a higher pedestal than those of a victim in the event of an accident where the owner(s) is one belonging to the aforementioned categories. In addition to this, the Act does not envisage a situation where the insurer refuses to pay the amount insured. No liability has been provided under the Act which accrues to the insurer in the event of his non-payment of the sum so insured. Thus, in such a situation a victim can claim compensation in two ways. Either he can file a suit for non-performance of the insurance contract against the Insurer in the capacity of a third-party benefciary[247] or he can wait till a suit is filed by the insured company ("owner") against the insurer for recovering the insured money. In the former situation, a suit for compensation will require the establishment of a contract and its breach which will likely take a considerable amount of time. This, in turn, fails the objective of the Act of providing immediate relief to victims of any such accidents. Likewise, in the latter case, the Act does not mandate a time period within which any such claim is to be made against the insurer by the owner. Therefore, the victim again becomes helpless and is left with no option but is at the mercy of the insured owner to file a suit against the insurer.[248]

A solution proposed by J. Bhagwati against the backdrop of the Bhopal disaster could be applied to the afore-mentioned situation. As per J. Bhagwati, the government should provide immediate compensation in events where any ensuing litigation stops the disbursement of relief.[249] Once litigation concludes, the government can always reimburse itself in such a situation since the liability in question is a no-fault liability. Thus, one can only hope that the government takes note of the Act's inadequacy immediately before any other major disaster breaks out.

Establishment of the Environment Relief Fund

Section 7 of the Act provides that the central government may, by a notification in the *Official Gazette*, establish a fund to be known as the Environment Relief Fund.[250] An owner has to pay an amount, in addition to the amount of premium, to the insurer which will be deposited by the insurer into the Environment Relief Fund.[251] This fund is to be utilized in the manner as provided under Section 7 of the Act.

Relief redressal mechanism

The Act mandates that the collector must verify the occurrence of an accident as envisaged in the Act and cause publicity to be given in such a manner he deems fit for inviting applications regarding claims for relief under Section 6.[252] An application for relief is to be made by the person who has sustained an injury or the owner of the property to which damage has been caused.[253] In the event of a death arising from the accident, the claim is to be made by the legal representatives of the deceased.[254] The Act does not provide any scope for claims being made by social action groups and participation of the public in claiming compensation under the Act.[255]

Under Section 7 (1) of the Act, the collector is to hold an inquiry into the claim for relief being made after he has given the parties an opportunity of being heard.[256] After that, the collector may make an award, specifying the persons to whom such amount of relief is to be made and determining the amount of relief which appears to him just. The Act further mandates that the award is to be made by following a summary procedure within three months of filing a claim for relief. Likewise, the payment of the award is also to be made within a set time period.[257]

These provisions have conferred discretionary powers on the collector which creates a scope for misuse of the power. The discretionary power so conferred goes against the express provision of Section 3, mandating compulsory compensation in the event of an accident.[258] Furthermore, Section 3 has not been mentioned under Section 7. As a result of this, there have been inconsistencies in the judicial interpretation of these provisions. While interpreting a question on the collector's power to grant relief under Section 7 of the Act, the Madhya Pradesh High Court reasoned that once the identity of the deceased's legal heir was finalized and the amount was paid as per the schedule mentioned in Section 3, the collector has no further role to play.[259] The court here expressed its discontent with the paltry amount given as compensation under the Act, but conceded that it was unable to legislate on the same. Recognizing the paltry compensation, an equitable interpretation of Section 7 was given by the Allahabad High Court.[260] In this case, the court was faced with the question of whether the competent authority lacked the jurisdiction to award compensation of more than the sum stipulated under Section 3 of the Act. The court went on to hold that compensation to be paid under Section 3 was a mandatory payment where the age, income, number of dependents or other factors were immaterial for awarding compensation, whereas Section 7 gives the collector the power to make an award determining the amount of relief which appears to him to be just and equitable.[261]

It was further clarified that compensation paid in pursuance of Section 3's mandate was independent of the provisions contained in Section 6 and 7 of the Act. This was because Section 3 is reflective of the "no-fault liability" principle and, thus, the representatives of the deceased will be entitled to compensation for every relevant accident encapsulated within this Act. Lastly, the court also explained that even if an application for compensation, under Section 3, was not made by the deceased's dependents, the collector can still award compensation under the same with regard to death and injury.[262] This interpretation has very well addressed the issue of paltry compensation being provided under the Act by interpreting it to meet its true purpose of being a piece of beneficial legislation. One hopes that courts, while addressing future claims made under this act, follow the latter court's reasoning to fulfill the Act's true purpose.

Furthermore, Section 8 provides that the right to claim relief under Section 3 is in addition to any other right of claiming compensation under any other law in force at the time.[263] Section 8 is of high relevance, as the remedies under the Act comprise of a paltry compensation being awarded under Section 3. In addition to this, there is an air of confusion relating to the extent of the collector's discretionary powers of awarding relief. Therefore, the only choice left for a victim is to resort to any other remedy as provided under any other law in force. As a result, the victim or his heir is left without any effective remedy as a claim in any other form would require proving negligence which might end up in unnecessary hardship.

On a keen perusal of relief dispensing mechanisms under this act, it will is safe to conclude that the Act is severely outdated and may lead to catastrophic results if not immediately overhauled.

Accident prevention

Section 9 of the Act mandates that, in order to ascertain compliance with the Act, any person authorized by the central government may require any owner to submit the necessary information.[264] Any person authorized by the central government has a right to enter the premises or place where a hazardous substance is being handled for the purpose of ascertaining that the provisions of this act are being complied with.[265] The authorized person can exercise this right only in the event of having a reason to believe that a hazardous substance is being handled in contravention of Section 4.[266] As a result of the search, if it is found that any handling of a hazardous substance has taken place then the authority may seize the s substance and other things which, in his opinion, will be useful to any potential proceedings under the Act.[267] The person can also dispose of the hazardous substance if he has a reason to believe that it is expedient to prevent an accident.[268] Moreover, the central government has the power to issue directions to any owner or any person, officer, authority or agency and such owner, person, officer, authority or agency to direct prohibition or regulation of handling the hazardous substance or regulating the supply of electricity, water or any other service.[269] The central government has also been given powers to make an application in a court of law to restrain an owner from handling hazardous substances in contravention of the provisions of this Act.[270]

Penalties

Section 14 of the Act mandates imprisonment for a term extending up to six years but not less than one-and-a-half years in the event of non-compliance with the requirements under Section 4, and failing to adhere to directions under Section 12 along with a fine of a minimum of a lakh of rupees.[271] Moreover, the Act also prescribes a penalty for obstructing the right of the person, so authorized by the central government, to carry on his functions under Sections 10 and 11.[272] It further includes the concept of corporate criminal liability where companies can be made liable for proceeding against offenses.[273] Lastly, the Act also envisages the possibility of proceeding against the heads of different government departments for committing an offense under this Act.[274]

Miscellaneous

The central government has been authorized, under the Act, to delegate its power to any person.[275] Further, Section 20 of the Act protects the government or any agency acting in good faith in relation to the provisions of this act.[276] In addition to this, the Act also provides that the central government establishes an advisory committee on matters relating to insurance policy under the Act, which in turn will include experts of insurance or hazardous substances.[277] Lastly, the provisions of this Act will have effect notwithstanding anything inconsistent contained in any other law.[278]

The National Green Tribunal (NGT) Act, 2010

In 2003, the 186th Report of the Law Commission of India on the "Proposal to Constitute Environmental Courts"[279] emphasized the need for the constitution of "environmental courts" in India. It observed that the previous National Environmental Tribunal Act, 1995[280] was yet to be notified and, even several years after its enactment, no tribunal had actually been established under the Act.[281] The tribunals, thus, remained non-functional and existed solely on paper.[282] The commission, after considering observations of the Supreme Court in previous judgments,[283] and taking into regard the inadequacies of the existing appellate authorities, which neither contained judges nor had the assistance of experts along with their limited jurisdiction, proposed to review the position with a view to bringing uniformity to the constitution and jurisdiction of bodies known as "environmental courts." It was further proposed that these courts should consist of judicial members assisted by technical experts.

The preamble to the National Green Tribunal Act, 2010 (hereinafter referred to as the NGT Act)[284] provides for the establishment of a National Green Tribunal.

> for the effective and expeditious disposal of cases relating to environmental protection and conservation of forests and other natural resources including enforcement of any legal right relating to environment and giving relief and compensation for damages to persons and property and for matters connected therewith or incidental thereto.

Moreover, in view of India's obligation to several international conferences,[285] as well as in recognition of the right to a healthy environment under Article 21 of the Constitution, it was considered expedient to establish such tribunals to deal with the multidisciplinary issues related to the environment.[286] The Act finally came into force and repealed two earlier enactments—the National Environment Appellate Authority Act (1997)[287] and the National Environmental Tribunal Act (1995).

The Act enables the tribunal, while passing any order or decision or award, to apply the principles of sustainable development, the precautionary principle and the polluter pays principle.[288] Under Section 18 of the Act, an application may be made to the tribunal by:

1 The person, who has sustained the injury.
2 The owner of the property to which the damage has been caused.
3 Where death has resulted from the environmental damage, by all or any of the legal representatives of the deceased.
4 Any agent duly authorized by such person or owner of such property or all or any of the legal representatives of the deceased.
5 Any person aggrieved, including any representative body or organization.
6 The central government or a state government or a union territory administration or the Central Pollution Control Board or a State Pollution Control Board or a Pollution Control Committee or a local authority, or any environmental authority established under the Environment (Protection) Act, 1986.

Tribunals

Chapter 2 of the Act contains the provisions for the establishment of the tribunals. Under Section 3 of the Act, the Central Government is empowered to establish a tribunal by way of notification.

Composition

The National Green Tribunal consists[289] of a full-time chairperson, who shall be accompanied by not less than ten and not more than 20 full-time judicial members and not less than ten and not more than 20 full-time expert members.

The chairperson has the power to invite one or more person,[290] for a particular case, with specialized knowledge in the related area to assist the court in the process of administration of justice.

The ordinary places of sitting of the tribunal as well its territorial jurisdiction shall be notified by the central government.[291] The central government may also after consulting with the chairperson of the tribunal, make rules regulating the practices and procedure of the tribunal including

1 The rules as to the persons who shall be entitled to appear before the tribunal.
2 The rules as to the procedure for hearing applications and appeals and other matters relating to the applications and appeals, including the circuit procedure for hearing at a place other than the ordinary place of its sitting falling within the jurisdiction.
3 The minimum number of members who shall hear the applications and appeals in respect of any class or classes of applications and appeals.[292]
4 Rules relating to transfer of cases by the chairperson from one place of sitting including the ordinary place of sitting to any other place of sitting.[293]

Appointment of members

The central government shall appoint a chairperson as well as the judicial members and expert members of the tribunal.[294] The chairperson shall be appointed by the central government in consultation with the Chief Justice of India.[295] The judicial members and expert members of the tribunal shall be appointed on the recommendations of a selection committee in the prescribed manner.[296]

Qualifications for appointment

Section 5 lays out the qualification requirements for appointment of members. A person is not qualified to be appointed as a judicial member unless he is, or has been, a judge of a Supreme Court or the Chief Justice of a High Court.[297] In order to be an expert member, a person has to have a Master's degree in Science (in physical sciences or life sciences) with a Doctorate, or a Master's of Engineering or Master's of Technology degree. They must also have 15 years' experience in the relevant field including five years of practical experience in the field of environment and forests (including pollution control, hazardous substance management, environmental impact assessment, climate change management, biological diversity management and forest conservation) in a reputed national-level institution, or have administrative experience of 15 years including experience of five years in dealing with environmental matters in the central or a state government or in a reputed national-or state-level institution.[298]

During their tenure, the chairperson, judicial members and expert members of the tribunal shall not hold any other office.[299] The chairperson and other judicial and expert members shall not accept any employment in connection with the management or administration of any person who has been a party to a proceeding before the tribunal under this Act, up to a period of two years from the date on which they cease to hold office.[300]

Tenure

The chairperson, as well as the members of both judicial and expert committees, shall hold their office for five years from the date of entering office but shall not be eligible for reappointment.[301] In the case of appointing a person who is or has been a judge of the Supreme Court, they will be required to retire at the age of 70 years. If a person who is or has been the Chief Justice of a high court has been appointed as chairperson or judicial member of the tribunal, he shall retire at the age of 67 years. If a former or present judge of a high court has been appointed as a judicial member of the tribunal, he shall retire at the age of 67 years. An expert member shall also not hold office after he has attained the age of 65 years.

Removal

Section 10 lays down the provisions on the removal of members. The central government may, in consultation with the Chief Justice of India, remove a person from the office of the chairperson or judicial member of the tribunal in the following cases. Namely:

1 Has been adjudged an insolvent; or
2 Has been convicted of an offense which, in the opinion of the central government, involves moral turpitude; or
3 Has become physically or mentally incapable; or
4 Has acquired such financial or other interest as is likely to affect prejudicially his functions; or
5 Has so abused his position as to render his continuance in office prejudicial to the public interest.[302]

A chairperson or judicial member may only be removed from office after an inquiry made by a judge of the Supreme Court, in which such chairperson or judicial member has been informed of the charges against him and is given a reasonable opportunity of being heard in respect of those charges under Section 10 (2).

The expert member may be removed from his office by an order of the central government on the grounds specified and in accordance with the procedure notified by the central government.[303]

Jurisdiction, powers and proceedings of the tribunal

The tribunal has jurisdiction[304] over all civil cases which involve a substantial question relating to the environment and/or if such question arises out of the implementation of the certain specified enactments[305] which consist of:

1. The Water (Prevention and Control of Pollution) Act, 1974.
2. The Water (Prevention and Control of Pollution) Cess Act, 1977.
3. The Forest (Conservation) Act, 1980.
4. The Air (Prevention and Control of Pollution) Act, 1981.
5. The Environment (Protection) Act, 1986.
6. The Public Liability Insurance Act, 1991.
7. The Biological Diversity Act, 2002.

The tribunal has the authority to hear and settle such disputes and pass orders.[306] An application for adjudication of disputes has to be made within a period of six months from the date on which the cause of action arose.[307]

It should be noted that the National Green Tribunals are not vested with powers to hear matters regarding the Wildlife (Protection) Act (1972) or laws pertaining to the preservation of forests preservation etc. enacted by several state governments. Any order passed under such laws cannot be challenged before the NGT.

Section 15 contains provisions regarding relief and compensation. The NGT has the power to grant relief and compensation to persons aggrieved by any orders passed under, or by any violations of the noted enactments. An application for the grant of any compensation has to be made to the tribunal within a period of five years from the date on which the cause for such compensation or relief first arose.[308] A claim of compensation can be made for:

1. Relief and compensation to the victims of pollution and other environmental damage arising under the enactments specified.
2. For restitution of property damaged.
3. For restitution of the environment for such area or areas.[309]

The NGT is not bound by either the procedure in the Code of Civil Procedure (1908) or the rules of evidence under the Indian Evidence Act 1872. It regulates its own procedures and acts under the principles of natural justice. In certain cases, the NGT has the powers of a civil court under the 1908 Code:

1. To summon and enforce the attendance of any person and examining him on oath.

2 To cases requiring the discovery and production of documents.
3 While receiving evidence on affidavits.
4 While requisitioning any public record or document or copy of such record or document from any office.
5 While issuing commissions for the examination of witnesses or documents.
6 To review its decision.
7 While dismissing an application for default or deciding it ex parte.
8 While setting aside any order of dismissal of any application for default or any order passed by it *ex parte*.
9 To pass an interim order (including granting an injunction or stay) after providing the parties concerned an opportunity to be heard, on any application made or appeal filed under this Act.
10 To pass an order requiring any person to cease and desist from committing or causing any violation of any enactment specified in Schedule I.
11 In case of any other matter which may be prescribed.[310]

The NGT has appellate jurisdiction under Section 16 to hear any grievance concerning order, decision or direction passed by the authorities under these powers. An appeal has to be made within a period of 30 days from the date of such order. If the tribunal finds a claim to be not maintainable, vexatious or false and disallows such claim, it may order costs including lost benefits due to any interim injunction.[311]

The relief awarded under this Act is in addition to the amount payable under the Public Liability Insurance Act, 1991.[312] Compensation or relief claimed under this Act, after consideration of public health, property or environment, may be payable under separate heads.[313] An application or appeal shall be dealt with expeditiously and disposed of within a period of six months from the date of fling the application or appeal, after giving an opportunity for a hearing for the parties.[314] An award made by the tribunal shall be executable as a decree of a civil court and shall be recoverable as arrears of land revenue or public demand.[315] Any person aggrieved by an order of the tribunal may file an appeal to the Supreme Court within 90 days of the date of communication of such award.[316]

Liabilities and penalties

Under Section 17, where the accident has resulted in the death or injury to any person other than a workman or damage to any property has resulted due to an accident or adverse impact of an activity, operation or process under any of the specified enactments, the person responsible is liable to pay relief or compensation for the death, injury or damage.[317] Moreover, if such injury or damage cannot be attributed to any single person but is the resultant effect of several activities or processes, the liability for relief or compensation may be apportioned on an equitable basis by the tribunal.[318] If the offender is a company or government department, the person responsible for conducting business or department head, respectively, shall be liable. However, if the accused shows that the offense was committed without his knowledge or that he exercised due diligence to prevent the offense, then he is not to be held to be liable.

The NGT Act penalizes[319] offenders with imprisonment that may extend up to three years, or with a fine of ten crore rupees, or with both. In case of failure or continuation of non-compliance, the offender shall be liable to pay an additional fine that may extend up to 25,000 rupees every day until such contravention discontinues. If the offender is a company, then it shall be liable to a fine which extends up to 25 crore rupees and in case of failure or continuation of contravention such company shall be liable to an extra fine of one lakh rupees every day that non-compliance continues.

The decision of the majority of members is binding. In case the opinion is equally divided among the members, the issue will be decided by the chairperson.[320] All proceedings shall be treated as judicial proceedings and the tribunal shall be deemed a civil court.[321]

Financial and administrative powers of the chairman

The chairperson of the tribunal shall exercise financial and administrative powers that are vested in him under the rules made by the central government. The chairperson may delegate his financial and administrative powers to any judicial member, expert member or officer of the tribunal subject to the condition that the member or officer, while exercising such delegated power, continues to act under the direction, control and supervision of the chairperson.[322] All officials are required to discharge their functions under the chairman. Under Section 35, the central government has the power to make rules.

To date, the NGT has passed several landmark verdicts on issues like environmental pollution, forest conservation, wildlife preservation, construction and development violating environmental safeguards. It has adopted a dynamic approach in several cases being critical of the existing policies, rather than having a passive stance. For instance, in *M. C Mehta v Union of India*,[323] the NGT observed the failure of government schemes in the past worth crores of rupees that have not only failed to contain the pollution of the river Ganga but have actually increased it manifold. Remarking that a change in strategy was much needed, it ordered a prohibition of dumping or landfill sites of any kind within 500 meters from the edge of the river or any of its tributaries from the Haridwar to Unnao stretch. It further directed a complete prohibition on disposing of e-waste, biomedical waste and municipal solid waste on the floodplain or into the river Ganga or its tributaries in this stretch. To reinforce its strict view on dumping, it also imposed a fine of 50,000 rupees on anyone guilty of violating the direction. The creation of a special monitoring cell in the Uttarakhand and UP Pollution Control Board for checking water quality was also directed, along with the creation of supervisory and implementation committees having both senior central and state government officials as members. The bench also allowed state governments to raise money from people if required to fund the cleaning process of Ganga.

The NGT has also dealt with cases regarding the dumping of hazardous waste. In *MS Ashok Vihar Mitra Mandel v The Govt. of NCT of Delhi & Others*,[324] toxic trade effluents (which after treatment also produced hazardous sludge) were received by the CETP. It was alleged that this hazardous waste generated by the CETP was being indiscriminately dumped onto green belts of the areas in question. The NGT, while passing the order, stated that the indiscriminate dumping must stop or it would eventually impact groundwater, the environment and ecology. Taking up the matters of pickling industries in this case, the court also prohibited their operations and stated that such prohibition would reduce effluent load, thus reducing sludge in the process.

In November 2016, when the air quality in Delhi began to deteriorate, ultimately resulting in an environmental emergency, the NGT played an important role in effectively managing the situation. It advocated for the phased deregistration of 15-year-old diesel vehicles in Delhi, placed strict rules on incineration plants and formed a committee to inspect gas stations. It also directed a ban on disposable plastics, in effect from January 2017. Construction activity was banned in the peak stages of this emergency.[325] All these measures reflected the NGT's stance that economic hindrances should not be prioritized over environmental degradation. This stance was reiterated again in 2017, when smog covered Delhi and the NCT region for days. The orders from the previous year involving construction activities were repeated—while ensuring that daily wages of workers were paid regularly. Disappointed at the lackadaisical attitude of the stakeholders, the NGT observed that

> Holding meeting and writing letters and shifting the blame to each other for non-performance and non-cooperation can hardly be an excuse for meeting such environmental emergency. No party, statutory bodies or even the citizens can be mere spectators to such environmental crisis and there has to be concerted effort in discharging of constitutional and statutory duty by all concerned to ensure that the people do not suffer from health hazards because of non-performance from the concerned quarters. The doctrine of preventive and precautionary principle

with greater emphasis on inter-generational equity has been violated, ignored at every relevant stages.[326]

Failing to find a "plausible explanation" for its prior orders not being followed, the NGT lashed out at civic bodies such as Central Pollution Control Board (CPCB) and Delhi Pollution Control Committee (DPCC) for not making any effort to test serious pollutants like carbon monoxide and sulfur dioxide. It also asked authorities to deregister diesel vehicles more than ten years old altogether. Regular cleaning of roads, preferably by manual vacuum along with sprinkling water, was also directed to prevent particulate matter from rising into the air.

The scheme of labeling environment-friendly products

In a resolution, the Ministry of Environment and Forests introduced a novel scheme that provides accreditation and labeling for household and other consumer products which meet certain environmental criteria, along with the quality requirement of the Indian Standards for that product, to be operated on a national basis[327]. The label shall be known as an "ECO MARK." Any product which is made, used or disposed of in a way that significantly reduces the harm it would otherwise cause to the environment could be considered an environment-friendly product.[328]

The scheme was introduced:

1 To provide an incentive for manufacturers and importers to reduce the adverse environmental impact of productivity.
2 To reward genuine initiatives by companies to reduce the adverse environmental impact of their products.
3 To assist consumers to become environmentally responsible in their daily lives by providing information to take account of environmental factors in their purchase decisions.
4 To encourage citizens to purchase products that have less harmful environmental impacts; and
5 To improve the quality of the environment and to encourage sustainable management of resources.[329]

The environmental criteria for each product category will be notified by the central government and, thereafter, shall be translated into Indian Standards by the Bureau of Indian Standards. The criteria shall be for broad environmental levels and aspects, but will be specific at product levels. Under this scheme, all products will be examined in terms of the main following environmental impacts:

1 That they have substantially less potential for pollution than other comparable products in production, usage and disposal.
2 That they are recycled, recyclable and made from recycled products or biodegradable where comparable products are not.
3 That they make a significant contribution to saving non-renewable resources, including non-renewable energy sources and natural sources, compared with comparable products.
4 That the product must contribute to a reduction of the adversary primary criteria which has the highest environmental impact associated with the use of the product and which will specifically set for each of the product categories.[330]

The Ministry of Environment and Forests recently put forward a proposal to introduce compulsory Environmental Impact Assessments (EIAs) for all industrial projects in both private and public sectors costing ten crores rupees or more. The proposal seeks to integrate environmental aspects at the project formulation stage itself.[331]

The preceding analysis gives a detailed account of the legislations, its provisions and the several resulting rules adopted on the management of hazardous substances in India. The debates, discussions and cases decided amply demonstrate their role of the legislation in protecting and safeguarding the environment in India.

Notes

1 Planning Commission, *Report of the Planning Commission of India—Sixth Five Year Plan 198–85* (New Delhi, 1981) 9.
2 The committee members were appointed for a two-year term. The members of NCEPC increased from 14 in 1972 to 24 in 1977 to 35 in 1979.
3 Armin Rosencranz, Shyam Divan, Martha L. Noble, *Environmental Law and Policy in India* (NM Tripathi Pvt Ltd, 1991) 43.
4 Government of India, Ninth 5-year plan, Environment and Forest Overview http://planning-commission.gov.in/plans/planrel/fiveyr/9th/vol2/v2c8.htm. Accessed 27 December 2017.
5 Ministry of Environment and Forests, National Environment Policy 2006, Government of India, http://www.moef.gov.in/sites/default/files/introduction-nep2006e.pdf. Accessed 27 December 2017.
6 No. 29 of 1986, 23 May 1988.
7 In passing the Act, the government felt that although existing laws generally focus on specific types of pollution or specific categories of hazardous substances they do not cover major or areas of environmental hazards. Further, control mechanisms to guard against the slow, insidious build-up of hazardous substances, especially new chemicals, in the environment are weak. See the *Gazette of India*, Extraordinary. Pt. II, Section 1, dated 26 May 1986.
8 Environment Protection Act 1986, Section 3(2) (VII).
9 Ibid., Section 3 (2) (iii).

10 Ibid., Section 3 (2) (iii).
11 Ibid., Section 3 (2) (iv).
12 Ibid., Section 3 (2) (v).
13 Ibid., Section 3 (2) (vi).
14 Ibid., Section 3 (2) (vii).
15 Ibid., Section 3 (2) (ix).
16 Ibid., Section 3 (2) (x).
17 Ibid., Section 3 (2) (xi).
18 Ibid., Section 6 (1). Under this Section the central government may, by notification in the *Official Gazette,* makes rules in respect of: "the procedures and safeguards for the handling of hazardous substances." Ibid., Section 6 (2) (c).
19 Ibid., Section 2 (d).
20 Ibid., Section 3.
21 Ibid., Section 6 (2) (b).
22 Ibid., Section 6 (2) (c).
23 Ibid., Section 6 (2) (d).
24 Ibid., Section 6 (2) (e).
25 Ibid., Section 6 (2) (f).
26 Ibid., Section 8.
27 Empowered to do so under Ibid., Section 10 (1).
28 Ibid., Sections 10 (1) (a) and (b).
29 Ibid., Section 11.
30 Appointed under Section 13 of the Act by the government from persons having prescribed qualifications.
31 Ibid., Section 12 (1).
32 Ibid., Section 10 (2).
33 Ibid., Section 10 (3).
34 Ibid., Section 15 (1).
35 Ibid., Section 15 (2).
36 Ibid., Section 18.
37 Ibid., Section 25 (2) (a).
38 Ibid., Section 25 (2) (b).
39 Ibid., Section 25 (2) (d) read with Section 11 (1).
40 S.O. 844 (E), dated 19 November 1986.
41 Made while exercising the powers conferred under Section 6 and 25 of the EP Act 1986.
42 Environment Protection Rules 1986, Rule 5.
43 Ibid., Rule 6.
44 Ibid., Rule 7.
45 Ibid., Rule 8.
46 Ibid., Rule 9.
47 Ibid., Rule 10.
48 Ibid., Rule 11.
49 Ibid., Rule 13.
50 The expert meeting was held from 22–24 August 1986.
51 Upendra Baxi, *Environment Protection Act: An Agenda for Implementation* (NM Tripathi 1987).
52 Transportation of Dangerous/Hazardous Substances by Road Order of Transport Commissioner, Maharastra State. Published in the *Maharashtra Government Gazette* (Part osl central Sr. No. 2, dated 1 January 1986) 5.
53 Ibid.

54 Upendra Baxi, *Environment Protection Act: An Agenda for Implementation* (NM Tripathi 1987) 68–69.
55 Transportation of Dangerous Hazardous Substances by Road Transport Commissioner. Maharashtra State. Order No. MVH 3885/D-II (2) THCR/on 1127 dated 1 July 1986.
56 Ibid.
57 Upendra Baxi, *Environment Protection Act: An Agenda for Implementation* (NM Tripathi 1987) 66.
58 Section 3 (1) of the Environment Protection Act 1986 provides: "subject to the provisions of this Act, the Central Government shall have the power to take all such measures as it deems necessary or expedient for the purpose of protecting and improving the quality of the environment and preventing, controlling and abating environmental pollution."
59 Government Order No. 287 was issued on 2 June 1989 in *Gazette of India* (1989) 142–56.
60 "Class label," in relation to any dangerous or hazardous goods, means the class label specified in column three of the table in Rule 137.
61 Rules and regulations in 1989 under Section 3(1) of Environment Protection Act 1986, Rule 130.
62 Ibid., Rule 131 (2).
63 See Table III, List of Hazardous and Toxic Chemicals, Government Order of 2 June 1989 [149–56].
64 GSR NO 395(E) dated 4 April 2016.
65 Initially, the Hazardous Wastes (Management and Handling) Rules were enacted in 1989. These rules were subsequently superseded in 2008 by the Hazardous Wastes (Management, Handling and Transboundary Movement) Rules. In 2016, these Rules were again re-notified by the Hazardous and Other Wastes (Management and Transboundary Movement) Rules.
66 Specified in Part B and Part D of Schedule III of the Hazardous Waste Rules 2016.
67 Hazardous and Other Wastes Rules 2016, Rule 2 (a) (b) (c).
68 Hazardous and Other Wastes Rules 2016, Rule 5 (1).
69 Hazardous and Other Wastes Rules 2016, Rule 5 (2).
70 Ibid., Rule 5 (3).
71 Ibid., Rule 6 (1).
72 Ibid., Rule IV.
73 Ibid., Rule 6 (2).
74 Ibid.
75 Given in Schedule IV of the Rules.
76 Hazardous and Other Wastes Rules 2016, Rule 6 (2).
77 Ibid., Rule 6 (3).
78 Ibid., Rule 6 (4).
79 Ibid., Rule 6 (7).
80 Ibid., Rule 6 (8).
81 Ibid., Rule 6 (5).
82 Ibid., Rule 8 (1) lists these cases: (1) small generators (up to ten tons per annum) up to 180 days of their annual capacity; (2) actual users and disposal facility operators up to 180 days of their annual capacity; (3) occupiers who do not have access to any treatment, storage, disposal facility in the concerned state; or (4) the waste which needs to be specifically stored for development of a process for its recycling, recovery, pre-processing, co-processing or utilization; (5) in any other case, on justifiable grounds up to 180 days.

83 Ibid., Rule 9 (1).
84 Ibid., Rule 9 (2).
85 However, the actual users shall ensure compliance to the standards notified under the Environment (Protection) Act 1986 (29 of 1986), for cement plant with respect to co-processing of waste and until the time the standards are notified, the procedure as applicable to other kind of utilization of hazardous and other waste shall be followed.
86 Hazardous and Other Wastes Rules 2016, Rule 12(1).
87 Ibid., Rule 12 (2).
88 Ibid., Rule 12 (3).
89 Ibid., Schedule VI.
90 Ibid., Rule 12 (6).
91 Ibid., part B of Schedule 3.
92 Ibid., Rule 12 (4).
93 Ibid., part D of Schedule 3.
94 Ibid., listed in part A and part B of schedule III and schedule VI.
95 Ibid., Rule 12 (7).
96 Ibid., Rule 12 (8).
97 Ibid., Rule 13 (1).
98 Ibid., Rule 13 (2).
99 Ibid., Rule 13 (3).
100 Ibid., Rule 13 (4).
101 Ibid., Rule 13 (5).
102 Ibid., Rule 13 (6).
103 Ibid., Rule 13 (7).
104 Ibid., Rule 13 (8).
105 Ibid., Rule 13 (9).
106 Ibid., Rule 13 (10).
107 Ibid., Rule 14 (1).
108 Ibid., Rule 14 (2).
109 Ibid., Rule 14 (3).
110 Ibid., Rule 14 (4).
111 Ibid., Rule 14 (5).
112 Ibid., Rule 14 (6).
113 Ibid., Rule 15 (1).
114 Ibid., Rule 15 (2).
115 Ibid., Rule 15 (3).
116 Ibid., Rule 16 (3).
117 Ibid., Rule 16 (4).
118 Ibid., Rule 16 (5).
119 Ibid., Rule 16 (6).
120 Ibid., Form 8 of the Rules.
121 Ibid., Rule 17 (2).
122 Ibid., Rule 18 (3).
123 Ibid., Rule 18 (4).
124 Ibid., Rule 18 (5).
125 Ibid., Rule 18 (6).
126 Ibid., Rule 18 (7).
127 Listed in column two of Schedule 7.
128 Rules for the Manufacture, Use, Import, Export and Storage of Hazardous Micro Organisms/Genetically Engineered Organisms or Cells 1989, Rule 7 (1); the three-month time period may be reduced by the concerned authority.

129 Ibid., Rule 8.
130 The report must be in accordance with the conditions laid down in Schedule 8. Which includes (1) the name and address of the person furnishing information; (2) description of the industrial activity; (3) description of the processes; (4) description of the hazardous chemicals generated; (5) information on the preliminary hazard analysis; (6) description of information on organizational systems used to carry on the industrial activity safety; (7) information on assessment of the consequences of major accidents; (8) information on the mitigation of major accidents; (9) description of safety relevant units and (10) information on the hazard assessment.
131 Rules for the Manufacture, Use, Import, Export and Storage of Hazardous Micro Organisms or Genetically Engineered Organisms or Cells 1989, Rule 10 (3).
132 Ibid., Rule 11 (1).
133 Ibid., Rule 11 (2).
134 Ibid., Rule 12.
135 As mentioned in column 2 of schedule 5.
136 Rules for the Manufacture, Use, Import, Export and Storage of Hazardous Microorganisms or Genetically Engineered Organisms or Cells 1989, Rule 14 (1).
137 This includes information relating to the nature, extent and likely effects offsite of possible major accidents.
138 Cases relating to existing industrial activities.
139 As outlined in part two of Schedule 1 and listed in column two of part two of Schedule 1. Part one of Schedule 1 deals with toxic chemicals, flammable chemicals and explosives and part two gives a list, of as many as 434 hazardous chemicals.
140 Schedule 9 provides the safety data sheet relating to chemical identity.
141 Manufacture, Storage and Import of Hazardous Chemicals Rules 1989, Rule 17 (3).
142 Ibid., Rule 17 (4).
143 As identified in column two of Schedule 5. As many as nine authorities are identified with legal backing.
144 Ibid., Rule 18 (2).
145 Ibid., Rule 18 (3).
146 Ibid., Rule 18 (4).
147 Ibid., as specified in Schedule 10.
148 Ibid., Rule 18 (5).
149 Manufacture, Storage and Import of Hazardous Chemicals Rules 1989, schedule 1
150 Ibid., Rule 19.
151 Ibid., Rule 20.
152 Notification of 5 December 1989. Published in the Gazette of India Extraordinary part II, s 3(1), 5 December 1989 1–19.
153 Rules for the Manufacture, Use, Import, Export and Storage of Hazardous Micro Organisms or Genetically Engineered Organisms or Cells, 1989; According to rule 3 (i) "Biotechnology" means the application of scientific and engineering principles to the processing of materials by biological agents to produce goods and services.
154 The seat of this committee is in the Department of Biotechnology.

155 Rules for the Manufacture, Use, Import, Export and Storage of Hazardous Micro Organisms or Genetically Engineered Organisms or Cells 1989, Rule 4 (2).
156 The RCGM consists of representatives from (a) Department of Biotechnology (b) Indian Council of Medical Research; (c) Indian Council of Agricultural Research; (d) Council of Scientific and Industrial Research; and (e) Other experts in their industrial activity.
157 Under Rule 4 (4) the Genetic Engineering Approval Committee consists of (1) chairman who is Additional Secretary, Department of Environment, Forests and Wild life, Representative of Department of Biotechnology who is the co-chairman; (2) Member representatives of the concerned Agencies and Departments, namely, Ministry of Industrial Development, Department of Biotechnology and the Department of Atomic Energy, as members; (3) Director General of Indian Council of Agricultural Research, Director General of Indian Council of Medical Research, Director General of the Council of Scientific and Industrial Research, Director General of Health Services, Plant Protection Advisor of the Directorate of Pliant Protection "Quarantine and storage; Chairman, Central Pollution Control Board and three experts in individual capacity, as expert members. The committee may even co-opt other members/ experts if necessary.
158 Environment Protection Act 1986.
159 The SBCC consists of the following members (1) Chief Secretary of the State as its chairman; (2) Secretary, Department of Environment; Secretary, Department of Health; Secretary, Department of Agriculture; Secretary, Department of Industries and Commerce; Secretary, Department of Forests; Secretary, Department of Public Works; Chief Engineer, Department of Public Health Engineering; State Microbiologists and Pathologists and Chairman of State Pollution Control Board as members. The SBCC may co-opt other members/ experts, if necessary.
160 The District Committee consists of the District Collector as its Chairman, Factory Inspector, a representative of the Pollution Control Board, Chief Medical Officer (CMO), District Agricultural Officer, a representative of the Public Health Engineering Department, District Microbiologists, Pathologist; Commissioner, Municipal Corporation and such other co-opted members, if necessary, as its members.
161 Rules for the Manufacture, Use, Import, Export and Storage of Hazardous Micro Organisms/Genetically Engineered Organisms or Cells 1989, Rule 4 (6).
162 Ibid., Rule 7 (2).
163 Ibid., Rule 7 (3).
164 The release is prohibited even for the purpose of experiment. But then in special cases under Rule 9 (2) the GEAC may give permission for deliberate releases.
165 Rules for the Manufacture, Use, Import, Export and Storage of Hazardous Micro Organisms/Genetically Engineered Organisms or Cells 1989, Rules 8, 9, 10 and 11.
166 Ibid., Rule 12.
167 Ibid., Rule 13 (2).
168 Ibid., Rule 13 (2) (a) (b) (c).
169 Ibid., Rule 13 as per Rule 14.
170 Ibid., Rule 14 (2).
171 Ibid., Rule 15.

172 Ibid., Rule 15 (3).
173 Ibid., Rule 15 (3).
174 Ibid., Rule 15 (4).
175 Ibid., Rule 16 (1).
176 Ibid., Rule 17 (2).
177 Ibid., Rule 18 (1).
178 Ibid., Rule 18 (2).
179 Ibid., Rule 19 (1).
180 Ibid., Rule 20.
181 The Factories Act 1948 (Act No. LXIII of 1948) came into force on 1 April 1948. The Act provides for the health safety welfare and other aspects of workers in factories. The Act is enforced by state governments through their factory inspectors.
182 Sumeet Malik, *P.L. Malik's Industrial Law* (25th edn, Lucknow Eastern Book 2017).
183 The First Schedule gives a list of 29 industries involving hazardous processes. They are: Ferrous Metallurgical industries, non-ferrous metallurgical industries, foundries, coal industries, power generating industries, pulp and paper industries, fertilizer industries, cement industries, petroleum industries, petrol chemical industries, drugs and pharmaceutical industries, fermentation industries, rubber industries, leather tanning industries, electroplating industries, chemical industries, insecticides, fungicides, herbicides and other pesticides industries, synthetic resin and plastic, man-made fiber industry, paints and pigment industries, manufacture and repair of electrical accumulators, glass and ceramics, grinding or glazing of metals, manufacture, handling and processing of asbestos and its products, extraction of oils and fats from vegetable and animal sources, manufacture, handling and use of benzene and substances containing benzene, manufacturing processes and operations involving carbon disulfide, dyes and dyestuff including their intermediates. Highly flammable liquids and gas. This list may be amended by way of addition, omission, or variation of any industry by the state government in the form of a notification in the **Official Gazette**.
184 Factories Act 1948, Sections 7 (2) (a) (b) (c) (d) and (e).
185 Ibid., s 7 (3).
186 Factories Act, s 38 (2).
187 Factories (Amendment) Act 1987, s 41A (1).
188 The Site Appraisal Committee consists of the following members:

(a) The Chief Inspector of the state who shall be its chairman.
(b) A representative of the Central Board for the Prevention and Control of Water Pollution appointed by the central government under Section 3 of the Water (Prevention and Control of Pollution) Act, 1974.
(c) A representative of the Central Board for the Prevention and Control of Air Pollution referred to in Section 3 of the Air (Prevention and Control of Pollution) Act, 1981.
(d) A representative of the state board appointed under Section 4 of the Water (Prevention and Control of Pollution) Act, 1974.
(e) A representative of the State Board for the Prevention and Control of Air Pollution referred in Section 5 of the Air (Prevention and Control of Pollution) Act, 1981.
(f) A representative of the Department of Environment in the State.
(g) A representative of the Meteorological Department of the Government of India.
(h) An expert in the field of occupational health; and
  (i) A representative of the Town Planning Department of a state government and not more than five other members who may be co-opted by the state government who shall be (1) a scientist with specialized knowledge of the hazardous process which

will be involved in the factory; (2) a representative of the local authority within whose jurisdiction the, factory is to be established;

(ii) not more than three other persons as deemed fit by the state government.

189 Factories (Amendment) Act 1987, Section 41(A) (2).

190 Ibid., Section 41(A) (4).

191 Ibid., Section 41(A) (3).

192 The information must include accurate information as to the quantity, specifications and other characteristics of wastes and the manner of their disposal—Factories (Amendment) Act 1987, Section 41 B (3).

193 Ibid., Section 41 B (2).

194 Factories (Amendment) Act 1987, Section 41 B (4).

195 This information must be given within 30 days if the factory engaged in a hazardous process before the commencement of the Factories Act, 1987. In cases where the factory proposes to engage in a hazardous process at any time after the commencement of the 1987 amendments to the Factories Act, the time limit to inform the chief inspector would be 30 days before the commencement of such process. Section 41B (5) (a) and (b) of the Factories Act.

196 License to a factory is issued under Section 6 of the Act.

197 Factories (Amendment) Act 1987, Section 41B (6).

198 Ibid., Section 41 B (7).

199 Ibid., Section 41 C (a).

200 Ibid., Section 41 C (u).

201 Ibid., Section 41 C (c).

202 Ibid., Section 41 D (1).

203 Ibid., Section 41 D (2)

204 Ibid., Section 41 D (3).

205 Ibid., Section 41 E (1).

206 Ibid., Section 41 E (2). As had been incorporated in the rules made under this act.

207 Ibid., Section 41 F (1).

208 Ibid., Section 41 F (2).

209 Ibid., Section 41 G (1). The reasons for exempting the setting up of such committees must also be given by a state government. The composition of the safety committee, the tenure of office of its members and their rights and duties must also be laid down.

210 Ibid., Section 41 H (1).

211 Ibid., Section 41 H (2).

212 See (1991) XXXII *Lucknow Law Times* 30–32.

213 Public Liability Insurance Act 1991, preamble.

214 The maximum relief under this act is Rs.25,000/per person for fatal accidents in addition to reimbursement of medical expenses, if any, incurred on the victim up to a maximum of 12,000 rupees. However, the availability of immediate relief would not prevent the victims to go to courts for claiming larger compensation. See the schedule to Section 3 (1) of the Public Liability Insurance Act, 1991, See Section 3 (1) (ii).

215 "Workman" under the explanation to Section 3, "workman": has the meaning assigned to it in the Workmen's Compensation Act 1923.

216 Md. A. M. Nomani, 'Law Relating to Environmental Liability and Dispute Redressal: Emergence and Dimension' (1996) XXIII (1 and 2) IBR (1996).

217 The Public Liability Insurance Act 1991, Section 2 (a).

218 Ibid.
219 Ibid.
220 World Nuclear Association, *Nuclear Power in India* (January 2017). http://www.worldnuclear.org/information-library/country-profiles/countries-g-n/india.aspx#ECSArticleLink1. Accessed 5 January 2017. The Atomic Energy Establishment was set up at Trombay, near Mumbai, in 1957 and renamed as Bhabha Atomic Research Centre (BARC) ten years later. The Indian Atomic Energy Commission is the main policy body. The Nuclear Power Corporation of India Ltd (NPCIL) is responsible for the design, construction, commissioning and operation of thermal nuclear power plants. At the start of 2010, it said it had enough cash on hand for 10,000 MWe of a new plant. The 1962 Atomic Energy Act prohibits private control of nuclear power generation, and 2016 amendments allowing public sector joint ventures do not extend to private sector companies, nor allow direct foreign investment in nuclear power, apart from the supply chain.
221 The Public Liability Insurance Act 1991, Section 2 (d).
222 Ibid.
223 S. N. Singh, 'Public Liability Insurance Act, 1991—Scope for making Provisions More Effective' [1991] 5 Corporate L Adv 234.
224 *U.P. State Electricity Board and another v District Magistrate, Dehradun and others* AIR 1998 All 1.
225 Ibid. 6.
226 The Environment (Protection) Act, 1986, Section 2(e); Hazard substance means any substance or preparation which, by reasons of its chemical or physico-chemical properties of handling, is liable to cause harm to human beings, other living creatures, plants, microorganism, property or the environment.
227 *M.P. State Electricity Board and Anr v Collector* and Ors. AIR 2003 MP 156; *Rahim and Another v Collector and Others* 2008 SCC Online All 1172; *Mankunwar v Chairman and Anr.*\ MANU/MP/0401/2010; *Smt. Sumta Tiwari v State of U.P. and Ors.* MANU/ UP/2631/2010; *Additional Secretary Officer In-charge of The Case Executive Engineer M.P. Poorv Kshetra Vidhyut Vitr v Siyaram Yadav* 2014 SCC Online MP 1438.
228 The Public Liability Insurance Act 1991, Section 2 (d).
229 Vikram Raghavan, Public Liability Insurance Act: Breaking New Ground for Indian Environmental Law, 39 [1997] JILI 108.
230 The Public Liability Insurance Act 1991, Section 2 (h) (ii).
231 Vikram Raghavan, Public Liability Insurance Act: Breaking New Ground for Indian Environmental Law, 39 [1997] JILI 108, '*Are Industrial Accident Victims Adequately Insured', The Financial Express* (20 June 2010) http://www.financialexpress.com/archive/are-industrial-accident-victims-adequately-insu red/635 999/. Accessed 24 December 2016.
232 The Public Liability Insurance Act 1991, Section 3.
233 Ibid., Section 3 (2).
234 A.K Tiwari, *Environmental Laws in India: Contribution of Supreme Court* (Deep & Deep Publications, 2006) 159.
235 Vikram Raghavan, Public Liability Insurance Act: Breaking New Ground for Indian Environmental Law, 39 [1997] JILI 108.
236 The Public Liability Insurance Act 1991, Section 3, explanation (i).
237 Ibid., Section 3 (1).
238 Ibid., schedule (ii).
239 Ibid., schedule (iii).

240 Ibid., schedule (iv).
241 Ibid., Section 6.
242 Ibid., Section 7 (7). (There have been conflicting interpretations on this topic which have been addressed later in the paper).
243 Ibid., Section 4.
244 Ibid., Section 4 (2A).
245 Ibid., Section 4 (2B).
246 Ibid., Section 4 (3).
247 Priyesh Sharma,'India: Treatment of Doctrine of Privity by the Indian Judiciary' *(Vaish Associates Advocates,* 11 June 2013) http:ZZwww.mondaq.com/india/xZ243778/Contract+Law/Treatment+Of+Doctrine+Of+Privity+By+Indian+Judiciary. Accessed 2 March 2018.
248 Once the said suit is filed by the insured owner, the victim will have to wait till a contractual breach is established and thereafter an order regarding compensation is passed.
249 P. N Bhagwati,'Supreme Court judgement on Bhopal gas tragedy' *(India Today,* 15 March 1989) http://indiatoday.intoday.in/story/supreme-court-judgement-on-bhopal-gas-tragedy/1/323236.html. Accessed 2 March 2017.
250 The Public Liability Insurance Act 1991, Section 7.
251 Ibid., Section 4 (2C).
252 Ibid., Section 5.
253 Ibid., Sections 6 (1) (a) and 6 (1) (b).
254 Ibid., Section 6 (1) (c).
255 A. K. Tiwari, *Environmental Laws in India: Contribution of Supreme Court* (Deep & Deep Publications 2006) 159.
256 Public Liability Insurance Act 1991, Section 7 (7A).
257 Ibid., Section 7 (3).
258 Ali Mehdi, 'the Public Liability Insurance Act, 1991—A Critical Appraisal' (1992) AIR Jour. 38.
259 *M.P.S.E.B. v The Collector and Ors.* MANU/MP/0489/2003.
260 *UP Power Corporation Ltd & Anr. v Kaleemullah & Ors.* (2010) 4 All LJ 11.
261 Ibid. 11.
262 Ibid. 12.
263 The Public Liability Insurance Act 1991, Section 8.
264 Ibid., Section 9.
265 Ibid., Section 10.
266 Ibid., Section 11.
267 Ibid., Section 11 (2).
268 Ibid., Section 11 (3).
269 Ibid., Section 12.
270 Ibid., Section 13.
271 Ibid., Section 14.
272 Ibid., Section 15.
273 Ibid., Section 16.
274 Ibid., Section 17.
275 Ibid., Section 19.
276 Ibid., Section 20.
277 Ibid., Section 21.
278 Ibid., Section 22.

279 Law Commission of India, *Proposal to Constitute Environmental Courts* (186th Report, September 2003) 6. http://lawcommissionofindia.nic.in/reports/186th%20report.pdf. Accessed 14 October 2017.

280 Due to the rising number of environmental problems in India, the National Environmental Tribunal Act 1995 was enacted to adjudicate cases on such matters and provide relief as necessary. It was repealed by the National Green Tribunal Act, 2010.

281 Law Commission of India, *Proposal to Constitute Environmental Courts* (186th Report, September 2003) 6. http://lawcommissionofindia.nic.in/reports/186th%20report.pdf. Accessed 14 October 2017.

282 Ibid.

283 Environmental courts were previously suggested in two judgments: In *M.C Mehta v Union of India* 1986 SCC 17, the Supreme Court stated that in as much as environment cases involve assessment of scientific data, it was desirable to set up environment courts on a regional basis with a professional judge and two experts, keeping in view the expertise required for such adjudication. There should be an appeal to the Supreme Court on the decision of the environment court. In *Indian Council for Enviro-Legal Action v Union of India* 1996(3) SCC 212, the Supreme Court further stated that environmental courts with civil and criminal jurisdiction must be established to deal with environmental issues promptly. See Law Commission of India, *Proposal to Constitute Environmental Courts* (186th Report, September 2003) 6 http://lawcommissionofindia.nic.in/reports/186th%20report.pdf. Accessed 14 October 2017.

284 The National Green Tribunal Act, 2010 (Act 19 of 2010).

285 India was a party to the decisions taken at the United Nations Conference on the Human Environment held in Stockholm in June 1972 which called upon the states to take appropriate steps for the protection and improvement of the human environment; India also participated in the United Nations Conference on Environment and Development held at Rio de Janeiro in June 1992, which called upon the states to provide effective access to judicial and administrative proceedings, including redress and remedy and to develop national laws regarding liability and compensation for the victims of pollution and other environmental damage. See the preamble to the National Green Tribunal Act (2010).

286 National Green Tribunal Act (2010), preamble.

287 It was enacted to set up National Environment Appellate Authority to hear cases where environmental clearances were required in certain areas. However, the Act was criticized for its limited mandate of providing a forum for reviewing the administrative decisions on environmental impact assessments. Apart from this, judicial members had also not been appointed for the authority for a long time. Hence, the Act was subsequently repealed.

288 National Green Tribunal Act 2010, Section 20.

289 Ibid., Section 3 (1).

290 Ibid., Section 3 (2).

291 Ibid., Section 3 (3).

292 The number of expert members shall, in hearing an application or appeal, be equal to the number of judicial members hearing the same.

293 Ibid., Section 4.

294 Ibid., Section 6 (1).

295 Ibid., Section 6 (2).

296 Ibid., Section 6 (3).

297 Ibid., Section 5 (1). A person who is or has been the judge of a high court shall also be qualified to be appointed as a judicial member.
298 Ibid., Section 5 (2).
299 Ibid., Section 5 (3).
300 Ibid., Section 5 (4). This provision will not apply to any employee under the central or state government, local authority, statutory authority or any corporation established by any central, state or provincial act or a government company.
301 National Green Tribunal Act 2010, Section 7; in case a person, who is or has been a judge of the Supreme Court, has been appointed as chairperson or judicial member of the tribunal, he shall not hold office after he has attained the age of 70 years. If a person, who is or has been the Chief Justice of a high court, has been appointed as chairperson or judicial member of the tribunal shall not hold office after he has attained the age of 67 years. If a person, who is or has been a judge of a High Court, has been appointed as a judicial member of the tribunal, shall not hold office after he has attained the age of 67 years. An expert member shall not hold office after he has attained the age of 65 years.
302 Under Section 10 (3), the person against whom the inquiry is being made may be suspended from office by the central government until an order is passed by the same on receipt of the report of such inquiry.
303 National Green Tribunal Act 2010, Section 10(5). The expert member shall not be removed unless he has been given an opportunity of being heard in the matter.
304 National Green Tribunal Act 2010, Section 14.
305 These enactments are specified in Schedule I of the Act.
306 Ibid.
307 Ibid., Section 14 (3); The tribunal may, if it is satisfied that the applicant had sufficient cause for not applying within the given period, allow it to be filed within a further period not exceeding 60 days.
308 The tribunal may, if it is satisfied that the applicant was prevented by sufficient cause from applying within the given period, allow a further period not exceeding 60 days. See National Green Tribunal Act 2010, Section 15 (3).
309 National Green Tribunal Act 2010, Section 15 (1).
310 Ibid., Section 19 (4).
311 Ibid., Section 23.
312 Ibid., Section 15 (2).
313 Ibid., Section 15 (4). Such heads are specified in Schedule II.
314 Ibid., Section 18 (3).
315 Ibid., Section 24.
316 Ibid., Section 22.
317 Ibid., Section 17 (1).
318 Ibid., Section 17 (2).
319 Ibid., Section 26.
320 Ibid., Section 21.
321 Ibid., Section 18 (5).
322 Ibid., Section 13.
323 *M.C Mehta v Union of India* order dated 13 July 2017, National Green Tribunal, Delhi. http://nmcg.nic.in/writereaddata/fileupload/39_NGTOrder.pdf. Accessed on 23 November 2017.
324 *M/s Ashok Vihar Mitra Mandel v The Govt. of NCT of Delhi & Others* order passed on 22 September 2016 National Green Tribunal, Delhi http://admin.ind

iaenvironmentportal.org.in/files/pickling%20industry%20Delhi%20NGT%20Order.pdf. Accessed on 23 November 2017.

325 Padampriya Govindarajan 'How India's National Green Tribunal Upheld Environmental Protections in 2016' 3 January 2017, *The Diplomat*. https://thediplomat.com/2017/01/how-indias-national-green-tribunal-upheld-environmental-protections-in-2016/. Accessed on 21 November 2017.

326 Delhi pollution case: multiple petitions were heard together. Order passed on 9 November 2017, National Green Tribunal, by its principal bench at Delhi. http://www.indiaenvironmentportal.org.in/files/ambient%20air%20quality%20NGT%20Order.pdf. Accessed on 21 November 2017.

327 Resolution of 20 February 1991 of the Department of Environment, Forests and Wildlife, Ministry of Environment and Forests, G.S.R. 85(E), Gazette of India Extraordinary; part II, 21 February 1991.

328 *Gazette of India* Part II (21 February 1991), Section 3 (1).

329 Ibid.

330 P.S Sangal, 'Some Recent Developments in the Field of Environment; Prospects for the Future' [1991] 13 Delhi Law Review 59.

331 Ibid., 61. See also Ministry of Environment and Forests, 'Achievements and Initiatives of Ministry of Environment and Forests during last 100 days' (1991) 2.

5 Disability, Disaster and the Law

Legislating Disability Inclusive Disaster Risk Reduction

Deepa Sonpal

Disaster laws ignore 'disability'

Is there a legal right for a person with disability to be protected against disasters? Is there a state liability in failing to ensure this right? Adrien A. Weibgen (2015, p. 2202) analyses the legal responsibilities of state agencies and departments towards marginalized communities in times of crisis and argues that people with disabilities (PWDs) have a 'right to be rescued', 'a legal right to have their unique needs accounted for and addressed in emergency planning'. He has argued that 'such planning is not merely morally correct; it is legally required, and it is critical that local governments get their plans in order before the next storms, and lawsuits, come'.

During post-tsunami, the news crew for Japan Broadcasting Corporation's Fukushi (Welfare) Network program me disclosed the much-anguished data that 'the mortality rate due to the Great East Japan Earthquake for persons with disabilities (2.06%) was twice that for the general population (1.03%). In addition, at facilities with many bedridden elderly residents, more than half of the residents perished. A survey of Hyogo prefecture clearly reveals that for the Great Hanshin-Awaji Earthquake, half of the fatalities were 65 or older, and according to the National Police Agency, at least 65% of victims in the Great East Japan Earthquake were 60 or older' (Nogiwa, 2013). Inclusive disaster policies and a disability-sensitive disaster law and management are a serious concern involving more and more researchers now from those who work on children, on the elderly, on various categories of disabilities. Disability is a much-debated concept globally as well as in the Indian context. There is no acceptable definition of disability that is followed, and hence there are variations in the enumeration and the prevalence rate. The World Health Organization (WHO-ICF, 2001; WHO-WB, 2011) has evolved an International Classification of Functioning,

DOI: 10.4324/9781003299561-5

Disability and Health or ICF which emphasises that environmental factors lead to disability – socio-cultural, economic, political and physical barriers in the environment – causing activity limitation and restricting participation in many aspects of life. The United Nations Convention on the Rights of Persons with Disabilities (UNCRPD) recognises that 'disability is an evolving concept and that disability results from the interaction between persons with impairments and attitudinal and environmental barriers that hinders their full and effective participation in society on an equal basis with others'.

The *World Report on Disability* (2011) claims that 15 per cent of the global population comprises of persons with disabilities. In India the Census 2001 and 2011 claims it to be a little above 2 per cent. Other informal sources have estimated around 5 to 6 per cent (WB, 2007). Disability is a phenomenon that may occur to any one at any point of time in their life cycle. Hence, the actual extent remains to be computed to be able to derive effective strategies of redressal, provisioning for budgeting and formulating any programme of action and for advocacy.

In recent times, the understanding of disasters has expanded due to issues faced in the context of global warming. Disasters are both natural and man-made which affect different sections of the populations differently depending on their coping mechanism and the context in which they are situated. Among the vulnerable/marginalised groups that are excluded from development processes, persons with disabilities remain the most alienated, specifically in disaster situations. Persons with disabilities are disproportionately affected by disasters, and disasters, in turn, can result in an increase in the number of persons with disabilities, from both direct and indirect actions (HI, 2005; CBM, 2013). For both these groups, the process of overcoming the short-term and long-term consequences of disaster is rather cumbersome due to their already-vulnerable states – the socio-economic status, lack of voice and the inaccessible evacuation, response and recovery efforts in most disaster situations. There is a greater likelihood of persons with disabilities being abandoned due to lack of planning, inaccessible transport, facilities (camps/shelters) and services (HI, 2005; CBM, 2013). Disaster situations create new impairments and disabilities. While persons impaired during a disaster may be visible, those that are more likely to be neglected are persons with disabilities existing prior to the disaster.

Persons with disabilities face stigma, abandonment, neglect and invisibility (Dalal, 2000), and this is enhanced during emergency and disaster situations where survival of the fittest prevails. Persons with disabilities are poorest of the poor and are entrapped in a vicious cycle of poverty and disability that gets aggravated in disaster situations (DFID,

2000; Elwan, 1999; Yeo, 2005). All vulnerable populations have specific needs. As persons with disabilities are not a homogenous segment, they are always confronted by intersectionality of class, caste, religious ethnicity, gender, type of disability and environmental context. Each person has specific needs depending on the type and extent of disability, socio-economic background, skills and orientation per se of the sensory, cognitive, psychological and mobility-related disability. (Unnati, 2006; HI, 2009; CBM, 2013). This chapter explores the specific international legal frameworks that aim to protect the rights of persons with disabilities, and at the same time emphasises the need for mainstreaming, integrating and including the rights of persons with disabilities within the global and national frameworks, policies and laws. It is absolutely essential to include the voices of persons with disabilities in the process of law making so that their needs, potentials and aspirations are considered to enable them to lead a dignified life on an equal basis with others (IFRC, 2010, 2013; UNDP, 2014).

International frameworks protecting the rights of persons with disabilities

The UNCRPD marks a paradigm shift in uplifting disability from a medico-charity approach/model to a social and rights-based model/ approach rendering full and equal participation to persons with disabilities on an equal basis with others. Article 11 of the UNCRPD focuses on the situation of risk and humanitarian emergencies and proposes all state parties to introduce a mandate in international humanitarian and human rights laws to include all measures to enhance the participation of persons with disabilities in situations of risk, including situations of armed conflict, humanitarian emergencies and the natural disasters.

United Nations Economic and Social Commission for Asia and the Pacific (UNESCAP), while launching the third Asia Pacific Decade of Persons with Disabilities (2013–2023), signed a treaty, the Incheon Strategy, to 'Make the Right Real' for the 650 million persons with disabilities in Asia and the Pacific (UNESCAP, 2012). Goal 7 of the Strategy ensures disability-inclusive disaster risk reduction and management. While clearly setting out the goal and targets to be achieved, specific indicators have been set for tracking progress that includes disaster risk reduction plans, training for service providers, provisioning for accessible goods and services in all the phases of disaster risk reduction – relief, shelters, assistive devices and technologies and ensuring the participation of persons with disabilities in preparation of community-based disaster management plans.

The Sphere Standards (2011) launched by a group of international NGOs for humanitarian aid has developed several tools to improve the quality of assistance to people affected by disasters and accountability of states including that of humanitarian aid to beneficiaries and donors. The Sphere Standards have included persons with disabilities including disability linked to age, gender and HIV/AIDS. The specific standards relate to participation and representation of all groups in assessment, response, targeting, monitoring and evaluation of programmes. The standards also refer to aid workers' competencies and responsibilities, management and support of staff.

The Asia-Pacific region is most adversely affected by disasters, including those caused by climate change. Persons with disabilities and other vulnerable groups are at higher risk of death, injury and additional impairments, as a result of exclusion from disaster risk reduction policies, plans and programmes. Public service announcements are often issued in formats and language that are not accessible by persons with disabilities. In addition, emergency exits, shelters and facilities tend not to be barrier-free (Unnati, 2006; CBM, 2013). Regular participation of persons with disabilities in emergency preparedness drills and other disaster risk reduction measures at the local and district levels could prevent or minimize risk and damage when disasters occur (HI, 2005). Physical and information infrastructure that incorporates universal design principles would improve the chances of safety and survival.

Disability is not as yet a part of the agenda of most development organisations, even though the social model (Albert, 2004) has led the focus away from the person-centred, health and welfare approach followed until very recently. Most examples of mainstreaming disability during disasters are reactive and not proactive wherein persons with disabilities need to be included before, during and after the disaster. Even the Hyogo Framework for Action (2005–2015) adopted by the World Conference on Disaster Reduction to make the world safer from natural hazards is not inclusive of disability. The Guidelines for the Domestic Facilitation and Regulation of International Disaster Relief and Initial Recovery Assistance – International Disaster Response Laws, Rules and Principles (also known as the IDRL Guidelines) – have mentioned disability as a sign of vulnerability (IFRC, 2011). Every framework needs to acknowledge the specific needs of persons with disabilities from a rights-based perspective on an equal basis with others basing the UNCRPD as the guiding and overarching framework. The Sendai Framework for Disaster Risk Reduction 2015–2030 – adopted on 18 March 2015 at the Third World Conference on Disaster Risk Reduction, held from 14 to 18 March 2015 in Sendai organised by United Nations Office for Disaster Risk Reduction (UNISDR) – is a step in this direction.

Developing national frameworks for disaster risk reduction from a disability lens

Articles 11 and 32 of the UN Convention on the Rights of Persons with Disabilities (CRPD) require that persons with disabilities benefit from and participate in disaster relief, emergency response and disaster risk reduction strategies. Article 11 states that 'States Parties shall take in accordance with their obligations under international law ... all necessary measures to ensure the protection and safety of persons with disabilities in situations of risk, including situations of armed conflict, humanitarian emergencies and the occurrence of natural disasters'. Further, Article 32 of the Convention ensures that any initiative on international cooperation should be inclusive of and accessible to persons with disabilities.

Disasters are affecting about 40 per cent of the global population residing in South Asia largely due to the inability or lack of adequate mechanisms to cope with them (IFRC, 2010). Persons with disabilities experience profound exclusion during disaster situations. Experience suggests that robust and stringent laws play a vital role in putting in place coping mechanisms demonstrating the power to equip vulnerable communities build better resilience (IFRC, 2010). Over-regulation leads to unnecessary bottlenecks, and under-regulation leads to uncoordinated efforts. Disruption of services post-disaster affects all and particularly persons with disabilities, as they are excluded from the mainstream services as well as processes of relief and rehabilitation. Moreover, the needs of persons with disabilities are likely to be ignored, more because other survival needs assume higher priority both among people and relief organisations (Unnati, 2006; HI, 2005; CBM, 2013). Also when resources are scarce, there is a possibility that persons with disabilities face neglect and discrimination. The kind and degree of follow-up and referrals that are required for physical and psycho-social rehabilitation are difficult as people relocate, and tracking processes are not so organised. Re-integration into normal activities of the community life like attending formal/ informal education centres or earning livelihood, accessing services of health and education is much slower due to the impairments and issues of accessibility.

Efforts for community-based disaster risk reduction and disaster preparedness are recent, and the role of vulnerable groups in disaster management processes, including that of persons with disabilities, remains unexplored. The needs of persons with disabilities continue to be excluded over the more long-term recovery and reconstruction efforts; thereby the opportunity to ensure that towns/cities are accessible and inclusively resilient to future disasters is often missed.

Even in normal situations, there is a dearth of trained rehabilitation experts, more so in rural areas. Mustering adequate human resources in disaster situations is even more difficult, especially on a sustained basis. Community-based skills in these areas are not honed to be able to fill in the gap. Girls and women with disabilities and persons with mental illness and multiple disabilities are the most vulnerable in disaster situations: disabilities that are not so obvious tend to be completely ignored.

In India there are no anti-discrimination laws to protect the rights of persons with disabilities. Currently, there are four laws related to disability – Persons with Disabilities (Equal opportunities, Protection of Rights and Full Participation) Act 1995, the National Trust for Persons with Autism, Cerebral Palsy and Multiple Disabilities Act 1999, the Mental Health Act 1999, and the Rehabilitation Council of India Act 1992. All these acts emanate from a medico-welfaristic perspective, offering rehabilitation support to persons with disabilities. As a signatory to the UNCRPD all laws of the country need to be harmonised with the spirit enshrined in this. Far from doing so, none of the laws related to disability even speak about the plight of persons with disabilities during and after disasters. Even the National Disaster Management Act 2005, fails to acknowledge the rights of persons with disabilities and fleetingly mentions them as one of vulnerable. The Rights of Persons with Disabilities Act, 2016, while it addresses the inclusion of persons with disabilities in disaster management plans and stipulates the maintenance of district level records on persons with disabilities by the Disaster Management Authority (Section 8), it does not legally bind the state to take necessary steps for persons with disabilities during disasters. Whereas specific laws, policies, protocols need to be developed from a disability lens, it is also crucial to disaster management policies that there exist documented evidences for non-compliance along with penalties for non-implementation of disability law. The following suggestions may be incorporated at each of the phases – relief, rehabilitation and reconstruction and disaster preparedness outlining the specific steps/protocols in consultation with persons with disabilities and their representation organisations. These need to be incorporated within the disability-specific and disaster management, laws, policies, rules and regulations and protocols, circulars and government orders issued at the national as well as the specific state-level policies. All programmes and schemes related to disability need to be revised and developed from a rights-based perspective that aims to empower and enhance the dignity of persons with disabilities in consultation with persons with disabilities and their representative organisations.

Administrative accountability and public liability during the 'relief – rehabilitation – reconstruction phase'

It is the responsibility of local administration to identify persons who have been injured at all rehabilitation centres and camps before developing an area-specific database. After surviving the disaster the harsh life of an evacuee does not end. They struggle desperately with toilets and other basic facilities inaccessible to them in temporary shelters; many of them who are provided wheelchairs as philanthropic measures of state activity get their wheel chairs stuck at fatal points, and some who survive the disaster die of this trauma and accident. While the visually challenged have no access to fliers posted as instructions, the hearing impaired are considered as silent and quiet people who are left behind to die unnoticed.

While it is the joint responsibility of the Ministries of Labour Welfare, Social Justice, and Health to come together under the umbrella of State Disaster Management Authority (SDMA), it is equally a mandatory task for SDMAs to design a structure where they could all plan a concerted action.

The SDMA should be collaborating with local hospitals and district administration for providing trauma care, curative, therapeutic and other supportive services like physiotherapy, occupational therapy, corrective surgery to persons with injuries to minimise the possibilities of these resulting into a disability; assistive and mobility devices, support services such as caretakers, sign language interpretation, adapted/accessible transportation services and information in accessible formats like Braille, large print, audio and visual announcements including early warning systems that can be understood by different persons with disabilities.

The same exercise is equally relevant for identifying the specific health care needs of persons with existing disabilities and providing them services at accessible centres or through community-based mechanisms and information in accessible formats. Developing a community-based mechanism for identification and rendering support to persons with disabilities works best by encouraging their participation. SDMAs and DDMAs (District Disaster Management Authority) should plan for developing a protocol for issuing/retrieving disability certificates for obtaining benefits of government schemes related to disability. Mapping of community-level resources and assets and strengthening the resources for sustained support to persons with disabilities for their basic health care and rehabilitation need to be added to the efforts on strengthening the implementation of social safety net programmes for most vulnerable groups. Enhancing and investing in recovery schemes especially psycho-social care and training, ensuring that the built environment is made barrier-free based on the principles of universal design for all in the reconstruction process and involving persons with disabilities and other vulnerable groups in the development, implementation and monitoring of the programmes improve efficiency and sustainable development, but the Disaster Management Act, 2005, fails to incorporate even the most basic needs of disability management. Much of this management requirement could be supported simply through a mandatory requirement from

SDMAs and DDMAs for maintaining a gender and disability disaggregated data and facilitating proactive disclosure of the same at all service provider levels. This could go a long way towards vulnerability and capacity assessments, contingency planning, constituting task force and disaster risk reduction committees by investing in capacity building such as developing places for rescue shelters within 2–3 kilometres vicinity that are accessible – this could even be the local school to help the evacuation process.

Laws have failed to create an enabling environment for mainstreaming disability through inclusive policies, bye-laws, information systems, infrastructure, attitudes of society on an ongoing basis. Therefore laws have drastically failed to curb violence and sexual harassment against children, senior citizens and women with disabilities. Administration follows no code of conduct in the absence of supervision, performance assessment and penalties for inflicting any form of ill treatment/violence/neglect/discrimination of persons with disabilities and specifically girls and women with disabilities.

Scientific tools have been missing for measuring progress by effectively designing indicators for monitoring the Hyogo Framework for Action, Sustainable Development Goals, Incheon Strategy, the Sphere Standards, national and regional disaster management plans and disability action plans developed by inter-agency groups. The disaster management curriculum in colleges and universities, school safety plans as well as in the training of first-responders, such as fire-fighters, ambulance and police personnel throughout the state, has yet to draw focus of the mainstream disaster laws.

In conclusion one could reiterate the words of Weibgen (2015, p. 2676) that 'the task of listening to marginalized people is not that of city agencies or federal judges alone – court orders cannot take the place of our own consciences. We must all continue to combat prejudice against people with disabilities outside of the courtroom, taking responsibility for meeting everyone's needs in times of disaster and in those of lesser crisis. While the law may serve to concretize and remind us of our obligations to each other, in the end, it is up to us to ensure that no one is left behind when the next storms come'.

References

Albert, B. (2004). Briefing Note: The Social Model of Disability, Human Rights and Development. *Enabling Disabled People to Reduce Poverty*, Disability KaR Research Project. Retrieved 24 January 2016 from www.enil.eu/ wp-content/uploads/2012/07/The-social-model-of-disability-human-rightsdevelopment_2004.pdf

Christoffel Blindenmission (CBM). (2013). *Disability Inclusive Disaster Risk Management: Voices from the Field and Good Practices*. Retrieved 1 January 2016 from

www.asksource.info/resources/disability-inclusive-disaster- risk-management-voices-field-and-good-practices
Dalal, A. K. (2000). Social Attitudes and Rehabilitation of People with Disabilities: The Indian Experience. *Journal of Rehabilitation*, *5*, 15–21.
Department for International Development (DfID). (2000). *Disability, Poverty and Development*, Issues Paper. London: Overseas Development Group.
Elwan, A. (1999). *Poverty and Disability: A Survey of the Literature*. Washington, DC: The World Bank.
Handicap International and European Commission Humanitarian Aid and Civil Protection DG. (2009). *Mainstreaming Disability into Disaster Risk Reduction: A Training Manual*. Nepal: Prevention Web. Retrieved from www.un.org/disabilities/default.asp?id=1546
Handicap International (HI). (2005). *How to Include Disability Issues in Disaster Management, European Commission: Handicap International*. Retrieved from www.globalprotectioncluster.org/_assets/files/tools_and_guidance/age_gender_diversity/HandicapInt_Including_Disability_Disaster_Management_EN.pdf
IFRC. (2010). *Disasters in Asia: A Case for Legal Preparedness*. Geneva: International Federation of Red Cross and Red Crescent Societies.
IFRC. (2011). *Introduction to the Guidelines for the Domestic Facilitation and Regulation of International Disaster Relief and Initial Recovery Assistance*. Geneva: International Federation of Red Cross and Red Crescent Societies.
Nogiwa, S. (2013). 'Issues and Lessons Learned from the Relief Activities for Persons with Disabilities Affected by the Great East Japan Earthquake' Tohoku Office: Association for Aid and Relief, Japan (AAR Japan), September. Retrieved 1 July 2016 from http://donate-japan.com/articles/view/458. html
UNESCAP. (2012). *The Incheon Strategy to 'Make the Right Real' for Persons with Disabilities in Asia and Pacific 2013–2022*. New York: United Nations.
Unnati. (2006). *Mainstreaming Disability Issues*. Ahmedabad: Unnati.
Weibgen, A. A. (2015). The Right to Be Rescued: Disability Justice in an Age of Disaster. *Yale Law Journal*, *124*(7), 2202–2679. Retrieved 1 July 2016 from www.yalelawjournal.org/note/the-right-to-be-rescued
World Bank. (2007). *People with Disabilities in India: From Commitments to Outcomes*. Washington, DC: World Bank.
World Health Organization. (2001). *The International Classification of Functioning, Disability and Health (ICF)*. Geneva: WHO. http://www.who.int/classifications/icf/en/.
Yeo, R. (2005). Disability, Poverty and the New Development Agenda. *Disability Knowledge and Research*, 1–33.

PART II

Families in Law

Property, Custom, and Violence

6 Family, Work and Matrimonial Property

Implications for Women and Children

Kamala Sankaran

B. Sivaramayya's illuminating book *Matrimonial Property Law in India* (1999) was perhaps the first comprehensive study of the subject in India. The book bears the imprint of his scholarship, the years of insight in the area of family law which many of us as former students, and later as colleagues, were fortunate to witness. Elaborating on the concept of matrimonial property, Sivaramayya (1999) went on to describe and analyse the different regimes of matrimonial property that exist in India and also focused on the way forward for a gender-just development of this key area of family law in the country. In the Introduction he highlighted the low ownership of property by women in the world. 'This position has arisen because of the social and legal failure to recognise marriage as an economic partnership also. The disproportionate holding of assets occurs primarily for three reasons: (1) Law and policies of the states do not recognise "domestic work" as "productive work"—even Marx does not. (2) Nature and nurture burden women with bearing and rearing of children. They are frequently forced to give up their careers to look after their homes. (3) Even when women take up jobs, they are confined to relatively low-paid ones' (Ibid.: xiii).[1] In this article, I explore these themes further, and examine in particular the gendered nature of work and the implications this has for women's and children's rights in matrimonial property.

Importance of property for a woman's well-being

It must be made clear at the outset that the issue of matrimonial property and its equitable division is a matter that concerns those families that have property; and that number is not small in India.[2] It is well-documented that the ownership of property, in the form of land and other assets, is highly skewed in favour of men worldwide. In 1980, the International Labour

DOI: 10.4324/9781003299561-6

Organisation (ILO) calculated that women do two-thirds of the world's work for 5-10 per cent of the income, and own one per cent of the assets. The importance of enhancing women's property ownership is for the sake of the empowerment of the woman, and also for the improved well-being of the family, particularly children. The link between women's agency and social change has been forcefully brought out by Amartya Sen in recent times: he notes that '[t]he ownership of property can also make women more powerful in family decisions' (1999: 189–203; 192).[3]

The importance of wealth, in the sense of property ownership, to a person's quality of life cannot be underestimated. Access to and control over property is a vital factor that determines a person's standard of living, avenues of future income and sense of economic security. Ownership of a piece of land, however small, would often permit a family to eke out a livelihood. Thus, it has been noticed that access to land is linked to incidence of rural poverty. In addition, it has been noted that having access to land 'serves as collateral for credit and as a mortgageable or saleable asset during crisis, and improves bargaining position with employers' (Agarwal 1997: 39). Owning a 'field of one's own' is important for the family as a unit, and more particularly for the woman. Her social status and well-being are directly connected to this ownership (Agarwal 1994). Of course, ownership of land by women may not necessarily lead to improved economic status. Decision-making over land is often in the hands of men. Brahmanical customs and social taboos prohibit women from handling tools and means of production (such as the plough) needed for tilling land.

In urban areas, access to housing is critical for survival. Huge sums are paid to gain the 'right' to set up a shop or slum on a pavement or plot of land. Access to housing implies that women who otherwise may not be able to venture out to work because of the need to look after small children or the aged, can engage in home-based work. Therefore the right to live in the matrimonial home (even if she does not have ownership rights over it) is an important right for the woman.

Ownership of income-creating assets is also a source to future incomes. The micro-finance movement in the country shows that loans of even small sums of money generate significant amounts of capital, and this is used by women and men to buy some income-creating asset or is used as seed money to set up small livelihood-sustaining enterprises.[4] In times of crisis, any asset owned by the woman can be sold or mortgaged. This provides her with a buffer and a fall-back option in times of need. In sum, ownership of property is an important, though not complete, guarantee against poverty. It is also important to recognise that having a source of regular income may often be an inadequate substitute for the sense of equality and empowerment that is provided by property ownership in an increasingly insecure environment.

Several writers have pointed to the positive link between women's access to property and enhanced bargaining positions both within the community and the family (see Jain and Banerjee 1985; Sen 1990). Thus, for instance, Bina Agarwal notes that this bargain involves both cooperation and conflict, and that '[t]he person who has a stronger fall-back position (better outside options), and/or whose claims enjoy greater legitimacy, would emerge with a more favourable outcome, although both parties would be better-off than if they did not co-operate' (Agarwal 1994:54–55). It has been noticed that women who have property are given greater respect and looked after better by their relatives. In the case of widows it has been noticed that those with access to property or income have a better status within the family and in society (Chen 1998). A recent study carried out in Kerala has shown that women owning immovable property (land or house) are found to face a significantly lower risk of marital violence than women with no property (Panda and Agarwal 2005). This would point to the need for women to have access to both property and incomes in order to improve their positions within the family and outside.

Property rights for women are important in another sense too. The extent to which their labour within the household and outside is rewarded with wages is also important given the manner in which household income is spent. It is well-documented that women's earnings often go towards meeting food and other basic needs of family members.[5] For instance, it has been noted that in 1989–99, 'one out of nine households [was] dependent on women's earnings to meet half or more of her expenditure' (Kishor and Gupta 2004: 694). Giving control over this income/property and thus also a voice in decision-making may be beneficial not only for the woman but other members of the family too.

Personal law and matrimonial property

Ownership of property is primarily obtained through inheritance. Women who inherit property from their fathers usually waive this right in favour of the male kin, generally brothers, in order to maintain good links with their natal family (cf Jaising 1997; Kishwar 1994: 2145–67). Property could also be acquired through savings out of one's earnings. This is the backdrop within which the concept of matrimonial property becomes crucial and its disposition and devolution critical to the position of women within the family and outside. The manner in which the property of spouses is controlled and its ownership determined, during marriage and at its dissolution, lie at the core of the debate over matrimonial property. Broadly speaking, in the regime of matrimonial property that we have for most communities in India, spouses continue to treat the property they bring into the marriage as their separate property. The property acquired by either spouse during the period of marriage continues to be the individual property of the spouse that acquired the property. The valuation of the matrimonial property that may take place at the time of the death of the husband or at the time of the dissolution of marriage follows what Sivaramayya referred to as the 'separation of property' model. Under such a system there is no corpus of 'matrimonial property' over which both spouses can exercise a claim, and related to that, there is no conception of an economic partnership between the spouses that would come into existence upon marriage. (While most of the country follows the separation of property model, in Goa, the *Civil Code of Goa* has elements of all these regimes (cf Sivaramayya 1999: 10–11).) As a result, for many women, the initial corpus of wealth that they have at the time of marriage (including *stridhan),* together with accretions to their property that are made by their own effort or through gifts or inheritance, alone constitute the property over which they exercise ownership at the time of the dissolution of marriage.

In many families in India, the 'breadwinner' is the male and the woman, even if educated, gives up her job in order to run the house and look after children. It comes as no surprise that women's chance of increasing their share of property during marriage (which also coincides with the bulk of their possible working life) is practically nil. In other cases, where the man is engaged as a self-employed businessman, small-scale entrepreneur, shopkeeper or farmer, the wife or child may well be engaged in helping out in his work. However, their role is perceived as that of a family helper and their contribution to the eventual income from the business/land is never separately calculated or credited to them.

The property of the husband (except for ancestral property in the case of Hindus belonging to the *Mitakshara* school) is treated as his exclusive property over which he has exclusive control.[6] In the case of communities like the Hindus, the man can even dispose of his property freely through his will and testament to the complete exclusion of his family members. Marriage not being an 'economic partnership' results in the limited capacity of the wife to claim rights over the property of her husband at the time of divorce.[7] This has profound implications for the rights of the wife over matrimonial property. Assets such as the matrimonial house or movable assets purchased by the husband are treated to be his exclusive property. The contribution of the wife in creating his savings in the first instance through performing (unpaid) household work is not a relevant factor in India.[8]

One of the most important properties over which the woman would like to exercise some control usually is the matrimonial home. In case of breakdown of marriage or otherwise, it is this matrimonial home which is her only place of residence, her shelter. Given the fact that most marriages in India are patrilocal, with the woman moving to the residence of her husband, dissolution of marriage or her leaving the husband's home because of domestic violence and her consequent loss of matrimonial home would also render the woman homeless. The Protection of Women from Domestic Violence Act 2005 now grants rights of residence (though not necessarily ownership) in the matrimonial home or shared household to the battered and estranged wife. The residence order passed by a magistrate under the Act can extend to restraining the respondent from alienating, disposing of or renouncing his share in the shared household or encumbering it. In certain cases, the magistrate can direct the respondent to provide the same level of alternate accommodation as enjoyed by the aggrieved person in the shared household or to pay the rent for such accommodation if the circumstances so warrant.[9] While this is no doubt a major step forward, we must not overlook the fact that the entitlement of the wife to the matrimonial property in the matrimonial home remains an unfulfilled demand. We must also note the implications of another recent amendment that has enhanced the residence rights of women. The limited rights of residence for daughters (married or unmarried) in their family home have been reversed with the recent amendment to the Hindu Succession Act 2005.[10]

Thus, despite the rights to residence which have been enhanced in recent times, given the separation of property model that exists in India, with no acknowledgement for the household work put in by the wife, she is not a joint owner of any assets acquired during marriage by the husband. In the event of the dissolution of the marriage through the husband dying intestate, the widow would be eligible for a share of his property according to the rules of the personal law governing them. The personal law for most communities accords the wife a status no higher than that of the children, thus completely ignoring her contribution to the household and family in the form of unpaid work. She is treated as a 'beneficiary' with no claims over the deceased husband's estate, and could be willed out of his estate should he wish to do so. Even the provisions of Section 27 of the Hindu Marriage Act 1955 (HMA) that speaks of distribution of property received at or about the time of marriage fall far short of incorporating equitable principles of distribution of matrimonial property. Explaining Section 27 of the HMA, the Supreme Court had clarified that '[t]he expression "property presented on or about the time of marriage" used in Section 27 has to be properly construed to include such property which is given at the time of marriage as also the property given before or after marriage to the parties to become their "joint property", implying thereby that the property can be traced to have connection with the marriage. All such property is covered by Section 27 of the Act.'[11] In another case, the Bombay High Court has cited this decision to clarify that property not given to the couple as their joint property cannot be the subject matter of an order under Section 27 of the HMA.

Property acquired by the couple by their own individual efforts and not given to them at or about the time of marriage to be held jointly would not be property covered by Section 27 of the Act. Thus, it is necessary that for an order under Section 27 to be passed, the property must have been presented at or about the time of marriage to become their joint property.[12]

In the event of the dissolution of marriage by divorce, the wife would no doubt be entitled to maintenance. However, the right to maintenance is at best only a right to a regular payment, and cannot be equated with a right to property. Even this right to maintenance is subject to many conditions being imposed upon the wife which she has to scrupulously fulfil in order to continue receiving maintenance. Maintenance is normally not granted as a capitalised sum in India, and thus, in the absence of a claim over matrimonial property the woman usually has no means of using a lump sum to purchase any income-creating asset. In fact, the provisions for maintenance of the spouse (usually the wife) have to be understood in the context of the legal position that any property owned/acquired by a spouse continues to be the sole property of the spouse (usually the male). Maintenance claims by the wife could thus be rationalised as the claims that the wife could make on the husband for the 'matrimonial duties' performed in marriage. Note however, that her claims upon the property of the spouse are restricted to a claim of *maintenance,* and never go so far as to claim a share in the *property* owned/acquired by the husband in the marriage. Again, in the case of the claim to maintenance, she must perform her wifely duties in order to maintain her claim. The same may be the case for children's right to maintenance.

The notion of a 'good wife' who performs her 'matrimonial duties' is a motif writ large in the different provisions of personal law in India. What exactly do these 'matrimonial duties' entail? Amongst other things such as the duty to engage in marital sexual intercourse (marital rape is not an offence in India), it would certainly include her duty to perform domestic work and run the household by performing all the household labour expected of a 'good wife'.[13] Added to this is the idea that the man is the breadwinner and therefore has the duty to maintain the wife,[14] and coupled with that the right to determine the location of the matrimonial home.[15] The notion that the man is engaged in production and the woman in reproduction, forms the basis of the notion that sexual division of labour is a universal truth.[16] This gendered understanding of the roles each spouse is traditionally expected to perform has never been seriously challenged by the courts. On the contrary, the failure to cook and look after children has been regarded as cruelty and constituting grounds to obtain divorce in India. This understanding—that there is an inherent division of labour within the household—appears to have been implicitly internalised by the courts.

Further, the performance of matrimonial duties only gives the wife a right to claim maintenance/alimony, but the law has not been willing to recognise this as giving rise to a right on the part of the wife who undertakes the bulk of the domestic and care responsibilities (whether with outside assistance or otherwise) to claim part of the husband's property upon divorce as a claim she has upon the 'matrimonial property'. The limitations in providing for the rights to maintenance alone when a marriage breaks up reveals itself in the greater impoverishment of women after divorce. It has been noted that marriage, for the woman, is an 'economic arrangement for life', and failure of the marriage often leads her into a life of poverty and dependence (cf Mukhopadhyay 1998: 35–76).

Unpaid work and the sexual division of labour

The gender stereotyping of women and the roles ascribed to women in the household are not unique to the personal law or to the manner in which the private domain is constructed. Domestic work is often monotonous, repetitive and physically taxing work. Cooking, taking care of children, and other arduous physical activity such as walking long distances to fetch water, or to collect firewood needed for cooking, to purchasing things from the weekly rural market are the kinds of chores most women perform on a daily basis. In urban areas it may entail being up all hours of the night for water, standing in queues for ration, dropping and collecting school-going children, etc. They could also be engaged in maintaining a kitchen garden or looking after household poultry and dairy activities (Kodoth 2004: 1914).

Sociologists have distinguished between 'family' and 'households' in India and use the term 'family' for a wider group connected to each other through kinship and marriage whose members may live in more than one household, whereas members of a household live together, sharing a common hearth and worship. For the present purpose, we are using the term 'household' while describing the work performed by women within it, while retaining the term 'family' to describe the property division between the spouses since 'family law' or 'personal law' are the expressions used in legal discourse.

A serious debate among scholars in different countries has concerned the question of how women's unpaid work within the household should be viewed, from the perspective of whether they contribute to the national economy, and whether this constitutes 'work'. Traditionally, only paid work was considered as gainful employment. The economist Alfred Marshall had made the point that if he hired a woman as a domestic help the national economy would increase, but if he married her it would go downl In the 1961 *Census,* economic data collection was based on the definition of 'work', defined as 'any person whose main activity was participation in any economically productive work either by his/her physical or by his/her mental activity' (Shimray 2004: 1698, 1702; Sen and Sen 1985: WS 49–56). In the 1971 *Census*, a 'worker' was one whose main activity in the reference year was economically meaningful work. In the 1981 *Census* it was recognised that people could work for different durations, and therefore two categories of workers emerged: main workers (working 183 days or more) and marginal workers (employed for less than 183 days). In all these cases, productive or meaningful work was understood as either work that was remunerative, i.e., in a context of an employer-employee relationship or self-employment outside the household for profit (Shimray 2004). In the earlier censuses, the unpaid work done on farm and in family enterprises did not get included as economically productive or meaningful work. However, in the 1991 *Census* those workers who did unpaid work on farms or family enterprises were included even though they did not receive wages for the work done. Subsistence activities, i.e., production for own consumption was also included in the case of certain crops. The scope of the definition of work was expanded in the 2001 *Census* to include production of milk for domestic consumption.[17]

The *Nairobi Forward-Looking Strategies for the Advancement of Women* (1985: Para 120) stated that 'remunerated and, in particular, the unremunerated contributions of women to all aspects and sectors of development should be recognised, and appropriate efforts made to measure and reflect these contributions in national accounts and economic statistics and in the gross national product. Concrete steps should be taken to quantify the unremunerated contribution of women to agriculture, food production, reproduction and household activities.' The *Copenhagen Declaration and Programme of Action: World Summit for Social Development* (1995: Para 46) recommended, 'Worldwide, most of this work is done by women who often face the double burden of remunerated and unremunerated work. Efforts are needed to acknowledge the social and economic importance and value of unremunerated work ... and to accord social recognition for such work, including by developing methods for reflecting its value in quantitative terms for possible reflection in accounts that may be produced separately from, but consistent with, core national accounts.' The Platform for Action adopted at the World Conference on Women in Beijing in September 1995 indicated that efforts should be made in the direction of devising 'suitable statistical means to recognise and make visible the full extent of the work of women and all their contributions to the national economy, including their contribution in the unremunerated and domestic sectors, and examine the relationship of women's unremunerated work to the incidence of and their vulnerability to poverty' (*The Beijing Declaration and the Platform of Action*, 1996: Para 68). Despite these international efforts, the position in many countries continues to fall short of granting visibility to women's unpaid work.

The United Nation's System of National Accounts (SNA) elaborates what could be considered productive in order to be counted towards the national accounts. These mainly correspond to what is considered 'productive' for the market (SNA activities). It 'lists a large number of productive activities undertaken within the household which are not included in the production boundary. For example, the production of domestic and personal services for consumption within the same household: preparation of meals, care and training of children, cleaning, repairs etc.' (Unni 2001: 2360, 2370). These activities have been termed 'extended SNA' activities, while 'activities related to learning, social and cultural activities, mass media and self-maintenance are categorised as non-SNA activities' (Ibid.). Thus, domestic work and 'care-work' or what is also termed the work of 'reproduction' as opposed to production have been treated as extended SNA activities.

In order to ascertain the amount of time spent by women on these extended and non-SNA activities, the National Sample Survey Organisation carried out a large-scale survey spread across six states in 1998-99.[18] Observing the time-use pattern of respondent households they were able to assess the time-use pattern of members over the span of a week (168 hours). On an average, women spent 19 hours a week on SNA activities (rural women spending up to 23 hours a week) while the corresponding figure for men was 42 hours. This can be understood in the context of the national accounts treating 'productive' work for the market alone as contributing to the national income. However, when it came to extended SNA (domestic work and care-work), the situation completely changed. Women spent longer hours, almost 35 hours a week compared to a low of less than four hours a week for men (roughly one-tenth the time spent by women) in these activities. Women reported that they spent about 2.1 hours per day on cooking food, about 1.1 hour on cleaning the household and utensils. Participation of men in these activities was just nominal. Taking care of children was also mainly the women's responsibility as they spent about 3.16 hours on these activities as compared to only 0.32 hours by males. In non-SNA activities, which pertain to learning, leisure and personal care, males spent about 8 hours more as compared to females.[19]

What are the implications of this for women? We can note from the data relating to SNA and extended SNA activities that women work longer hours a week compared to men. The view that women's work never ends is borne out. The proportion of women's work compared to the total of men and women's work works out to roughly 55 per cent.[20] Thus, if extended SNA activities were treated as economic activities the share of women would be greater.

It must be noted that while there is a need for more activities performed by women to be treated as economic activities for the purpose of assessing their contribution to the household and the national income, much of the work of this nature that is performed is unpaid (even though an economic value may be imputed to it). Such activities may be performed either by family labour or through exchange labour. For the six states combined, payment was not made for about 38 per cent of the time spent in SNA activities. The amount of unpaid activities was higher in the case of women (51 per cent) as compared to men (33 per cent). The predominance of females in unpaid activities, which was visible in all the states, had great regional variation too. The percentage of time spent by women in unpaid activities was highest in Haryana (86 per cent) and the lowest for Tamil Nadu (32 per cent). No doubt social, cultural and economic factors play a role in the regional variations.

Where time has been used as a unit for measurement, as in the time-use surveys mentioned above, the amount of time spent by women to do domestic work has been a factor to incorporate unpaid work as economically productive work. Another way to do so has been to impute a monetary value to this work. According to experts, the most accepted method for this is the 'third-party principle' according to which 'domestic production refers to unpaid activities that can be performed by a third person for pay. Clearly this criterion includes tasks such as shopping, cleaning, food preparation and childcare; it does not include leisure or personal activities such as watching television or getting dressed' (Beneria 1999: 295).

What is very clear is that what Marx had referred to as the activities needed for the 'reproduction of labour', i.e., those activities carried on within the household for the worker to recoup and report for work the next day, are also now getting acknowledged as having value. Not just use-value, but these can have a monetary value ascribed to them as well. Thus, while examining the quantum of minimum wages payable under the Minimum Wages Act 1948 we can observe that while the law is silent about what elements the minimum wage should seek to cover, policy prescriptions and judicial decision have filled this lacuna. The minimum wage should *at least* meet the bare sustenance of an employee and his family. It also includes expenses necessary for his other primary needs, such as medical expenses, expenses to meet some education for his children, and in some cases transport charges, etc. The Supreme Court has approved the norms for fixation of minimum wages approved by the Tripartite Committee of the Indian Labour Conference held in New Delhi in 1957.[21] The five norms have been emphasised and enhanced in further cases. The Court has held that in calculating minimum wage (i) the standard working-class family should be taken to consist of three consumption units for one earner, the earnings of women, children and adolescents should be disregarded; (ii) minimum food requirement should be calculated on the basis of a net intake of calories, for an average Indian adult of moderate activity; (iii) clothing requirements should be estimated as per capita consumption of 18 yards per annum which should give, for the average worker's family of four, a total of 72 yards; (iv) in respect of housing, the rent corresponding to the minimum area provided for under the Government's Industrial Housing Scheme should be taken into consideration in fixing the minimum wage; and (v) fuel, lighting and other 'miscellaneous' items of expenditure should constitute 20 per cent of the total minimum wage. The Supreme Court added the following additional components as a guide for fixing the minimum wage (vi) children's education, medical requirement, minimum recreation including festivals/ceremonies and provision for old age, marriage etc., which should constitute 25 per cent of the total minimum wage.[22] The Court emphasised that the above six components are nothing more than a minimum wage at subsistence level which the employees are entitled to at all times and in all circumstances. It may be noted that no amount has been set aside for the cost of processing of food, as the cost of the purchase the required calorie intake in its unprocessed form is provided. The cost of cooking, cleaning, care-work and other domestic work performed by the woman is left out of minimum wage calculations. It may be argued that the minimum wage fixed by assuming that the invisible domestic work is cost-less in effect results in the woman's domestic work subsidising the cost to the employer in employing a worker at the (reduced) minimum wage. It is in this sense that the links between patriarchy and capitalism may be understood.

What implications does this debate have upon the law of matrimonial property? No doubt the family members' perception of women's contribution to the household income would be coloured by popular and economists' conception of what constitutes 'work'. Thus, invisibility of women's work in the public domain would have serious implications for undervaluing the share of women in matrimonial property. While the question can remain open about whether household work like cooking, cleaning and child-care contribute to the national income, there can be no doubt that they contribute to the family income and well-being as well, the two being interlinked. There are many aspects to this argument. The subsistence work put in by women due to the sexual division of labour has been shown to be the basis that allows males to go out to work and for their employers also to absorb the surplus value created. Thus patriarchy—which sustains the sexual division of labour within households—also creates the basis for the creation of surplus value for the capitalists (see Dalla Costa and James 1972; Mies 1982).

Women often increase their burden of housework and caring in times of crises and as a coping, survival strategy for the family in times of poverty and unemployment. It has been argued that the presence of a large pool of unpaid workers in the form of women act as 'shock absorbers' for the family to respond to the cyclical crises of capitalism (Glazer 1980: 259). The effect of the position of women in the economy also has an impact on the position of women within the family.

I have already noted that under the separation of property model that we have for matrimonial property in India, woman's property consists of the property she brings into the marriage and additions made to it. Assets purchased during the marriage usually by the husband are often times because of the unpaid work put in by women that contribute to the husband's savings. If we were to use the 'replacement cost' model to ascertain the economic contribution of the woman in the household, we would no doubt arrive at a figure that captures her share in the 'separate' property acquired by the husband during the marriage. This has in fact been the basis for the laws of many countries accepting the notion of matrimonial property. There is urgent need for the Indian law to incorporate some such similar system of matrimonial property (see Pradhan Saxena 1993; Sivaramayya 1999).

The care-work performed by women also reduces the burden that families place upon support services provided by the state. Thus women's labour allows the abdication of its duties to its citizens by the state. Poor hospital care, lack of adequate and affordable child-care and care services for the sick and aged add to the burden of women within the household. Caring labour which provides personalised attention and care to members of the family may be motivated by feelings of love and compassion, but as feminist thinkers have pointed out it is also a gender-specific responsibility borne by women alone. (We see, for instance, that paternity leave is granted in limited circumstances in India, mainly to government employees.) While it may or may not have an economic value assigned to it, caring labour is essential for the proper development of members of the household, most particularly children and the aged. This is done often at the cost of personal careers or at the expense of other income-generating activities, but is difficult to reduce to an economic worth, particularly at the time of divorce. The debate over matrimonial property is only now beginning to take into account the caring labour performed by women, while the domestic unpaid work component has been incorporated in several jurisdictions.

It is not just women who perform unpaid work within households but also very often children, particularly the girl child. For instance, it has been pointed out that statistics on child labour frequently show a preponderance of boys rather than girls engaged in child labour. However, if unpaid activities are included under child labour, more girls than boys are engaged in child labour (Greenwork 2002). According to NSS data, the incidence of child labour was 3.8 per cent in 1999–2000 whereas it was 5.1 per cent according to the 1991 *Census* data. However, based on time-use surveys 20 per cent of boys and girls in the age group of 6–14 years participate in economic activities. They are engaged in unpaid or subsistence activities such as animal grazing, collection of fuel and fodder, farming and other services (Dev 2004: 741).

This brings us to the obvious question of whether matrimonial property should be a matter that is an issue only between spouses? How do we assign shares for the unpaid work performed by children in the family, and how do we take care of their independent contribution to economic assets in matrimonial property at the time of divorce? Unpaid family labour is an integral part of the lives of many children growing up in India. The Child Labour (Prohibition and Regulation) Act 1986 specifically acknowledges this work and makes clear that it is outside the scope of legal regulation.[23] This is, in fact, the basis for the distinction that is often made between child labour and child work (Sankaran 2004). This is an area that the developing law of matrimonial property must acknowledge and provide for. The models of matrimonial property regimes that we have of other countries focus on the division of matrimonial property among the spouses. This does not take into account the contribution that children of the house have made towards the corpus of 'family' property.[24] Both where children perform paid employment outside the home and in cases where they perform unpaid work for the household or household enterprise/farm, there is a definite contribution towards household income and hence property.

It may, no doubt, be argued that the parents are responsible for the welfare and upbringing of the children and therefore it would not be correct that the children be allotted a share in the division of matrimonial property. However, in the event where the children in the family perform paid or unpaid work, the situation could change. In order to give agency to the child it would be necessary that the child too be allotted a share commensurate with his/her contribution to the family property. To deny them their due would in fact constitute unjustified enrichment of the property of the father (and mother) in the case of a division of matrimonial property in the event of a divorce, or other heirs in the event of the death of a parent. Such a position would protect the child's interest and be in conformity with the Convention on the Rights of the Child 1989.

Occupational segregation by sex and the earnings gap

Women's property holdings within the family are currently low for reasons related to their (lower) employment levels and wages as well. Their capacity to obtain paid employment is lower than that of men, hence their earning—and therefore savings—capacity is reduced. The Labour Force Participation Rate (LFPR) is uniformly lower for women as compared to men. According to the *Census* 2001, rural LFPR for woman was 30.98 compared to 52.36 for men, and the corresponding figures for urban areas were 11.55 and 50.85 respectively (Dev 2004: 736). Even when women work outside the house, they work in low-paid jobs, their work is systematically undervalued and thus their earning capacity is reduced. Women workers are often found as agricultural labourers, construction workers and domestic workers—all of which are low paying (Ibid.: 739). In fact it has been commented that 'women are found to own and control so remarkably fewer assets and income than men, and are so significantly less educated that it has been suggested that their class positions are uniformly lower than men' (Harriss-White 2004: 27). The common feature of the work performed by women is that they work in low-paid occupations.

Women are often to be found in the lowest paid jobs that are repetitive, and often replicate the kind of work they perform at home. Thus, domestic workers, who are invariably women, perform for remuneration the work they undertake within their own households. This aspect alone helps to keep the wages for domestic work low, as it is perceived as women's work and thus not as valuable. The low significance and economic value ascribed to it within the household and the economy is mirrored in the lower levels of wages earned for similar kinds of work outside. It could be speculated that, in the long term, acknowledging the work done within the house by women as having economic worth would reflect in the higher comparable worth ascribed to work involving similar levels of skill, effort and responsibility in the workplace.

The clustering of women into low-end jobs is also not entirely attributable to their lower educational qualifications, indicating strong gender-based segregation at work in the labour market (Anant and Sankaran 2003). The gender segregation of women into low-end jobs is a feature that is to be found in all countries in the world. A law to deal with gender discrimination such as the Equal Remuneration Act 1976 can deal with discrimination between men and women who are differentially paid for performing same or similar work; yet this law cannot cope with occupational segregation where women are clustered in low-status and low-paying jobs.[25]

Women are often concentrated in those jobs that reflect the care-work they perform at home such as in nursing and teaching. It has been noted that women's earnings, as compared to men's, reflect an earnings gap in India. This is despite the fact that occupational segregation by sex is lower in countries in Asia in comparison with the rest of the world (Anker 1998). The gender gap in earnings and the persistent payment of lower wages in jobs where women are employed has been a feature of women's employment world-wide.[26] Women's wages are uniformly lower than those of men everywhere, and in agriculture, for instance, women on an average earn only 71 per cent the wages of those earned by men (Harriss-White 2004: 28).

The implication of this earnings gap is that even where women work, their contribution to household income, and therefore accretion to matrimonial property, is diminished. This is a factor that should be borne in mind while developing models for the distribution of matrimonial property. While working women may bring in lesser amounts into the family kitty due to diminished wage levels at the workplace, we often find that their contribution to domestic and care-work is in no way diminished or shared because of their status as working persons. The double, nay triple, burden cast upon working women has often been commented upon. Thus, the future or present earning capacity of women should not be a factor to discount the amount of matrimonial property they ought to be entitled to receive upon the dissolution of marriage. Not only do women earn less, their earnings are almost entirely spent on maintaining the household, leaving them with little or no savings. Thus, even within the family the working women's capacity to create assets is far lower than that of men; yet at the time of the dissolution of marriage, this imbalance is not taken care of.

Should the aspect of occupation segregation and the earnings gap be taken into consideration while deciding issues of the division of matrimonial property during a divorce? This does not appear to be the case internationally. Some of the problems that would confront law-makers and judges would be the difficulty (in the absence of empirical data) of determining by how much to compensate a working wife for such factors. While the gendered nature of work outside the house is a factor adversely affecting women, we must not lose sight of the fact that working women often increase their bargaining positions within the household. Characterising these as 'co-operative' conflicts, Amartya Sen (1990) points out that a woman's ability to obtain employment outside the home considerably improves the perception of her contribution within the family to its economic resources. Restrictions that are placed by cultures in not allowing a woman to seek employment outside the home constitute an infringement of her liberty and quest for gender equity (Sen 1999). Should such deprivations be compensated while dividing the corpus of matrimonial property at the time of divorce? This is another issue that merits consideration. Thus, the economic factors that typically cast women into low-paying jobs, and the cultural prohibitions that prevent women from entering employment should be distinct factors that need to be kept in mind while developing a regime for matrimonial property division.

Those who engage in care-work and domestic work within the house reduce their future earning capacity should they ever enter the labour market. The skills required for housework and care-work are not recognised as highly skilled, and they also have lower value ascribed to it. This is especially the case should there be a divorce, and women have to support themselves. 'The human capital that housewives and/or househusbands acquire is less transportable than that of a partner who specialises in market work, leaving them in a weaker bargaining position in the family and economically vulnerable to separation or divorce' (Lee Badget and Folbre 1999).

Conclusion

There is a lacuna in the law inasmuch as it does not recognise a notion of matrimonial property in India. Barring the limited case of the Civil Code of Goa, the personal laws in India have yet to acknowledge this gap. Section 27 of the Hindu Marriage Act 1955 does not suffice, as Sivaramayya himself convincingly argued. Given the limited rights to inherit property that women have in many religious personal laws and their lower levels of participation in the labour force, it comes as no surprise that the property ownership of women is limited. There can be no debate that ownership of assets is invaluable in the process of empowerment of women (cf. Agarwal 1994).

Developing a suitable regime of matrimonial property in India would clearly require a close examination of the function of marriage and the role played by women in nurturing and caring for the members of the household. There is an urgent need to broaden the concept of what constitutes matrimonial property and develop a true recognition of a woman's contribution to the wellbeing and wealth of the household.[27] The sexual division of labour within the household and the so-called 'natural' roles cast upon women to perform these tasks must be subject to close scrutiny. While women may freely wish to continue to perform these roles, the question of the democratisation of relations within the household and ascribing adequate worth, and therefore respect, for the women who perform this work is a matter of great importance for women's equality. The skewed nature of the distribution of domestic and care responsibilities cast upon women in the household has to be recognised and made visible. Further, the close connections between the perceptions of the nature of this work in the 'public' domain, the lack of adequate recognition of its economic worth and its invisibility in national accounts, on the one hand, and the reduced value ascribed to such work in the 'private' domain of the family by economics and personal law must be highlighted. Economics and law must inform each other in order that a real and correct picture of the contribution of women's work to the well-being of the family is incorporated in a matrimonial property law in India.

Notes

1 I use the term 'matrimonial property law' in the sense in which Sivaramayya used it, namely the 'appropriate principles that should guide the division of assets on the termination of marriage' (Sivaramayya 1999: 1).
2 Agarwal (1994: 362) notes that in 1982, the percentage of landless (i.e., owning neither agricultural nor homestead land) to total rural households in India was 11.3 per cent. However 62.4 per cent of these land-owning households had merely between 0.002–1.00 hectares (Ibid.: 364).
3 Sen draws attention to the overlap between the 'agency' approach and the 'well-being, welfarist' approach while maintaining the distinction between the two conceptions.
4 See, for instance, the *First Report of the Committee on Empowerment of Women [2004–05]* cited in 'The Promise of SHGs' (2005).
5 The greater responsibility of women towards maintaining the household has been noted in Sardamoni (1991) and Menscher (1988), cited in Kodoth (2004: 1914).
6 This discussion does not take into account the matrilineal systems of property devolution we have in some parts of India.
7 The wife's right to inherit the husband's property is, of course, not under dispute. However, the fact that the husband is free to treat his property as entirely his own is borne out by the unlimited right to will away his property defeating claims of his wife in many religious personal law systems. And this right to inherit is not relevant when the marriage ends in dissolution.
8 Cf Sivaramayya (1999) for a comparative perspective on this issue.
9 Thus, the Protection of Women from Domestic Violence Act 2005 provides for the rights of women to secure housing. It provides for the right of the woman to reside in the matrimonial home or shared household, whether or not she has an right or title to reside in such home or household. This right is secured through a residence order passed by a magistrate. Perhaps, in a notional sense then, the Act provides for each woman to 'have a room of one's own' in the sense mentioned by Virginia Woolf (1929) given the small size of the dwelling units in most Indian homes. It must also be borne in mind that the Domestic Violence Act 2005 deals not only with the wife as the aggrieved person, but extends to those related by consanguinity, marriage or those living in a joint family.
10 The Hindu Succession (Amendment) Act 2005 has deleted Section 23 and now given all daughters—whether married or unmarried—the equal rights of residence, and to demand partition in the family dwelling home as sons.
11 *Balkrishna Ramchandra Kadam v. Sangeeta Balkrishna Kadam* AIR 1997 SC 3562.
12 *Kamalakar Ganesh Sambhus v. Master Tejas Kamalakar Sambhus* AIR 2004 Bom 478. In this case, even though the wife showed that she had made half the contribution for the construction of the house property, the Court held that this could not be the subject matter of an order under Section 27 of the Act, and set aside the order of the Family Court on these grounds.
13 See *Kalpana Srivastava v. S.N. Srivastava* AIR 1985 All. 253 where the court held that failure by the wife to prepare tea for the husband's friends, among other factors, amounts to cruelty. This could be read to be sufficient grounds to allow him to divorce her.

14 See, for instance, the gender unequal duty to maintain the wife that is cast upon the husband alone under the Hindu Adoption and Maintenance Act 1956.
15 See *Kailashwati v. Ayodhya Prakash* (1977) 79 PLR 216, *Tirath Kaur v. Kirpal Singh* AIR 1964 Punj. 28, *Swaraj Garg v. KM. Garg AIR* 1978 Del 296.
16 It has been shown that, in agriculture, it is women who do the actual work in several communities in India. See Mazumdar and Sharma (1990: 185–97).
17 In the 1991 *Census,* cultivation of certain crops even for self-consumption was treated as economic activity. The scope of the term 'cultivation' was expanded in the 2001 *Census* to include certain other crops such as tobacco, fruits, all types of flowers, roots and tubers, potatoes, chillies and turmeric, pepper, cardamom, all types of vegetables and fodder crops, etc. This meant that activities related to production of all the above-mentioned crops for domestic consumption has been classified under 'plantation' in the *Census of India,* 2001. See http://pondicherry.nic.in/open/depts/ecostat/ census/population.htm. The National Sample Survey Organisation also provides data on women's employment. These surveys are conducted once every five years. They adopt a broader notion of work—it encompasses all activities pursued for pay, profit or family gain. Thus its data about the extent of women in the labour force is higher than that reached by the *Census* data. For further details see *Report of the Study Group on Women and Child Labour* (2001).
18 A Time-Use' Survey was conducted in 18,591 households spread over six selected states, namely, Haryana, Madhya Pradesh, Gujarat, Orissa, Tamil Nadu and Meghalaya between 1998 and 1999. The main objectives of the survey were to collect data for properly quantifying the economic contribution of the women in the national economy and to study the gender discrimination in the household activities. For details see http://microdata.gov.in/nada43/index.php/catalog/140. Accessed on 3 May 2022.
19 In order to place this data in an international context, we can compare the Indian data on time use with the data provided for selected developing countries. Women worked 116 percentage of the time worked by men. Of the total work time the proportion of time spent by men on market and non-market activities was 72 and 21 respectively On the other hand women spent proportionately less time on market activities (40) and more on non-market activities (60) on an average.
20 *The Human Development Report* 1995, UNDP, notes an average figure of 53 per cent world-wide.
21 *Standard Vacuum Refining Co. of India v. Its Workmen* 1961 2 LLJ 227 (SC); AIR 1961 SC 895.
22 *Workmen v. Reptakos Brett & Co. Ltd.* 1992 1 LLJ 340, AIR 1992 SC 504.
23 Section 3 of the Child Labour (Prohibition and Regulation) Act 1986.
24 I do not use the term 'matrimonial' property here for obvious reasons.
25 India does not yet have a legislative framework dealing with comparable worth allowing us to compare jobs performed by men and women. One reason for this is the reluctance of the government to bring about an amendment to the Equal Remuneration Act 1976 to replace the expression 'same or similar work' with the ILO mandated 'equal pay for work of equal value' contained in the ILO's Equal Remuneration Convention No. 100 (1951).
26 The Equal Remuneration Act 1976 in India mandates that men and women should be paid equal wages for 'same or similar work'. The ILO's Equal Remuneration Convention 1951 (No. 100) uses the concept of equal pay for work of equal value—a formulation that has the potential to deal with occupation segregation by sex.

27 For an account of the legislative attempts relating to married women's property, see Agnes (2000: 184, 255), and Menski (2003: 468).

References

Agarwal, B. 1994. *A Field of One's Own*. Cambridge: Cambridge University Press.

______. 1997. 'A Field of One's Own: Gender and Land Rights in South Asia, Salient Features of the Book', in Nitya Rao and Luise Rurup (eds), *A Just Right: Women's Ownership of Natural Resources and Livelihood Security*. New Delhi: Fredrich Ebert Stiftung, pp. 37–43.

Agnes, Flavia. 2000. *Law and Gender Equality*. Delhi: Oxford University Press.

Anant, T.C.A., and Kamala Sankaran. 2003. 'Economic Growth, Employment Generation and Fundamental Principles and Rights at Work', Background Paper for ILO-CIE Conference on 'Globalisation, Decent Work and the ILO Declaration on Fundamental Principles and Rights at Work', Kolkata, 24–25 February.

Anker, R. 1998. *Gender and Jobs: Sex Segregation of Occupations in the World*. Geneva: International Labor Office.

The Beijing Declaration and the Platform of Action. 1996. New York: The United Nations.

Beneria, Lourdes. 1999. 'The Enduring Debate over Unpaid Labour', *International Labour Review*, vol. 138: 287–309.

Chen, Martha Alter (ed.). 1998. *Widows in India*. New Delhi: Sage Publications.

The Copenhagen Declaration and Programme of Action: World Summit for Social Development. 1995. New York: The United Nations.

Dalla Costa, Mariosa, and Selma James. 1972. *The Power of Women and the Subversion of the Community*. Bristol: Falling Wall Press.

Dev, S. Mahendra. 2004. 'Female Work Participation and Child Labour', *Economic and Political Weekly*, vol. 39(19): 736–44.

Glazer, Nona. 1980. 'Women and Household Labour', in Susan Fenster-maker Berk (ed.), *Women and Household Labour*. Beverly Hills: Sage Publications.

Greenwork, Adriana Mata. 2002. 'Gender Issues in Labour Statistics', in Martha Fetherholf Loutfi (ed.), *Women, Gender and Work: What is Equality and How Do We Get There?* Geneva: International Labour Office, pp. 3–20; rpt Rawat publications, Jaipur.

Harriss-White, Barbara. 2004. *India Working: Essays on Society and Economy*. New Delhi: Foundation Books.

Jain, Devaki, and Nirmala Banerjee (eds). 1985. *Tyranny of the Household: Investigative Essays in Women's Work*. New Delhi: Vikas Publishing House.

Jaising, Indira. 1997. 'Women's Inheritance Rights in Contemporary Jurisprudence', Nitya Rao and Luise Rurup (eds), *A Just Right: Women's Ownership of Natural Resources and Livelihood Security*. New Delhi: Fredrich Ebert Stiftung, pp. 110–21.

Kishor, Sunita and Kamla Gupta. 2004. 'Women's Empowerment in India and its States', *Economic and Political Weekly*, vol. 39(19): 694–712.

Kishwar, Madhu. 1994. 'Codified Hindu Law: Myth and Reality', *Economic and Political Weekly*, vol. 29(33): 2145–161.

Kodoth, Praveena. 2004. 'Gender, Property Rights and Responsibilities for Farming in Kerala', *Economic and PoliticalWeekly*, vol. 39(19): 1914–920.

Lee Badgett, M.V. and Nancy Folbre. 1999. 'Assigning Care: Gender Norms and Economic Outcomes', *International Labour Review*, vol. 138(3): 311–26.

Mazumdar, Vina, and Kumud Sharma. 1990. 'Sexual Division of Labor and the Subordination of Women: A Reappraisal from India', in Irene Tinker (ed.), *Persistent Inequalities: Women and World Development*. New York: Oxford University Press, pp. 185–97.

Menscher, Joan P. 1988. 'Women's Work and Poverty: Women's Contribution to the Household in South India', in Daisy Dwyer and Judith Bruce (eds), *A Home Divided: Women and Income in the Third World*. Standford: Stanford University Press, pp. 99–119.

Menski, Werner. 2003. *Hindu Law*. New Delhi: Oxford University Press.

Mies, Maria. 1982. *Lacemakers in Narsapur: Indian Housewives Produce for the World Market*. London: Zed Books.

Mukhopadhyay, Maitrayee. 1998. *Legally Dispossessed: Gender, Identity and the Process of Law*. Calcutta: Stree Publications.

The Nairobi Forward Looking Strategies for the Advancement of Women. 1985. New York: The United Nations.

Panda, Pradeep and Bina Agarwal. 2005. 'Marital Violence, Human Development and Women's Property Status in India', *World Development*, vol. 33(5): 823–50.

Pradhan Saxena, Poonam. 1993. 'Concept of Matrimonial Property', in Kusum (ed.) *Women March Towards Dignity: Socio-Legal Perspectives*. Delhi: Regency Publications, pp. 74–86.

Report of the Study Group on Women and Child Labour. 2001. Government of India: National Commission on Labour.

Sankaran, Kamala. 2004. 'Strategies to Eliminate Child Labour', in Ved Kumari and Susan Brooks (eds), *Creative Child Advocacy*. New Delhi: Sage Publications, pp. 301–14.

Sardamoni, K. 1991. *Filling the Rice Bowl: Women in Paddy Cultivation*. New Delhi: Sangam Books.

Sen, Amartya. 1999. *Development as Freedom*. Delhi: Oxford University Press.

Sen, A.K. 1990. 'Gender and Cooperative Conflict', in Irene Tinker (ed.), *Persistent Inequalities: Women and World Development*. New York: Oxford University Press, pp. 123–49.

Sen, Gita and C. Sen. 1985. 'Women's Domestic Work and Economic Activity', *Economic and Political Weekly*, vol. 20: WS 49–56.

Shimray, U.A. 2004. 'Women's Work in Naga Society', *Economic and Political Weekly*, vol. 39(19): 1698–711.

Sivaramayya, B. 1999. *Matrimonial Property Law in India*. Delhi: Oxford University Press.

The Human Development Report 1995. United Nations Development Project.

'The Promise of SHGs'. 2005. *Economic and Political Weekly*, 40(9): 796–97.

Unni, Jeemol. 2001. 'Gender and Informality in Labour Market in South Asia', *Economic and Political Weekly*, vol. 36(19): 2360–377.

Woolf, Virginia. 1929. *A Room of One's Own*. New York: Harcourt, Brace & Co.

7 Sex-selective Abortion and Reproductive Rights

A Syncretic Feminist Approach

Bijayalaxmi Nanda

Civil and political rights which originated with the American and French Revolution did not extend to women, nor did the full range of economic and social rights which emerged thereafter. This exclusion of women from the full exercise of their rights continued till the end of the eighteenth century. The nineteenth century saw a questioning of this exclusion by liberal political thinkers. By the middle of the twentieth century a full-fledged movement to demand substantive women's rights spread throughout the world. While liberal feminists spoke about equal rights to education and employment, socialist feminists spoke about both relations of production and reproduction and radical feminists focused mainly on reproduction. Feminists since the nineteenth century have elaborated on the idea of reproductive rights by articulating the principle of a woman's right to 'control her own body' (Dixon-Mueller 1993: 4).

Gender discrimination and inequality as a rights issue has been traced to the writings of British feminist Mary Wollstonecraft in *Vindication of Rights of Woman* written in 1792. The famous liberal political thinker John Stuart Mill and his wife Harriet Taylor Mill elaborated further on women's rights in their *Subjection of Women* (1869). Both these texts raised demands in terms of civil and political rights for women. They questioned the discriminatory practices that obstructed women's entry into the public sphere of education and employment. They advocated for the recognition of women's rights in these fields in order to counter discrimination and bring about gender equality. Engels's *Origin of Private Property, Family and State* (1884) strived to establish how women became the first slaves due to the emergence of private property and how in the family the man was the bourgeoisie and the woman the proletariat. They were of the belief that with the abolition of private property women and men would be equals. Socialist feminists like Heidi Hartmann (1981) and Zillah Eisentein (1979)

DOI: 10.4324/9781003299561-7

disagreed with this narrow, reductionist idea. They examined the role of reproduction in women's lives and made causal linkages with the sexual division of labour to provide answers to the reasons for gender discrimination and inequality. Radical feminists emphasized only the women's body as a cause for the inequality and discrimination she faced. Kate Millett's *Sexual Politics* (1971) questioned the public–private distinction which relegated women to the private sphere and failed to recognize the politics of power-structured relationships which led to a male dominated society. The feminist slogan 'the personal is political' raised by her can be considered the foundational principle of reproductive rights. Catherine Mackinnon, Andrea Dworkin and Shulamith Firestone in their respective writings nuanced the understanding on reproductive rights by examining issues around abortion, rape and reproductive technologies.

The female body became the site for competing claims for rights. State policies often engaged with the control of women's fertility for the purpose of demographic goals, and communitarian, cultural and religious structures have pronatalist agendas, while feminists emphasize on the right to bodily integrity, privacy and choice. Connected in complex and contradictory ways, these competing discourses reveal the collaborative and combative nature of the terrain of gender discrimination.

In this chapter an attempt is made first to study the evolution of the idea of reproductive rights, next there is an examination of the conflictual and complex understanding of reproductive rights in the phenomenon of sex-selective abortion in India, then the competing discourses on the issue emerging from the global, state and civil society narratives is discussed. It lays down the story of the struggle to counter sex-selective abortion in India, the roots of the contradictions of some of those discourses when it comes to reproductive rights and the relevance of the same for the status of women in India. In the final analysis the syncretic feminist perspective combining principles from various feminist positions is provided as an approach to resolve some of the debates and dilemmas regarding reproductive rights and countering sex-selective abortion as gender discrimination in India today.

The evolution of reproductive rights

The feminist position on reproductive rights has been examined earlier. As a theoretical discourse reproductive rights owe their origin to the writings of socialist feminists and radical feminists. In terms of inalienable and indivisible rights it found its first expression in the 1966 Declaration on Population by World Leaders (United Nations 1975: 9), which recognized family planning as a means of 'assuring greater opportunity to each person' and of 'freeing man to attain his individual dignity and reach his full potential'

(Dixon-Mueller 1993: 12). The Convention on the Elimination of All forms of Discrimination Against Women (1979) also confirms women's rights to family planning and equal rights with men to decide on the size of the family. It also speaks about right to maternity and child care benefits especially in terms of preventing discrimination at work. The convention emphasizes the obligation of states to reform their cultural and customary practices which are discriminatory to women. It thus addresses three concepts of rights: *natural rights* deriving from the theory of individual liberties, *social rights* from the theories of state responsibility and *customary rights* deriving from traditional beliefs and practices. It recognizes that the achievement of gender equality requires gender-specific policies and programmes. It emphasizes the requirement to eliminate cultural and customary practices and attitudes that are responsible for the gap between the rhetoric of legislation and the reality of its practice. The document serves the purpose of being a directive to action, a commitment to gender equality and a feminist tool to assess gender inequality (Dixon-Mueller 1993: 10).

It was in 1994 that the International Conference of Population and Development (ICPD) in Cairo laid down and elucidated the basic principles of reproductive and sexual rights in their Plan of Action. The rights for women include: (a) the right to decide about pregnancy – if, when and how often, (b) the right to have access to safe, effective, affordable and acceptable methods of family planning, (c) the right to a satisfying and healthy sex life, (d) the right to a safe pregnancy, childbirth and a healthy infant and (e) the right to control over one's body and bodily integrity.

Reproductive rights were again emphasized in the Beijing Platform of Action in 1995, popularly known as the Platform for Action for women (United Nations 1995). It is here that Hilary Clinton, who was then chairing the opening session, said the famous words 'Women's rights are human rights', thereby proclaiming rights for women as an inalienable part of the discourse on rights. The comprehensive idea of the right to control one's body is a feminist principle that stresses women's right to their sexual and reproductive capacity. It includes their right to informed and empowered consent and choice. This understanding of the right to one's body is an integral part of liberal and Marxist principles too.

In India the National Population Policy (NPP) 2000 (Government of India 2000) takes its basic philosophy from ICPD PoA and from the concerns of women's organizations in the country, thereby taking into consideration the changing understanding on population, reproductive health, equity and rights. With the shift in international perspective influenced by ICPD, the government reflected its change of approach in the NPP 2000 by eliminating the use of contraceptive targets. The NPP is a historic document which reflects a shift from the earlier demographically driven, targetoriented policies to one that addressed special concerns of reproductive health. The NPP addresses the unmet needs for basic reproductive and child health services, supplies and infrastructure (Population Foundation of India 2010).

The dilemmas and debates regarding reproductive rights of women are played out most clearly when one examines the issue of abortion. In the West abortion has increasingly become caught in a double bind. This is largely because the feminist understanding of reproductive rights and choice is eclipsed by the conservative response of the right to life of the foetus to be upheld over women's rights. The persistent attempts by feminists to recover abortion rights for women continue to be their most major battle in the US.

In India abortion services are available to women as a limited medical right under the Medical Termination of Pregnancy Act 1974. However, issues of safe and accessible abortion services remain. Intense son preference complicates the subject of abortion in the country. It leads to sex-selective abortion, which in turn shapes the dynamics of the relationship between reproductive rights and feminist activism in fundamental ways. The contradictions and contestations embedded in these issues may pose challenges and have over time divided feminists; they nevertheless raise a critical point about women's lives and their choices regarding matters of reproductive rights.

Sex-selective abortion in India

The deficit of women in India and the possible factors responsible for it have engaged the attention of demographers, social scientists and social activists in India (Agnihotri 1995; Bose 2001, 2002; Patel 2007; Shiva 2002). What has been convincingly demonstrated is that the primary factor contributing to the deficit of women in India is the anomalous higher mortality among women compared to men (Visaria 2006). The decennial census reports are the primary source of accurate information on sex ratio. The deficit of females, especially in the age group 0 to 6 (what is called child sex ratio), has increased between 1981 and 2011. This deficit has triggered alarm bells since it has increased in spite of the overall improvements in mortality situation and a greater increase in life expectancy of women compared to that of men.

Statistics show that the decline in the child sex ratio between 1981 and 2011 cannot be solely explained by discrimination against girls practiced in this region for several decades, because at no other time in the history of census taking has the sex ratio of children declined so drastically (Visaria 2006). Although there has been a consistent decline in sex ratio, an increase in the deficit of young girls noted in the four decennial censuses of 1981, 1991, 2001 and 2011 is indicative of a strong possibility that the traditional methods of neglect of female children have increasingly been replaced by not allowing female children to be born.

The practice of female infanticide has been known to exist in certain regions like Punjab, Haryana, Rajasthan and other states in the North-Western region (Malhotra 2002; Oldenberg 2003). With the advent of new reproductive technologies, this traditional gender-discriminatory practice has been replaced by sex-selective abortion. These reproductive technologies, which include amniocentesis and ultrasound for sex determination followed by sex-selective abortion, have spread to other parts of the country which essentially did not practice female infanticide.

It was the third wave of the women's movement in India, especially the Committee on the Status of Women in India in 1974, that recognized sex ratio as a composite indicator of women's status. The decline in child sex ratio and the issue of 'missing girls' were raised by women's groups. Due to their persistent lobbying and through seminars, debates and research, the issue gained prominence and was provided an appropriate environment to take firm roots in domains of enquiry – be it research, policy, advocacy or campaigns (Rustagi 2006). This eventually led to a ban of sex-determination tests in government hospitals in 1976.

However, it only meant a partial ban, as it led to the proliferation of private clinics/hospitals offering the facility. Since then, different parts of the country have witnessed several campaigns against the misuse of science and technology for continued discrimination against women. In 1982, the Centre for Women's Development Studies (CWDS) launched the first campaign. It was initiated by Vina Mazumdar and Lotika Sarkar in Delhi as a protest against an advertisement for Bhandari Antenatal Sex Determination Clinic in Amritsar, Punjab. The clinic was openly advertising its services through press, in railway compartments and in other public places. The advertisement referred to daughters as 'liabilities' to the family and a threat to the nation and exhorted expectant parents to avail the services of the clinics to rid themselves of this 'danger' (Nanda 2007).

More campaigns like the Forum Against Sex Determination and Sex PreSelection (FASDSP) in 1985 in Maharashtra and the Campaign Against Sex-selective Abortion (CASSA), Tamil Nadu came up. FASDSP lobbied to regulate the practice of sex determination in Maharashtra by formulating a separate legislation, instead of modifying the Medical Termination of Pregnancy (MTP) Act, 1971, that had the danger of curtailing women's right to abort. As a result, the Maharashtra Regulation of Use of Prenatal Diagnostic Techniques Act, 1988, came into being.

Serious drawbacks in the state legislation and poor implementation caused the awakening of interest in the issue across the entire country. A move for an all-India ban on sex-determination tests gained momentum, and the Pre-Natal Diagnostic Tests (Regulation and Prohibition of Misuse) Act, 1994 (called the PNDT Act), came into existence.

Though the PNDT Act came into force in January 1996, no visible evidence of decline in the practice of sex selection came forth. Lack of concern and political will to implement the legislation by the Centre and states led to a Public Interest Litigation (PIL) in the Supreme Court. The PIL was filed by three petitioners – Dr. Sabu George, a social activist, Mahila Sarvangeen Utkarsh Mandal (MASUM) and Pune and Centre for the Enquiry of Health and Allied Themes (CEHAT), Mumbai, in February 2000. In May 2001, the Supreme Court directed the Central Government to implement the PNDT Act in all its aspects and called upon all state governments to take necessary steps to implement the Act. However, a further dip in Census 2001 sex ratio suggested that this gender-discriminatory practice continued unabated in spite of the laws against it (Nanda 2007).

In the light of new techniques available to determine sex before birth, it was felt necessary to amend the Act. From February 14, 2003, the Pre-natal Diagnostic Techniques (Regulation and Prevention of Misuse) Amendment Act, 2002 came into force. After incorporating a few important changes, the PNDT Act 1994 was renamed as 'the Pre-conception and Pre-natal Diagnostic Techniques (Prohibition of Sex Selection) Act (PCPNDT Act)'.

Given these conditions it is important to understand sex-selective abortion in a wider perspective and along with debates on abortion in India. In 1965 a UN mission evaluating India's population policy recommended legalizing abortion (Menon 2004). In 1966 the Shantilal Shah Committee submitted its report recommending that access to abortion be liberalized in order to put an end to a large number of illegal and unsafe abortions (Jalnawalla 1974). This Act, known as the Medical Termination of Pregnancy Act (MTP Act), was passed in 1971 quite independently of the women's movement. It is, thus, believed that it is within imperatives of population control that the Indian state moved towards the legalization of abortion. Clearly then the legal sanction for abortion does not arise from feminist principles at all, but it exists nevertheless (Menon 2004). In fact, there exists a very influential school of thought in India which justifies the selective abortion of female foetuses as a form of population control (Contractor and Duggal 2003). While there is a need to recognize the right to abortion as a right for women to have control over their bodies, given that they have very few bargaining or negotiation powers when it comes to their reproductive choices, it is only a limited medical right that has been sanctioned to them by a population-control lobby. The gender dimensions which are present in the phenomenon of sex-selective abortion and its perpetuation through coercive population policies must be examined further (Rao 2001).

Evidence from some parts of India suggests that termination of pregnancies was resorted to not for the reasons stated under the MTP Act but because there is a strong son preference leading to sex-selective abortions. The gender bias was flagrantly aided by a combination of medical technology on the one hand and the liberal abortion laws that helped couples to abort female foetuses on the other (Visaria 2006). Therefore, the issue of sex-selective abortion brings into the fore the discrimination against women in society at multiple levels. First, there is a barrier at the level of birth; and secondly, women's fertility and reproductive choice are controlled by societal conditioning premised on the 'worth of girls'. The proliferation of new reproductive technologies and a consumerist market use a pro-choice language to reinforce anti-women practices, i.e., in negating the right to be born as females.

The state in India and policy responses

The state in India follows two distinct approaches in terms of policy response to the issue. The first addresses the demand for sex-selective abortion from families, which is in the form of providing financial incentives to enhance the worth of girls. The other is to address the supply of new reproductive technologies for sex determination by legislation, that is, the PCPNDT Act. These two approaches are common to most policy responses regarding gender justice. In discussing discourses of the state in Britain regarding gender equality, Kantola mentions the crime discourse which associates the state with providing law and order and the equal opportunities discourse where the state had a role in providing women and men with the same chances (Kantola 2006: 157). So in this vein of the crime discourse and the equal opportunities discourse the state in India has unfurled a comprehensive national legislation, that is, the PCPNDT Act and a Conditional Cash Transfer (CCT) strategy in many states in order to counter sex-selective abortion and provide for gender justice.

The PCPNDT Act (Pre-Conception and Pre-Natal Diagnostic Techniques Act), 1994 (as amended in 2003), is a comprehensive piece of social legislation which emerged due to active involvement of women's groups and a sustained campaign. As the law stands today, it has two objectives to fulfil. The first is to regulate the prenatal diagnostic procedures, and the second is a total prohibition of 'sex selection', a term defined primarily to denote any kind of pre-conception test or method used for sex selection (Jaisingh 2007). The Act is largely unused due to a complex nexus among medical practitioners, families seeking the service and the government machinery.

The other issue that impacts the implementation of this legislation is related to the feminist groups, especially a section of the pro-abortion feminists. They are of the opinion that a strict implementation of the PCPNDT

Act will lead to essential abortion services going underground. As women and families begin to feel the pressure of these external campaigns, they might begin to resort to unlicensed providers and resist medical care, endangering the health of women and their babies (Sarkaria 2009). This section of the pro-abortion feminists thus wants to steer clear of the issue of sex-selective abortion. Since they make their arguments for abortion on the basis of choice, they feel it is untenable for them to make a case for denying women the choice to determine the sex of the foetus. Other sections of the pro-abortion feminist group, however, continue to engage with the complexities of the issue at hand. Sarkaria elaborates upon this in the context of the United States. According to her, pro-abortion feminists in the reproductive justice movement perceive the narrow notion of individual choice as exclusionary and even incompatible with the reality of many women's lives. The movement seeks to expand the concept of choice. She cites April Cherry, who states that 'the right to choose means very little when women are powerless' (Sarkaria 2009: 940).

The criminalization of sex-selective abortion is thus important because it takes into account the implausibility of an empowered choice in a context where women may be coerced or conditioned to do sex-selective abortion. It also critiques the basic reason for the choice, which is the prejudice against daughters in society. It highlights the role of the medical practitioners who provide sex determination and conduct sex-selective abortion in rampant violation of the Act. While the pro-choice feminists' approach to abortion is to protect individual women's decisions, sex selection and sex-selective abortion fall outside this ambit of choices.

The government has unfurled a number of schemes, both at the Centre and in the states, to incentivize the birth of girls in India. Most of them are CCTs. They include the Girl-Child Protection Scheme in Tamil Nadu, Balri Rakshak Yojana in Punjab, the Ladli scheme in Delhi and Haryana and many others and the Beti Bachao Beti Padhao (BBBP) campaign in 100 districts of India which have the lowest child sex ratio. The schemes except for the BBBP are mostly in the form of financial incentives of cash deposits which are delivered at the end as a lump sum between Rs. 12,000 in some states and Rs. 1 lakh in others. The scheme, which seems benign and well intentioned, comes with a set of eligibility criteria and conditionalities. The eligibility criteria are tied up with restricting the number of children and the income criteria of parents. Feminists have questioned the population-control mindset of the government. According to studies by feminist research scholars, the linking of financial incentive schemes for girls to an insidious population-control policy has an adverse impact on girls. It can increase sex-selective abortion and also the vulnerability of girls who fall outside the ambit of the schemes. Moreover, it stigmatizes the poor, making them seem like the guilty when it comes to sex-selective abortion, whereas it is clear that the poor are the last in the queue to discriminate against girls. The BBBP campaign combines the strict implementation of the PCPNDT Act to counter sex determination with incentivizing education for girls in order to break the myths and stereotypes about daughters being liabilities.

Feminists have thus critiqued these schemes and have asked for a review of the same in order to rid them of their gender-insensitive and contradictory elements. So while pro-abortion feminists critique the PCPNDT Act for overlapping on the right to abortion and ask for its complete withdrawal, others would like to see this law retained while protecting the right to safe and legal abortion. Some outrightly reject the conditional cash transfers for protecting girls, while some believe it can be retained if reviewed in the light of the critique presented by them on its gender-insensitive elements.

The emphasis thus is to understand the importance of each feminist position and suggest ways to reconcile them in order to engage with the issue of sex-selective abortion. This reconciled position can be defined as a syncretic feminist perspective. The aim here is to demonstrate that a syncretic feminist position with an in-depth and holistic understanding of reproductive rights is the most appropriate approach to be used in the context of countering sex-selective abortion in this country.

Discourses: debates and dilemmas

The discourse on rights is best exemplified in the various debates and dilemmas present in the state and global narratives concerning sex-selective abortion in India. The situation of competing rights – the conflicting claims of the family to choose the sex of the foetus – and the right to life of the foetus are poised against each other. The rights of women to exercise their reproductive choices and not to be either coerced or conditioned to abort it because of it being female is not effectively articulated in this scenario. The discourse therefore is by no means a simple one; however, the significance of reproductive rights in its holistic and syncretic sense cannot be overridden. The predominant frames of the debates are three, which I elucidate here – the Equality versus Demographic Discourse, the Crime versus Justice Discourse and the Rights versus Ethics Discourse. A detailed examination of the same follows here.

(a) The equality discourse versus demographic discourse

Feminist voices on sex-selective abortion have raised concerns about declining sex ratio as a significant indicator of women's status. The approach of the syncretic feminist perspective is to view women as equals who are denied their equal status due to a multitude of factors. Some of these factors include: fewer access to opportunities in education, employment, political participation as well as entrenched patriarchal structures and institutions at play. The significance of equality to feminists here is marked by their efforts to persuasively establish a dichotomy between the Medical Termination of Pregnancy (MTP) Act and the Pre-Conception and Pre-Natal Diagnostic Techniques (PCPNDT) Act, to constructively critique the misuse of reproductive technologies and to emphasize improving the status of women in society. The affirmation of women's role as central to development represents a major victory for women's movements and gender equality advocates who have been struggling to make their voices and perspectives heard by policymakers. At the same time, there is a concern about the extent to which these commitments get translated into reality on the ground and the widening gap between policy pronouncements and practice (Menon-Sen 2013: 162).

The state has in this sense remained distanced from the substantive equality model. The conditional cash transfers which were available remained steeped in a cultural context of daughters who are devalued and the social constraints that exist for their family due to their birth. In some states there are no separate conditional cash transfers for girls. A few CCTs that may exist focus on reproduction with maternal and child health as their major concern. The central government's National Rural Health Mission (NRHM) is the overarching framework for both regions in this matter. The Janani Suraksha Yojana (JSY) is invoked as the panacea for all maternal and child health issues.[1] The value structures that inform the states in their negotiation of the idea of gender equality are flawed. There is an instrumental construction of women as mothers or in the context of the demographic narrative as numbers which are 'missing' and need to be restored in order to bring about balance in population.

In Punjab, which had the dubious distinction of being the worst state when it came to its child sex ratio (CSR) in 2001, the state unfurled a range of policies and programmes, donor-driven activism and funded projects when the 2001 census reports came out. The dubious distinction of having the worst child sex ratio in India made sex-selective abortion a priority issue to be tackled by the state. Once the child sex ratio showed marginal improvements, all such programmes were put on the back burner. In some states in the eastern zone like Odisha for example, the 2011 census did reveal a decline, but since the decline is not stark compared to other states, serious engagement on the issue is still not visible. The demographic discourse emerged through the writing of Amartya Sen and others, and feminist perspectives highlighted it in order to alert the state to the dismal status of women. However, the state's tendency has been to construct the notion of gender equality here in sex-neutral rather than sex-specific ways.

An acknowledgement of the personhood of women and the range of structural, cultural and material inequalities they face remain on the fringes of state discourses. The capacity for the state to re-imagine women in terms of equal citizens whose constitutional guarantees are being undermined by sex-selective abortion is a far cry. The obligation upon governments and state agencies to protect and promote the right to equality for women are seldom fulfilled, nor is its enforceability a mandate. The approach of the state is to address and redress the issue as a demographic concern and as a social evil. It is not surprising since the baggage of cultural factors which are seen as immune to state intervention has defined the lack of equality for women in India in the context of sex-selective abortion. Daughter aversion has been seen by the state as emerging from a cultural context where families due to cultural beliefs and superstitions eliminate them. It is worthwhile to note that institutional norms, practices, incentives, disincentives, rules and regulations are equally responsible for obstructing women's right to equality. The critical examination of conditional cash transfers has revealed how, while they were ostensibly tied to enhance the worth of the girl-child for the family, they were ironically linked to gender-disempowering elements like limiting number of children, sterilization, age limit and such other matters.

The state in India is, thus, driven by the demographic narrative. The decline in numbers of women in India figures in world statistics and reports. It leads to a lower rank of India in terms of its position on the Human Development Index (HDI) and other forms of measurement like the Gender Empowerment Measure (GEM) and Gender Development Index (GDI). The state has utilitarian arguments about the need for women as wives and mothers. Many of the initiatives of the state have exemplified this where the state's instrumental rationality of women's health is seen in terms of focusing only on childbirth visible in the reproductive and child health programmes as well as in the intent and objectives of the NRHM. Many of the communication materials, especially in Punjab and Haryana where there is a deficit of women, also reveal other elements of this utilitarian stance.

By presenting contemporary examples of how men now find it difficult to get brides because of the dwindling numbers of women, they implore families to keep their daughters for this reason. This fails to take into account that in many parts of India the decline in the number of women has led to a double burden on them. The practice of coerced polyandry has resulted in daughters getting eliminated, even as brides are bought and sold. Given this reality, the utilitarian argument about women's 'use' as 'providers of sex and sons' is essentially anti-women (Nanda 2013). There is very little attempt to perceive the inequalities within marriage, its predominantly patriarchal structure and the potential for violence within it. The state discourse is also about restoring balance in the ratio through various interventions to enhance the value of the girl-child.

This discourse, therefore, is premised, as is the case with the global discourse, on an instrumental distinction between rights of the girl-child and of women. The benign and emotive subject of the right of girls to be born is pitted against the image of regressive families which let their cultural backwardness obstruct that right. At the same time any reference to gender equality remains purely incidental. While misuse of new reproductive technologies stands defined under an available legislation, i.e., the PCPNDT Act, the state remains an unwilling partner here in terms of fixing blame.

(b) The justice discourse versus crime discourse

While the dominant global discourse does engage with legislation in terms of banning sex determination, it is a complex one. Thirty-six countries across the world have banned sex selection either totally or for social non-medical uses in Europe, Asia and North America. Twenty-five such countries are in Europe and eight in Asia, in addition to Canada in North America and Australia and New Zealand (Darnovsky 2009). The United States is a major exception in the West, which has no such legislation at the national level.[2] However, a bill known as Prenatal Non-discrimination Act was introduced by Representative Trent Franks, Republican of Arizona, a state which already has such a legislation, which would punish doctors with up to 5 years in prison for performing sex-selective abortions and race-selective abortions because the parents seek a child of the other sex. The bill was defeated in the house on 31 May 2012 and could not become a law.

Apart from the main opposition to the bill in terms of it being restrictive of women's choice for privacy and being anti-women (Steinhauer 2012), its racial overtones also came for pronounced criticism. The introducer of the bill had cited studies which showed evidence of sex-selective abortion among Chinese-, Indian- and Korean-American families through the US Census 2000 data. However, it was pointed out that the study was not detailed enough to pinpoint the cause of the disparate ratios – whether it was due to pre-pregnancy techniques involving fertility treatments or sex-selective abortions. In addition, they commented that these three ethnic communities constitute a very small proportion of the US population. The introducers of the bill had also relied on interviews with 65 immigrant Indian women, a sample too small to inform a national legislation (Barot 2012). Clearly the opponents of the bill in general and Asian women's rights groups in particular feared targeting of Chinese, Indian and Korean communities through this legislation.

> Reproductive justice and Asian women's rights groups, in fact, cite myriad problems that sex-selective abortion bans could create. At the most practical level, such restrictions are neither enforceable nor effective, as already demonstrated internationally. And various attempts to enforce them, they stress, would only perpetuate further discrimination in their communities through stereotyping and racial profiling of Asian women whose motivations for an abortion would be under suspicion. In a recent op-ed explaining their opposition to PRENDA (Prenatal Non-discrimination Act), the executive directors of NAPAWF (National Asian Pacific American Women's Forum) and the National Latina Institute for Reproductive Health wrote: 'Immigrant women already face numerous barriers to accessing health care of any kind, including reproductive health care and abortion, and this ban would make an already difficult situation far worse'.
>
> (Barot 2012)

By making efforts to ban sex-selective abortion, to curtail abortion rights in general and to target select Asian communities in particular, such discourses create barriers for ethnic populations, especially Indian and Chinese. The justification for this perceived discrimination is derived from the demographic profile of the ethnic population in terms of female deficit and also inferred from attitudinal studies of the community revealing an intense son preference. At the same time, remarkably, the legislation to control the development in reproductive technologies, especially for more specific 'baby shopping', does not exist.

Baby shopping is being made possible through genetic engineering with the help of eugenics where prospective parents can flip through a catalogue and shop for traits to 'design' their children. Genetic engineering is the deliberate modification of an organism through the alteration of its genetic code. By removing sections of an organism's DNA and replacing them with new segments, geneticists can artificially select for certain traits. These techniques are being perfected through experiments on plants and animals and as scientists continue to uncover the secrets of the human genome. Engineered organisms, such as glow-in-the-dark cats, abnormally muscular cows and insect-resistant corn, have already been successfully developed, and designer babies may be next (Catalano 2012). A designer baby is defined as 'a baby whose genetic make-up has been selected in order to eradicate a particular defect, or to ensure that a particular gene is present' by the Oxford English Dictionary.[3] The Human Genome Project has already mapped out every gene and chemical base pair of the human genome, and scientists continue to uncover the effects and interactions of each gene. And now the process of in-vitro fertilization provides access to the genetic material within. This reproductive technology is being promoted without any considerations of regulations and the implications for sex selection.

Michael Sandel is one of the most influential critics of the research to create perfect babies whose eye colour, tastes, intelligence and sex can be genetically mapped and coded and produced.

> Perhaps the most inevitable nonmedical use of bioengineering is sex selection. For centuries parents have been trying to choose the sex of their children. Today biotech succeeds where folk remedies failed.... If sex selection by sperm sorting is objectionable, it must be for reasons that go beyond the debate about the moral status of the embryo. One such reason is that sex selection is an instrument of sex discrimination – typically against girls, as illustrated by the chilling sex ratios in India and China.
>
> (Sandel 2004)

The idea of regulating such research through legislation has been likened to controlling cures for baldness by proponents of eugenics. The regulation of sex determination for only the ethnic communities like Indian, Chinese and Korean in the United States and Europe has also been critically examined. In UK abortion purely on the grounds of sex is banned by the Abortion Act, 1967. However, it does not ban the doctor from communicating the sex of the foetus to the parents during ultrasound scans. New reproductive technologies like sperm separation for pre-conception sex selection are not covered by any law. In the United States, like in other developed parts of the world, sex determination is allowed. Its use is rationalized on the basis that couples in their countries are essentially gender sensitive, so their desire to have gender variety or balance in family size and composition should be allowed.

However, the practice of targeting South Asian immigrants through making these tests illegal or difficult for them to acquire has also been criticized for leading to a stigmatization of the community. Doctors, clinics and ethicists in countries like the United States have delineated this part of the practice as being sexist and therefore unethical while continuing to argue that sex-selective family balancing is ethical. This has served to limit the discussion on the other gender aspects embodied in the use of these technologies. Malik argues convincingly that there is a need to articulate clearly the universality of the gendered context of the use of these technologies for sex selection in all socio-cultural milieus. In other words, there is a need to move away from son preference as the only measuring yardstick to evaluate the sexist use of these technologies. She further highlights the need to oppose the growing trend of the use of reproductive technologies for non-medical, non-compelling reasons. Family balancing is one such 'cosmetic use'. We need to emphasize that non-medical use of these technologies does not necessarily mean they do not carry reproductive health burdens for women as a result of the use – a fact that is often ignored (Mallik 2003).

The International Human Rights Clinic at the University of Chicago Law School, the National Asian Pacific American Women's Forum and Advancing New Standards in Reproductive Health at the University of California, San Francisco, released a report on sex-selective abortion laws and policies in the United States recently. The findings of the report allude to the stigmatization of Indian and Chinese families due to the presence of such laws. The report says in its findings 'though Asian Americans are most discussed by lawmakers trying to pass sex-selective abortion laws, two countries, Lichtenstein and Armenia, have male skewed sex ratios at birth as high or higher than India and China' (Citro 2014).

In India the legislation is mainly concerned with the misuse of reproductive technologies, especially in terms of sex determination. The low conviction rate in terms of the magnitude of the crime, as defined under the PCPNDT Act, is a cause for concern. It is also a testimony to the fact that it has not received serious attention from policymakers and implementers. The state discourse here is that since there is a nexus between the families seeking sex determination and the doctors providing it, it is very difficult for the state to intervene in the matter and to be able to catch the culprits. The abject helplessness that the state ostensibly demonstrates in the face of rampant misuse of reproductive technologies also reveals limitations in terms of defining the issue. The state discourse, similar to the global discourse, views it as a crime against the unborn girl-child by their families. It also regards it in terms of cultural backwardness of the community which indulges in such practices. The medical professionals offering the service do not figure in concrete terms within the state discourse.

This discourse in India, like the global discourse, is thus underpinned by the cultural norm. The demand for gender justice here tends to be legitimate only from the position of protecting the rights of the unborn girlchild rather than in terms of women's rights, choice and agency. In fact as stated earlier, the state discourse as well as popular discourse defines it as a crime of mother vs. daughter or mother-in-law versus daughter-in-law. The appeal highlighted by communication materials which are developed to create awareness generation are highly emotive, mostly pleadings of the daughter to the mother.[4]

In Punjab the monitoring or tracking of pregnancies of women demonstrates this crime discourse clearly. It is not defined in the language of the justice paradigm that is central to the feminist perspectives, which view it as a crime against women and as one emerging from a range of causes which are inextricably linked. In a succinct study on laws favouring son preference in India, leading legal feminist Kirti Singh deconstructs legal instruments which directly or indirectly influence son preference in India and thereby lead to sex selection. She critically examines the elements and features in the laws which are favourable to sons and perpetuate gender discrimination. She also points out how justice is also denied by the attitudes and orientations of law-implementing agencies like the judiciary. A close reading of judgements and judicial process which has been examined in the study has brought these facts to the fore (Singh 2013).

Mitu Khurana, who is a woman complainant under the PCPNDT Act, believes that she faced the maximum opposition from implementing authorities and the judiciary. Her struggle for justice which is now 6 years in court is symptomatic of most such cases. The lackadaisical approach of the law-implementing authorities within the government and the judiciary reveal the limitations of the efficacy of these laws and their adjudication. In her reflections Mitu has gathered together the statements of different judges who have been sitting on her cases. The various statements include:

> If you want to save your daughters from harassment, withdraw your cases and do a settlement with your husband. Otherwise I will see to it that you have to bring your daughters to the court on every hearing. Laws are meant only for books and lectures. Do not think you will get anything from the courts.
>
> Tell your price. What will you take to withdraw your cases?
>
> You are the enemy of your daughters; you are destroying their life only because of your ego [. . .][5]

A slew of more punitive laws on sexual harassment and rapes have emerged in India following a much-reported gang rape and murder of a paramedic student in Delhi in December 2012.[6] Ratna Kapur, who in her earlier work had taken a position that legal interventions are useful when it comes to gender justice (Kapur 1996, 1999), has complicated her opinion since then. According to Kapur today too much of legislation, especially with stringent punitive implications, may be counterproductive as far as achieving gender justice is concerned (Kapur 1996). The record of patriarchal judicial systems and victimization of the victim in courtroom proceedings also add to the obstacles. Ratna Kapur disagrees with Nussbaum's idea in *Sex and Social Justice* (Nussbaum 1999). She does not outrightly reject the liberal ideas posed by Nussbaum but critiques the hegemonic ideals of liberalism in a multi-layered and nuanced manner. Speaking about sexuality, Kapur points out how laws and culture can interact and overlap with each other creating a nexus which is reinforcing conservative and patriarchal positions about women. Through her focus on women's sexuality in India, Kapur reveals how self-appointed guardians of Indian culture reaffirm dominant gender ideologies. She uses the track of the controversies surrounding the films *The Bandit Queen* and *Fire*, anti-sodomy law (Section 377) and the anti-trafficking law (the Immoral Traffic Prevention Act) to do so.

In Mitu's situation, the statements of judges and implementing authorities on her case do show the reflection of their patriarchal consciousness and the intermeshing of women's sexuality within it. The legitimate role of women to be considered within the institution of marriage and their fertility and sexuality to be defined within the norms of marriage makes it difficult to have a gender-egalitarian position. So a liberal rights discourse as supported by Nussbaum which emphasizes that feminism and social justice have common concerns misses the way in which an enabling legislation can be subverted by the ideological consciousness of its implementers. It also does not recognize the possibility that some of the legislation irrespective of their genesis, i.e., having developed through feminist struggle, may continue to have gender-discriminatory elements or gender-neutral elements where the interpretation by a patriarchal judicial authority may not deliver the goods so to speak. By 'gender neutrality' one is referring to those elements in the law that are in a neutral language to mark their objectivity.

The PCPNDT Act was enacted with the purpose of not overlapping over the right to abortion of women in India. The intent of the law is quite clear. It is meant to be a gender-enabling legislation. However, in its provisions and its specifications there is reference to gender discrimination only in two places. In one place it mentions 'female foeticide' and in another it says 'the woman will be presumed innocent unless proven otherwise'. The rules and procedures of the law are detailed, cumbersome and written with technical details especially about medical services. Although a lot has gone into the making of this law and it is comprehensive, the so called technical features, which make sense perhaps to the experts in the field and feminists and activists who have been involved in the making of this legislation, make little sense to authorities who implement the law. In comparison, the simple outlaying of laws like Protection of Women from Domestic Violence Act and Protection of Women from Sexual Harassment at Workplace Act makes it difficult to a great extent for implementing authorities, irrespective of patriarchal attitudes, to interpret the law according to their mindsets.

The syncretic feminist position will, however, mean combining elements from both Nussbaum and Kapur here. While understanding that liberal rights talk may be hegemonic or counterproductive as Kapur says, it is important to retain a basic minimum from the rights talk as purported by Nussbaum. It is also important to negotiate with that kind of universal rights talk and expose its limitations and reveal the problems of the specific cultural and ideological consciousness in the locations and sites where these rights are being talked about. Strategizing the field in order to counter gender discrimination is very significant here. The application of the strategies and theories to the lived reality of sex-selective abortion in India requires an ability to go beyond critique and engage with the emancipatory potential of its elements.

Theoretical understandings on justice go beyond ideas of mere procedural legal justice. The most ambitious attempt to answer this question was provided by John Rawls in his 1971 book *A Theory of Justice*. Rawls argues that 'A well-ordered society is effectively regulated by a public conception of justice'. This means that all citizens would use their reason to choose the same principles of justice. To put Rawls's conclusion succinctly, we would insist on being treated equally while permitting those inequalities that benefit everyone, especially the least prosperous among us. The principles for protecting the life chances of the disadvantaged members of the community are chosen because we adopt 'the veil of ignorance' to conceal our own natural talents and our social circumstances that might bias our thinking, we would fear that we might be among the least well-heeled (Schumaker 2010). This egalitarian idea of justice has been put to many criticisms. Notable amongst them are Sen and Nussbaum's capability approach and Okin's feminist critique.

Sen's sophisticated argument is that by concentrating on the means to freedom rather than on the extent of freedom, Rawls's theory of a basic structure of society has stopped short of paying adequate attention to freedom as such (Sen 1995: 86). Based on this understanding, Sen developed his capabilities approach. The assessment of individual claims is not in terms of the resources held but the freedom they actually enjoy leading the lives they value (Sen 1995: 81). Nussbaum considers the capabilities approach an alternative to Rawls. In her own words, 'the alternative then, is the capabilities approach, an approach that has been developed in somewhat different ways by me in philosophy and by Amartya Sen in economics' (Nussbaum 2006: 70). She goes on to further add,

> In *Women and Human Development* and elsewhere, I argue that the best approach to this idea of a basic social minimum is provided by an approach that focuses on human capabilities, that is what people are actually able to do and to be, in a way informed by an intuitive idea of a life that is worthy of the dignity of the human being.
>
> (Nussbaum 2006: 70)

She identifies a list of central human capabilities, arguing that all of them are implicit in the idea of a life worthy of human dignity. In her work *Frontiers of Justice* she analyses three social issues which could not be resolved or even partially addressed by traditional theories of justice. These include the problem of achieving justice for persons with physical and mental disability, of extending justice to all citizens of the world and lastly the problem of doing justice in relation to the treatment of non-human animals. Her critique of Rawls is premised on the ground that there is no watertight definition of what justice is in the contemporary context (Nussbaum 2006).

The approach, both in Sen's understanding and Nussbaum's expansion, is more than just a theoretical engagement with the idea. It explores its application in the real world. In fact, in her most recent work Nussbaum makes a case for love in matters of justice (Nussbaum 2013). According to Nussbaum, a decent political culture cannot survive without cultivation of some emotion. She categorizes three emotions that pose problems for what she terms 'compassionate citizenship'. These include envy, fear and shame. There is a need for emotion and compassion to motivate and sustain altruistic actions and egalitarian institutions. She talks about political emotions rooted in love, which she explains as:

> embracing imperfection while striving for justice. Just as personal love and friendship are at their best when they are directed not at ideal images of the person, but, instead, at the whole person with flaws and faults (not, of course, without criticizing or arguing), so too with love of a city or country: it gets under one's skin, is undeterred by imperfection, and thus enables diverse people, most of them dissatisfied with reality, but in many different and incompatible ways, to embrace one another and enter a common future.
>
> (Nussbaum 2013: 393)

Okin's well-known criticism of Rawls's theory of justice in *Justice, Gender and the Family* is devoted to exposing the way in which contemporary political philosophers fail to take sexual difference into account, despite their use of gender-neutral language (McKinnon 2011: 275). She argues that any theory of justice which is silent about the inequalities within the family is an incomplete one. Carole Gilligan argues for the feminist ethics of sentimental care to replace the masculinist sense of justice. Wolff and De-Shalit say that the government's responsibility in the attempt to achieve social justice should be to 'decluster disadvantage', which would be, in effect, to arrange society so that there is no clearly worst-off group (McKinnon 2011: 187).

The theoretical terrain of justice is rich and variegated. It raises questions of rights, entitlements, equality, capability, sensibility, disadvantage, choice and freedom. But the state in India in general and in the context of sex-selective abortion in particular chooses to restrict itself to the crime and the equal-opportunity discourses. The crime discourse, which is about restoring law and order, is stated clearly in the state policies and programmes, best exemplified by the PCPNDT Act. However, as stated earlier, the implementation of the law leaves a lot to be desired. The spirit of the law decriminalizes women, but the implementing authorities do tend to see it as an issue which is gender neutral. Secondly, in the equal-opportunities discourse, the CCTs are unimaginatively rolled out with contradictory elements which actually enhance gender discrimination. The justice discourse, for all practical purposes, thus, remains distanced from the ambit of state interventions.

While the notion of legal justice is validated through the legislation (PCPNDT Act), it becomes diluted due to states' overemphasis of sex-selective abortion as a social evil. That this is an expression of misogyny and gender discrimination, as underlined by feminist perspectives, has not been recognized by the state. Thus, the substantive idea of gender justice is also undermined. In short, the state remains unresponsive to questions of justice in countering sex-selective abortion.

(c) The rights discourse versus ethics discourse

That 'little girls' are 'mercilessly' aborted by their parents due to an intense son preference and daughter aversion makes a case for an ethics discourse. The ethical claim of the little girls' right to life here acknowledges the impact of socio-cultural factors, but it is used to further drive a point about the right to life of foetuses. Many pro-life organizations supported by the church and other missionary agencies, in both the global and the local domains, have used the issue to demonstrate the ethical issues regarding abortion. Campaigns have been mounted on the issue sanctifying the right to life. They have tried to challenge the arguments of the pro-choice lobby for abortion by citing the concerns around sex-selective abortion.

Eight states in the United States currently have laws prohibiting sex-selective abortion. Twenty-one states and the United States Congress have considered bills banning sex-selective abortion. Proponents of laws banning sex-selective abortion in legislatures and civil society groups around the country claim that the laws will prevent gender discrimination. However, upon closer examination it becomes clear that restricting access to abortion is the general motivation for sex-selective abortion bans in the United States. In the United States Congress and state legislatures across the country, politicians who sponsor sex-selective abortion bans are at the forefront of the movement to make abortion illegal (Citro 2014: 22).[7] Proponents of sex-selective abortion bans have explicitly stated that the laws are actually part of the effort to restrict access to abortion entirely. In 2008, Steven Mosher, the head of the Population Research Institute (a leading anti-abortion group), stated, 'I propose that we – the pro-life movement – adopt as our next goal the banning of sex and race-selective abortion' (Citro 2014: 21). The report of the Human Rights Clinic of the Chicago law school says that

> the language used in laws banning sex-selective abortion also suggests that lawmakers are concerned primarily with restricting access to abortion generally, rather than combating gender discrimination. For instance, the language used in the bill pending in the United States Congress consistently refers to the 'unborn child' and defines abortion based on sex as intentional killing.
>
> (Citro 2014: 23)

There is an appeal to ethics here which highlights the necessity and significance of protecting the right to life. By using the example of sex-selective abortion, the pro-life lobby globally has strived to build a strong case to strike down the right to abortion for women.

The state in India has steered clear of the ethical claims. Since abortion in India is steeped in the population discourse of controlling numbers through curbing women's fertility, the pro-life arguments are not tenable here. However, in terms of communication materials generated by the state for awareness, overlaps on the right to abortion do exist. Use of religious groups for advocacy also leads to ethical and moral claims around right to life which demonstrate the importance of life per say without engaging with the nuances of gender. In Punjab for example, the *Akal Takht* gave the first call against sex-selective abortion.[8] Religious tropes have been liberally used in the campaigns to talk about the girl-child. Even global bodies like the United Nations Fund for Population (UNFPA) and the United Nations Children's Fund (UNICEF) have used religious groups to campaign for the cause of the girl-child.[9]

This overlap of the pro-life discourse is also visible in various initiatives of the state in Punjab, where the burden of punitive measures falls on the mother of two daughters. The monitoring of pregnancies in order to curb sex-selective abortion has identified her as the most likely culprit. The overlap over the right to abortion as well as the right to privacy and bodily integrity of women have been against the very notion of reproductive rights espoused in the state's National Population Policy, Reproductive and Child Health Programme, Medical Termination of Pregnancy Act, etc. (Government of India 2001).

To take up the case of Odisha as a contrasting example, issues of infant and maternal mortality have received more serious attention. Sex-selective abortion has not been couched in terms of the right-to-life issue. In fact, the tendency in Odisha was to reject the premise of sex-selective abortion and to term it as abortion arising out of 'illegitimate pregnancies'. So the ethical concerns were about the lack of morality in 'young unmarried women' whose 'promiscuous behaviour' gave rise to unwanted pregnancies. The official position is that it is these unwanted pregnancies that led to abortions which have been wrongly identified as sex-selective. More crucially for Odisha, the devaluation of daughters noted in the 2011 census has not been found significant enough for the state to be actively involved in the issue. So the ethical discourse emerging from the state, as evident from the research, revolves around three elements: the pro-life approach, the role of women in terms of reproduction and the understanding around women's sexuality. The state defines women's bodies in terms of their reproductive role. Policies and programmes which refer to women are usually in the domain of reproductive and child health, maternal health and so on and so forth. The other engagement of the state in this arena is with the issue of sexual harassment, sexual violence and domestic violence. In this engagement the sexuality of women comes to be defined and circumscribed around honour and marital status. The child's right to life is a very powerful argument against the woman's right to choice. The state's emphasis on monitoring pregnancies emerges from this high moral stance. Since first-trimester abortion is off limits due to a legislation allowing it, and also because of its utility to the state in controlling population, the next best method has been seen to monitor women's pregnancies.

In Odisha this scenario has veered to another form by placing blame on women by defining their sexual boundaries. The emphasis on marriage as a significant indicator of women's status, the circumscribing of women's legitimate sexual role, as wives has a bearing on the issue. So instead of a set of inalienable rights emerging on the basis of autonomy, informed and empowered choice and freedom, the state, as evident by the official engagement in both the disparate regions, views the issue as a 'social evil' not amenable to state intervention. It also views women as the primary cause of the problem. The criminalization of women not so much in convictions but in official engagements, courtroom discussions and popular understanding is a matter of central concern in this study. Women as litigants, supplicants and activists become a source of irritation to the state, as 'problems' to be dealt with (Sunder Rajan 2003: 28).

What sort of rights discourse is then most suitable to examining sexselective abortion? Ronald Dworkin's explanation of rights creates a support for the claims derived from constitutional guarantees. The idea of 'rights as trumps' describes the status of those constitutional rights that are used by courts in some jurisdictions to override legislation, even if that legislation has been democratically endorsed and serves the public good (Mckinnon 2011). Then there is the set of negative rights making claims for autonomy based on the notion of freedom from state intervention supported by Locke in the classical liberal ideas to contemporary libertarian Nozick. The debate between negative liberals and positive liberals on rights is basically about freedom from and freedom to. This debate is echoed in the political theorization of liberal egalitarians and libertarians (Dworkin 1977). However, the complexity of the practice of sex-selective abortion makes it difficult for the range of liberal ideas to sufficiently ground it. The question of whose rights becomes of paramount significance. Then emerges the question of freedom from what? And freedom to do what?

The rights of women to choose have been extended to arguments about choosing the sex of the foetus. The right to have children, not to have children, the right to a range of contraception including abortion and the right to bodily integrity and autonomy all resound with a liberal rights paradigm. However, determining the sex of the foetus and terminating it if found female is difficult to justify in this context. The feminist perspective is that the basic premise of this choice is derived from a negative notion of women's worth. Tied up with this idea is the notion of 'self-esteem' of women which is derived from a society which tends to devalue females. This notion of self which leads to the conceptualization of autonomy and agency for women has been a central focus of feminist theorizations. There are two possibilities here for feminists. Either they reject the idea of an individual self, unencumbered by socialization and social expectation, or they accept that women do act on their own. The syncretic feminist perspective, while accepting the notion of a 'self' dependent on societal norms and expectations, also believes and encourages the possibility of an 'individual self' which has agency and autonomy (Agarwal et al. 2006).

The idea of reproductive rights popularized by radical and socialist feminists has offered answers in terms of a range of rights (Petchesky and Judd 2001). The link between rights and capabilities is also a significant one. It is hard to theorize a rights discourse on the issue, but it is not impossible. Feminist theorizing offers a range of possibilities with categories established on specificities and commonalities. The notion of sex-selective abortion as gender discrimination is derived from a feminist academia and activist perspective. The dominant global perspective has been to examine it in terms of an ethical claim of the right to life. However, the global discourse from rights-based bodies like the UN and others has been concerned about the rights of women and in this context specifically about reproductive rights.

The analysis of these discourses illustrates the overlap and consensus between state and global discourses on the issue of sex-selective abortion. In these discourses, the place of women is in the reproductive role of mother, and the idea of gender equality is restricted to the right to life of the girl-child. The political economy of new reproductive technologies, both globally and locally, and its severe impact on this issue remains peripheral to the discourses. The ethical claims are underpinned by the pro-life discourse without any allusion to choice, agency and rights of women in this context. Both at the theoretical level and at the level of actual policies and schemes directed at women, the engagement with gender discrimination here remains full of contradictions, contestations and challenges.

The competing discourses which are informed by feminist perspectives, both at the local and global levels, provide an alternative understanding of the issue. The integration of these feminist discourses into state and global structures, institutions and reflections may create a critical space to explore the context here in a manner which will stimulate and revitalize the much-needed commitment to counter gender discrimination.

The syncretic feminist perspective with an intersectionality approach

The UNFPA in India has been working closely with the issue of sex-selective abortion for the last 12 years. They have supported civil society initiatives to counter the issue. They have also steadfastly followed a consultative process of working by listening both to feminists in activism and academia and to grassroots organizations working on the issue. The reproductive rights discourse is common to most global bodies working on human rights and gender. The basic framework of the discourse is drawn from a combination of elements from liberal, socialist and radical feminism. The rights include reproductive health as a component of overall health, throughout the life cycle, for both men and women; reproductive decision making, including voluntary choice in marriage, family formation and determination of the number, timing and spacing of one's children and the right to have access to the information and means needed to exercise voluntary choice; equality and equity for men and women to enable individuals to make free and informed choices in all spheres of life, free from discrimination based on gender; and sexual and reproductive security, including freedom from sexual violence and coercion, and the right to privacy.[10] The engagement here is with women's rights and not with child rights or a pro-life approach.

The other common strategy of rights-based global and local bodies is to follow a life cycle approach addressing issues of gender violence and discrimination through laws and entitlements and capacity building. This approach is also derived from multiple feminist perspectives. Liberal feminist belief is that rights, entitlements and political participation would entail gender justice. Radical feminist perspective relies on the idea of patriarchy and remains doubtful of the patriarchal state. Marxist feminism is a critique of capitalism. Socialist feminist perspective is underpinned by the complex relationship between relations of production and reproduction.

Post-modern feminist perspective focuses on diversity and difference. It also keeps in mind an intersectionality approach, i.e., the considerations of the class, caste, gender and age interconnections.

A single feminist perspective is limited in terms of its vision to engage with the issue at hand. Formal guarantee of rights is available within the Indian constitution. However, it is in the accessing of these rights that problems emerge. So liberal feminism fails to explain why women have not been able to achieve equality irrespective of rights and entitlements formally guaranteed to women and girls. The 'patriarchal state' engages in making women-friendly laws, thereby offering a challenge to the radical feminist understanding of the state. While intersectionality and heterogeneity are important issues to be considered as posed by postmodern feminism, there remains a need to examine the relevance of 'strategic essentialism'. According to Spivak it refers to 'a position that accepts that organizing for political purposes necessarily entails uniting under a single banner and thereby some form of exclusion, but that this is a provisional necessity and not a categorical matter' (Bowden and Mummery 2009: 118).

Jill Steans discusses the notion of strategic essentialism as developed by Spivak in the context of feminist strategies to bring about gender equality. According to Steans, while the diversities between women in terms of class, race and other categories need to inform feminism, it is also important to recognize the commonalities which exist between women. The common experience of gender discrimination and violence for women irrespective of their differences needs to be privileged at certain moments in order to be able to provide meaningful context for developing useful measures for change (Steans 2014). Nussbaum's capabilities approach is also one which straddles different feminist perspectives. The capabilities approach, of which she is the most influential proponent, is a critique of the rights discourse. However, Nussbaum herself does believe in strict binaries. According to her the idea of capabilities is a complex one. It requires the fostering of internal capability through education, healthcare and supportive relationships as well as ascertaining that her efforts are not thwarted by unequal legal, financial or physical obstacles. It requires looking at how laws, movements, groups and social institutions enable women (Nussbaum 2003: 17). So in her own words, 'A capabilities approach is closely linked to a rightsbased approach and can be understood as one way of further specifying a rights-based approach' (Nussbaum 2003: 18).

Susan Okin arguments are an intermeshing of liberal, radical and socialist feminist principles, although she would be categorized as a liberal feminist (Kymlicka 2002). Nancy Fraser believes that postmodern feminists need to go beyond Foucault's analysis of power, by hanging on to radical feminism's sense of moral outrage and modifying this with recognition of the diversity of women's condition of life (Kantola 2006: 16). Ackerly talks about 'curb-cut feminism'. She defines it as 'a destabilizing epistemological perspective, familiar to feminists, that requires the theorist to be especially attentive to oppression and to the possibility of exclusion, exploitation, powerlessness, value imperialism, marginalization, invisibility, violence, ignorance, silencing, domination and hegemony' (Ackerly 2008: 35).

The feminist discourse in India which is largely a combination of liberal and socialist feminism has also raised similar critiques of the state discourse on sex-selective abortion. The women's movements in India have played a very significant role in critically laying down the basic parameters of discussion on the issue of sex-selective abortion. By emphasizing the need to make a distinction between the law on abortion (MTP Act 1971) and sex determination (PCPNDT Act 1994), it has circumscribed the issue around gender discrimination and violence. The right to safe, accessible abortion has remained a concern. It has questioned the market, coercive population policies as well as the state. It remains sceptical about the state in terms of its ability to be wholly gender sensitive in its structures and institutions but works 'at bringing the state back in' to deliver its promises to women.

Global bodies and institutions like UNFPA and UN for Women are alert to the dynamics of local feminist discourses. They engage in consultations, workshops and supporting direct advocacy and research interventions in the field. They also lobby with policymakers to strategize change. The syncretic feminist perspective is evident in the UNFPA's approach of emphasizing the three As. The three As of tackling daughter aversion as purposed by them include:

- **Assets:** Assets with girls/women, earning income, owning and inheriting property and ownership of land are essential for tackling daughter aversion. These are also protective barriers against violence. To promote these aspects it is required to have policies that improve financial standing of women through employment and tax rebates.
- **Autonomy of women and girls:** Autonomy of women and girls to be enhanced through emphasizing on ability, power, providing choices, ensuring physical safety and mobility by making laws work for women and to improve safe public spaces, transport, etc.
- **Ageing to be addressed:** Access to social protection for women and men which sees to it that children cannot be the only source of support. The idea is that policy response to ensure social care should be a must.

(Brahme 2012)

The global perspective here is alert to the rights and bodily integrity of women. The critique of the inflexibility, unimaginativeness and anti-women elements of the CCTs were brought out by a UNFPA study (Sekher 2012), and so also were the anti-women, anti-Dalit elements of coercive population policies like the two-child norm. Interestingly, the two-child norm and other coercive population policies have been critiqued by feminist scholars and activists also. The partnership between these global bodies and the feminist researchers and activists is very strong. For example, a recent publication of the UNFPA which has discussed in detail all laws favouring son preference in India is written by a leading legal feminist of India who is a member of the self-funded All Indian Democratic Women's Association (AIDWA) (Singh 2013). Such synergies are common and reflect the openness of the global discourses to the learning from the field.

Alternative discourses which exist in non-funded movements and activism in the field are also based on syncretic feminist perspectives. They are nuanced with their in-depth analysis of class and caste. Saheli in Delhi is a non-funded women's group.[11] Its research and activism on sex-selective abortion is refined and sophisticated in offering the distinction between prolife and pro-choice arguments and the critique of the market which offers sex determination. The Centre for Advocacy and Research (CFAR) is not a feminist organization, nor does it profess to be one. It started as a media advocacy centre. The CFAR is a registered public-interest research and advocacy group committed to interventions on gender and development issues with a focus on HIV/AIDS, education, women's health, sustainable development, child rights and elimination of violence against women and children. The focus of CFAR has been monitoring media and developing the expertise to use this knowledge for strategic advocacy through and with the media. Women's active engagement in tribal movements in Odisha to protect their land and the complex issues that they have raised about their lives are also important for the global and state-level discourses to engage with.

The women's movement in India has actively associated itself with the campaign to end sex-selective abortion. In essays on the women's movements in India the issue of sex-selective abortion is contained within the discussion on the autonomous women's movement in India and mostly within the understanding of violence against women (Agnihotri and Mazumdar 1995). Within the women's movements, however, there has been some unease working on the issue. The divide reveals that even within the movements there have been debates. Some feminist groups have refused to work on the issue, citing the persistence of an overlap over abortion leading to the crackdown on abortion services and the unavailability of safe, affordable and legal abortion for women. Others have paid special attention to it and sustained their efforts to maintain a strict distinction between safe, legal abortion services and the practice of sex determination leading to sex-selective abortion to the detriment of girls and women. The overall Indian scenario did reveal that the women's movement along with feminist academia are engaged in discussions, debates and seminars on the issue, but in terms of radical commitment of the movements to guarantee widespread change on the issue, a lot must be done.

The challenges before the women's movements on the issue have been manifold. Firstly, there is a divide between groups on the issue as mentioned earlier. Secondly, the proliferation, the accessibility, affordability and availability of new reproductive technologies have made it difficult for the movement to control it. It requires extensive efforts, an open and dynamic engagement with the state as well as the market in order to curb it. Even some efforts which exist may be in need of supplementary support by a more concerted civil society, media and state action. The women's movement's discourse has by and large invoked a limited syncretic feminist perspective which has emphasized gender equality focusing on rights, capabilities, empowerment and political activism. The challenges before the movements have made it difficult for this perspective to be broadened and strengthened and to percolate down to all. Thirdly, the syncretic ideas of feminism within the women's movements also need to be broadened and strengthened.

There are exclusions here. Within the alternative discourses on the issue, which include that of the women's movements, the UN bodies and the civil society initiatives, some have become hegemonic while some have been excluded from being linked with global discourses. The syncretic feminist perspective needs to be derived from all positions here which look at issues of marginalization and oppression specifically for women and girls and beyond them. Issues of tribal communities losing land to corporate giants, of environmental degradation, of working-class men losing employment, of farmers committing suicide because of agrarian crises are to be taken within its fold. What Ackerly succinctly puts forth for the 'curb-cut feminism' can be used to highlight the syncretic feminist perspective too. She says,

> In political theory jargon, feminist curb cutting is a destabilizing epistemological device set out to enact, not just announce contestability. In plain English, it reminds us of our fallibility and encourages our humility; however, it does not allow us to enact contestability through self-reflection alone. It requires that we enact our theory in the real world, proving (in both senses of the word) its emancipatory potential.
> (Ackerly 2008: 157)

Thus, the syncretic feminist perspective brings in the two dimensions of inclusion and reconceptualization here. Inclusion of women and girls within programmes and their access to political, economic and social rights are derived from the principles of liberal feminism. The idea of reconceptualization is derived from radical and post-modern feminism. While the liberal feminist perspective would emphasize formal equality and political participation, the radical feminism's main concern here would help to question the power structures at play whether within the state agencies or other institutions and structures. Postmodern feminism cautions about treating women as a homogeneous category, and the intersectionality approach would be to delve into the class, caste, community, race and ethnicity and age dimensions.

The implications of this theoretical framework in this context are that countering gender-discriminatory programmes in India demands much more than just cash transfers and monitoring women's pregnancies. They require addressing many challenges like implementing gender-sensitive laws, building women-friendly educational institutions, and providing quality education which counters gender stereotypes and creates a truly egalitarian ethos. It should also include leveraging markets for the poor and marginalized women, along with skill development and vibrant collectives with ideas based on participation and self-sustainability.[12]

Way forward

After critically assessing the significance of the state in addressing gender discrimination, the relevant question to be asked here would be whether the state should at all be invoked. As stated earlier, the syncretic feminist perspective believes in the centrality of the role of the state. Due to its character and location, the state can offer a common ground for all stakeholders on the issue to get involved, engaged, interact and intersect on the issue. The significance of a syncretic feminist perspective in order to engage with gender discrimination therefore can work best with the state as its primary actor. In an examination of social protection schemes rolled out by the state in India, Dreze and Goyal (2003) say that the answer did not lie in abandoning schemes but in improving the quality, 'to go forwards rather than backwards'. Similarly, Kabeer believes that it is important to realize three things about social protection schemes and other forms of intervention which are rolled out by the state:

- Social protection schemes need to accommodate a more pro-active role of the state while understanding that the state may not always be a benevolent representative of public good.
- The state can also be a site for struggles over the interpretation of needs and the allocation of resources.
- Building the capacity of the marginalized and excluded groups to participate in these struggles is indispensable to the promotion of more

inclusive systems of social protection and to the achievement of gender equality and justice (Kabeer 2010).

Towards a conclusion

Does this mean that the strategies emerging from the syncretic feminist perspective will be the magic bullets to counter sex-selective abortion? By withdrawing coercive population control elements from the CCTs, will girls get better life chances? By penalizing doctors for their unethical and illegal medical practice of sex determination, will families be sensitive to the value of daughters? These are questions for further research and probing. The aim here is to point out the political significance of the feminist perspectives to create space for critical discourses regarding women as persons with rights, entitlements and capabilities which are being denied to them due to material, structural and cultural impediments. It is also to look beyond rights offered by the state, at heterogeneous structures and institutions like the market, civil society initiatives, vibrant movements and the relevance of these plural bodies in their extension of a critical space to women and girls.

This chapter has also emphasized the need to focus on the state and its contexts, structures and discourses which are amenable to change due to both global and local reflections. When informed by the syncretic feminist perspective with an intersectionality approach, this change can be towards achieving gender justice by providing women and girls an enabling environment to be persons of their own free will and choice.

An attempt has been made to complicate our understanding of the state and the shifting discourses, debates and dilemmas in the context of sex-selective abortion in India. It has desisted from offering any simplistic, teleological explanation for sex-selective abortion as gender discrimination in India. The syncretic feminist perspective has the potential to expose the limits of state institutions and structures, to make evident the dominant discourses which work against women and girls and to reveal the importance of comparative analysis between state, regions, civil society initiatives and movements. It sensitizes state agencies to the importance of the context. The aim of the perspective is to point out the need of the coexistence of multiple discourses and practices here.

However, the focus on the multiplicity of state institutions, structures and bodies is to also challenge at all levels the conceptualization of gender discrimination by them and the interconnections at the level of their policy-making and policy-implementation framework. A systematic combination of syncretic feminist perspectives within state discourses and their actors and institutions will be able to exert an influence across the terrain of policymaking and policy interconnections. It will also be able to influence the market and other players in the field. Feminists themselves will become aware of their own limited stance if isolated from each other. The importance or articulating alternative discourses which challenge the state on the issue and to effectively and strategically partner is also essential here.

Challenging the norms and understanding of sex-selective abortion as gender discrimination by the state will require the feminists to look inwards at their active engagement on the issue and beyond the state. The need is to also get interlinked with movements, both global and local, which may not be openly articulating a rights talk but may have effectively challenged discrimination and marginalization in their own context. The state should recognize the significance of such voices by making itself sufficiently fragmented and neutral enough to allow various points of access. The inculcation of a syncretic feminist perspective with an intersectionality approach by the state as well as the feminists, activists, civil society bodies and other influential actors will make it possible to explicitly address gender discrimination and expand reproductive rights and create a notion of equality and justice that would be helpful for studying all aspects of oppression and marginalization.

Notes

1 Janani Suraksha Yojana (JSY) is a safe-motherhood intervention under the National Rural Health Mission (NRHM). It is being implemented with the objective of reducing maternal and neonatal mortality by promoting institutional delivery among poor pregnant women. The scheme is under implementation in all states and Union Territories, with a special focus on states performing low on maternal and neonatal mortality indicators. As a conditional cash-transfer scheme a fixed amount is paid to women for these institutional deliveries. For more details see http://nhm.gov.in/ nrhm-components/rmnch-a/maternal-health/ janani-suraksha-yojana/ background.html (accessed on 24 June 2017).

2 Eight states in the United States have introduced laws against sex-selective abortion in 2012 to ban the procedure, and three states – Arizona, Pennsylvania and Oklahoma – have banned sex-selective abortions. A similar law in Illinois was scrapped by state courts. See O'Keefe (2012).

3 As defined by the Oxford English Dictionary https://en.oxforddictionaries. com/ definition/designer_baby (accessed on 24 June 2017).

4 Information, Education and Communication (IEC) materials of government and NGOs in the public domain are in general insensitive to such gender concerns. Also see Naqvi (2006).

5 Personal communication with Mitu Khurana and observation of her legal battle in the Tis Hazari court and high court during the research period.

6 On 15 December 2013, a young paramedic student was brutally raped in a moving bus by five men which included the bus driver, conductor and helper. She later succumbed to her injuries in hospital. The brutality involved in this rape case led to a massive public outburst in Delhi which later spread to different parts of India. Popularly known as the Nirbhaya Case, it led the Central Government to constitute a committee under the retired Chief Justice of India, Justice J. S. Verma. The Verma Committee Report gave wide-ranging suggestions

for improvement of safety of women along with recommendations to strengthen anti-rape laws. The report led to the passage of the Criminal Law (Amendment) Act, 2013.

7 Also see Kalantry (2013), pointing out that the proponents of sex-selective abortion bans in the United States present information about son preference in India in a narrow and misleading lens to push for the bans in the United States.

8 The Akal Takht which is the main religious clergy of the Sikh gurudwara and has a huge influence upon the largely Sikh population in Punjab was called by the government to support them on the issue. The Akal Takht issued a decree (Hukam Nama) called the 'kudi mar' (daughter murderer) decree, which exhorted the Sikh families to stop murdering their daughters, as it was immoral, unethical, evil and hence a sin. The decree declared that any Sikh found practicing sex-selective abortion would be excommunicated.

9 The first religious body meeting on the issue was facilitated by the state (the Ministry of Health and Family Welfare) and UNICEF in 2002. The religious leaders who attended the meeting spoke about the duties of motherhood, glorifying the role and the emphasis on the right to life of the foetus in the womb, and the word 'bhrunhatya' (foeticide) replaced the word 'female foeticide' in their speeches and resulted in an overlap over the right to abortion which is legally available under the MTP (Medical Termination of Pregnancy) Act 1971.

10 Reproductive Rights as defined by UNFPA www.unfpa.org/rights/rights.htm (accessed on 24 June 2017).

11 Saheli was set up in 1981 in New Delhi, India, primarily as a crisis intervention centre. It is an integral part of the autonomous women's movement in India. Writings in their newsletters on the issue include 'More Teeth to the PNDT Act – Favourable Changes on the Anvil, The Business of Sex Selection – The Ultrasonography Boom' (2006), *Sex Selection-Trying to Tame The Tiger* (2003), *Law on Sex-Determination-Amendments and Developments* (2002), *Law Against Sex-determination – Souvenir* (1995), *Sex Determination and child Birth-Critique of The New Bill* (1995), *Campaign Against Sex Determination and Selection-Report Of National Protest Day* (1998).

12 In South Korea a strategy of combining legal enforcements with property rights and other forms of social protection for women and girls have led to a remarkable improvement in the sex ratio at birth. For more details see Chung and Das Gupta (2007).

Bibliography

Ackerly, Brooke A. 2008. *Universal Human Rights in a World of Difference*. Cambridge: Cambridge University Press.

Agarwal, Bina et al. (eds.). 2006. *Capabilities, Freedom and Equality: Amartya Sen's Work from a Gender Perspective*. New Delhi: Oxford University Press.

Agnihotri, Indu and Vina Mazumdar. 1995. 'Changing Terms of Political Discourse: Women's Movement in India, 1970s–1990s', *Economic and Political Weekly*, 30(29): 1869–1878.

Agnihotri, Satish B. 1995. 'Missing Females: A Disaggregated Analysis', *Economic and Political Weekly*, 30(33), August 19: 2074–2084.

Barot, Sneha. 2012. 'A Problem-and-Solution Mismatch: Son Preference and Sex-Selective Abortion Bans', *Guttmacher Policy Review*, Spring, 15(2), www.guttmacher.org/pubs/gpr/15/2/gpr150218.html (accessed on 25 June 2017).

Bose, Ashish. 2001. 'Census of India 2001 and after', *Economic and Political Weekly*, 36(20), May 19.

Bose, Ashish. 2002. 'Curbing Female Foeticide: Doctors, Governments and Civil Society Ensure Failure', *Economic and Political Weekly*, February 23: 696–697.

Bowden, Peta and Jane Mummery. 2009. *Understanding Feminism.* New Delhi: Rawat Publications.

Brahme, Dhanashree. 2012. 'Policy Response to Sex Selection: A Case of Little and Lots'. Paper presented at the workshop on *Mapping the Adverse Consequences of Sex Selection and Gender Imbalance: Findings and Policy Implications*, Rajiv Gandhi Institute of Contemporary Studies, New Delhi, 9–10 November.

Catalano, Michael. 2012. 'The Prospect of Designer Babies: Is It Inevitable?', *PIT Journal*, Cycle 3, North Carolina.

Census of India. 1981, 1991, 2001, 2011. Registrar General of India, GOI.

Chung, Woojin and Monica Das Gupta. 2007. 'Why Is Son Preference Declining in South Korea? The Role of Development and Public Policy, and the Implications for China and India', *Policy Research Working Paper*, 4373, The World Bank, October.

Citro, Brian et al. 2014. 'Replacing Myths with Facts: Sex-Selective Abortion Laws in the United States', *Cornell Law Faculty Publications*, Paper 1399, http://scho larship.law.cornell.edu/cgi/viewcontent.cgi?article=2536&con text=facpub (accessed on 25 March 2017).

Contractor, Qudsiya and Ravi Duggal (eds.). 2003. *Sex Selection-Issues and Concerns: A Compilation of Writings*. Mumbai and Pune: CEHAT.

Convention on the Elimination of All forms of Discrimination against Women. 1979. www.un.org/womenwatch/daw/cedaw/ (accessed on 26 February2017).

Darnovsky, Marcy. 2009. 'Countries with Laws or Policies on Sex Selection', *Centre for Genetics and Society*, April, https://pdfs.semanticscholar.org/5495/da6a0ad4f 1758bf2b17b94c41a72f7faca8c.pdf (accessed on 25 June 2017).

Dixon-Mueller, Ruth. 1993. *Population Policy and Women's Rights: Transforming Reproductive Choice*. Westport: Praeger Publishers.

Dreze, Jean and Aparajita Goyal. 2003. 'The Future of Midday Meals', *Frontline*, 20(16), August 2–15, www.frontline.in/static/html/fl2016/stories/ 20030815002208500.htm (accessed on 20 March 2017).

Dworkin, Ronald. 1977. *Taking Rights Seriously*. Cambridge, MA: Harvard University Press.

Eisentein, Zillah R. 1979. *Capitalist Patriarchy and the Case for Socialist Feminism* (pp. 271–353). New York: Monthly Review Press.

Engels, Frederick. 1984. *Origin of Private Property, Family and State*, www.marx-ists.org/archive/marx/works/1884/origin-family/ (accessed on 23 February 2017).

Government of India. 2000. *National Population Policy-2000*, www.hsph.harvard. edu/population/policies/india.pop.pdf (accessed on 12 May 217).

Government of India. 2001. *National Population Policy-2000*, Ministry of Health and Family Welfare, New Delhi.

Hartmann, Heidi. 1981. 'The Unhappy Marriage of Marxism and Feminism: Towards a More Progressive Union', in L. Sargent (ed.), *Women and Revolution*. Montreal: Black Rose Books.

ICPD Cairo. 1994. www.unfpa.org/icpd (accessed on 24 March 2017).

Jaisingh, Indira et al. 2007. *From the Abnormal to the Normal: Preventing Sex Selective Abortions through the Law*. New Delhi: Lawyers Collective.

Jalnawalla, Sarosh Framroze. 1974. *Medical Termination of Pregnancy Act, a Preliminary Report of the First Twenty Months of Implementation*, www.jogi.co.in/articles/files/filebase/Archives/1975/oct/1975_588_592_Oct.pdf (accessed on 20 June 2017).

Kabeer, Naila. 2010. *Gender and Social Protection Strategies in the Informal Economy*. London, New York, and New Delhi: Routledge.

Kalantry, Sital. 2013. 'Sex Selection in the United States in India: A Contextualist Feminist Approach', *UCLA Journal of International Law and Foreign Affairs*, 61: 68–75.

Kantola, Johanna. 2006. *Feminists Theorise the State*. New York: Palgrave Macmillan.

Kapur, Ratna. 1996. *Secularism's Last Sigh? Hindutva and the (Mis)Rule of Law*. New Delhi: Oxford University Press.

Kapur, Ratna. 1999. *Subversive Sites: Feminist Engagements with Law in India*. New Delhi: Sage Publications.

Kymlicka, Will. 2002. *Contemporary Political Philosophy: An Introduction*. New Delhi: Oxford University Press.

Malhotra, Anshu. 2002. *Gender, Caste and Religious Identities: Restructuring Class in Colonial Punjab*. New Delhi: Oxford University Press.

Mallik, Rupsa. 2003. '"Negative Choice" Sex Determination and Sex Selective Abortion in India', in *Urdhva Moola*, 2(1). Mumbai: Sophia Centre for Women's Studies and Development.

McKinnon, Catriona. 2011. *Issues in Political Theory*. New Delhi: Oxford University Press.

Medical Termination of Pregnancy (MTP) Act 1971. India.

Menon, Nivedita. 2004. *Recovering Subversion: Feminist Politics beyond Law*. New Delhi: Permanent Black.

Menon-Sen, Kalyani. 2013. 'Women in India's National Population Policy: Is Empowerment Enough?', in A. K. Shiva Kumar et al. (eds.), *Handbook of Population and Development in India*. New Delhi: Oxford University Press.

Mill, John Stuart. 1869. *Subjection of Women*. London: Longmans, Green, Reader, and Dyer.

Millett, Kate. 1971. *Sexual Politics*. London: Harr Davis.

Nanda, Bijayalaxmi. 2007. 'Campaign against Female Foeticide: Perspectives, Strategies and Experiences', in Tulsi Patel (ed.), *Sex-Selective Abortion in India: Gender, Society and New Reproductive Technologies*, pp. 357–365. New Delhi: Sage Publications.

Nanda, Bijayalaxmi. 2013. 'Does the Girl Child Count? Census and Other Stories', *Mainstream*, L1(15), March 30.

Naqvi, Farah. 2006. *Images and Icons: Harnessing the Power of Mass Media to Promote Gender Equality and Reduce Practices of Sex Selection*. New Delhi: BBC World Service Trust.

Nussbaum, Martha C. 1999. *Sex and Social Justice*. New York: Oxford University Press.

Nussbaum, Martha C. 2006. *Frontiers of Justice: Disability, Nationality, Species Membership*. New Delhi: Oxford University Press.

Nussbaum, Martha C. 2013. *Political Emotions Why Love Matters for Justice*. London: The Belknap Press of Harvard University Press.

Nussbaum, Martha C. et al. 2003. *Essays on Gender and Governance*. New Delhi: UNDP.

O'Keefe, Ed. 2012. 'Bill Banning "Sex-Selection Abortions" Fails in the House', *The Washington Post*, May 31, www.washingtonpost.com/politics/bill-banning-sex-selection-abortions-fails-in-the-house/2012/05/31/gJQAaWFd5U_ story.html (accessed on 25 June 2017).

Oldenberg, Veena Talwar. 2003. *Dowry Murder: The Imperial Origins of a Cultural Crime*. New Delhi: Oxford University Press.

Patel, Tulsi. 2007. 'Foeticide, Family Planning and State-Society Intersection', in Tulsi Patel (ed.), *Sex Selective Abortion in India Gender, Society and New Reproductive Technologies*. New Delhi, Thousand Oaks, and London: Sage Publications.

Petchesky, Rosalind and Karen Judd (eds.). 2001. *Negotiating Reproductive Rights: Women's Perspective across Countries and Cultures*. London and New York: Zed Books.

Population Foundation of India. 2010. *Advocacy Papers on Population Issues*, http://populationfoundation.in/files/fileattached/Fileattached-1480403702-Advocacy-Papers-on-Population-Issues.pdf (accessed on 12 May 2017).

Pre-conception and Pre-natal Diagnostic Techniques (Prohibition of Sex Selection) Act (PCPNDT Act) 1994. India.

Rao, Mohan. 2001. 'Population Policies: State Approve Coercive Measures', *Economic and Political Weekly*, 36(29), July 21.

Rustagi, Preet. 2006. 'Future of the Girl Child'. Paper Presented at the Workshop on the *Well Being of India's Population: A Compendium of Perspective*, Institute for Human Development, New Delhi, January. A revised version available at https://tspace.library.utoronto.ca/bitstream/1807/9397/1/ Rustagi.pdf (accessed on 25 June 2017).

Sandel, Michael J. 2004. 'The Case against Perfection: What's Wrong with Designer Children, Bionic Athletes, and Genetic Engineering', *The Atlantic*, April 1, www.theatlantic.com/magazine/archive/2004/04/the-case-against-perfection/302927/ (accessed on 16 March 2013).

Sarkaria, Mallika Kaur. 2009. 'Lessons from Punjab's Missing Girls: Towards a Global Feminist Perspective on Choice in Abortion', *California Law Review*, 97.

Schumaker, Paul (ed.). 2010. *The Political Theory Reader*. West Sussex: Wiley-Blackwell.

Sekher, T. V. 2012. *Special Financial Incentive Schemes for the Girl Child in India: A Review of Select Schemes*. New Delhi: United Nations Population Fund.

Sen, Amartya. 1995. *Inequality Reexamined*. New Delhi: Oxford University Press.

Shiva, Mira. 2002. 'Skirting the Issue: The Girl Child', in *Seen But Not Heard*. New Delhi: Voluntary Health Association of India.

Singh, Kirti. 2013. *Laws and Son Preference in India: A Reality Check*. New Delhi: United Nations Population Fund.

Steans, Jill. 2014. '"Feminist Strategies" at the Centre for Political Studies'. Paper Presented at Jawaharlal Nehru University, New Delhi, February 19.

Steinhauer, Jennifer. 2012. 'House Rejects Bill to Ban Sex-Selective Abortions', *The New York Times*, May 31, www.nytimes.com/2012/06/01/us/politics/ house-rejects-bill-to-ban-sex-selective-abortions.html (accessed on 25 June 2017).

Sunder Rajan, Rajeswari. 2003. *The Scandal of the State: Women, Law, and Citizenship in Postcolonial India*. Ranikhet: Permanent Black.

United Nations. 1975. *Status of Women and Family Planning*. New York: United Nations.

United Nations. 1995. *Beijing Declaration and Platform for Action*, www.un.org/womenwatch/daw/beijing/pdf/BDPfA%20E.pdf (accessed on 27 April 2017).

Visaria, Leela et al. 2006. 'Two Child Norm: Victimising the Vulnerable', *Economic and Political Weekly*, 41(1): 41–48.

8 Adjudicating Domestic Violence in the Courts

Shalu Nigam

> "*And yet the wife is the actual bond servant of her husband: so far as the law is concerned, she is as subordinate to him as slaves, commonly so called, are to their masters. She promises life-long obedience to him at the altar, and is legally held to that all through her life. She can do no act whatever without his at least tacit permission. She can acquire no property for herself: the instant something becomes hers, even if by inheritance, it automatically becomes his. In this respect the wife's position under the common law of England is worse than that of slaves in the laws of many countries The two are called 'one person in law,' for the purpose of inferring that whatever is hers is his, but the parallel inference is never drawn that whatever is his is hers; the maxim is not applied against the man, except to make him responsible to third parties for her acts, as a master is for the acts of his slaves or of his cattle. I'm not claiming that wives are in general no better treated than slaves; but no slave is a slave to the same extent and in a full a sense of the word as a wife is. Hardly any slave is a slave at all hours and all minutes; in general, he has his fixed task, and when it is done he disposes up to a point of his own time and has a family life into which the master rarely intrudes. however brutal a tyrant her husbands lave is – even if she knows that he hates her, and/or it is his daily pleasure to torture her, and/or she finds it impossible not to loathe him – he can claim from her and ·legally· enforce the lowest degradation of a human being, that of being made the instrument of an animal function contrary to her inclinations*".[1]

John Stuart Mill, in 1869 in his thesis on the *Subjection of Women*,[2] while questioning women's subordinate status within marriage, argued that man as a master not only wants a woman's labor but also her sentiments, and he conspires to exploit in order to accomplish this desire for a submissive docile slave over whom he could have an absolute control. Mill rejected the 'cult of domesticity' and wrote that marriage is a form of slavery that confers power to men and "not only to good men or decently respectable

DOI: 10.4324/9781003299561-8

men, but to all men, including the most brutal and most criminal" are benefitted by it.[3] Based on such a critique, reforms have been made in the laws in some countries, but in India, laws are still propagating the norms that enslave women. Though a domestic violence law has been enacted to prohibit, criminalize and condemn any act of abuse which has been socially accepted, normalized and routinized by the social norms by providing legal recourse and remedy against such actions, these laws are construed narrowly in the courtrooms. The purpose of the law is lost in the technicalities and subjectivities involved in translating and interpreting laws.

The object of the law seeks to right the wrongs by equalizing and tilting the power balance in favor of women who are at the receiving end and are socially disempowered and marginalized within their homes. The larger aim is to create a culture that promotes constitutional values and promotes a rule that sternly prohibits violence in all forms within a household. It is expected that through this law the message is being spread that domestic violence is unacceptable and intolerable and that the one who is being victimized is entitled to obtain remedies. The law is therefore created with the goal to attack inequitable and unjust social norms.

Courts, as the custodian of justice, constitutional values and the rule of law, play a significant role in defining and shaping the legal and social norms and ensuring that those who are powerless are rendered justice. In normal parlance, the courts are considered temples of justice by ordinary people. It is expected that the courts, with their progressive and fair attitude, condemn all forms of violence and enforce the law in an innovative manner to provide justice to the women who face abuse. However, analysis of everyday proceedings in the courtrooms reveals the manner in which sexism operates and is reinforced in daily decisions, orders, conversation, jest, reasoning and assumptions based on the ideology that subjugates women despite the fact that the constitution guarantees affirmative provisions in favor of women. Courts often use stiff legal language; are objective, stern and righteous; and are known to instill discipline and authority, and, at times, mirror the society where a frequently benevolent paternalistic and patriarchal attitude is being used to control and fix behavior. Contradictions exist because a litigant approach the court with the expectation of righting the wrong but ends up receiving paternalist sermons. The patriarchy exhibits itself in various forms day in and day out in the courtrooms, while the male-dominated courts often act hostile to women's concerns. Seemingly, what is important is not the voice of a woman, but rather protecting the rule of men.

This chapter looks at the situation in the courts and the manner in which judiciary is interpreting the provisions of domestic violence law to provide relief to women complainants. It concludes that in domestic violence cases, the courts neither provide rights-based justice nor do they offer rehabilitation to the victims of violence. What the courts propose is a network of family ideology and traditional values filtered through the prism of law and subjective biases, an idiosyncratic style and their discretion to decide good or bad, right or wrong. Experience reveals that often, in the layered, hierarchical, patriarchal society, the courts frequently reinforce deeply embedded masculine values and androcentric morals while ignoring the fact that their prime concern is to implement the law and disburse justice as per the constitutional norms. The court in cases of domestic abuse work with the aim of preserving the family, rather than the protecting the rights of an individual woman who has faced hurt. Patriarchal norms are privileged over constitutional or human rights. Morality is redefined and reinterpreted in the courtrooms to deny women their rightful claims. The ideals relating to rights and justice find no space within the private domain of the family, and specifically when the questions relate to the rights of women. Women are discriminated against as wives and daughters in families and as citizens in the courts and other public spaces.

Marriage is not construed as a companionship

> "A wife should be administrator in purpose, slave in duty, Lakshmi in appearance, Earth in patience, Mother in love, Prostitute in bed",[4] wrote the Kerala judge while quoting a Sanskrit *shloka* to interpret the duties of a woman in a matrimonial relationship.
>
> (2018)

Thus, as per the court, a wife should be capable of adopting multiple roles. She must be perfect in work and appearance, should be caring and loving and yet must work as a slave. The role of a wife is painted with high expectations, whereas no such roles are prescribed for husbands by the court. As per this notion, a woman can attain salvation only if she obeys her husband, because for her, her husband is a lord and a master beyond which she cannot have a separate existence. The traditional conservative notions about the 'good woman' who is obedient, compliant, docile and does not question the norms is still prevalent within and outside the courtrooms and prevents many women from seeking justice using the legal system.[5] In fact, the conventional stereotype of an 'ideal uncomplaining wife' is reinforced by the judicial system that reiterates that a devoted and a loyal wife will suffer torture silently. The paternalistic attitude that operates within and outside the courtrooms hinders many women from negotiating for their rights or to obtain justice. In fact, marriage is construed as a sacred relationship and not a tie that is based on companionship. As per this approach, it is a *dharma* or the duty of the wife to look after her family subserviently without questioning. Marriage is considered to be a pious '*Dharmic*' institution[6] which is 'made in heaven but broken on earth'.[7] Much emphasis is laid on the performance of ceremonies such as the *Saptapadi* as per the rituals[8] to accentuate the sacramental nature of the relationship that involves a union of souls that extends not only to one but to seven lives.[9]

Since the colonial era, the courts have been relying on ancient Hindu texts as coded in *Vedas* and *Smritis*. Many of these texts have been interpreted as putting the wife on a lower level, considering a woman to a *dasi* or a slave. The intersection of caste and gender hierarchies is reproduced to arrive at the interpretation of ancient religious literature while construing rights and wrongs within marriage, rather than the constitutional values or legal norms. For instance, the Bombay High Court[10] adduced that as per *Shastras*, in an *anuloma* marriage, marriage between a man from a higher caste to lower-caste woman is valid, and children born out of such a tie are legitimate. However, the children born out of a relationship between Shudra men and a Brahmin mistress or a *pratiloma* marriage, which is declared invalid under the Hindu law, are not *dasiputra* and therefore cannot claim inheritance in their father's property. While using the Brahmanical texts, gender and caste parameters are utilized to deprive a *Brahmin* woman and her children of their rights and penalize her for marrying a lower-caste man.[11] This trend of interpreting rights in marriage narrowly continued in the independent India.[12] Contrary to the constitutional values of equality, justice and liberty, such orthodox ideas and stereotypes are being embedded in personal laws morally, religiously and socially and are evident in the spate of rulings and verdicts pronounced by the courts.

Colonial mind-set operating in post-colonial India

The imperial rulers reinforced the dominant androcentric ideology while also introducing the narrow constricted moral codes of Victorian notions while suppressing women's status. Thomas Babington Macaulay, an officer appointed by the British rulers, when drafting the Indian Penal Code[13] narrowly interpreted the 'Indian culture' and ignored the practices of the majority.[14] He adopted the orthodox Brahmanical understanding while inferring the laws of *Manusmriti* and combined it with the imperial morality to codify the law, and this has been retained and continued to today, propagating the constricted attitude and mind-set that subjugate women. Macaulay and his fellow Englishmen could not recognize the fact that laws propounded by Manu were flawed, as these ingeniously manipulated the values and philosophy of Hinduism.[15] This unreasonably androcentric colonial jurisprudence survived despite unending talks on the modernization of the legal system in free India.[16] Narrow-minded misogynist interpretations of the religious laws deterred the cause of gender equality and gender justice.[17] Currently, the situation is that the penal code as operated in the courts is penalizing the women complainants the most.[18]

The reasoning of the law simply seems to have been stuck in the colonial morality. For example, when deciding the Rukmabai's case, Justice Pinhey evoked the pristine moral past and the logic of native customs to decide a case of a young woman who refused to join the company of her husband, Dadaji, who pleaded for the provision of restitution of conjugal rights.[19] Discourse on law and morality, justice and emancipation, civilization and barbarism, masters and slaves, colonial justice and local customs was raised then to sift justice through the labyrinth of hegemonical interpretations to arrive at a dominant logic to justify the pathological stand while shaping righteousness. Sarkar[20] noted that while adjudicating the matter of Phulmonee, a ten-year-old bride in 1890 who was raped to death by her husband, the English judge exonerated the accused without questioning the husband, who insisted on sleeping with the child, or the barbaric custom which allowed him to do so with impunity because colonial rulers do not want to meddle with the customs of the natives for reasons of political expediency. This approach continues to exist today whereby the state does not wish to interfere with the private violence inflicted within the sanctity of the home.

During the colonial period different standards and scales of justice are utilized by the state to deal with cases pertaining to marriage. In fact, Section 259 and 260 of the Civil Procedure Code of 1877 was revised in 1882 to provide that if a spouse refused to comply with the decree awarded in the suit for restitution of conjugal rights, then he or she should be punished with imprisonment or a fine or both. These decrees were often used against women. Earlier, women could garner the support of extended families in cases of violence by husbands, but the wording of Section 259 was amended to provide that the extended family could not interfere and also Section 260 worked against women who had little property.[21] Thus, colonial rulers "effectively helped Bengali males 'to create a state within a state' by insisting that the household remains a zone of autonomy and self-rule for a Hindu male".[22]

The 'women question' in post-independence India

This trend of neglecting the 'women question' continued in post-colonial India, where the patriarchal structure remained one of the major causes of the oppression of women. The narrow-minded patriarchal interpretations of the religious laws deterred the 'social reforms' that were initiated in the post-colonial period and could not address the realities relating to the persistent discrimination against women. The promise of gender equality as made by the constitution remained on paper only and failed to reach a vast majority. This significant social document failed to create a revolution or achieve a new social order, even though it calls for social justice and democratic governance and is accompanied by a spirit of modernization and development.

The framers of the constitution, departing from the then prevalent norms, introduced the framework of egalitarianism within marriage through Article 42 of the draft constitution[23] that reads:

> The State shall endeavour to secure that marriage shall be based only on the mutual consent of both sexes and shall be maintained through mutual cooperation, with the equal rights of husband and wife as a basis. The State shall also recognise that motherhood has a special claim on its care and protection.

This provision has the potential to address inequalities within heterosexual marriages; however, it was dropped from the final draft of the constitution without a debate. Kannabiran,[24] while analyzing case law, opined that constitutional provisions, laws and facts are intertwined and intermeshed with notional elements of a patriarchal system which 'puts in place an ideological apparatus for juridical understanding of sex-based discrimination'.

In the post-colonial legal discourse too, the 'women question' was subsumed and merged with the questions of groups and communities. The Hindu Code Bill introduced by Dr B.R. Ambedkar envisaged major changes in the situation of Hindu women and dealt with the questions that particularly affected women's lives such as those relating to succession, maintenance, marriage, divorce, adoption and guardianship.[25] For the first time, the bill suggested that married daughters should get half of what sons are entitled to. It also abolished caste as the basis for marriage and adoption. Most importantly, it recognized the principle of monogamy and granted the right to concubines to claim maintenance. The bill was recognized as a "progressive measure of reform in regard to personal freedom of women".[26] However, protest from the orthodox quarters were loud. The bill was then sent to a committee and while succumbing to pressure from the conservative members, the bill was dropped on the eve of the first general elections. Ambedkar then resigned as the law minister. Explaining his disappointment on the stalling of the Hindu Code Bill which sought to stop the reproduction of the Brahmanical patriarchy, Ambedkar said,

> To leave inequality between the class and class, between sex and sex which is soul of the Hindu Society untouched and go on passing legislation relating to economic problems is to make farce of our Constitution and built a palace on a dung heap. This is the significance I attached to the Hindu Code.[27]

It was only in 1955–1956 that parts of it were pushed as the Hindu Marriage Act, the Hindu Succession Act, the Hindu Minority and Guardianship Act and the Hindu Adoption and Maintenance Act while diluting the provisions given in the earlier bill. These new acts by no means advanced the rights of women. On the contrary, this codification put an end to the diversity of Hindu laws practiced in different regions and in the process destroyed existing, liberal customary provisions. These legal correctives did not go beyond what is phrased as "typecasting women as wombs to bring forth babies, lips to utter sweet nothings, and laps to cuddle infants."[28] The Constituent Assembly Debates maintained the tradition of ignoring women's concerns. Rather, the Indian state infantilized women by giving decision-making powers to the male guardians, taking away women's agency and patronizing them in the guise of providing 'protection'. The woman's body was construed as a marker of male honor and the metaphor of vulnerability and therefore needs to be controlled and protected. What is stressed is the fact that women belong to their families and their communities but not to their own person, which positioned women as wives and mothers and not as independent citizens with the right to autonomy. According to Menon and Bhasin, "Family, community and state emerge as the three mediating and interlocking forces determining women's individual and collective destinies."[29]

This trend continues to dominate, and even today, the courts in general are following the similar regressive approach where the right to equality within families is interpreted parsimoniously by the courts. The courts refuse to apply constitutional values in the domain of the family.[30] The principle to preserve the institution of marriage has been reinforced in several cases,[31] and in *Saroj Rani vs Sudarshan Kumar*[32] while overruling the decision of Andhra Pradesh High Court in *T Sareetha vs T Venkata Subbaiah*,[33] it was determined that the state must refrain from entering the private domain of the home. The public–private dichotomy is thus used to deny women their rightful entitlements under the law. Those who enforce the law discriminate between men and women unconsciously, and this reflects a traditional and rigid attitude toward women.[34]

The state sanctions dowry and domestic violence

The laws relating to dowry or domestic violence have been enacted under pressure; however, the state is not keen to preserve women's rights, as has been indicated in numerous stances where cases have been decided such that a husband is granted immunity to abuse his wife, and therefore the courts promoted domination in the guise of love and discipline. The analysis of decisions pronounced indicate that the rule of men supersedes the rule of law. Regulation of marital violence is covered in the language of husbands' prerogative to justify unequal marital relations. Wife battering is not viewed as criminal conduct by a violent husband; rather, it is justified as an expression of emotions that need to be adjusted and rechanneled into marriage, and the wife is entrusted with the duty of doing so.

For instance, in *Sham Lal vs State of Haryana*,[35] Neelam Rani was set ablaze on 17 June 1987 and died because she could not fulfill the dowry demand. She was facing extreme cruelty in her marital home. The accused persons, including her husband, father-in-law and grandmother, pled that because of frustration that she could not give birth to a child and could not adjust to the village life, she committed suicide. The session court convicted her husband and her father-in-law under Section 302, 304B and 498A IPC. On appeal, the High Court acquitted the father-in-law but convicted her husband on the basis of the findings that she had been doused with kerosene and burned alive. The apex court on appeal in its decision on 20 February 1997 observed that as there was nothing on record to show that she was treated with cruelty or harassed for the demand of dowry, the conviction of her husband was set aside under Section 302 and 304B but he was held guilty under Section 498A. As he has already served three years in prison, he was acquitted. Though Neelam Rani was maliciously burned alive, the insensitive court, unconcerned about the seriousness of the crime, let off the accused with a lighter punishment on technical grounds. Perhaps those guilty of burning her knew that they will be able to escape easily from the clutches of the law. The murder of a woman is not a matter of concern to a male-dominated state. This attitude has led to a culture of impunity.

The criminal law prioritizes the rights of the offenders over the rights of the victim while deciding the case. Technical defects have been pointed out to exonerate the perpetrators of the crime, while the courts turn a blind eye to the suffering of victims. For instance, in the matter of *State of West Bengal vs Orilal Jaiswal*,[36] Usha, a 20-year-old woman, committed suicide within a year of her marriage. Despite giving sufficient dowry as per the demands made by the accused persons, Usha was tortured physically as well as mentally. Her husband used to assault her. She was taunted for bringing a substandard quality of dowry and was also mocked for bringing evil luck to the family. The deceased complained several times to her natal family but later she committed suicide. The postmortem report showed signs of death by hanging. The doctor noted abrasion marks on her body. The session judge noted the lapse on the part of the IO and found the husband and mother-in-law guilty under Section 306, 498A and 34, IPC. On appeal, the High Court set aside the conviction. The Supreme Court convicted both of the accused under Section 498A, but considering the age of the mother-in-law, her sentence was reduced to two years imprisonment. The court acquitted both the accused for the charges under Section 306 while giving them the benefit of the doubt. Thus, no one was held guilty for the torture Usha underwent within ten months of her marriage, and no one could be held accountable for her suicide. No attempts were made to look at the psychological trauma or physical brutalities she underwent, as if her life seems to have no value. The persons who compelled Usha to commit suicide are absolved from their criminal culpability.

In *State of Punjab vs Iqbal Singh*[37] Mohinder Kaur, who was working as a teacher, set herself and her three children ablaze at her matrimonial home on 7 June 1983. Married seven or eight years ago, she was harassed for dowry. She wrote a letter to the DSP complaining of her ill treatment and seeking police protection. Her husband frustrated her efforts to seek a transfer from the school where she was working. Her mother-in-law and sister-in-law encouraged her husband and conspired to kill her by sprinkling kerosene, but their plan misfired. Fed up, Mohinder wrote a letter to her mother sharing her agony and committed suicide the next day. Her mother lodged an FIR. The trial court convicted her husband, mother-in-law and sister-in-law; hence an appeal was made before the High Court, which acquitted all of them on the grounds that the prosecution could not prove the ingredients of Section 306 relating to the abetment of suicide. The Supreme Court, while considering her ill treatment and the atmosphere of terror created for her, restored the conviction of her husband but acquitted his sister. The courts insisted on technicalities and not on the fact that Mohinder Kaur was continuously and brutally tortured to an extent that she killed her three children and committed suicide.

In *Arvind Singh vs State of Bihar*[38] the daughter of Phulmati was burned alive. The deceased disclosed that her husband and other family members forcibly poured kerosene and burned her entire body. The girl was tortured because she was 'ugly looking' and because the demands for dowry for Rs 10,000/ and a gold ring could not be fulfilled. The apex court, during the trial, dwelled on the forms of the burn injuries, the technicalities of the dying declaration, nonexamination of the IO and other evidences and set aside the imprisonment under Section 302 or 304B and 498A because no dowry demands were made prior to the date of the occurrence of crime. Those who murdered Phulmati's daughter with impunity, burned her and then refused to take her body to the hospital knew that the system upholds a mind-set where burning women alive is not considered a deadly crime. Perhaps it is easy to entangle justice in the web of technicalities, nitty-gritty and legal procedures.

Similarly, in *Sher Singh vs State of Haryana*,[39] Harjinder Kaur committed suicide on 7 February 1998 by ingesting aluminum phosphate because she was brutally tortured for not fulfilling the demand for a motorcycle and a fridge. Her husband contested that she was hot-tempered, wanted him to shave his hair and forced him to live separately from his parents. The session judge convicted her husband, father-in-law, mother-in-law and brother-in-law under Section 304B and 498A IPC. The High Court on appeal acquitted all others expect her husband on the grounds that the prosecution failed to establish their role. The Supreme Court acquitted the husband while noting,

> What motivated or compelled her to take this extreme and horrific step will remain a mystery, as we are not satisfied that the prosecution has proved or even shown that she was treated with such cruelty, connected with dowry demands, as led her to commit suicide.
>
> The court could not accept the fact that for a motorcycle and a fridge, a woman was barbarically tortured to an extent that she committed suicide while she was pregnant.

In *Ramesh Kumar vs State of Chhattisgarh*[40] the court undermined the seriousness of the law while holding that a presumption of abetment of suicide by a married woman made under Section 113A of the Indian Evidence Act is not mandatory but permissive. Also, it held that there is a need to establish a cause-and-effect relationship between cruelty and suicide. Even in dowry death cases where Section 304B is applicable and the burden of proof rests on the accused, the courts have demanded that the prosecution prove its case beyond a reasonable doubt. For instance, in *Sanjiv Kumar vs State of Punjab*,[41] the court acquitted the accused while holding that though the deceased was subjected to harassment and cruelty by the appellant and his family members, because the family of the appellant is relatively prosperous compared to the family of deceased, they would not demand petty things such as a TV, refrigerator or cash of Rs 10,000/ and also the deceased had an illicit relationship with her brother-in-law because she went and stayed at his house despite opposition from her husband, leading to incriminating circumstances. This reasoning devalues women where her economic status and character are utilized as grounds for acquittal.

More recently, a court awarded six years' imprisonment to Mohd Abdul Alim who poured boiling water on his wife Noorjahan on 9 March 2013 when she came back from work and was resting. She was taken to Safdarjung Hospital with 50 percent burns on her body, and she died seven days later.[42] In her dying declaration, she accused her husband, as he was suspicious of her character. The court noted that the police failed to establish the fact of her murder and convicted him only for causing grievous hurt. "There in nothing in the postmortem report to show that burns were sufficient in the ordinary course of nature to cause death of the deceased", noted the court. Noorjahan lost her life, yet the accused is not held guilty for causing her death.

There are cases after cases where the courts have upheld the logic of the patriarchy while acquitting the accused persons. Women have died in compelling circumstances. The testimony of witnesses and other material evidence indicates that women have been brutally murdered or were compelled to commit suicide because of unreasonable motives or coercive demands. Yet it does not matter to the state if women are killed brutally – the accused husband and in-laws should not face punishment and therefore in the process, the courts have overlooked material evidence and acquitted the accused person on flimsy grounds, technicalities and an anti-women interpretation of law or while pointing out the fault of women as wives the acquittal of accused persons is upheld. While I was finalizing this work, I came across a news item which states that the world is debating about saving species which may become extinct due to climate change,[43] and here I am pondering murder, suicide and torture of wives and the approach of courts whereby the violent husbands are being let off easily. Perhaps women here are treated as lesser beings than those species on the verge of extinction.

Technical defects are evoked to exonerate violent men

Technical defects have been evoked in domestic violence and dowry death cases to exonerate the violent husbands and in-laws. For instance, in *Satvir Singh vs State of Punjab*[44] the court observed "It is not enough that harassment or cruelty was caused to the woman with a demand for dowry at some time, if Section 304B is to be invoked. But it should have happened 'soon before her death'". This reasoning has been taken in many other cases.[45] In another case, a trial court judge, based on technical defects in recording the dying declaration of the victim, exonerated the accused of all charges.[46] This was later set aside by the High Court. In *Narsingh Prasad Singh vs Raj Kumar*,[47] the High Court reduced the sentence of abusers who had mercilessly beaten a victim with a wooden stick and planned to burn her alive to the fine of Rs. 1000 without providing a reason as to why the sentence should be reduced. In *Krishan Lal vs Union of India*[48] it was assumed that "With the passage of time after marriage and birth of children, there are remote chances of treating a married woman with cruelty by her husband or his relatives". In *Mohd Hashim vs State of UP*[49] the accused persons were convicted under Section 498A, 323 IPC and Section 3 and 4, Dowry Prohibition Act; however, the apex court allowed the appeal of the offenders to reduce the sentence under the Probation of Offenders Act. Arguments have not been raised regarding the protection of the rights of the victim, nor have the courts showed concern for substantive justice. In fact, the circumstances have not been considered while pronouncing the decision, and the arguments remained limited to the technical issue around applicability of the law.

In *Mohd Miyan vs State of UP*[50] in a meeting of complainant wife with her husband, mother-in-law and their nine relatives demanded dowry and when she refused, her husband became enraged. It was alleged that her mother-in-law and sisters-in-law caught her hair, and her husband hit her with his fist, breaking one of her teeth. The complainant filed an FIR under Section 498A, 323, 325, 504 and 506 IPC besides invoking Section 3 and 4 of the Dowry Prohibition Act. The accused persons approached the High Court to quash the proceedings, and the court dismissed the petition. In the Supreme Court it was argued that in the FIR, the complainant stated that her divorce took place four years ago. The apex court held that a prosecution is not sustainable under Section 498A IPC or under the Dowry Prohibition Act. The insensitive court turned a blind eye to the fact that the husband and his relatives were demanding dowry when cruelty was inflicted on the wife. The court could not see the physical cruelty being inflicted on her but instead sympathized with the accused and his relatives. The court did not imagine the manner in which a power structure operates when the nine people surrounded one person to extract dowry from her and forced her physically to concede to the demands.

In several matters,[51] pleas of limitation and territorial jurisdiction have been invoked to exonerate the accused persons. The courts failed to consider that the women have been tortured, brutalized and murdered while allowing the appeal of the accused persons. What is prioritized is technicalities, procedural complexities or the rights of the accused, and what is negated in the process is the sufferings of the victims, the humane element and the object of enacting the law. Justice is denied while twisting and manipulating the law to protect the accused persons and, in the process, the purpose of the law is lost behind the technical maze and complications.[52]

In *Appasaheb vs State of Maharashtra*[53] Bhimabai died because her parents could not fulfill the continuous demands for dowry made by her husband and his mother. The postmortem report showed that the cause of her death was insecticide poisoning. The Supreme Court ruled that a demand for money on the account of financial stringency or for meeting some urgent domestic expenses cannot be termed as a demand for dowry, and therefore the conviction of appellants cannot be sustained. In *Vipin Jaiswal vs State of AP*,[54] the victim received severe burn injuries that she eventually died from. Her husband and in-laws were demanding Rs 50,000/. The trial court convicted the accused under Section 304B and 498A. The Supreme Court on appeal ruled that the demand was made six months after the marriage because the accused husband wanted to purchase a computer to start a business, and therefore this coercion cannot be construed as a dowry-related demand. Thus, the message conveyed is that even if coercive demands are made for any reason after marriage and women were murdered, the same will not be construed as dowry demand and the husband or in-laws could not be held guilty for committing brutal murders.

In cases pertaining to dowry death or suicide, where the accused persons – husbands and in-laws – have tortured women for years and murdered them brutally because their greed is not satiated, they are being let off by the courts on technical grounds such as gaps in the investigation, or not producing crucial witnesses or evidence, or while interpreting the law.[55] In many cases brutal murders were tried as simple cases of suicide. In numerous other cases brides have been burned, murdered, killed, forced to commit suicide or even tortured brutally, but the courts could not hear their painful screams and refuse to see the evidence of serious crime. Rather, the utterly sympathetic courts have protected the men on the grounds of technical gaps, procedural defects or the nitty-gritty of law. The entire machinery is geared to save the 'innocent men' irrespective of the fact that these men have murdered, tortured and burned their wives alive. Though a thorough analysis of the court's decisions is further required, a mere glimpse at many decisions shows that lives of women are considered cheaper than daily household items such as a fridge, TV, cooler, motorcycle, car or cash. Women have been ill treated pitilessly for days, months and years and are murdered because demands were not fulfilled, yet no action is being taken to punish the guilty. Also, apart from not bringing dowry, many of them were subjected continuously to ruthless abuse, humiliation and torture for reasons such as skin color, bringing evil luck, being 'ugly looking' and similar other non-reasons. Yet the learned courts acquit the accused persons on flimsy, technical grounds and in doing so, not only deprive victims of justice but also perpetuate the culture of violence and impunity. The courts do not protect women's rights as wives, but what the courts uphold is men, their might and their privileges. This shows that the logic of patriarchy prevails over the rule of law and reinforces the rule of men.

A woman is painted negatively with suspicion and assigned low credibility in the courts

Courts often do not trust women complainants. A woman's testimony is viewed with suspicion, and she is assigned low credibility as a witness or a litigant. Women who are challenging the patriarchy and questioning the dominant notions relating to marriage or family are viewed with suspicion by the courts. For instance, in *Indrasing Raol vs State of Gujarat*[56] Kailsba got married in February 1986 and committed suicide on 7 March 1987 because she was constantly tortured for dowry. She was reduced to a "bag of bones" and her "miseries know no bound". A few days before she committed suicide, her husband, who employed with the army, after consuming liquor at midnight, beat her indiscriminately, kicking and hitting her because she refused to accompany him. The police therefore registered a FIR under Section 498A and 306 IPC. On appeal, the High Court while acquitting the violent husband argued,

> A woman would prefer to end her life, if continuous, or recurring unabated harassment or cruelty grave in nature, is intolerable or unendurable. Highly sensitive impulsive, reckless, or touchy woman may on one incident end her life, but that exception to the rule is not envisaged by the Section. It should also be stated that after marriage sometimes emotional disorder is created, and that results into frustration and pessimism. A woman sometime becomes psychotic and develops tendency to end her life. A woman being highly sensitive and sentimental, or reckless, or if tired of her life either because her dreamt expectations are not satisfied or found to be the mirage, or for any other reason may become dejected and desperate and may develop suicidal tendency, and end her life.
>
> (para 17, 1999)

The court with one stroke not only generalized the nature of women but also overlooked the fact that the deceased in this case was continuously harassed by her husband. The court contradicts its own statement where initially it stated that because of constant torture, Kailasba was reduced to a bag of bones and an object of misery and later to acquitted her violent husband, thus drawing different conclusions based on a single episode of violence. Her worth is discredited in the process. The subjectivities, biases and prejudices held sway, and the truth is discarded in the process when the court becomes blind to the fact that within a short span of her marriage, Kailasba was tortured so severely that she ended her life. In many cases, it is the woman – her work, her character, her personality – that is being questioned. A man, even if he is a drunkard, vile, criminal or violent, is not viewed with suspicion. Fricker[57] has called this testimonial injustice when a speaker's credibility is defeated by the prejudices of the hearer while blocking the flow of truth. The male-dominated society deems women to have no credibility. Judges subject women to stereotypes and prejudices, because of which women suffer harm, and their concerns are overlooked in the process of delivering justice.

The law questions women, not men

In many cases, the courts have reduced the sentences or acquitted the violent men. Even in cases where women have been burned alive or have been compelled to commit suicide, the courts frequently, while sympathizing with the accused men, ignore the brutalities committed on women. For instance, in the well-known Naina Sahani *Tandoor* Murder case,[58] the apex court commuted the death sentence to life imprisonment "because murder was the outcome of strained personal relationship. It was not an offence against the society". Maxwell Pereira in his book titled *The Tandoor Murder*[59] reconstructed the gruesome crime scene that took place on the night of 2 July 1995 when Constable Kunju, deployed at the Connaught Place police station, discovered that 'a murdered woman's corpse' was being cremated in the middle of night in a secret manner. He went on to describe the turbulent journey from investigation to trial where witnesses turned hostile because the high-profile accused used all his muscle and money power to escape. The trial court handed down a death sentence to the accused, which was confirmed by the High Court. The apex court partly allowed the appeal of the accused and ended up commuting his death sentence while ignoring the ruthless murder.[60] The bench said

> Considering the social status of the deceased, it would be difficult to come to the conclusion that the appellant was in dominant position qua her. The appellant was deeply in love with the deceased. The evidence on record shows that he suspected her fidelity and the murder was the result of this possessiveness.

The apex court revived the history of the relationship and erroneously sent the message that in the case of a 'private' relationship between a man and a woman, if a man loves her, he also has a right to brutally murder her with impunity if he suspects her character. The state will not take such violence seriously, as it is not considered as a crime against society. The legal system took recourse to a conservative myopic vision and reinforced that a man has authority and prerogative to discipline and control a woman if he suspects her character or is possessive.

In *Waghmare vs State of Maharashtra*[61] Sarla Waghmare was emotionally and physically abused by her husband and his family. They regularly beat her and harassed her for a motorcycle, and after two months of marriage, her brother-in-law poured kerosene on her and set her on fire, which resulted in serious injuries. The Bombay High Court held that these incidents of violence were not sufficient to force her to commit suicide and that the demand for a motorcycle was not a dowry demand. The court acquitted the guilty persons because the wife had not acted according to 'conventional' pattern of wifely behavior and was not 'consistent' because "she withdrew the complaint of being burned by her brother-in-law two months after her marriage". The court ignored the fact that there is intense pressure on a woman to withdraw the complaint to preserve the marriage. Courts measure the "'rightness' of women's action by applying stringent rules of wifely behavior and condone violence by men".[62]

Courts uphold conservative notions and not constitutional values

MacKinnon[63] argued that society as a whole and its constitutive parts, including law, institutions and private relations, are hierarchically organized on the basis of sex and are designed to create and maintain male dominance. This work also suggests that a biased attitude continues to operate within the legal system. In the courts, women are routinely disrespected and infantilized. The relationship matrix is utilized to adjudicate the women's claims. For instance, in *S. Hanumantha Rao vs S. Ramani*,[64] the husband alleged that his wife's unwillingness to wear *mangalsutra* was the evidence of mental cruelty.

Custodial torture within the four walls of the home was neglected for the sake of upholding tradition and culture. The courts construct an image of an ideal stereotype of a good wife who is subservient, submissive and perfect. Any deviation from this norm causes a woman to be considered bad. Such a presumptive culture disregards the fact that men use their abusive power to assault women, create fear and demand compliance as well as authoritative control. In *Arup Hazra vs Manashi Hazra*[65] the husband filed the divorce application on the grounds of cruelty that his wife has "refused to cook food and serve meals to the husband and any members of his family, and used to move out of home without permission". The wife alleged that her husband was harassing her because her family refused to pay Rs. 50,000 as a dowry. The court allowed his application for divorce on the grounds of desertion.

In *Sonia vs Vinod*[66] despite of the report by the PO that the aggrieved woman was in dire need of protection, the Magistrate stated that there was no evidence of violence; rather, the complainant was not cooperating with her husband and harassing him on trivial matters and was not behaving in a traditional manner towards her husband and his family; therefore, the court dismissed the application. In this case, the wife complained that she was harassed and beaten up for the dowry and that her husband used to consume alcohol habitually and mistreated her and therefore she requested a protection order. The magistrate subjectively constructed the image of a 'woman' as a perfect daughter-in-law and a wife who should cooperate with her husband and his family. As the *khap panchayats*, courts uphold the traditional norms rather than upholding constitutional values.

Similarly, in another case, the court held that as "the wife is not performing her pious obligation but she was so much mesmerized by her political thoughts and quiet adamant that she failed to understand the consequences of her negligent attitude".[67] In yet another case, divorce was granted because the wife "taunted the husband for not being able to satiate her sexual desires on account of his [. . .] heavy weight".[68] Patriarchal courtrooms often set boundaries to limit the autonomy, dignity and freedom of a woman and decide her place in society, control her body and mind, regulate her sexual being and control her interactions and her relationships, including controlling her womb and her desires determining each and every step of her life from being an unmarried girl, to a wife, to a mother. The courts opined that in case a wife is forgetful or is "devoid of etiquettes and courtesy", her husband has a right to chastise her.[69] Similarly, if a wife does not have a compromising temperament, this gives the husband the right to get annoyed and angry, and in such a state he could beat his wife. Also, per a ruling by the Supreme Court,

> teasing by the accused-appellant of the deceased, ill treating her for her mistakes which could have been pardonable and turning her out of the house, also once beating her inside the house at the odd hours of night did amount to cruelty within the meaning of Section 498A of IPC.

Courts often presume that violence within marriages occurs due to conflict and stress and that both parties are equally responsible for the dispute. This assumption ignores the reality of the power differential within the relationship in addition to the structural factors that govern the nature, dynamics and social reality of domestic violence. Morality is a part of the legal discourse, and many decisions are couched in a preaching tone while using a patriarchal lexicon and ignoring the impact of violence on women and children. The Bombay High Court, in a public interest litigation,[70] split "violence" down the middle while stipulating that women facing "severe physical" domestic violence must be brought before the court to secure a protection order, but for all other types of violence, pre-litigation "joint counselling" may be conducted by the police and non-governmental organizations to amicably settle the dispute, even while conceding that the "assurances" have no legal binding.

Construing an ideal woman as a perfect wife through a judicial lens

Basu and Jaising[71] observed that often women who approach the courts are viewed with the androcentric moral lens while stereotypes and prejudices operate in the courtroom. While examining Justice J. D. Kapoor's book *Laws and Flaws in Marriage*[72] Basu and Jaising show the manner in which the courts frequently push the gendered norms and reward women who conform to a traditional role of a wife.

High expectations are laid for women as wives by the courts, though no preaching is done on the conduct of a man as a husband. For instance, while dealing with a case of divorce, the division bench of the Bombay High Court observed that the wife should be like the goddess Sita, who should follow her husband, Lord Rama, even during his isolation in a forest, but for a man to be Rama could not be imagined by the misogynist court.[73] "Implicit in a number of judgements is a notion of culture relativism which suggests that Indian women are accustomed to a certain amount of violence and therefore violence against them is not considered as a serious infringement on women's rights",[74] rightly observed a study.

There are many decisions which see women as 'good' wives, mothers or daughters-in-law and uphold a conservative sexual morality. In *Suman Kapur vs Sudhir Kapoor*[75] the court upheld that when women focus on their career, they neglect their household duties. The court failed to appreciate the fact that a woman may seek opportunity to advance her career, and in marriage, being an equal partnership, men should cooperate and actively contribute to the household responsibilities such as managing the household or taking part in the child care rather than misusing the provision of restitution of conjugal rights to force their wives to give up their careers. In *Praveen Mehta vs Inderjit Mehta*[76] it was articulated that the wife's illness could not excuse her lack of cooperation for sex. The court openly upholds the patriarchal logic that the husband could not enjoy the company of his wife because of her ill health. Also, in *Birdichand Sarda vs State of Maharashtra*[77] the wife was visualized as an extremely 'sensitive' person who made unreasonable demands to seek the undivided attention of her busy husband.[78] In *Savitri Pandey vs Prem Chandra Pandey*[79] the court, while strictly interpreting the context of cruelty, held that

> Cruelty, however, has to be distinguished from the ordinary wear and tear of family life. It cannot be decided on the basis of the sensitivity of the petitioner and has to be adjudged on the basis of the course of conduct which would, in general, be dangerous for a spouse to live with the other.

Courts preach on the duties of wives but not about the role of husbands

In a patriarchal society, gendered norms place different social burdens upon men and women. In the specific familial context, expectations are based on the gender of the members such that women are in a disadvantageous position. While propagating the family ideology, in *Narendra vs K Meena*,[80] the court opined that separating a husband from his family amounts to 'cruelty' without recognizing the fact that a girl who is separated from her natal family at the time of marriage also has moral or legal obligations towards her natal family. The Supreme Court stated

> It is not a common practice or desirable culture for a Hindu son in India to get separated from the parents upon getting married at

> the instance of the wife, especially when the son is the only earning member in the family. A son, brought up and given education by his parents, has a moral and legal obligation to take care and maintain the parents, when they become old and when they have either no income or have a meagre income.... As stated hereinabove, in a Hindu society, it is a pious obligation of the son to maintain the parents. If a wife makes an attempt to deviate from the normal practice and customs of the society, she must have some justifiable reason for that and in this case, we do not find any justifiable reason, except monetary consideration of the Respondent wife. In our opinion, normally, no husband would tolerate this and no son would like to be separated from his old parents and other family members, who are also dependent upon his income. The persistent effort of the Respondent wife to constrain the Appellant to be separated from the family would be torturous for the husband and in our opinion, the trial Court was right when it came to the conclusion that this constitutes an act of 'cruelty'.
>
> (2016)

The text points out the manner in which pre-conceived traditional notions, stereotypes, biases and prejudices operate within courtrooms. The term cruelty is interpreted against the backdrop of social norms regarding what constitutes appropriate behavior. The repressive mentality is reflected when the court upholds male supremacy and privilege and reinforces the position of women as second-class citizens. It considers women an appendage to men and the male as an authoritative figure and a breadwinner, while reinforcing the gender and cultural stereotypes. The court upheld conservative notions while reinterpreting the hegemonic understanding of Hinduism.[81] It defined the duties of wives but cast no obligations on the husbands. What is ignored is the fact that in the patrilocal society, a woman is forced to leave her natal home upon marriage and therefore she is isolated. Her parents invest in her education and marriage, and therefore she owes a duty toward them. Moreover, in cases where families only have daughters, it is the duty of daughters to care for their parents. The fact of her marriage cannot take away her responsibility towards them.

Courts on the issue of marital rape

> "I don't think that marital rape should be regarded as an offence in India, because it will create absolute anarchy in families and our country is sustaining itself because of the family platform which upholds family values," Former Chief Justice of India, Justice Dipak Mishra
>
> (2019)[82]

On the issue of marital rape, the state has followed a regressive approach.[83] In a matter before the Supreme Court, the center defended the provisions under Section 375(2) that permits a man to rape his legally wedded wife even if her age is less than 18 years, and the court agreed that marital rape cannot be considered a criminal offense.[84] In consonance with the traditional regressive ideology of glorifying motherhood and preserving the institution of the family, the court failed to see the fact that a person below 18 years of age is a minor and any such attempt to legitimize the rape of such a child for the sake of protecting the institution of marriage will have a detrimental impact on the health of the child. The Child Marriage Prevention and Redressal Act recognizes that marrying a girl below 18 years of age is invalid, yet while ignoring these provisions, the court legitimized the rape of minors while upholding the sanctity of marriage.[85] In other words, the court upheld child marriage which is "actually a 'solemnized invasion' of a girl, her bodily integrity, her sexuality and her mind."[86] The Protection of Children from Sexual Offence Act 2012 contradicts the provisions as laid down under the Penal Code.

Thus, legally, there is no uniformity in defining the age of consent, and different pieces of legislation prescribe different ages. Such an approach systematically pushes back women's rights and liberties while upholding the institution of marriage and undermining women's rights as citizens. The notion of controlling sexuality of women guides such decisions. The issue of consent was not raised while adjudicating, and the court ignored the aspects of women's bodies, mind, agency or autonomy. The bodily integrity and dignity of women are sacrificed at the altar of preserving the institution of marriage and upholding the patriarchal structures of power.

Domestic violence is a continuous offense, not episodic

Domestic violence is a continuous offense, where the victim lives in a state of continuous fear and terror. However, the courts rarely take this fact into account. In *Sujata Mukherjee vs Prashant Mukherjee*[87] the court recognized this fact, and

> that in view of allegations in the complaint that the offence was a continuing one having been committed in more local areas and one of the local areas being Raipur, the learned Magistrate at Raipur had jurisdiction to proceed with the criminal case instituted in such court.

In *Jagdish vs State of Rajasthan*,[88] the court held,

> If repeated demand for dowry is made and harassment is meted out to a woman which may be physical or mental is an act of cruelty. It is not necessary that the husband or his relatives must be present at

> the time when the house wife is subjected to cruelty. If their act or conduct, omission or commission is of such a nature which results in mental and physical harassment it will amount to an act of cruelty to a woman and it is immaterial that the woman is living at that relevant time at her matrimonial home or at her parents' house. The offence under Section 498A is a continuing office and if the act of cruelty continues even while, the woman is living at her parents' house, the offence is triable by both the Courts in whose territorial jurisdiction the act of continuing offence of cruelty has been committed at matrimonial home or the parents' house.

The Supreme Court in several cases[89] dealt with the matter of retrospective operation of the act and held that the past conduct of the parties, even if prior to the act coming into effect, were relevant for passing orders under Sections 18, 19 and 20. However, as discussed previously, not in many cases is cruelty seen as a continuous offense, and this is problematic.

Standards of cruelty as a matrimonial offense are different from cruelty in criminal law

In *Dastane vs Dastane*,[90] the court held that

> To marry or not to marry and if so whom, may well be a private affair but the freedom to break a matrimonial tie is not. The society has a stake in the institution of marriage and therefore the erring spouse is treated not as a mere defaulter but as an offender. But this social philosophy, though it may have a bearing on the need to have the clearest proof of an allegation before it is accepted as a ground for the dissolution of a marriage, has no bearing on the standard of proof in matrimonial cases.[91]

The court opined that spouse who inflicts cruelty be treated as an offender; however, this presumption is not applied in cases where erring husbands inflict cruelty on wives. Though the law states that the standard of proof in the criminal matter and the matrimonial or civil proceedings are different, the courts maintain dual standards while dealing with cruelty as defined under the matrimonial laws as compared to those elaborated under the criminal law. "In the criminal proceedings, the charges have to be established beyond reasonable doubt whereas standard of proof in matrimonial proceedings is that of preponderance of probabilities".[92] Yet the consequences of two different proceedings have serious implications on the situation of women as these are interpreted by the courts in favor of men.

In *Bhagat vs Bhagat*,[93] it is illustrated that,

> While arriving at such conclusion, regard must be had to the social status, educational level of the parties, the society they move in, the possibility or otherwise of the parties ever living together in case they are already living apart and all other relevant facts and circumstances which it is neither possible nor desirable to set out exhaustively.

Thus, the term 'cruelty' may have different interpretations depending in the facts of the case,[94] yet the courts do not see that the act of cruelty may have deeper implications for women because of the uneven structural implications. But the same courts set different standards while dealing with the criminal liabilities of the deviant husbands who inflict cruelty on their wives. In *Raj Rani vs State*,[95] the court held that the allegations must be of a very grave nature and should be proved beyond a reasonable doubt. In *Girdhar Shankar Tawade vs State of Maharashtra*,[96] it was observed that "'cruelty' has to be understood having a specific statutory meaning and there should be a case of continuous state of affairs of torture by one to another". Hence, cruelty per se is hardly punished. Rather, it is acknowledged only in serious cases when a woman dies. A perusal of several judgments under this law reveals that there was hardly an instance in which the accused were held guilty under 498A on its own. The judiciary is reluctant to punish or convict men even when there is enough evidence to indicate the guilt of the accused.[97]

The fragile masculinity of the androcentric courts

The courts are composed mostly of men as judges, as lawyers and as court staff, and they use a masculine lens to filter the complaints of women. As in other institutions, in the courts, too, men dominate the higher-level positions. Frequently, human subjectivities pour in while interpreting the facts and circumstances of the case, and any grievance is viewed as man versus a woman's issue. The fragility of masculine courts is often displayed in cases relating to intimate men–women relationships. For instance, in X versus Y,[98] the husband, while challenging one of the orders passed by the family court, filed a defamation suit against the wife because in her pleadings, she used the word 'impotent' toward him. The magistrate found that a prima facie case had been made and issued a process which was challenged by the wife in the High Court. The High Court observed that

> prima facie the word 'impotent' when understood in its plain and grammatical sense, reflects adversely upon the manhood of a person and has a tendency to invite derisive opinions about such person from others. Therefore, use of such word and its publication as contemplated under Section 499 of IPC would be sufficient to constitute, in a prima facie manner, the offence of defamation punishable under Section 500 of IPC.

Perhaps a fragile ego got injured because of the use of one word. Despite the clarification provided by the counsel for the wife, the court refused to grant relief to her while focusing on the concept of 'manhood'. The court overlooked the fact that frequently in a country where litigants are hardly aware of the technicalities of the law, lawyers draft the pleading on behalf of the client; therefore, holding a woman guilty would hardly serve any purpose.

Frequently, the discourse on gender-based violence is embedded in the language of the 'protection of women as daughters, wives or mothers'. This discourse seeks to communicate ownership and control of women by men. It perpetuates inequality and strengthens the power imbalance in the relationship and reaffirms discriminatory gender norms and practices. The perpetrator of violence asserts power over the person targeted. Yet the juridical discourse justifies roughness and rationalizes men's control over women rather than recognizing women's independent identity, existence or dignity. Often the courts provide remedies to women who fit into the image of a 'good woman or an ideal victim'. The residential, educational or economic status of women is used to decide whether she is entitled to protection orders or monetary orders. The language of rights is not used, and further the approach is deeply engrained in the patriarchy. This situation calls for re-examining the legal system by making it more gender friendly as well as building more accountability and transparency while adjudicating the matters with a focus on rights-based justice.

Courts penalize woman for giving dowry and not the husbands for demanding dowry

The courts in several cases have pronounced that the bride and her family should be penalized for giving dowry rather than punishing the grooms for making coercive demands and even murdering wives in case their natal families failed to give dowry. In *Neera Singh vs State*[99] the court reasoned

> A perusal of the complaint would show that as per allegations dowry demand was made even before marriage i.e. at the time of engagement and an AC was demanded from her father by her in-laws and her father had assured that AC would be given at the time of marriage. However, she told her father 'You have given car and AC at the demand of in-laws, what will happen if they demand a flat tomorrow?'. Despite her this conversation with her father and despite her knowing that dowry demand had already been made, she married in the same family irrespective of the fact that she was well-educated lady and was an engineer and her brother was in police. In fact, these kinds of allegations made after breakdown of the marriage show the mentality of the complainant. I consider where these kinds of allegations are made, the police should

> simultaneously register a case under Dowry Prohibition Act against the parents of the complainant as well, who married their daughter despite demand of dowry. Section 3 of the Act prohibits giving and taking of dowry. If a woman of grown up age and well educated gets married to a person despite dowry demand, she and her family becomes accomplice in the crime under Dowry Prohibition Act.
>
> (2007)

The flawed logic ignored the fault in the coercive action by the husband and his family members, who demanded dowry and taunted the woman for the same. Further, the judge erroneously reasoned that the practice of dowry is growing because the parents of the bride fulfilled the demands that were made:

> Nowadays, exorbitant claims are made about the amount spent on marriage and other ceremonies and on dowry and gifts. In some cases, claim is made of spending crores of rupees on dowry without disclosing the source of income and how funds flowed. I consider time has come that courts should insist upon disclosing source of such funds and verification of income from tax returns and police should insist upon the compliance of the Rules under Dowry Act and should not entertain any complaint, if the rules have not been complied with. Rule 2 of the Dowry Prohibition (Maintenance of List of Presents to the Bride and Bridegroom) Rules, 1985.

It was added,

> [T]he Metropolitan Magistrates should take cognizance of the offence under the Act in respect of the offence of giving dowry whenever allegations are made that dowry was given as a consideration of marriage, after demand. Courts should also insist upon compliance with the rules framed under the Act and if rules are not complied with, an adverse inference should be drawn. If huge cash amounts are alleged to be given at the time of marriage which are not accounted anywhere, such cash transactions should be brought to the notice of the Income Tax Department by the Court so that source of income is verified and the person is brought to law.

The court finds no fault with the persons who demand dowry and taunt, insult, humiliate, abuse, torture and murder women for dowry but instead recommended strict actions against the givers of dowry. The takers of dowry or the people who demand dowry are nowhere found to be at fault. No suggestions have been made to level the hierarchical relationship between the bride and the groom's family or to eliminate patriarchal biases.

Courts impose penalties on women for filing false complaints

The PWDVA provides for remedies to the complainants and recommended penalties against the respondents for a breach of orders passed under the law. Nowhere does the law state that the penalty may be imposed on the women complainants in any circumstances. Yet contrary to the legal provisions, in *Sumana Bhasin vs Niraj Bhasin*,[100] the zealous court imposed a penalty on the aggrieved woman for filing a 'false complaint'. In an application under the PWDVA, the trial court ordered for Rs 25,000/ pm maintenance along with Rs 5,00,000/ as compensation which was later stayed by the High Court. The judge, while relying on the technical aspect that the onus of proof lies on the person who makes allegations, dismissed the application of the aggrieved woman while imposing cost of Rs. 1,00,000/ on her. The judge stated that "[t]he imposition of cost is in furtherance of the principle that wrongdoers should not get benefit out of frivolous litigations". It was further held that

> Imposition of actual, realistic cost would go a long way in controlling the tendency of false pleadings and forged and fabricating documents by litigants. It is a fit case which calls for imposition of exemplary cost on the complainant, so that likeminded people are dissuaded from resorting to such malafide practices. The testimony of the complainant throws light on the conduct of the complainant and the extent, to which she has falsified and concocted various allegations and has suppressed important facts in order to harass the respondents and had misused the PWDV Act as a tool to extort unjustified money from the respondent no1 for unjustified personal gain. In such glaring circumstances, the Court cannot be expected to be sit as a mute spectator, where the Law, which is enacted solely for Protection of protect victims of Domestic Violence, is being misused and abused and made a tool of harassment and extortion.

The court therefore, instead of facilitating access to justice to women, created a hindrance while interpreting the affirmative law in an adverse manner. The courts do not penalize a man who delays or avoids paying maintenance or otherwise tries to delay the proceedings. No cost is imposed on men who strategically use tactics to deprive women of their due claims or who intentionally avoid following the orders pronounced by the courts. However, in the case of women, the same courts quickly impose costs or suggest penalties.

An analysis of judgements indicates that a backlash is growing in terms of efforts made to establish women's rights. The lobbying by men's groups to dilute the provisions of the domestic violence law, both civil and criminal, is impeding the process of accessing justice, whereby the state is also blindly repeating the facts without looking at the available data and statistics or without conducting any neutral research. This backlash is a critical and understudied dimension that is working towards the dilution or the complete abolition of vital legal protections for women, and this needs to be looked at from a gender point of view. Utilizing cyber forums, public protests and print media, the anti-women groups are disseminating narratives of women wreaking destruction on the family and weakening family bonds through their alleged misuse of "gender-biased" laws. They conspire to distort reality without any logical facts and jeopardize ongoing any advocacy efforts made by the women's movement. The judiciary, which is influenced by this trend, is dismissing the complaints at the cost of the safety and vulnerability of women, as highlighted in *Arnesh Kumar vs State of Bihar*.[101] The bench, while dropping the charges of cruelty and harassment against a husband, noted, "Petty quarrels cannot be termed as cruelty to attract the provisions of Section 498A, IPC". The order was made without realizing the fact that delays in arresting the accused could jeopardize a woman's life and security in cases where she is a victim of abuse. The court in this matter failed to distinguish the fine line between 'domestic violence' and 'the domestic dispute'. Another disturbing aspect is that this debate continues without any empirical basis. The opinions are not based on in-depth investigations, nor are they informed by theoretical or academic understanding. Dominant stereotypes prevail to form an ill-informed perception of existing laws and dictate the functioning of both the executive and the judiciary.

In *Rajesh Kumar vs State of UP*[102] the Supreme Court, without examining the reality or referring to any research, concluded that the law is misused by "vengeful" women and sees men as victims of this "cruel law". The court took an anti-woman stance where the judges expressed their anguish and pronounced that this law is abused and therefore suggested measures to dilute it. The courts see women through a stereotypical lens and brand them as "disgruntled women" who are "vengeful", "gold diggers" and "liars" while doubting the veracity of their complaints. Courts refuse to look into the data available on dowry death, women's suicide and violence, or the profiles of those lodged in the jails. The courts have not looked into the manner in which this law is implemented at the ground level through the existing paraphernalia consisting of CAW cells, counselling centers, family courts or mahila courts where counselling is done mandatorily and guidelines have been laid down pertaining to the arrest of the accused persons. What is ignored is the fact that the conviction rate is low in such cases because of coercive mandatory compromises or settlements enforced at various levels which start before the registration of the case. Women are discouraged from speaking the truth and are intimidated to remain silent while de-recognizing the historical background of patriarchal structural discrimination. The courts thus mirrored the oppressive culture and uphold orthodox values rather than safeguarding the spirit of the constitution or promoting the rights of women. While closing its eyes to the structural imbalance of power within the relationship, the court reinforces male domination while normalizing violence and coercing women to internalize the subjugation. In one stroke, the court took away the fundamentally guaranteed liberty, dignity and autonomy of a woman. In one stroke, the court breached the sacrosanct, non-negotiable rights of a citizen.

Filing a complaint under Section 498A is construed as cruelty by the wife

In *Christine Lazarus Menezes vs Lazarus Peter Menezes*[103] it was observed that lodging a false case under Section 498A by the wife is cruelty against the husband, and he can seek divorce on this basis. The Gujarat High Court in *Natubhai Somabhai Rohit vs State of Gujarat*[104] quashed the FIR on the ground that it is registered against ten members of the family, and even earlier the complainant filed a complaint under the PWDVA wherein she has roped in all family members, which shows her tendency to indulge in allegations and filing complaints. In another case it was held that women are using the law for the purpose of extorting money from their husbands.[105] The courts deny relief to women[106] while using the lens of morality.[107] Several judgements portray the complainants in a negative light. For instance, in the Batra's case,[108] the complainant was depicted as a woman who has terrorized her in-laws and has been asserting her rights while aggressively utilizing the law in her favor. In Kavita Dass's case,[109] the complainant was seen as a victim who is also a mother and a good woman, as she has been fulfilling all her duties diligently. The judicial reasoning is guided by the moral construct and stereotypes of a 'good woman' and a 'bad woman', and the decisions are informed by the patriarchal assumptions. Kapur,[110] too, has asserted that the legal discourse has the power to create binary assumptions regarding men and women, femininity and masculinity and culture and sexuality. Therefore, the law reinforces the dominant construction of women as weak, biologically inferior, modest and incapable of protecting themselves, on one hand, and evil, bad women as those who do not conform to the traditional norms, on the other.

The doctrine of battered woman syndrome in India

This discussion relating to misuse of the law by women has failed to acknowledge that in the cultural context where women's subordination is a norm and often they are socialized to silently tolerate the oppression, the law does not consider several significant elements. The legal system recognizes cruelty in marriage, yet it still fails to understand the intricate social and psychological complexities of the situation of a woman victim of domestic violence. For example, the history of abuse, pattern of violence and a woman's psychological state or experience are factors in domestic violence cases which may have a major impact on the outcome of the criminal litigation.

The courts in India have hardly dwelt on the same while adjudicating the matters until recently, when the Delhi High Court in one of its landmark decisions, while applying this doctrine, held an accused man guilty of abetting the suicide of his wife. In *State vs Hari Prashad*[111] under Section 306 IPC for abetting the suicide of the victim, the court upheld the doctrine of battered woman syndrome and stated that a victim could defend herself by launching a counter-attack. The court opined that, "Pushpa could not do so because biologically she was weaker ... The provocation by Hari Prashad became her compulsion to end the domestic relationship and she did by taking the extreme step of suicide". Though the court portrayed the woman as a docile, obedient wife "who has made every endeavor to stand against torture", they negated the women's agency or autonomy while valorizing her virtues of tolerance and patience, as only "when she was hoaxed" did she take the extreme step of ending her life. Thus, the court utilized the doctrine of battered woman syndrome to understand the situation of a woman in her matrimonial home. In this matter, the court innovatively applied this doctrine to the situation where the victim was already dead, yet it found the accused guilty of abetting the suicide of his wife. Battered woman syndrome is not used here as a defense; however, it has been utilized to establish the guilt of the accused in this particular case based on the reality of the situation.

Can a mother-in-law file a complaint against the daughter-in-law?

The PWDVA has been used to address the situation of women who face domestic violence within their homes. It is common knowledge that once a daughter-in-law asserts her right to reside in the matrimonial home, her husband and in-laws deploy various tactics and strategies to deny her this claim. In most of the cases where the household belongs to a joint family, the usual strategy deployed by the in-laws is to throw out both the woman and her husband of the matrimonial house, as this also helps them to show that they cannot be held liable under Section 498A, and also they can deprive her of her right to reside in the shared household. Often, false claims are made that both the son and daughter-in-law harass the old parents. While implementing the law, the male hegemony slyly deploys the strategy of pitting the rights of the mother-in-law against that of the daughter-in-law while absolving men of their responsibilities. For instance, the Delhi High Court in *Kusumlata vs State*[112] held that the mother-in-law is an aggrieved person and can file a complaint against the daughter-in-law. The court observed, "This phenomenon of the daughters-in-law harassing their mothers-in-law especially who are dependent is not uncommon in the Indian society". The court generalized the situation and made the daughter-in-law a culprit because she raised her voice against her violent in-laws. This argument ignores the social hierarchies and the power dynamics that operate within the family and feeds into the patriarchy by reinforcing male power. It colludes with the male interest of oppressing women within families.[113]

This argument overlooks the fact that a woman, given no economic or social independence in a patriarchal family, derives her power solely from men – be it as his mother or as his wife. The power struggle between two women in such a structure therefore becomes inevitable. A mother-in-law, by the virtue of her years of marriage or by producing a son, enjoys an authoritative position in comparison to a new entrant. She acts as a carrier of a culture legitimizing and preserving patriarchy while training young women to accept their inferior position within the household.[114] She often feels socially and financially insecure when a new wife enters the household, and because of the internalization of patriarchy, she may abuse her daughter-in-law for a desire for power or to subordinate the weak. Kishwar noted that an ideal family venerates the mother–son relationship, where a woman's status as a mother or a maternal figure is considered more important than that of a wife, who represents a sexualized image of a woman and therefore deserves less respect.[115] This power struggle does not take place in the relationship between a father-in-law and a son-in-law because their spheres of operation are different from each other by the virtue of the fact that they live in separate households.[116] Moreover, in a patriarchal setup, a mother trains her daughter to accept the patriarchy through rigid social and sexual control, yet such authority is accepted as normal and desirable in a misogynist setup, and no voices are raised when women as daughters are abused within the natal family. The courts hardly look into power dynamics or examine the interplay of patriarchal forces within the relationships and act against the interests of women while pronouncing decisions. The courts thus act as mirror and reflect the notions, biases, prejudices and stereotypes that exist in society. Instead of socially transforming the society while pronouncing against the embedded biases, the courts often end up reinforcing the values that are unfair and discriminatory.

The PWDVA: the male is a respondent

Section 2q of the PWDVA clearly defines "respondent" as any male adult person who has been, or is, in a domestic relationship with the aggrieved person. Initially, it was understood that an application can be filed only against a male respondent[117] and a proceeding could not be continued against a female, but the Kerala High Court,[118] MP High Court[119] and the Delhi High Court[120] have held that an aggrieved wife or a female living in a relationship in the nature of marriage may also file a complaint against a relative of the husband or the male partner. It was settled by Supreme Court that in proviso to Section 2(q), a relative of the husband or male partner includes female also and a female relative of husband or male partner may also be seen as a respondent.[121] The court held that the gender-specific nature of the PWDVA was a reasonable classification in view of the act's object and purpose and that the act was therefore constitutional. Nevertheless, in *Hiral P. Harsora vs Kusum Narottamdas Harsora*[122] the Supreme Court struck down the words "adult male" from Section 2(q) of the act, to include women and minors as respondents under the law. This verdict implies that women and minors, and not just men, could be charged for committing acts of domestic violence. The thrust of the judgement is formal equality without looking at the disadvantageous position of women and while ignoring the notion of the substantive equality as guaranteed in the constitution. The court overlooked the fact that the PWDVA has been created specifically to deal with violence against women rather than promoting the notion of formal equality between men and women. The court's logic behind this verdict was based on the fact that the Delhi High Court, in Kusum Lata's case,[123] had already held that a mother-in-law could lodge a complaint against her daughter-in-law under the PWDVA. The SC ruling to change the PWDVA from 'gender specific' to 'gender neutral' has rendered its object invalid and the law regressive, as it provides an adult male an opportunity to have his wife evicted from the shared household by getting other women in the household to file a complaint. It disregarded the need for specific provisions for women and overturned battered women's right to access justice. Any attempt by women to access the PWDVA is already inviting counter-complaints by the female in-laws present in the same household. This gender-neutral provision is further being manipulated and engineered by the men to maneuver the law in their favor. When the court includes children and other female relatives under the ambit of Section 2q, it fails to contextualize the fact that law was originally formulated to create an interim space for a woman "in a domestic relationship" to protect her from violence.[124] This decision was reiterated by the Karnataka court,[125] where it was held that any person, whether male or female, aggrieved and alleging violation of the provisions of the act, can invoke the provisions under the act, though later this order was withdrawn.

A live-in relationship is not considered a domestic relationship

The PWDVA specifically provides protection to a woman in a live-in relationship. However, the courts in interpreting the law have constricted the scope of such relationships while upholding the concept of the sanctity of a marital relationship. Without acknowledging the fact that it is the women who suffer in any such relationship, the courts, while emphasizing the technical aspects of the legal definition of live-in relationship, have adversely interpreted the rights of women while negating the object of the law. In Velusamy's case[126] the apex court held that only legally married people and not live-in partners could access the PWDVA, clearly ignoring the fact that according to Section 2(f) of the act, the definition of "domestic relationship" includes a "relationship in the nature of marriage". The court stated that "If a man has a 'keep' whom he maintains financially and uses mainly for sexual purpose and/or as a servant it would not, in our opinion be a relationship in the nature of marriage". While referring to a woman as a 'keep' and implying that a woman could be used for sexual purposes, the court used gendered language and dehumanized women while promoting the unfettered rights of men to indulge in polygamy. The act clearly states that the "relationship in the nature of marriage" fulfills the noted requirements, yet the court negated this aspect while interpreting the law.

In *Aruna Parmod Shah vs Union of India*[127] the court, while referring to the concept of domestic relationship, pronounced that,

> We find no reason why equal treatment should not be accorded to the wife as well as a woman who has been living with a man as his common-law wife or even as a mistress. Like treatment to both does not in any manner, derogate the sanctity of marriage since an assumption can fairly be drawn that a 'live-in relationship' is invariably initiated and perpetuated by [the] male.

Thus, the court made a moral assumption while promoting the sanctity of marriage and assumed that only men can initiate and perpetuate live-in relationships. These assumptions derogate women when courts utilize their own yardstick of defining a woman as a "wife, keep or the mistress". It is indeed worrisome when the courtrooms act as the moral guardians and the custodians of patriarchal values rather than as upholders of the rule of law or justice in cases relating to women. Effort is made to preserve order and morality, and women's rights are sacrificed in the process. Courtrooms do not see women as citizens with autonomy or independence. Rather, the claim of a woman is viewed with reference to her social background and embedded in the web of her relationship as somebody's daughter, wife, mother or sister.

This inhuman logic was reiterated in *Indra Sarma vs VK Sarma*[128] where it held that the "Appellant was aware that the Respondent was a married person even before the commencement of their relationship, hence the status of the applicant is that of a concubine or a mistress, who cannot enter into the relationship in nature of marriage". The court failed to appreciate the fact that the law was enacted to protect women, and it nowhere implies that a person entering into a long-term relationship with a married man cannot seek protection. Relying on the aforesaid principle, the Bombay High Court[129] observed that the lady who knew that the applicant was married and his wife had opposed their relationship cannot say that she was an "aggrieved person" and she was not entitled to any relief under the PWDVA. In fact, the courts while interpreting the law failed to appreciate the fact that due to the social stigma attached to such relationships, women need more protection. In *Manmohan Attavar vs Neelam*[130] it held that 'domestic relationship' is necessary to permit a party to occupy the shared household. These different interpretations by the court created confusion rather than resolving difficulties. The courts assume that heterosexual marriage as an ideal relationship and any other form of existence is stigmatized while ignoring the fact that women in such relationships are abused and violated. This approach ignores the fact that the term 'relationships in nature of marriage' can convey long term partnership and a woman is thrown out of the household because she is not being recognized by the society as a wife, thus making her situation more vulnerable.

Erasing entitlements: misinterpreting the right to reside in the shared household

The right to reside in the shared household has been considered as a significant right that seeks to prevent a survivor of violence from being dispossessed of the matrimonial home. However, despite the laudable objective of the law in upholding the wife's right to reside in the matrimonial home, it often gets nullified because the courts insist on rules, procedures and evidences besides linking it to the right to property division or the ownership of the household. The act does not create a new right. Earlier, this remedy could be availed under the Civil Procedure Code to apply for injunctions. Yet the courts with their patriarchal mind-set are overreacting in their zeal to save families and property owners rather than looking it as a simple entitlement to stay in the matrimonial home. Rather than providing remedies or relief to the victims of violence, what is being emphasized is the fact that the property of the family should be protected. Frequently, magistrates have been routinely rejecting the petitions for protection orders with respect to the matrimonial home; more specifically, if it is owned by the in-laws, the courts have been bringing in the rights of inheritance against a woman's right to reside in a shared household. The Supreme Court in *SR Batra vs Tarun Batra*[131] refused to grant residency rights to the woman in the house belonging to her mother-in-law. The apex court specified that 'shared household' implies the house belonging to or taken on rent by the husband or house, which belongs to the joint family in which the husband is one of the members. Property exclusively owned by the mother of the husband cannot be called a 'shared household'. The court's decision narrowly interpreted the provisions of the law and defeated the very purpose of the legislation. While there are judgments that reaffirm the wife's right to reside in the shared household by virtue of her marriage, irrespective of whether the property is rented or owned by the husband, the repercussions of the (in)famous *Batra vs Batra* case continue to be felt in the lower echelons of the judiciary.

The case has resonance in other decisions too.[132] In several other cases, the High Courts have held that the daughter-in-law has no right to reside in the house of the parents of the husband against their consent or wishes.[133] Delhi High Court elaborated that an adult son or daughter has no legal right to occupy self-acquired property of the parents against their wishes.[134] In *B Sakunthala vs Vasantha*,[135] the court quashed a complaint filed by the widow against her father-in-law and sister-in-law. In this matter, the house was sold by the father-in-law to the sister-in-law in order to deny the widow her right to reside in the matrimonial home. The sister-in-law initiated the proceedings under the Rent Control Act in order to evict the petitioner. Thus, in many cases, while linking the right to residence to property rights, the courts have denied women their rights to reside in the shared household against the object of the act, thereby rendering women homeless or destitute.

However, there are cases where a different view has been taken. In *Shumita Didi Sandhu vs Sanjay Singh Sandhu*, the marriage was solemnized, yet the wife was not allowed to enter the matrimonial home.[136] She filed a suit, claiming the right to reside in the matrimonial home. The husband argued that she had no such right as she had not "lived" in the house. The court concluded that the woman has no right to reside there, as the house was owned by her mother-in-law, yet she could be dispossessed only with "due process" of the law and cannot be physically thrown out. This judgment makes available to the woman safeguards that are otherwise granted to tenants and trespassers. In *P. Babu Venkatesh vs Rani*,[137] the Madras High Court upheld a residence order application filed on the behalf of a wife. The court found that her husband transferred the house to his mother's name, intending to defeat her right to reside there. The court held that pending divorce proceedings did not affect grants of relief under the PWDVA and directed the police to break open the lock of the house and provide protection to the aggrieved person to reside in the shared household.

Thus in several circumstances, High Courts have held that the aggrieved person has the right to reside in the shared household, such as cases where the property is in the name of the husband and the in-laws[138] or where the husband has a right, title or interest in the property for the purposes of Section 17 of the PWDVA.[139] In *Vandana vs T. Srikant Krishnamachari*,[140] the Madras High Court ruled that where the husband has a right, title or interest in the property for the purposes of Section 17 of the PWDVA, it is shared household and it is immaterial whether the parties have cohabitated in said property. In such cases, by virtue of being a wife, the aggrieved woman has a *dejure* right of residence in the shared household. In *Kavita Choudhury vs Eveneet Singh*[141] and in *Roma Tiwari vs Rajesh Tiwari*,[142] the courts have upheld the aggrieved person's right to reside in the shared household, irrespective of whether she has any right, title or interest in the said household or when the husband has no ownership right in the property. In several cases, High Courts have emphasized the fact that a woman must be provided with a roof over her head.[143] In *Sujoy Sanyal vs Shakuntala Sanyal*[144] and in *Natasha Kohli vs Manmohan Kohli*[145] it has been held that the wife's right of residence must be respected not only because of the statutory mandate but also on the principles of equity. In *Ishpal Singh Kahai vs Ramanjeet Kahai*, the court,[146] while upholding the injunctions orders by the family court, directed the respondent to remove himself from the shared household and made a specific note on right to residence:

> The human right of a person has little to do with her ownership rights in property. It is therefore immaterial to consider in whose name the matrimonial home stands. In a case of domestic violence, the court has only to appreciate the abuse and protection against such abuse. Section 17 of the PWDVA recognizes right to reside in shared household irrespective of right, title or ownership over, interest over the property.

In *Kavita Dass vs NCT of Delhi*,[147] the Delhi High Court stated that the "court cannot ask the aggrieved person to vacate the house, even though it may be on rent". In this case, the couple was living in a rented accommodation. The husband left the wife and colluded with the landlord to file an eviction suit against her. The wife initiated proceedings under the PWDVA petitioning for the rent and maintenance. She then moved to the husband's rented apartment with the help of a PO under the interim orders. The magistrate observed that the house cannot be held as a shared household and ordered her to evict the house. The wife appealed against it, but her appeal was dismissed. An FIR was also filed against the wife; however, the Delhi High Court reversed the orders while keeping in the spirit of the

PWDVA and focused on providing substantive justice to the victim; following the Supreme Court decision in *Kanwal Sood vs Nawal Kishore*[148] this court held that 'shared household' includes any household owned or tenanted by either of the parties in respect of which either the woman or the respondent or both, jointly or singly, have any right. The court held that a wife has a right to live with the respondent, whether he lives in an ancestral house, his own acquired house or a rented house.

In *B.P. Achla Anand vs Appi Reddi*[149] the decision related to tenanted premises where the husband and the wife were staying prior to filing the application under the PWDVA. In this matter, the issue related to the suit for eviction filed by the landlord against the tenant. The question pertained to whether the wife of the tenant can contest the suit when her husband was not interested in contesting the same. The Supreme Court held that "such a wife would be entitled to raise all such pleas and claim trial thereon, as would have been available to the tenant himself and no more." It has been further held that

> a deserted wife continuing in occupation of the premises obtained on lease by her husband, and which was their matrimonial home, occupies a position akin to that of an heir of the tenant-husband if the right to residence of such wife has not come to an end. The tenant having lost interest in protecting his tenancy rights as available to him under the law, the same right would devolve upon and inhere in the wife so long as she continues in occupation of the premises. Her rights to obligations shall not be higher or larger than those of the tenant himself.

The court also noted that

> A Hindu wife is entitled to be maintained by her husband. She is entitled to remain under his roof and protection. She is also entitled to separate residence if by reason of the husband's conduct or by his refusal to maintain her in his own place of residence or for other just cause she is compelled to live apart from him. Right to residence is a part and parcel of wife's right to maintenance. The right to maintenance cannot be defeated by the husband executing a Will to defeat such a right. The right has come to be statutorily recognised with the enactment of the Hindu Adoptions and Maintenance Act, 1956.

Thus, while analyzing the many judgements relating to the right of a woman to reside in the shared household, it may be said that there is a lack of clarity about the women's rights secured under the PWDVA. The courts have given mixed interpretations of the law where various factors come into play while deciding the matter.

Quantum of monetary relief

Section 20(2) of the PWDVA provides for monetary relief. However, experiences show that the execution of the maintenance order is difficult. Several matters have reached the Supreme Court where the respondents have deployed tactics and strategies to avoid paying maintenance.[150] In *Francis Cyril Cunha vs Lydia Jane Cunha*[151] an application for the discharge of maintenance was filed, and the trial court summoned the husband for committing an offense under Section 31 of the PWDVA for the breach of the order. The matter went to the High Court, which held that nonpayment of maintenance is not an offense on technical grounds, thus depriving women of their legal rights provided under the law. The Sixth Monitoring and Evaluation Report by the Lawyers Collective in 2013 showed that women are denied rights when they approach the courts under the PWDVA. Thus, interpretation of the provisions of this law is chaotic, inconsistent and marred by confusion. In addition, its implementation was further been problematic, as it is compromised and diluted because of the subjective biases, stereotypes and prejudices of those who enforce this law. Instead of using a proactive approach to expand the provisions of the law, the remedies are denied on excuses based on patriarchal notions, dominant ideologies and traditional ideas about the position and the status of women. This is also made evident by the fact that the state, instead of investing in institutional capacity or the infrastructure, has been shying away from fulfilling its responsibilities.

The basic premise behind domestic violence remains unchallenged

Domestic violence in India is premised on several notions, as follows:

1. The marital relationship is hierarchical and inegalitarian. Women are not accorded equal legal status within a marriage and the family, where a man is considered the master of the household.
2. The husband and his family have authority to beat the wife in addition to demanding dowry. Chastisement is a prerogative granted to a husband who can commit violence against his wife in the guise of love and discipline.
3. A violent husband is not made accountable even if he brutally murders the woman. The law grants immunity to violent husbands even if the husband is a drunkard, vile or a criminal.
4. The family is a private realm, and no one – not even the law – should interfere with the privacy of such an institution. Domestic harmony is prioritized over safety of a woman.
5. The doctrine of marital unity as propounded by Blackstone persists, which prevents those who frame the law and those who implement it

from seeing complainant wives as citizens demanding protection under the law.

6 Courts are expected to uphold constitutional values but instead are enforcing family ideology.
7 The law has been used symbolically and superficially to address violence, but no steps have been taken to address the root cause; for instance, the dowry law has failed to eliminate dowry or address dowry-related violence.
8 The legal discourse focused on blaming the victim, stigmatizing her and penalizing women for not 'adjusting' within their families.
9 Due to a backlash, the focus is shifting away from reality, from 'bad men' who are battering or burning their wives, to 'bad or terrible women' who are misusing the law.

Most of these premises are never questioned even in a court of law. The law does not utilize the principles of rationality while adjudicating the claims of battered or murdered wives. It legitimizes and reiterates social inequalities within the institution of marriage.

Few attempts have been made to change the approach and the attitude of those who implement the law to see women as partners and citizens with equal rights. Legal reforms could not make a dent on the construction of women's 'natural' position within an existing power structure that creates their everyday reality of their life within and outside the family. Additionally, the justice system is part and parcel of a larger patriarchal society where the system is corrupt and inefficient. Courts have used logic relating to the chastisement prerogative and marital privacy while prosecuting men in cases of wife beating. The language of hierarchy, love and discipline is used to protect violent men, and the tropes of both hierarchy and interiority is used to cover bias in the hierarchical marriage arrangements. The regime of immunity is utilized to justify brutal violence while utilizing the dimensions of feelings and domestic space.

The justice system has failed to meet the changing needs of society

Analysis of many judgements shows that women are being tortured, brutalized, burned alive, murdered or forced to commit suicide, yet, tragically, the current judicial discourse focuses on the misuse or abuse of the law by women. The cases relating to dowry deaths, murders of wives, suicide of women in marriage and domestic violence found little space in the media. No sensitivity is being displayed when a wife dies – rather, such cases are normalized and trivialized, and what is prioritized are fake concerns raised by the fragile masculinity, probably because women's concerns are no longer deemed relevant by the patriarchal society. Dowry deaths were highlighted during the 1980s, and the laws have been reformed since then; however, no monitoring or follow-up has been done to ensure that the system of dowry coercion is eliminated. Similarly, domestic violence cases are being reported in increasing numbers, yet no accountability has been fixed to ensure that actions could be taken to monitor the situation. The system has not devised ways to monitor if the police are following the procedures or conducting an investigation seriously. The criminal justice system has failed to respond to the changing situation. Similarly, civil law ignores the realities of women's lives. Perhaps the state is not willing to accept the agency of women challenging and defying patriarchal norms. Yet with the existence of the strong constitutional paradigm in addition to advancements in terms of education, awareness and enhanced aspirations, women are challenging the conventional stereotype and are defying age-old norms. However, once women enter the courtrooms, they face the similar patriarchal restrictions which they have been dealing with outside the court spaces. The courts and investigative agencies dominated by men have failed to transform at the same pace, and this lag in the expectations of women and the working of the state is creating complications. Therefore, there is a need to renovate the mindset and the attitude of the state towards women's concerns.

Summary

This chapter scrutinizes the operation of law and highlights that though domestic violence was criminalized in India in 1983, the legal system continues to treat wife beating as an offense different from other cases of assault and battery. Also, the authorities intervened only occasionally in cases of marital violence. Men who beat their wives are offered formal and informal immunities, while the courts uphold the concept of 'family harmony' and endorse the chastisement prerogative of the husband. The legal system treats the family as a private space where a public law cannot be applied. It concludes that the law uses the gendered notions of citizenship while adjudicating the cases of violence against women.

Notes

1 Mill, John Stuart (1869) *The Subjection of Women*, www.earlymoderntexts.com/assets/pdfs/mill1869.pdf pp. 17–18 accessed on 20.3.18.
2 Ibid.
3 Ibid. p. 47.
4 Quoted by the lower court in the matrimonial appeal 360/2013 decided on 1.8.18 in VV. Prabhakaran vs Chandranath AIR 2018 Ker 179.
5 Sathe, S.P. (1999) 'Gender, Constitution and the Courts'. In *Engendering Law, Essays in Honour of Lotika Sarkar*, edited by Amita Dhanda and Archana Parashar, Lucknow: Eastern Book Company.

6 Prabhubhai Ranchhodbhai Tailor vs Bhartiben Prabhubhai Tailor 004 (3) MhLJ 487; Shiva Mohana Reddy vs Aparna Reddy on 3.9.2004 Andhra HC.
7 Bajrang Gangadhar Revdekar vs Pooja Bajrang Revdekar on 18.8.2009 Bombay HC AIR 2010 Bom 8/MANU/MH/0811/2009.
8 Samit Subhash Agarwal vs Kamlesh Laltaprasad Gupta 27.4.2018 Bombay HC 2019 (1) Bom CR 133.
9 Ajay Lavania vs Shobhna Dubey 28.7.2011 Allahabad HC MANU/UP/1647/2011.
10 Ramchandra Doddappa Naik vs Hanamnaik Patil (1935) 37 BOMLR 920.
11 This view has been taken in many cases, such as Narain Dhara vs Rakhal Gain (1876) ILR 1 Cal 1, Rahi Wife Of Teja Kurad vs Govinda Valad Teja, ILR 1 Bom 97, Ram Saran Garain vs Tek Chand Garain ILR 28 Cal 194, Sukurmoni vs Kirpal Narain Tewari (1892) ILR 19 Cal 91.
12 Shakuntalabai vs LV Kulkarni, 1989 AIR 1359, Kashibai Jadhav vs Yamunabai Namdeo Jadhav 25.2.2016, Bombay HC, Jairam S More vs Sindhubai I (2001) DMC 407, Yamanaji H. Jadhav vs Nirmala AIR 2002 SC 971.
13 Hancher, M. (2013) 'Reading and Writing the Law: Macaulay in India' *Law and Language: Current Legal Issues*, 15 (1) 187.
14 Chan, W., Wright, B. and Yeo, S. (2011) *Codification, Macaulay and the Indian Penal Code: The Legacies and Modern Challenges of Criminal Law Reform*, London: Routledge.
15 Rege, Sharmila (2013) *Against Madness of Manu: BR Ambedkar's Writings on Brahmanical Patriarchy*, New Delhi: Navayana.
16 Kolsky, E. (2010) 'The Body Evidencing of Crime: Rape on trial in Colonial India, 1860–1947,' *Gender and History*, 22 (1) 109–30.
17 Sinha, K. (2016) 'Be It Manu, Be It Macaulay: Indian Law and the Problem of Female Body,' *Journal of Indian Law and Society*, 5, 61–94.
18 Nigam, S. (2005) *Understanding Justice from the Perspective of Women Litigants as Victims of Domestic Violence in India*, Occasional Paper No. 35, CWDS, New Delhi. Also, Nigam, S. (2017) 'Fighting for Justice in the Patriarchal Courts,' *Countercurrents*, August 30.
19 Chandra, Sudhir. (1998) *Enslaved Daughters: Colonialism, Law and Women's Rights*, New Delhi: Oxford University Press.
20 Sarkar, Tanika (2001) 'Conjugality and Hindu Nationalism: Resisting Colonial Reason and Death of Child-Wife'. *In Hindu Wife Hindu Nation: Community, Religion and Cultural Nationalism*, New Delhi: Permanent Black, pp. 119–225.
21 Anagol, P. (2008) 'Rebellious Wives and Dysfunctional Marriages: Indian Women Discourses and Participation in the Debates Over Restitution of Conjugal Rights and the Child Marriage Controversy in the 1880s and 1890s'. In *Women and Social Reform in Modern India: A Reader*, edited by Sumit Sarkar and Tanika Sarkar. Bloomington: Indiana University Press.
22 Ibid., p. 283.
23 Kannabiran, Kalpana (2009) 'Judicial Meanderings in Patriarchal Thickets: Litigating Sex Discrimination in India,' *Economic and Political Weekly*, Review of Women's Studies, 44 (44): 88–98, Quoted Rao Shiva B (1968) *The Framing of Indian Constitution: A Study*, New Delhi: Indian Institute of Public Administration.
24 Ibid.
25 Hindu Code (1948) *Constituent Assembly Debates*, Vol. VII (April 9) p. 3628.
26 Pattabhi, Sitaramayya (1948) *Constituent Assembly Debates*, Vol. VII (9 April) p. 3635.

27 Rege, S. (2013) *Against the Madness of Manu,* New Delhi: Navayana.
28 Mahanta, Aparna (1994) 'The Indian State and Patriarchy'. In *State and Nation in the Context of Social Change*, edited by TV Sathyamurthy, Vol. I, New Delhi: Oxford University Press, p. 94.
29 Menon, Ritu and Bhasin, K. (1998) *Borders and Boundaries: Women in India's Partition,* New Delhi: Kali for Women, p. 255.
30 AIR 1984 Delhi 66 para 33.
31 Rani vs Kumar (1984) 3 SCC 90.
32 1984 AIR 1562.
33 AIR 1983 AP 356.
34 Gonsalves, L. (1993) *Women and the Law*, New Delhi: Lancers.
35 1997 (9) SCC 579.
36 AIR 1994 SC 1418.
37 1991 AIR 1532.
38 2001(3) SCALE 549.
39 Criminal Appeal 1592/2011 decided on 9.1.2015.
40 (2001) 9 SCC 618; also State of West Bengal vs Orilal Jaiswal (1994) 1 SCC 73.
41 (2009) 16 SCC 487.
42 Singh, Namita (2019) 'Man Sentenced to Six Years RI for Injuries Which Led to His Wife's Death,' *The Hindustan Times*, April 29.
43 *The Hindustan Times* (2019) 'Million Species at Risk of Wipeout: Draft UN Study,' April 24.
44 (2001) 8 SCC 633.
45 Harjit Singh vs State of Punjab (2006) 1 SCC 463; Thakkan Jha vs State of Bihar (2004) 13 SCC 348.
46 Kamalakar Nandram Bhavsar vs State of Maharashtra (2004) 10 SCC 192.
47 (2001) 2 SCR 984.
48 1994 CrLJ 3472.
49 Cri Appeal 1218 of 2016 SLP Cri 6104/14 decided on 28.11.16.
50 Cri Appeal 1048 of 2018 SLP Cri 4122/16 decided on 21.8.18.
51 Rudrakant Jha vs State of Jharkhand, Jharkhand HC, Cri MP 1204/ 2007 decided on 7.5.12; Sudhir Kapur vs State in Crl.M.A. 799/2009 decided on 10.08.2010; Bimla Rawal vs State (NCT of Delhi) in WP (Crl.) 1541/2007 decided on 03.01.2008; Bhura Ram vs State of Rajasthan (2008) 11 SCC 103; Y Abraham Ajit vs Inspector of Police, Chennai (2004) 8 SCC 100; Onkar Nath Pandey vs State of Jharkhand, Jharkhand HC Cr MP 1100/ 2013.
52 Suo Moto vs Ushaben Kishorbhai Mistry Spl Cri Application 5313/ 2015 decided on 27.11.15, MANU/GJ/1108/2015.
53 (2007) 9 SCC 721.
54 2013(3) SCALE 525.
55 Durga Prasad vs State of MP (2010) 9 SCC 73; Gurdeep Singh vs State of Punjab (2011) 12 SCC 408; Kala Ram vs State of Haryana (2012) 10 SCC 763; Biswajit Haldar vs State of West Bengal (2008) 1 SCC 202; Rajesh Bhatnagar vs State of Uttarakhand AIR 2011 SC 363, Kishori Lal vs State of MP 2007 3 RCR Cri 385, Shailender vs State 169 (2010) DLT 563; Satvir Singh vs State of Punjab (2001) 8 SCC 633, Shanti vs State of Haryana AIR 1991 SCC 1261; Kansraj vs State of Punjab 2000 (5) SCC 207; State of West Bengal vs Orilal Jaiswal 1994 (1) SCC 73; Ramesh Kumar vs State of Chhattisgarh (2001) 9 SCC 618; State of Gujarat vs Avinas Dinkar Joshi, Gujarat High Court Cri App 900 of 2000 decided on 9.4.2013; Indrasing Raol vs State of Gujarat II (2000) DMC 239; State of Maharashtra vs Ashok Shukla AIR 1997 SC 3111 and many others.

56 II (2000) DMC 239.
57 Fricker, M. (2008) 'Epistemic Injustice: Power and Ethics of Knowing,' *Theoria*, 61, 69–71.
58 Sushil Sharma vs State NCT of Delhi (2014) 4 SCC 317.
59 Pereira, Maxwell (2018) *The Tandoor Murder: The Crime That Shook the Nation and Brought the Government to Its Knees*. Chennai: Westland Publications.
60 It is not that the author is in favor of the death penalty; rather, the arguments given to commute the death sentence are unreasonable.
61 1990 Cri LJ 407.
62 Gangoli (2007) supra.
63 MacKinnon, C.A. (1987) *Feminism Unmodified: Discourses on Life and Law* London: Harvard University Press.
64 1999 3 SC 620.
65 AIR 2009 CAL.135.
66 Application No. 1192/1 PS Sultanpuri, MM Rohini Court decided on 15.9.07.
67 Usharani Pradhan vs Braj Kishore Pradhan, MAT No. 104 of 2011 High Court of Orissa, order dated 23.9.11.
68 SA vs AA MAT Appeal 68/2012 decided on 22.3.2016, Delhi HC.
69 Ramesh Kumar vs State of Chhattisgarh, supra.
70 PIL No 104 of 2015.
71 Basu, Asmita and Jaising, Indira (2005) *Violence Against Women: A Statistical Overview, and Challenges, Gaps in Data Collection Expert*, Paper presented at Violence Against Women: A Statistical Overview, Challenges and Gaps in Data Collection and Methodology and Approaches for Overcoming UN Division for Advancement of Women, Geneva.
72 Kapoor, J.D. (2002) *Laws and Flaws in Marriage: How to Stay Happily Married*. New Delhi: Konark Publishers.
73 *The Times of India* (2012) A Wife Should Be Like Goddess Sita: Bombay HC, May 8, https://timesofindia.indiatimes.com/city/mumbai/A-wife-should-be-likegoddess-Sita-Bombay-HC/articleshow/13054421.cms.
74 Sandanshiv, D.N. and Mathew, Jolly (2005) 'Legal Reform in Dowry Laws.' In *Issues in Contemporary Indian Feminism: Dowry and Inheritance*, edited by Srimati Basu. London & New York: Zed Books, p. 73.
75 AIR 2009 SC 589.
76 AIR 2002 SC 2582 5.
77 AIR 1984 SC 622.
78 The women's group in Maharashtra initiated a signature campaign and a poster exhibition titled '*Mein Ek Manjushree*'. From Haksar N and Singh A (1986) *Demystification of Laws for Women*, Lancers, New Delhi.
79 (2002) 2 SCC 73.
80 SCC OnLine SC 1114.
81 Kapur, Ratna (2016) 'Hindu Divorce Case: Retrograde Gender Politics on the Bench,' *The Wire*, October 8.
82 Kadidal, A. (2019) 'Marital Rape Should Not Be a Crime in India: Ex CJI Misra,' *Deccan Herald*, April 9.
83 *Livelaw Network* (2017) Criminalizing Marital Rape May Destabilize Institution of Marriage: Center Tells Delhi HC, August 29, www.livelaw.in/criminal ising-marital-rape-may-destabilise-institution-marriage-centre-tells-delhi-hc/.

84 Sinha, Badhra (2017) 'Govt Defends No Action for Legal Exception Allowing Forced Sex with Minor Wife,' *The Hindustan Times*, August 10.
85 *The Telegraph* (2017) 'Marriage Defence for Rape,' August 10.
86 Sinha, Shanta (2017) 'The Centre Has Solemnized the Invasion of Girls' Bodily Integrity, Sexuality and the Mind,' *The Wire*, August 14, https://thewire. in/ 167674/child-marriage-invasion-of-body-mind-sexuality/.
87 (1997) 5 SCC 30.
88 1998 Cri.LJ. 554.
89 VD. Bhanot vs Savita Bhanot (2012) 3 SCC 183 also Saraswathy vs Babu AIR 2014 SC (Cri.) 493.
90 AIR 1975 SC 1534.
91 Para 27.
92 Kajal Roy vs Prasanta Roy (2005) 2 CALLT 567 HC, para 26.
93 1994 AIR 710.
94 Shobha Rani vs Madhukar Reddy 1988 AIR 121.
95 AIR 2000 SC 3559.
96 AIR 2002 SC 2078.
97 Wazir Chand vs State of Haryana, 1989 AIR 382. Also, State of Maharashtra vs Ramesh Damodar More Bombay HC Cri Appeal 12/2003 decided on 11.5.17.
98 Criminal Application APL 774 of 2017 Bombay HC, Nagpur Branch decided on 2.11.2018, para 24.
99 I (2007) DMC 545.
100 Criminal Complaint No. 316/3/2007 PS NFC MM Court Saket Pronounced on 27.5.2015.
101 (2014) 8 SCC 273.
102 *2017* (8) SCALE 313.
103 Bombay HC Family Court Appeal No. 150/2008 decided on 21.4.17.
104 Cri Misc Application 20679/2013 decided on 6.4.17.
105 Case No. 3/2010, Sonepat, Haryana.
106 Crl Appeal 10/2010, Delhi.
107 Case No. 3132/2010, Uttarakhand, Kashipur.
108 Supra.
109 Supra.
110 Kapur, Ratna (2006) 'Revisioning the Role of Law in Women's Human Rights Struggles.' In *The Legalization of Human Rights: Multidisciplinary Perspectives on Human Rights and Human Rights Law*, edited by Saladin Meckled-Garcia and Başac Çali. London & New York: Routledge, p. 105.
111 Cri Appeal 333/2000 on 10.2 2016.
112 Cri MC No 725 of 2011 decided on 2.9.2011 Delhi HC.
113 Gangoli (2007) supra.
114 Yuval Davis, N. (1997) *Gender and Nation*. London: Sage.
115 Kishwar, M. (1997) 'Women, Sex and Marriage: Restraints as a Feminist Strategy, *Manushi*,' 99, 23–36.
116 Menon, Nivedita (2012) 'Feminism and the Family – Thoughts on International Women's Day,' *Kafila*, March 8.
117 Ajay Kant vs Alka Sharma (2008) Crim. LJ. 264 (MP HC) 7.
118 Vijayalekshmi Amma vs Bindu 2010(1) KLT 79.
119 Sarita vs Umrao (2008) 1R Cr D Rajasthan HC, Nand Kishore vs Rajasthan (2008) RLW 3432 Rajasthan HC.
120 Varsha Kapoor vs UoI WP (Crl.) 638 of 2010, 3.6.2010 Delhi HC.

121 Sandhya Manoj Wankhde vs Manoj Bhimrao Wankhde (2011) 3 SCC 650.
122 Civil Appeal 10084/2016, SLP civil 9132/2015 on 6.10.2016.
123 Supra.
124 Ghose, Sanjay (2016) 'A Gender-Neutral Domestic Violence Law Harms Rather Than Protects Women,' *The Wire*, November 3.
125 Mohd Zakir vs Shabana Criminal Petition 2351/2017 Karnataka HC decided on 18.4.17.
126 Velusamy vs D. Patchaiammal, 2010 AIR SCW 6731.
127 WP (Crl.) 425 of 2008.
128 AIR 2014 SC 309.
129 Deepak vs State of Maharashtra 2015 CRI. LJ 4833.
130 Civil Appeal No. 2500 of 2017 Supreme Court decided on 14.7.2017.
131 (2007) 8 SCC 2675.
132 Raj Kumari vs Preeti Satija IA 500/2011 in CS (OS) 85/2010 Decided on 13.1.2012; Pal Singh vs Priyanka Singh Manu/DE/7325/2011.
133 K Rajendran vs Ambikavathy Cri. Rev Case 482/2012 decided on 8.1.13, Madras HC, Also, Neetu Mittal vs Kanta Mittal AIR 2009 Delhi 72.
134 Sudha Mishra vs Surya Mishra, RFA. 299/2014, Order 25/7/2014, Delhi HC.
135 Crl OP 8503 of 2016 and Crl MP (MD) 4117 and 4118/2016 decided on 7.9.2016 Madras HC.
136 MANU/DE/8160/2007.
137 MANU/TN/06/12/2008.
138 Jyotsana Sharda vs Gaurav Sharda, MANU/DE/3520/2009.
139 Rajkumar Pandey vs Sarita Pandey MANU/MH/1295/2008.
140 (2007) 6 MLJ 205 (Mad).
141 MANU/DE/3497/2010.
142 WPC 10696/ 2017 Bombay HC decided on 12.10.2017.
143 Ruma Chakraborty vs Sudha Rani Banerjee (2005) 8 SCC 140, 147.
144 MANU/WB/0597/2010.
145 MANU/DE/2506/2010.
146 MANU/MH/0385/2011.
147 2012 ILR 3 Delhi 747.
148 (1983) 3 SCC 25.
149 2005(3) SC 313.
150 Shalu Ojha vs Prashant Ojha 2017 (3) SCC (Cr) 744.
151 Criminal Rev Petition No. 758/2015 decided on 18.12.2015, Karnataka HC.

9 Feminist Activism, Violence in the Family, and Law Reform in India

A Three Decadal History

Kalpana Kannabiran

Introduction: contextualizing personal laws in India

> The State shall endeavour to secure that marriage shall be based only on the mutual consent of both sexes and shall be maintained through mutual cooperation with the equal rights of husband and wife as a basis. The state shall also recognize that motherhood has a special claim upon its care and protection.
>
> *Draft Article 42 of Constitution of India, dropped without debate (Rao 1968: 323)*

India is a constitutional, secular democracy, with the principles of equality and secularism written into the Preamble of the Constitution. The fundamental rights chapter (Part III) of the Constitution of India guarantees equality before the law (Article 14), non-discrimination based on sex, religion, caste, race, place of birth, or any other category (Article 15), the right to life and personal liberty (Article 21), and the right to freedom of religion (Article 25).

Alongside this constitutional framework, and intersecting with it, are religious laws that govern matters related to the family (marriage, divorce, inheritance, adoption, maintenance, succession, and guardianship). In the main, there are three sets of religious personal laws – Hindu, Muslim, and Christian – that have figured in public debates and jurisprudence, especially in terms of their specific relationship to the Constitution and other public law (notably criminal law). There is, of course, a diversity within these traditions as well that has been extensively debated in sociological discourse. The important aspect of these three traditions is that they immediately bring into play the question of the rights of minorities and the (written and unwritten) privileges of the majority in the country – rights and privileges that are not restricted to family laws alone but often bleed into the

DOI: 10.4324/9781003299561-9

discourse on family law from a larger, often embattled debate on majoritarianism and the disentitlements of minorities in post-colonial, independent, democratic, plural, and multicultural India.

Tracing the historical context of the majority–minority dichotomy in India, Robinson argues that it was introduced by British colonial rulers

> who viewed particularly the Hindus and Muslims essentially through the lens of religion and saw them as bounded and un-differentiated communities ... The application of such categories and of the rigid notion of cultural/communal identity that accompanied them is ... far from the localized, criss-crossing, and overlapping nature of identities that existed prior to British interventions.
>
> *(Robinson 2012: 6)*

The codification of Muslim Personal Law (MPL) (not the *reform* of MPL) was crucial to this process of constructing minority identities (Williams 2012). Scholars have argued that "India's minority rights policies have weakened the capacity of the state to protect the rights of women as equal citizens of a secular democracy" (Robinson 2012: 34) and assert that the state cannot become "an ally of social conservatism" or allow the undermining of its authority to legislate equal rights (Mahajan 1999, cited in Robinson 2012: 34). However, there is also a tendency to fix the aberrational presence on "the case of Muslims" as distinct from "Hindu Personal Law which has been amended from time to time by the state and Christians who have come together to make more gender-just the provisions of Christian Personal Law" (Robinson 2012: 34).

This chapter will focus on violence in the family and the approach of litigants, courts, legislatures, and the political elite to the elimination of such violence and/or neglect, tracing the relationship between laws criminalizing gender-based violence and personal laws that govern the family. To anticipate our argument, the cases and campaigns unravel for us the complexities in the interconnections between women's status across communities irrespective of, or despite, reform – the Muslim woman not really emerging as the oppressed exception in an otherwise fair and equal world for women of other communities. However, there is another field in which gender simultaneously plays out – Muslim women in an increasingly stridently majoritarian society are denied agency and viewed as victims of an oppressive community, as evident from the debates around triple *talāq* and the Uniform Civil Code (UCC).

While acknowledging the vast and complex terrain occupied by the family in women's lives, this chapter focuses on one aspect of feminist struggles in India – struggles against violence against women (VAW) in the family – and traces feminist debates, advocacy, legal reform, and the growth of jurisprudence and public policy (national and international) around the question of domestic violence (DV) and its interlinkages with gender-based discrimination in family laws from the early 1980s to 2016.

Background of women's rights in India: 1970s and beyond

The early 1980s witnessed the rise of new feminist voices in India. This was the period immediately after the Emergency of 1975, which also witnessed the growth of struggles for civil liberties and democratic rights across the country. The articulation of women's rights, however, was independent of the dominant human rights discourse, often raising questions of civil and political rights within the state, and, more importantly, within groups – communities, movements, families – and forcing the state to resolve contending claims. As women's rights movements gained momentum, a number of mass movements and democratic rights groups recognized the need to frame women's rights as part of a broader analysis of human rights, such as the Dalit and Adivasi rights movements.

With the rise in right-wing Hindu nationalism and communalism however, especially in the aftermath of the demolition of Babri Masjid in 1992,[1] one witnesses a shift in public discourse and feminist articulations, especially with respect to the rights of women in the family. Shades of strident majoritarianism are of course evident even in the 1980s, consolidating itself in the next decade.

Most women's groups were small, city/town-based, and worked primarily on consciousness raising, campaigns, and individual casework. This period witnessed the rapid growth in women's organizations, and a large number of women of different generations from all walks of life entered activism as a politically conscious choice. Women's rights groups across India, as elsewhere in the world, sprang from the need to reckon with gender discrimination and to find the theoretical tools to do this effectively. Feminist campaigns brought women's issues into public view through a multi-pronged strategy that included media exposure, strategic litigation, case work, public protests, consciousness and awareness raising at the local and national levels, and lobbying for changes in the law. As Gandhi and Shah argue, feminist mobilization on issues of VAW politicized what was up to that point understood as a "social issue" (Gandhi and Shah 1992: 94).

Voices from the struggle

I begin my account of law reform with three voices from the early 1980s, because the women speaking here are women who have had a lasting influence on the articulation of women's rights in the family. Flavia Agnes is one of the leading lawyers for women's rights in the country; Shahnaz Sheikh was the first Muslim woman to challenge triple *talāq* in the Supreme Court of India, while Satyarani Chadha is known as the face of the anti-dowry movement – her fight to have her son-in-law prosecuted for her daughter's murder resulted in far-reaching changes in the criminal law on dowry deaths in the early 1980s:

> The first time he said I'll beat you, I thought he was joking. No one had said these words to me all my life. When he beat me the first time with his hands I was shocked. The second time – with a wooden hanger … The third time it was the belt, the buckle hurt the nose and the bridge broke. I was numb not so much with pain, but despair. No one had warned me marriage included this.
>
> *(Agnes 1984: 11)*

Shahnaz Sheikh writes of her experience:

> In 1983, I filed a writ petition in the Supreme Court challenging Muslim Personal Law as being discriminatory to Muslim women. I was divorced by the utterance of triple talaq and thrown out at midnight by my ex-husband. Life was difficult … It was [my husband's] word against mine. I consulted five qazis [magistrates or judges of Sharia courts], each of whom gave me a different version of my divorce.
>
> I did not know what my legal marital status was. Was I married or divorced? That was when I decided to hire a lawyer and challenge this form of divorce and Muslim Personal Law in the SC [Supreme Court] on grounds of equality guaranteed by the Constitution. This was the first case of its kind in the Court.
>
> *(Sheikh 2016)*

Satyarani Chadha's twenty-year-old pregnant daughter died of burns within a year of marriage:

> I lost my daughter 35 years ago but in that process I saved thousands and thousands of others. But in the end, what did I get? He is alive, married and absconding, he is not in prison, but my daughter is dead. This disillusionment with law will always stay with me.
>
> *(Jain 2014)*

The debate on social reform, especially as it impacts women's lives, has an old history. While in its earliest phases the debate focused on the subjugation of Hindu women, particularly high-caste Hindu women, the voices of reform that focused on marriage, conjugal practices, and family have arisen from different regions and, within each religion, from different groups.

Yet it is also true that heightened violence during conflict and the anticipation of violence post-conflict do give rise to community-driven spaces of collective mobilization to offer support to survivors. Vahida Nainar observes that advocacy during the conflict phase improves narrating violence and bearing witness. Victim-survivor communities experience a sense of agency (and even empowerment) as they recall each other's experiences of violence – the space of the camp is transformed into a space of community and solidarity.[2] This is indeed the solidarity that Zakia Soman speaks about when she recounts the cascading effect of community-based advocacy post-conflict into homes in an effort to stall the economic violence of eviction from the matrimonial home and dispossession from assets that come with the unilateral pronouncement of divorce under Muslim law.[3]

There are widely divergent experiences of working with survivors of family violence – especially spousal violence – across religious community, caste, region, and class in India. While some advocates observe that the only women who come to them for relief under public law are women from the majority community, suggesting also that Muslim women go either to Muslim lawyers or to Qazi courts, there are others in the same city like the counselors from Shaheen, a women's support group in the Old City of Hyderabad, managed by survivors, that point to the fact that across social locations, the women who have come to them have suffered from very similar problems. This difference in access to constituencies perhaps also derives from (a) spatial location – lines of contact in the new city being drawn in very different ways from lines of contact in the Old City of Hyderabad, and (b) the distinction between professional legal practice on the one hand and cross-community counseling, paralegal services, and victim support on the other. Sultana, from Shaheen, is a survivor of gruesome assault by her husband when she was pregnant; now, fifteen years later, she is a leader in the counseling center, with a keen sense of the practicalities of justice delivery and the indispensability of providing relief to women in difficult circumstances. She observes that polygamy is a problem for Muslim and Hindu Backward Class (BC) women, while severe restrictions on mobility are a problem with Muslim, Hindu BC, and Dalit women. She also notes that from her experience of a decade as counselor, not all women want to opt out of an abusive marriage or relinquish custody of their children. Several want to remain with the family but want the violence to abate, especially the routine sexual violence. In a context where both the men and women are poor, lack regular employment, and are socially vulnerable, the heightened vulnerability of women in the family can sometimes be reduced through counseling services by women's collectives like Shaheen that are able to bring violent husbands to the counseling table, using their goodwill with the Qazi and their presence in the community and neighborhood.[4]

It is useful to recall Solanki's delineation of two approaches to governing the family. The first she calls the "society-centred" approach, which suggests "group autonomy for cultural groups, especially minorities, in the regulation of the family." Here, she cites Chatterjee's view that a "strategic politics of difference" may be invoked whereby "cultural communities can refuse to be homogenized in the name of dominant reasonableness by developing an 'inner democratic forum' " (Solanki 2011: 5). The second approach is "state-centric" with difference relegated to the private sphere – with the state as the only locus of law (Ibid.: 5–6).

Feminist reasoning

The significant aspect of the reform initiatives triggered by feminist groups in India is that there were a series of institutional responses – pre-legislative, legislative, and jurisprudential – that brought about a significant shift in the public discourse on VAW in the family. The purpose of undertaking this journey into feminist deliberations over thirty years is to understand the ways in which feminist advocacy has interwoven with legislation and statutory interpretation to shift the standards of interpretation of women's place in the family in India – a shift that has immediate implications for public discourse, the treatment of individual women in families, the response of the justice system (formal and community-based), and the political responsibility of elected representatives.

There have been two distinctive strains of feminist legal reasoning in debates around women's rights amidst claims to cultural (and religious) autonomy across the board – from minority to majority religions: the first has argued for a UCC that will govern practitioners irrespective of faith; the second has argued for a robust recognition of religio-cultural diversity, even while posing the question of equality, entitlements, and protections for women within community spaces.

The debates have been complicated by the fact that: (a) in the first set of arguments in favor of the UCC, the most strident appropriation of the debate has happened in the dominant Hindu right-wing political formations, where the separate spheres argument has been challenged as "appeasement of Muslims" by allowing specific practices like polygamy, unilateral divorce (especially the form that has come to be known as triple *talāq*), and maintenance for divorced/separated Muslim women under the Muslim Women's (Protection of Rights on Divorce) Act, 1986, rather than under the standard provision of Section 125 Criminal Procedure Code; (b) on the second track, where democratization of community spaces has been advocated, right-wing, conservative Muslim clergy and political parties (overwhelmingly male) have resisted every move for internal reform that could reduce the vulnerability of women to structural violence in the family, by insisting on the complete autonomy of community spaces under Article 25 of the Constitution of India; and (c) on the third track, where feminists, especially those from the dominant Hindu groups, have set themselves apart from fundamentalist or communal positions on women, there has not been a clear critique of patriarchal biases in Hindu laws of marriage and divorce and also the "hinduization of the Special Marriages Act" (Agnes 2008a: 504–505).

Advocate Albertina Almeida poses pertinent questions in relation to the current debate on the UCC, drawing on the experience of Goa in retaining the uniform code:

> [E]ven as the UCC is being touted as the panacea for the violations of women's rights, nobody asks what really is the UCC in Goa. What is meant when the civil code is said to be "uniform"? Why was it retained in Goa? And how is it working for different sections of women?
>
> *(Almeida 2016)*

Cautioning us that uniformity does not presume equality, that it can mean uniformity of discrimination across all religions, and that treating unequals equally results in inequality in effect, she presents an analysis of the Goan experience with uniform codes, which is quite specific and bears lessons for the ongoing national debate in India (Ibid.).

Across all positions, to put it in a nutshell, equality must be understood in a manner that does not suggest uniformity but rather suggests a framework that ensures parity between groups (especially religious groups) and democracy within groups (Solanki 2011).

Dowry deaths, Hindu women, and law reform: the 1980s

The late 1970s witnessed the deaths of large numbers of young women, in their matrimonial homes, especially from burns; these women were recently married (mostly Hindu, in endogamous marriages within their castes), urban for the most part, and educated. The use of kerosene stoves was rapidly expanding across the country and consuming the lives of newly married women. These deaths were being reported by the husbands' families as suicides:

> Satyarani Chadha did not have the benefit of either vernacular or English education, nor the privileges of an elite class. She was a shy, middle class family woman until the tragic death of her 20 year old, six month pregnant daughter Kanchanbala, with 100% burns in her

> marital home. This event in 1979 ... changed her into an activist and a relentless crusader for women's rights and justice. Along with the parents of over 20 dowry victims, she spent 27 years of stubborn pursuit and dogged determination, battling legal cases and visiting courts, till she finally got justice when the High Court upheld the conviction of her son-in-law for abetting Kanchanbala's suicide.
>
> Turning her grief into courage and deriving strength from her personal trauma Satyarani embarked on a life long struggle through her organization Shakti Shalini for women survivors facing DV, dowry abuse and harassment in their marital homes. She spent many years guiding, counseling and supporting parents and girls facing harassment and violence at the hands of their husbands and in-laws for dowry.
>
> *(Jain 2014)*

Feminists insisted that dying declarations of women who had "attempted suicide" be treated as evidence and that police procedures be tightened up; protests against these deaths cascaded (see Kumar 1990: 115–126), with demonstrations, street theater, and sustained campaigns. In 1978, a year after the nationwide protests began, the Prime Minister of India, Mr. Charan Singh, assured a women's delegation that "measures to stop the maltreatment of women for dowry" would be introduced in the next Parliamentary session (Ibid.: 120).

Following up on the demand by women's rights groups that matrimonial matters need to be adjudicated in a space that "mitigate[s] disequilibrium inherent in marriage relationships by creating new obligations and modifying old ones," family courts were set up under the Family Courts Act, 1984, with jurisdiction over criminal and civil matters relating to the breakdown of marriage: divorce, restitution of conjugal rights, alimony, maintenance, and child custody (Agnes 2008b: 276–277; see also Basu 2014). These courts were structured to create a more easily navigable space for women and were an important part of the structural and institutional changes brought about through feminist lobbying with the government. On another, related, track, India signed CEDAW in 1980 and ratified it in July 1993 with some reservations.

A survey of one hundred reported cases of deaths of women in their matrimonial homes between 1995 and 2004 shows that although there are problems in the interpretation of women's position in the family arising from the patriarchal mind-sets of judges and lawyers, and although the number of women dying in matrimonial homes remains alarmingly high – women being poisoned, burned, battered, drowned, shot, hanged, and strangled within the "safe and harmonious" confines of the family – there is a marginal increase in the rate of convictions in cases where women have died gruesome deaths and a perceptible shift in the judicial conscience.[5] This impact is not as perceptible however in cases where the woman survives and escapes the cruelty of the matrimonial home. In these cases, the hostility to the survivor for not acquiescing to the codes of patriarchal conjugality (which is constituted by spousal violence) is evident in accounts of encounters with the criminal justice system. On another level, while most of the violence that women are subjected to within their matrimonial homes is premeditated and intentional, *mens rea* (criminal intent) is not read into murders of wives in the same way as it is read into murder per se. As Nainar observes, it is very difficult to argue that DV is torture – that is, giving these acts the gravitas that torture has – unless we are able to shift the focus from the actor to the acts.[6] The family relationship is always the mitigating factor in sentencing policy, although the family relationship in fact renders these women more vulnerable to assault.

Still, justice delayed is better than no justice at all, which is demonstrated amply by the judgment in the case of the murder of Satyarani Chadha's daughter in 1979, which triggered the whole movement for criminal law reform. The Delhi High Court ruled that with respect to presumption, Section 113A of the Indian Evidence Act, although it came into force after the incident, "did not create any new offence and as such it does not create any substantial right but it is merely a matter of procedure of evidence and so retrospective in its application."[7]

Through all of this however, the 1980s saw the emergence of a new common sense – in the public domain, the legislature, the executive, and the judiciary – on women's rights and entitlements within the family. The contradictions were deep, but the debate opened up a space for a different level of engagement, and the law forced an institutional engagement with the problem of VAW and an understanding of the crimes within the family that women were subjected to on a daily basis. Despite this, when the Protection of Women from Domestic Violence Act (PWDVA) was being debated two decades later, eminent jurists asked Indira Jaising, "What is this thing called 'domestic violence'? The law recognises no such thing" (Jaising 2013: xv). The thing called domestic violence had to wait till 2006 to be defined in law.

Muslim women organizing around rights in the family, 1986–2016

It is apt to begin the discussion on family laws and Muslim women with the statement issued on 20 October 2016 by over a hundred "Muslims and people of Muslim descent" in India, which opposes triple *talāq*, the UCC, the Hindu right-wing ruling party's (the Bharatiya Janata Party) "new found love for Muslim women," and the appropriation of the Muslim voice by the All India Muslim Personal Law Board.[8] Here I discuss the textures of advocacy on Muslim women's rights in different parts of the country, focusing on the relationship between family laws and the larger political debates and projects on the status of minorities in India.

In the view of noted political scientist Zoya Hasan, religion, feminist politics, and the question of Muslim women's rights need to be understood so that the intersection between minority rights and women's rights is accounted for. A second issue concerns

> the strategies deployed by minority groups to preserve their distinctive identity in response to threats to it, on the one hand and how Muslim women-led networks are challenging the authority of the religious elite to represent the "Muslim community" while reframing the category "Muslim women" in order to assert political agency to enhance women's rights, on the other.
>
> *(Hasan 2014: 264)*

The nuanced articulation of the rights of Muslim women as put forth in Hasan's statement is a core aspect of the recent article by Shahnaz Sheikh, the first Muslim woman to challenge triple *talāq* in the Supreme Court of India, in 1986 (Sheikh 2016).

The single "positive" outcome of the genocidal VAW in Gujarat,[9] according to Zakia Soman, a founder of the BMMA (Bharatiya Muslim Mahila Andolan or Indian Muslim Women's Movement), was that ordinary women came out of their homes to speak about the violence they had witnessed or experienced. There was anger among women. They simply refused to accept the situation and stepped out of their homes to become first-generation activists – 200–300 women in the first instance. In the face of numbing, targeted assault, survivors were not stigmatized or ostracized by their family or community. There was also insecurity in the minds of parents, which led to mass marriages of very young girls – thirteen to sixteen years of age – post-conflict in the relief camps conducted by camp organizers and supported by Muslim organizations. Soman recounts that the act of stepping out and speaking about anti-Muslim violence led quite naturally to women speaking up about injustice and violence in the family – DV, *talāq*, second marriage without informing the first wife, and sudden demands for dowry. While initially they met as Aman Samuday (Peace Coalition), they realized soon that they needed to meet as women, and called meetings under the banner of Niswaan. Soman recounts their first meetings as a women's group:

> I remember a lot of women had come. Some of the women had come in a full-fledged burkha. But once we all got into the room we said, "there's nobody here, we can all be free here, *Ab uthar do, ab burkhe ki*

> *zaroorat nahi hai*" [now you can remove your burkhas, there is no need for burkhas now]. And they had taken off their burkhas. I had seen their faces for the first time; I'd known them otherwise in the burkha, because they were coming for some rally or dharna [protest] over the Gujarat riots – I had only seen them through their eyes.[10]

The first issues that were brought to the group were *talāq* and polygamy. Where women faced violence and needed to be moved out of the matrimonial home, the fact that the organizers were involved in post-conflict support had built trust in the community so they did not face resistance in retrieving a victim's personal belongings from her husband's home. In terms of law, they used a combination of instruments that worked – Muslim personal law, 125 CrPC for maintenance, PWDVA, 498A IPC, and negotiation and mediation with an abusive husband – anything that was just and brought relief to a woman in a particular situation. Most importantly, the BMMA felt both codification of Muslim law and access to public remedies were both necessary and important.

In the context of working with Muslim women, Noorjehan Safia Niaz observed that violence is not just physical – the threat of divorce, polygamy, and denial of child custody are all forms of violence commonly deployed against women.[11] While it may be desirable to use formal legal institutions such as the courts, women have no control over legal proceedings and poor women cannot afford the expenses incurred in court proceedings. Most prefer a settlement in the Women's Sharia Courts set up by the BMMA. Reiterating Zakia Soman's viewpoint, Noorjehan felt that after the demolition of Babri Masjid and the violence across the country against Muslims, there was a rise of Muslim women's organizations and women found their own voice within the community. Looking back on the early cases like Shah Bano,[12] she feels the difference is that in the mid1980s there were individual women fighting their battles, whereas now, Muslim women's collectives and movements were backing individual women's struggles. Although there is a very vocal opposition to their work (whether on the topics of *talāq* or women's entry into the Haji Ali *dargah* [tomb]), she feels that it is a sign of the tacit support they enjoy that there has been no fatwa issued against them to date. And she does not believe that it will be possible for regressive forces to gain control over them.

Muslim communities in Tamil Nadu are governed by the Jamaat, an all-male body that interprets Sharia law in adjudication of cases related to family law, especially marriage and divorce. Women, by definition, were excluded from the Jamaat and represented by male kin, even when matters directly concerning them were heard by the Jamaat. In 2004, around the same time that Zakia Soman began to work with Muslim women in post-conflict Gujarat, Sherifa Khanum formed the Tamil Nadu Muslim Women's Jamaat in the southern state of Tamil Nadu:

> Whenever the jamaat wanted to subjugate women, they cited Quran as their guide. So we understood that it was the authority they drew from Quran that they used to oppress women. We then read Quran and re-examined our realities as women. This strengthened our resolve. The word that crystallised their actions and their authority was "jamaat" – a word that carried immense weight. And so in the course of our discussions, the idea was born. Why should we not form a jamaat ourselves?[13]

In 2002, Jameela Nishat founded the Shaheen Women's Resource and Welfare Association to work among women in the riot-affected areas of the Old City of Hyderabad. Taking a different route and working with the office of the Qazi alongside courts dealing with family law – rather than setting up women's jamaats or Sharia courts – in an interview Nishat underscored the difficulties of providing relief to women. Straddling criminal courts, family courts, and Qazi courts, Shaheen calibrates the options available to women who want to leave abusive homes. Recounting her work with the office of the Chief Qazi, she pointed out that the Qazi's records show an overwhelming number of cases of *khula*, where the woman asks for divorce and secures it. She cautioned against reading this as an expression of women's freedom.[14] Rather, in the experience of Shaheen, it indicates that there is so much violence that women are unable to bear it and choose to opt out of marriage.

The All India Muslim Women's Personal Law Board (AIMWPLB), led by Shaista Amber, was set up as the women's wing of the All India Muslim Personal Law Board in 2005. It was perhaps born at this precise moment in response to the growing demand for reform by Muslim women across the country:

> The Muslim woman today continues to face the brunt of a discriminatory law. She is divorced either orally, or in writing, and unilaterally, she gets meagre or no mehr[15] amounts, her husband continues to remarry with impunity; her consent is not taken at the time of marriage, she is forced to undergo halala,[16] she faces intolerable restrictions during her iddat[17] and so on. It is a tragedy that while Quran bestows many rights on the Muslim women, they are not able to access them. The Quranic injunctions must be made legally enforceable by adding it to the constitution of India.[18]

AIMWPLB's *Khuli Adalat* (open court), a mobile adjudicatory forum, provides women facing difficult situations, especially in the family, to place their problems for consideration before Islamic scholars.

In general, the experience of Muslim women and the debate on personal law reform vis-à-vis the UCC has resulted in binaries in public discourse that thwart the possibilities of organic solutions emerging and crafted by the women themselves. Despite this, we have seen the various ways in which women have been able to negotiate the system – if the formation of a women's Jamaat is one route, women's Sharia courts and *Khuli Adalats* are another, and working with the Qazi's office to ensure that women get a fair hearing and decent maintenance in the case of *khula* is a third way.

In addressing the question of law reform for Muslims, in 2005 AIMWPLB put out a Model *Nikahnama* (marriage contract), while in 2015 Soman and Niaz circulated a Draft Muslim Family Law for signatures.[19]

What is of particular interest through all these initiatives is the effort expended to integrate the constitutional principles of justice and equality for women with religious law. Within all these moves, there is a cascading feminist common sense across social location that interrogates violence in the family and searches for alternatives – through counseling, dissolution on mutually consensual terms, negotiated settlements for the return of peace, the right to residence, and importantly in the domain of public law, strategic litigation, legislative reform, and legislative impact assessments on a regular ongoing basis, among others. It is with these questions before us that we move to a consideration of case law and problems in statute and interpretation in the three major religious traditions in India – Hindu, Muslim, and Christian.

Family law jurisprudence: an interreligious snapshot

Two discriminatory statutes that governed Hindus were challenged in *Gita Hariharan v. Reserve Bank of India* (AIR 1999, 2 SCC 228) – the Hindu Minority and Guardianship Act, 1956 and Section 19(b) of the Guardians and Wards Act, 1890.[20] In the first petition, Gita Hariharan was refused recognition as her minor son's guardian when she applied for Reserve Bank of India Relief Bonds in his name. In the second petition, Vandana Shiva claimed custody of her minor son, challenging the legal norm of the father as natural guardian to the exclusion of the mother. The Supreme Court reinterpreted the statutory provisions in both these acts in favor of substantively equal status of mother and father vis-à-vis a minor child. In doing this, the court cited provisions from CEDAW, the Beijing Declaration, and Article 2 of the Universal Declaration of Human Rights (UDHR) (see de Alwis and Jaising 2016 for a detailed analysis). It must be stressed that the route to personal law reform has been distinctive in each of the major religions. The reforms around anti-dowry legislations that primarily affected Hindu women were described in an earlier section, as well as the efforts at mobilizing Muslim women around issues of DV, imbuing new meaning to the idea of plural jurisprudence and legal pluralism.

Tracking the relationship between legislative and judicial action with respect to family laws, Subramanian observes that the Christian clergy and mobilizers were more inclined to reform in the post-1980s period than were Muslim leaders (Subramanian 2014). As a result, the initiative for Christian law reform came from the legislature, whereas Muslim law reform was pushed through statutory and constitutional interpretation, faced as it was with no legislative initiative and demands by aggrieved women litigants for entitlements, especially on dissolution of marriage. Even prior to the deliberations around reforming the Christian law of divorce, however, the 1986 case of *Mary Roy v. State of Kerala* (1986 AIR 1011, 1986 SCR (1) 371) removed gender-based discrimination in the inheritance of property among Syrian Christians in Kerala, although her lawyer, Indira Jaising, recalls, importantly, that what Mary Roy was primarily asserting was not ownership, but her right to usufruct, in the property of her natal family to whom she returned after her divorce.[21]

Although there was a fair degree of unanimity that Christian law of divorce, the Indian Divorce Act, 1869, provided very limited and unequal grounds for divorce to men and women, legal reform itself was considerably delayed. It was the case of *Mary Sonia Zachariah v. Union of India* (1995 (1) Ker LT 644 (FB)) that saw the coming together of religious organizations and rights organizations, which included two of Kerala's important reformed Orthodox churches, Christian reform organizations, and rights groups such as the Joint Women's Programme.

The specific points on which the court deliberated in *Mary Sonia Zachariah* were the limited grounds for the availability of divorce (denied to women on grounds of cruelty or desertion alone) and the unequal access to divorce for Christian as compared to other religious groups. The latter point, the court felt, defeated the constitutional guarantee to equality and non-discrimination on grounds of religion and gender. The denial of cruelty as a ground for desertion, the court felt, violated women's fundamental right to life and personal liberty.

The second judgment, *Pragati Varghese v. Cyril George Varghese* (AIR 1997 Bom 349), introduced an easier availability of divorce to Christian women than to Christian men, riding on the crest of Christian reform advocacy. It justified such asymmetry by taking recourse to the "muscularly weaker physique of the woman, her general vulnerable physical and social condition and her defensive and nonaggressive nature and role particularly in this country."

The legislative amendment to the Indian Divorce Act in 2001 was comprehensive and equalized the divorce rights of Christian men and women. It

(a) made divorce available to men and women upon mutual consent; (b) removed the requirement of high court confirmation of lower court divorce decrees; (c) increased alimony entitlements, and (d) removed the punitive approach to adultery that authorized transfer of the property of adulterous women to their husbands and children on divorce.

Section 125 of the Criminal Procedure Code (New) adopted in 1974 required men to support their dependent ex-wives. For Muslim men, this meant extending support beyond *iddat*, until such time that the ex-wife found support either through employment or through remarriage. Although in deference to pressure from conservative Muslim legislators a qualification was added in Section 127(2)(6) that exempted Muslim husbands from providing support to their ex-wives beyond *iddat*, decisions on maintenance claims by divorced Muslim women varied in applying these two sections between 1974 and 1985. There was a preponderance in the judicial view that husbands were required to pay permanent maintenance – in contrast to decisions involving Hindu or Christian women, where alimony was the norm after 1974. The case that brought the question of maintenance for a divorced Muslim woman to the national stage was the case of Shah Bano, decided by the Constitution Bench of the Supreme Court of India.[22]

While the arguments of Shah Bano's advocate and legal scholar Danial Latifi were crafted with a keen and nuanced understanding of Muslim law, the author of the judgment, Justice Y.V. Chandrachud, rather than building on the arguments presented, interspersed his judgment with statements such as the "fatal point in Islam is the degradation of woman," and called for a UCC (Subramanian 2014).

The furore that followed this judgment, especially among Muslims, led to Shah Bano herself renouncing the alimony that the court had decreed. In response to the demand of conservative sections, the Muslim Women (Protection of Rights on Divorce) Act, 1986 (MWPRDA) was passed. According to this act, the natal family of the woman and community trusts (*waqf*) would bear the responsibility of providing economic support for women beyond *iddat*.

However, the act was ambiguous about the man's responsibility to maintain his ex-wife beyond the *iddat* period – there was no clear statement that men would not be required to support their ex-wives beyond *iddat*. Women therefore continued to seek maintenance both under 125 CrPC and through other plural mechanisms described in the earlier section. Section 125 CrPC itself was amended in 2001 to remove the ceiling of Rs. 500 per month on maintenance.

In 2001, in *Danial Latifi v. Union of India* (2001 (7) SCC 740), lawyers who had represented Shah Bano argued that Muslim men owed their ex-wives permanent alimony even after the passage of the MWPRDA. Without overruling Shah Bano, or the MWPRDA, the Court followed an established standard of judicial construction – construing statutory law in the light of the Constitution – and asserted that it is "difficult to perceive that Muslim Law would place the responsibility for economic support for a divorced woman entirely on people unconnected to the matrimonial relationship" (cited from Subramanian 2014). Also, importantly, by the time the Latifi decision came, the political climate in the country had turned stridently anti-minority. Given its accommodative and careful approach to interpretation, the Latifi judgment came to bear without much resistance from those who had protested against Shah Bano earlier.

Finally, after decades of opposition to the practice of "triple *talāq*" by Muslim women's organizations, in August 2017 the court in *Shayara Bano v Union of India and Others*[23] finally applied the principle of manifest arbitrariness to strike down the practice of triple *talāq*.

Protection of Women from Domestic Violence Act, 2005

The PWDVA came into effect on 26 October 2006, to provide for "more effective protection of the rights of women guaranteed under the Constitution *who are victims of violence of any kind occurring within the family*" (PWDVA, Statement of Objects and Reasons, cited in Jaising 2014: 3, emphasis added). As Senior Advocate Indira Jaising points out, the legislative invocation of the Constitution in a law on DV is testimony to a feminist journey through the rugged patriarchal terrains of law, where we have come full circle from the point where a judge of a high court famously declared that introducing constitutional law in the home is "like introducing a bull in a china shop."[24] The home, under this law, was conceived as a shared space with entitlements to residence that did not flow from ownership. Jaising points out that the idea of "shared household" in PWDVA "is in keeping with the family patterns in India, where married couples continue to live with their parents in homes owned by their parents" (Jaising 2014: 3). DV under this law is not limited to spousal violence, and "matrimonial relationship" is displaced by "domestic relationship."[25] In the history of feminist support to survivors of DV, dispossession from both the natal home on marriage and the matrimonial home through cruelty has not addressed the survivors' needs for sustenance and shelter. The combination of criminal and civil elements in this legislation, therefore, is aimed at ensuring the abatement of violence *and* the securing of other needs of the woman. The fact was that "women were getting relief all under one roof, where they didn't have to run separately for maintenance, separately for custody, separately for compensation, and then the right to residence – which was a big deal."[26]

The PWDVA was enacted after three decades of struggle to end violence in the home, which included legislation, legislative impact assessment, the deliberations of a Parliamentary Standing Committee, and close monitoring and evaluation (Jaising 2014). In fact, it would not be far from the truth to state that the PWDVA is a direct result of these actions.

What is particularly interesting about the trajectory of this legislation is the different institutional realms and practices it has intertwined with. The PWDVA recognizes public health facilities as service providers and addresses for the first time *within a legislation* the issue of violence as a public health concern (Bhate-Deosthali et al. 2012: 67). The significance of this lies in the fact that it is perhaps the first time that redressing VAW has involved a close engagement with the public healthcare system – both from the need for evidence gathering in a medico-legal case and to address the need for emergency treatment, care, and trauma counseling.[27] The dominant view until this point was that DV was a "personal" problem, with the healthcare provider only providing symptomatic relief.

Women's experiences of violence exist across a continuum. Several advocates interviewed for this chapter observed that the *Nirbhaya* case has had a marked impact in women naming marital rape and sexual violence as DV – despite the fact that criminal law in India does not recognize the crime of marital rape, and by these accounts the threshold of tolerance for domestic violence has dropped, with natal families in several instances coming out in support of daughters.[28]

Further, approaches to justice are plural – and not all cases go through the public law system. Yet one of the remarkable characteristics of feminist advocacy against violence has been that the cumulative sensibilities that are crystallized in the PWDVA (for example) have in small but significant measure made inroads into spaces of personal law, providing important standard-setting tools in different locales. With the PWDVA itself being central to the thick nesting of activism around CEDAW, international debates, standards, and stories filter through to the smallest initiatives through an array of practices in strategic litigation – the women's Jamaat, the Qazi court, the *biradari panchayat* (informal caste councils), the court of the magistrate, the constitutional court, or the CEDAW sessions that call governments to account.

The most important lesson that this legislation bears for our understanding of the changed position of women in the family, according to Indira Jaising, is that it represents a departure from protectionism by the state and the emergence of the woman's autonomous and inalienable rights within the family – to a life free from both violence and from dispossession.[29]

Conclusions

This chapter has attempted to provide a bird's-eye view of the intersections in India between feminist struggles against VAW in the family, the rise of feminist legal scholarship, the campaigns for law reform, and the afterlives of feminist engagements with law.

The rise of violent Hindu majoritarianism has had very specific discursive effects on the rights of women, especially from minority groups, both within the courts and in the public domain. The successful challenge in the Supreme Court of India to the practice of triple *talāq* by Muslim women, and the appropriation of this discourse by the ruling party through the enactment criminalizing the pronouncement of triple *talāq* for instance, to serve the Hindutva agenda of stigmatizing minorities for their shabby treatment of "their" women has rendered the pitch extremely difficult to navigate for women generally, but especially for Muslim women who have been fighting for reform within personal law traditions.[30] The observation is poignant and true that witnessing/surviving collective anti-minority violence makes the narration of violence (within the family) possible. This larger context of bitterly contested majority-minority politics within which Muslim women – from Shahnaz Sheikh and Shah Bano in the 1980s to Shayara Bano in 2016[31] – have stood their ground against both Muslim orthodoxy and Hindutva politics is one that shines the torch on the strength of feminism in India even in times of siege.

An important aspect of this engagement is that the resolution of cases has steadily taken place with simultaneous recourse to the courts and to community-based adjudicatory spaces – those driven by women, like the Muslim women's Jamaat (Dhanraj 2011), as well as through creative interventions in Qazi courts.[32] In terms of its demonstration of a wider praxis for feminist legal reform, the indispensability of plural legal spaces, and the calibrated use of each space to wrest more ground for women, is most significant (see Vatuk 2017).

This review has attempted to signpost the various ways in which legal reform efforts have historically taken shape in India. Codification is not always the answer, as we have seen – it could result in the dispossession of women in insidious ways; nor, as Indira Jaising has argued, is the right to property alone the answer. Across communities, women who leave abusive marriages (or are thrown out) find themselves on the edge of survival. Those who anticipate these troubles and stay are often killed. The campaigns for reform of criminal law introducing the new offence of torture and murder for dowry in the 1980s fueled a new turn in feminist mobilization. And yet, two decades later, the CEDAW Committee marked the rise in dowry deaths as a matter of concern and the Law Commission of India (2007) published a second report on dowry deaths recommending the death penalty.

Important lessons from the campaign against domestic violence, however, are: (a) the ways in which we can resurrect older practices of fairness contained in personal laws and ousted through codification, for a new template of justice; and (b) the ways in which feminist interventions in legal reform intersect. The focus in the PWDVA on shared residence, drawing as it does, on the older right to usufruct that women enjoyed, makes a sharp departure from an approach of state protectionism towards women towards their *right* of residence. This was also the basis of the earlier challenge posed by Mary Roy to Christian women's right to inheritance, which focused on Roy's right to *use* the family property.[33] Similarly, several accounts stressed the fact that the uprising against sexual assault in 2012 and the subsequent reform of rape law has reduced the threshold of tolerance for domestic violence,[34] with survivors of marital rape reporting this at public hospitals.[35] While on the subject, the importance of treatment (of physical and psychological injury) and recording of medical evidence of survivors who approach healthcare facilities is rarely discussed as an intrinsic part of law reform on VAW. The case of the Centre for Enquiry into Health and Allied Themes (CEHAT) in Mumbai illuminates this path for us (Bhate-Deosthali et al. 2012 and Bhate-Deosthali et al. 2013).

The core strengths of the feminist movement against violence in India have been the steady emergence of survivors as leaders of the movement to end violence and the intersectional approach to women's rights. This mapping of the trajectories of rights advocacy, legislation, and the rise of new sensibilities and consciousness, we hope, will serve twin purposes: providing a template through which we may begin to understand other social movements, and offering a template to think through transversal politics for women's rights, in which engagements with legal regimes/lawscapes are critical.

Acknowledgements

I am grateful to Yakın Ertürk and the WLP team for their support and feedback. I gratefully acknowledge the support of Vasanth Kannabiran, Stanley Thangaraj, and Bandana Purkayastha. I thank Jameela Nishat, Shaheda, Sultana, and Suman from Shaheen, Hyderabad; Zakia Soman and Noorjehan Safia Niaz from Bharatiya Muslim Mahila Andolan (Indian Muslim Women's Movement), Ahmedabad and Mumbai; Padma Bhate- Deosthali and Sangeeta Rege from the Centre for Enquiry into Health and Allied Themes (CEHAT), Mumbai; Anuradha Kapoor from Swayam, Kolkata; Advocates Renu Mishra, Anchal Gupta, Priyanka Singh, and Abhay Pratap Singh from the Association for Advocacy and Legal Initiatives (AALI), Lucknow; Vahida Nainar, women's rights and human rights activist, Mumbai; Advocate Vasudha Nagaraj, Hyderabad; and Senior Advocate Indira Jaising, Lawyers Collective, Delhi, for sharing with me their views and valuable materials from their archives.

Notes

1 On 6 December 1992, the Vishva Hindu Parishad and the Bharatiya Janata Party organized the demolition of the Babri Mosque in Ayodhya, Uttar Pradesh, involving 150,000 'volunteers'.The crowd overwhelmed security forces and tore down the mosque, resulting in months of heightened communal tension, widespread protests against the demolition, organized violence against Muslims, and the deaths of at least two thousand people.
2 Interview with Vahida Nainar, 23 December 2016.
3 Interview with Zakia Soman, 21 December 2016.
4 Interview with Sultana, Shaheda, and Suman, Shaheen Women's Resource and Welfare Association, 28 December 2016.
5 These are cases reported from various high courts and the Supreme Court. Details are available on file with the author.
6 Vahida Nainar interview, 23 December 2016.
7 *Subhash Chander and Anr. v. State on 16 December 1991*, 46 (1992) Delhi Law Times 366.
8 http://thewire.in/74667/triple-talaq-statement-muslims/There are many decisions on triple *talāq* and unilateral male repudiation among Muslims. For a detailed list of cases, see Subramanian 2014: n. 98.
9 In 2002, more than a thousand people were killed over the course of two months in genocidal violence against Muslims in Gujarat, a state then led by Narendra Modi, now India's prime minister.
10 Interview with Zakia Soman, 21 December 2016.
11 Interview with Noorjehan Safia Niaz, 2 January 2017.
12 In 1978, Shah Bano, a sixty-two-year-old Muslim mother of five from Madhya Pradesh, was divorced by her husband. She filed suit in India's Supreme Court and won the right to alimony. However, under pressure from Islamic leaders, the Indian Parliament subsequently reversed the judgment.
13 Sherifa Khanum in *Invoking Justice*, a documentary film on the Tamil Nadu Muslim Women's Jamaat directed by Deepa Dhanraj, 2011.
14 Interview with Jameela Nishat, 26 December 2016.
15 *Mehr* (*mehrieh* in Farsi) is a mandatory payment, in the form of money or possessions paid or promised to pay by the groom to the bride at the time of marriage, which legally becomes her property.
16 *Halala* is a situation in which the divorced woman is forced to marry another man and consummate that marriage, divorces that man, and remarries her original husband.
17 *Iddat* is the period a woman must observe after a divorce or the death of her spouse, during which she may not marry again.
18 Website of All Indian Muslim Women Personal Law Board, www.aimwplb.com/about.
19 They also put into circulation a draft legislation on Muslim family law (Soman and Niaz 2015).
20 This discussion of cases, judicial interpretation, and reform in this chapter is based on Subramanian 2014.
21 Interview with Indira Jaising, 5 February 2017.
22 *Mohammad Ahmed Khan v. Shah Bano Begum*, 1985 SCR (3) 844.
23 Writ Petition (Civil) 118 of 2016.
24 *Harvinder Kaur v. Harmander Singh*, AIR 1984 Del 66.

25 Domestic relationship includes "all relationships based on consanguinity, marriage, adoption and even 'relationships in the nature of marriage'" (Jaising 2014: 9).
26 Interview with Anuradha Kapoor, Swayam, Kolkata, 21 December 2016.
27 Interview with Padma Bhate-Deosthali and Sangeeta Rege, 27 December 2016.
28 Interviews with Advocate Vasudha Nagaraj, Hyderabad, 29 December 2016, and Noorjehan S. Niaz, 2 January 2017. The *Nirbhaya* case refers to the sexual assault and murder of a young woman on the streets of Delhi in December 2012 that resulted in amendments to the rape law in 2013.
29 Interview with Indira Jaising, 5 November 2017.
30 Muslim Women (Protection of Rights on Marriage) Act 2017 passed in December 2017, in Section 4 sets out imprisonment for three years and a fine as punishment for men pronouncing triple *talāq*.
31 *Shayara Bano v. Union of India*,Writ Petition (Civil) 118 of 2016.
32 Interviews with Jameela Nishat, 26 December 2016, and Sultana, Shaheda, and Suman, Shaheen Women's Resource and Welfare Association, 28 December 2016.
33 Interview with Indira Jaising, 5 February 2017.
34 Interviews with Vasudha Nagaraj, 29 December 2016, and Renu Mishra and AALI team, 5 January 2017.
35 Interview with Padma Bhate-Deosthali and Sangeeta Rege, 27 December 2017.

References

Agnes, Flavia (1984) *My Story ... Our Story, of Re-Building Broken Lives*, Bombay: Women's Centre.

——— (2008a) "Women's Movement in a Secular Framework: Redefining the Agendas," in Mary E. John (ed.), *Women's Studies in India*, Delhi: Penguin: 501–508.

——— (2008b) "Family Courts: From the Frying Pan into the Fire?" in Mary E. John (ed.), *Women's Studies in India*, Delhi: Penguin: 272–278.

Almeida, Albertina (2016) "Goa's Civil Code Shows That Uniformity Does Not Always Mean Equality," *The Wire*, 8 August 2016, https://thewire.in/57211/goas-uniformcivil-code-is-not-the-greatest-model-to-follow/.

Basu, Srimati (2014) "Dreaming a Better Court for Women: Adjudication and subjectivity in the Family Court of Kolkata, India," in Ravinder Kaur and Rajni Palriwala (eds.), *Marrying in South Asia: Shifting Concepts, Changing Practices in a Globalising World*, Hyderabad: Orient Blackswan: 351–370.

Bhate-Deosthali, Padma, T.K. Sundari Ravindran, and U. Vindhya (2012) "Addressing Domestic Violence within Healthcare Settings: The Dilaasa Model," *Economic and Political Weekly*, Vol. *XLVII*, No. 17, 28 April: 66–75.

Bhate-Deosthali, Padma, Sangeeta Rege, and Padma Prakash (eds.) (2013) *Feminist Counselling and Domestic Violence in India*, New Delhi: Routledge.

CEDAW (2007) Concluding Comments of the Committee on the Elimination of Discrimination against Women: India, 37th session, 15 January–2 February, www.un.org/womenwatch/daw/cedaw/cedaw25years/content/english/CONCLUDING_COMMENTS/India/ India-CO-3.pdf.

——— (2014) "Concluding Observations on the Combined Fourth and Fifth Periodic Reports of India, 1219th and 1220th sessions," CEDAW/C/IND/CO/4-5, 18 July; http://tbinternet.ohchr.org/Treaties/CEDAW/Shared%20Documents/Ind/CEDAW_C_IND_ CO_4-5_17678_E.doc.

De Alwis, Rangita de Silva and Indira Jaising (2016) "The Role of Personal Laws in Creating a 'Second Sex,' " *Faculty Scholarship*, Paper 1681, http://scholarship.law.upenn.edu/faculty_scholarship/1681.
Dhanraj, Deepa (2011) (Dir.) *Invoking Justice* (documentary film).
Gandhi, Nandita and Nandita Shah (1992) *The Issues at Stake: Theory and Practice in the Contemporary Women's Movement in India*, New Delhi: Kali for Women.
Hasan, Zoya (2014) "Religion, Feminist Politics and Muslim Women's Rights in India," in Kalpana Kannabiran (ed.), *Women and Law: Critical Feminist Perspectives*, New Delhi: Sage: 264–273.
Jain, Juhi (2014) "A Tribute to Satyarani Chadha, the Face of the Anti Dowry Movement," 7 July 2014, http://feministsindia.com/tribute-satyarani-chadha-face-indias-anti-dowry- movement/.
Jaising, Indira (2013) "Foreword," in Padma Bhate-Deosthali, Sangeeta Rege, and Padma Prakash (eds.), *Feminist Counselling and Domestic Violence in India*, New Delhi: Routledge: xv–xviii.
——— (2014) "Bringing Rights Home: Review of the Campaign for a Law on Domestic Violence," in Kalpana Kannabiran (ed.), *Women and Law: Critical Feminist Perspectives*, Delhi: Sage: 1–31.
Kumar, Radha (1990) *The History of Doing: An Illustrated Account of Movements for Women's Rights and Feminism in India, 1800–1990*, New Delhi: Zubaan.
Law Commission of India (2007) *202nd Report on Proposal to Amend Section 304B of Indian Penal Code.*
Rao, B. Shiva (1968) *The Framing of India's Constitution: A Study*, New Delhi: Indian Institute of Public Administration.
Robinson, Rowena (2012) "Introduction," in Rowena Robinson (ed.), *Minority Studies* , New Delhi: Oxford University Press: 1–48.
Sheikh, Shahnaz (2016) "Why I Took on Triple Talaq and Why I Oppose the Uniform Civil Code," *Indian Express*, 16 November 2016, http://indianexpress.com/article/opinion/columns/triple-talaq-uniform-civil-code-indian-constitution-4377532/.
Solanki, Gopika (2011) *Adjudication in Religious Family Laws: Cultural Accommodation, Legal Pluralism, and Gender Equality in India*, New Delhi: Cambridge University Press.
Soman, Zakia and Noorjehan Safia Niaz (2015) *No More Talaq Talaq Talaq: Muslim Women Call for a Ban on an UnIslamic Practice*, Mumbai: Bharatiya Muslim Mahila Andolan.
Subramanian, Narendra (2014) *Nation and Family: Personal Law, Cultural Pluralism and Gendered Citizenship in India*, Stanford, CA: Stanford University Press. E-book.
Vatuk, Sylvia (2017) *Marriage and its Discontents: Women, Islam and the Law in India*, New Delhi: Women Unlimited.
Williams, Rina Verma (2012) "Making Minority Identities: Gender, State and Muslim Personal Law," in Rowena Robinson (ed.), *Minority Studies*, New Delhi: Oxford University Press: 73–94.

Abbreviations in Case Citations

AIR: *All India Reporter*; Bom: Bombay; Del: Delhi; ILR: *Indian Law Reports*; Kar LJ: *Karnataka Law Journal*; Ker LT: *Kerala Law Times*; SC: Supreme Court; SCC: *Supreme Court Cases*; SCR: *Supreme Court Reports*

10 Saving Custom or Promoting Incest? Post-Independence Marriage Law and Dravidian Marriage Practices

Patricia Uberoi

In this article I seek to bring both a social anthropological and a feminist perspective to bear on certain provisions of the Special Marriage Act of 1954 (SMA) and the Hindu Marriage Act of 1955 (HMA),[1] and on the legislative debates surrounding their enactment and amendment. In particular, I look at the Acts' provisions regarding 'prohibited relationships'—what anthropologists might term *rules of exogamy*—violation of which, under either Act, renders a marriage 'null and void'.

While feminist authors have been quite vociferous in their critique of the political horse-trading that preceded the enactment and amendment of the personal law regime of independent India, the various provisions of the laws concerned, and their mode of application and adjudication, in fact the 'prohibited relationships' clauses have attracted negligible attention as a 'gender' issue. Partial exceptions are comments by B. Sivaramayya, to whose gender-sensitive work on Indian personal law we are all much indebted, and by feminist legal sociologist, Flavia Agnes.[2] In both these instances, however, the concern was with what we might call the effective 'de-secularisation' of the Special Marriage Act by a 1963 Amendment which (in line with The Hindu Marriage Act) allowed of a violation of the 'prohibited relationships' provisions of the SMA such that 'where a custom governing at least one of the parties permits of a marriage between them, such marriage maybe solemnized, notwithstanding that they are within the degrees of prohibited relationship'.[3] It was understood that this back-door concession to 'custom' was made in the light of the existing marriage practices of many communities in South India which permit—nay, even *prefer*—marriage between certain categories of close kin that otherwise fall under the definition of 'prohibited relationships' in both Acts.

I begin by outlining, in a rough-and-ready way, the formal features of the northern and southern kinship systems, and the connections made in recent social scientific and feminist literature between the respective systems

DOI: 10.4324/9781003299561-10

of kinship and marriage and various social and demographic indicators of women's 'status' in society. I then consider the tortuous process of the enactment and amendment of the 'prohibited relationships' sections of the SMA and the HMA, and the positions articulated in the process. Finally, I consider, somewhat inconclusively it must be said, aspects of the rather sparse case law in this particular area of the marriage laws. The overall intention is simply to draw attention to a 'gender' dimension of the contemporary legal regulation of marriage which is not generally seen as meriting feminist scrutiny.

North and South Indian kinship

Anthropologists have long recognised that North and South India exhibit two qualitatively distinct systems of kinship and marriage. These differences roughly parallel the subcontinental distribution of two major language families—the Indo-Aryan (or Indo-European) and the Dravidian—and are encoded, *mutatis mutandis,* in the structure of the respective kinship vocabularies.[4] Among other features, kinship terminologies of the Dravidian type make a distinction between what anthropologists term 'parallel' and 'cross' cousins (the children of same-sex siblings *versus* those of opposite sex siblings), and conflate the terms for mother's brother, father's sister's husband, and father-in-law. These and other features are believed to point to the practice of preferential cross-cousin marriage (that is, marriage of a man with the daughter of either his mother's brother or his father's sister), matched by a corresponding proscription on parallel cousin marriage (marriage with the daughter of his father's brother or mother's sister). On the other hand, the structurally contrastive Indo-Aryan kinship terminologies class *all* cousins as quasi-siblings (and thereby unmarriageable), and terminologically distinguish the mother's brother, father's sister's husband and father-in-law. Indeed, in the region of north Indian kinship, where marriage between close kin *of any type* is disapproved, marriage is seen as a means to forge new bonds and extend the range of social influence, rather than—as in the southern system—as a means of reiterating and consolidating pre-existing affinal ties.

Two women anthropologists, writing in the 1950s and 1960s, were instrumental in suggesting that there might also be an important 'gender' dimension to all this 'kinship algebra', and to the generic distinction thus posited between North and South Indian kinship. In her long standard, but latterly rather neglected work, *Kinship Organization in India* (originally published in 1953),[5] Irawati Karve drew on the evidence of kinship terminologies in the first instance, and the ethnographic record by way of supplement, to differentiate four main varieties of kinship organisation in the Indian subcontinent, coordinating with the distribution of language families. The major division, and the chief focus of Karve's attention, was that between (1) the North Indian or 'Indo-Aryan' system, which she saw as continuous with the model represented in the classical Sanskrit legal texts;[6] and (2) the southern region of 'Dravidian' kinship. Between these two she posited (3) a 'Central' kinship zone with mixed features, covering Maharashtra, Gujarat and parts of Rajasthan through Madhya Pradesh to Orissa, while (4) a non-contiguous 'Eastern' zone, effectively a residual category in her scheme of things, included speakers of the Sino-Tibetan and Austro-Asiatic language families.

Aside from the features already referred to, Karve pointed to a number of other differences in kinship and marriage practices that may express or entail a moderation of the strongly masculinist emphasis evident in North India. For instance, North Indian customary rules of exogamy require not only a ban on marriages within the localised patrilineal descent group, but sometimes extend this exogamous prohibition to cover *all* co-villagers, whether distantly or only putatively related under the same patronymic, or completely unrelated (see below);[7] in South India, by contrast, intra-village marriage is generally permitted. Thus, in the north, women typically marry total strangers, often at a considerable distance, and thereafter take up residence with their husbands' families, whereas in the southern kinship system women may marry within the kin network, possibly within the same village, and have greater flexibility in regard to post-marital residence arrangements. Add to this the higher prevalence of dowry marriage in the north, and you have in that region a family system which is qualitatively and experientially different from that in the south, *at least from a woman-centered perspective.*

Karve's picture of regional differentiation in kinship practices was further amplified by anthropologist Pauline Kolenda in a series of papers from 1967.[8] Utilising materials from a number of ethnographic studies of the 1950s, along with household and other information from the 1961 Census, Kolenda sought to correlate the incidence of different household types—particularly the patrilineal joint household—with factors such as caste status, size of landholding, and rural/urban residence. To these she added a set of proxy-measures of women's domestic 'bargaining power', referring to the emotional or material leverage that a young married woman might bring to bear on her husband to persuade him to set up house independent of his patrikin:[9] high or low rates of divorce and remarriage; bridewealth or dowry payments; and stronger or weaker ties with the wife's kin (uxorilaterality *versus* virilaterality). Kolenda's studies indicated the higher prevalence of joint households in the northern zone; conversely, factors enhancing women's bargaining power appeared to be stronger in the south. As she also noted, these regional differences in the prevalence of joint household arrangements appeared to correlate with certain other significant social phenomena that are now widely touted as indicators of 'social development'.[10]

Though Karve and Kolenda were chiefly interested in describing and mapping patterns of family and kinship *per se,* exegesis of regional differences in family practices has subsequently been coopted to other, and wider, explanatory ends: in the first place, to explain the 'cultural' dimension of regional patterns of demographic behaviour; and, more broadly (but not unrelatedly of course), to explain contrasting patterns of economic and social development and gender empowerment. 'The main states of India', Dyson and Moore wrote in an exceedingly influential paper in 1983,

> can be broadly grouped into *two basic demographic regions.* In contrast to the north, states in the south and east are characterized by the following: relatively low overall fertility; lower marital fertility; later age at first marriage; lower infant and child mortality; comparatively low rates of female to male infant and child mortality and, largely as a consequence, relatively low sex ratios.[11]

Dyson and Moore related these differences in demographic indicators—in particular, the regional asymmetry of sex ratios[12]—to the different levels of 'female autonomy' enabled by the respective family and kinship systems: low in the north, higher in the south.[13]

A major demonstration of the homology between regional patterns of kinship and marriage and other factors that may enable or inhibit women's 'bargaining position' in the family and society is offered in economist Bina Agarwal's densely documented *A Field of One's Own* (1994).[14] This study seeks to map women's customary and statutory rights of inheritance through South Asia (India, Pakistan, Bangladesh, Nepal and Sri Lanka), specifically, women's inheritance rights in *arable land,* which is the most important resource and chief means of livelihood for some three-quarters of the region's population. In this respect, too, Agarwal's study reveals a noticeable north/south India dichotomy, women in the south being more likely to inherit land under customary law as wives or as daughters, or to be apportioned land as dowry. She also found a similar patterning in respect of a number of other factors that are presumed to affect women's bargaining position in the family: (i) rules of post-marital residence; (ii) close kin marriage; (iii) purdah practices; (iv) controls over women's sexuality and freedom of divorce and remarriage; (v) rural female labour force participation rates; (vi) rural literacy rates; (vii) total fertility rates; and, rather more problematically in my opinion, (viii) measures of land scarcity.[15] Taken together, Agarwal suggests, south India has customarily allowed women superior access to material resources, resulting in their better bargaining power in the family and better leverage in availing of the gender-equal inheritance rights that were provided in the Hindu Succession Act (HSA) of 1956. The crucial explanatory factor in Agarwal's account is the distinctiveness of the south Indian kinship system (in particular, the different rules of marriage and norms of post-marital residence), along with the co-presence in the southern region of pockets of matrilineal and bilateral succession, stretching down into Sri Lanka.

A number of other economists have similarly drawn attention to north-south regional differences in respect to a range of indicators of social development, gender equity, and distributive justice. On measures of female literacy and levels of education, health delivery, maternal and child survival, male and female life expectancy and, as already mention, sex ratios, southern India (and most notably the southwestern state of Kerala) has an outstanding profile in comparison to the north and northwestern states.[16] Reflecting on this phenomenon in the light of the revelations in the 2001 Census of an increased anti-female sex bias in natality and post-natal child mortality, Amartya Sen has asserted 'something of a social and cultural divide across India'.[17] Even the 'partial misfit' in the picture, the state of Tamil Nadu, he said, does not really detract from the 'astonishing finding' that

> the vast majority of the Indian States *fall firmly into two contiguous halves*, classified broadly into the north and the west, on the one side, and the south and the east, on the other. Indeed, every State in the north and the west ... has [a] strictly lower female-male ratio of children than has every State in the east and the south..., and this indeed is quite remarkable.[18]

It will be clear from this albeit cursory survey of a truly vast literature that social scientists have placed considerable explanatory weight on aspects of the south Indian system of kinship and marriage, related to levels of 'female autonomy', as factors accounting for that region's superior track record in South Asia in respect of patterns of demographic behaviour and indices of economic and social development. In this light, it is surely something of a conundrum that post-independence family law legislation—legislation that was supposedly aimed at improving the social position of Indian women—actually *de-legitimised* Dravidian marriage practices, while ultimately, contradictorily and grudgingly, allowing their retention as 'custom' under specified conditions.

In exploring this conundrum, this article returns to the legislative debates of the 1950s and 1960s around the 'prohibited relations' provisions of the Special Marriage Act (1954) and the Hindu Marriage Act (1955) to reflect on the complex regional and gender politics of this gesture. There are several aspects of the puzzle that will be highlighted here. *First,* controversy over the 'prohibited relations' sections of the new Acts (i.e., the sections that effectively if inexplicitly outlaw Dravidian marriage practices) was—*relatively speaking*—quite mild compared to the much more vociferous controversies on issues of monogamy, divorce, and age of marriage. However, as this account will indicate, there was obviously a behind-the-scenes struggle going on through a decade and more before a compromise solution was finally reached. *Second,* the delegitimization of Dravidian marriage practices has attracted minimal interest and comment in legal circles.[19] *Third,* as noted, case law is surprisingly sparse in respect to the 'prohibited relations' provisions of the two Acts, though other grounds for nullity and the voidance of marriage are exploited to the hilt in this notoriously litigious environment. *Fourth,* notwithstanding the presumed positive correlation between Dravidian kinship and marriage practices and higher levels of women's autonomy (see above), the undercutting of Dravidian marriage practices has not been flagged as a significant 'gender' issue. By contrast, many *other* aspects of the new legal regime of marriage—for instance, the not-unrelated issue of the 'future of matriliny' under colonial and post-colonial legal regimes, and the very fraught question of the desirability or otherwise of 'religious' personal laws (versus a Uniform Civil Code)—have generated intense and continuous feminist attention.[20] *Fifth,* a supposedly universal and scientific 'eugenic' discourse has clearly played a significant role in muting both feminist and 'Dravidian' pockets of resistance, though this mediating factor remains both unacknowledged and—as yet—unchallenged.

I must now confess that this article offers no solution to the conundrum thus set out, and certainly no recommendations for legal intervention and feminist activism. The intention is simply to open up to feminist scrutiny an issue that has been brushed under the carpet of legal and social reform for half a century or more.

Legislating marriage in post-independence India

As is well known, the enactment of the new Hindu Law Code in the mid-1950s was a tremendously controversial affair that stretched over more than a decade.[21] The process had begun, piecemeal as it were, with the 19th and early 20th century social reform movements, and consequent legislative enactments in British India and in 'progressive' native states like Mysore and Baroda. The demand for a comprehensive Code for all Hindus and for all aspects of Hindu personal law came as a recommendation of the B.N. Rau Committee, constituted in 1941 to consider lacunae in the Hindu Women's Rights to Property Act (1937). The work of the Committee was stayed by War, resuming in 1944, and the Report eventually submitted to the Legislative Assembly in 1947. The Hindu Code was hotly but intermittently debated through the next four years, ultimately provoking the Law Minister, B.R. Ambedkar, to resign in protest against what he believed to be deliberate delaying tactics motivated by narrow electoral calculations.

The family law Bills were taken up once again following the first general elections and the constitution of the new Parliament. The Special Marriage Bill was presented first, as presumably the less contentious of the set, and the expressly Hindu personal law divided into four separate Bills, the better to ensure their smooth passage through the House. The Special Marriage Act (SMA) and the Hindu Marriage Act (HMA) were passed in 1954 and 1955 respectively, to be followed by the Hindu Succession Act, the Hindu Minority and Guardianship Act and the Hindu Adoptions and Maintenance Act, all in 1956. Here we are concerned primarily with certain provisions of the Special Marriage Act and the Hindu Marriage Act which bear on South Indian marriage practices.

The purposes of the two Marriage Acts, it must be said by way of beginning, were rather different. The SMA was essentially a reenactment of the 1872 Special Marriage Act,[22] retaining a notable penalty of the earlier Act, namely, severance of the parties marrying under this Act from Joint Family property.[23] ('Either he should have the wife or the property', as one unsympathetic Member put it.[24]) It was billed at the time as a secular and territorial law of marriage and divorce which, notwithstanding its problems, was at least 'a step in the right direction' towards the ultimate goal of a Uniform Civil Code.[25] It was thought that the SMA would encourage frugal marriage ceremonies, rather than the extravagant festivities associated with religious rituals,[26] and contribute to national unity by enabling inter-caste and inter-religious marriages.[27] Changing sociopolitical circumstances, it was said, commended a new, 'progressive' and 'contractual' approach to marriage.[28] 'Democracy', said D.C. Sharma during consideration of the Bill, 'means freedom of choice':

> We can choose in marriage anybody we like. I think this Bill gives us that freedom of choice. This is a freedom which cannot be denied to men and women. It cannot be denied to persons when they receive high education, when they are brought up in a democratic atmosphere, and when they are taught that they should love freedom. If they can have political freedom in other spheres of life, I do not see why they should not have freedom in their choice of partners.[29]

The explicit and stated purposes behind the promulgation of the Hindu Law Code were quite different, namely, to bring 'certainty' into the operation of Hindu law; to 'unify' the various schools of classical and customary law; to eliminate restrictive practices and antiquated rules; and—at least for some—to provide a benchmark of progressive legislation en route to the Uniform Civil Code.[30] Specifically, the HMA sought: (i) the abolition of caste [endogamy] as a necessary requirement of a valid marriage; (ii) the enforcement of monogamy; and (iii) the facility for divorce or the dissolution of marriage on certain grounds.[31] As remarked, the 'monogamy' and 'divorce' provisions were the heart of the controversy over the Bill: the former because it interfered with a 'right' to which a section of Hindu men felt entitled (whether by 'tradition' or by comparison with the rights of Muslim men); the latter because it was seen to controvert the indissoluble, 'sacramental' character of Hindu marriage. Nonetheless, Law Minister Pataskar took pains to assure the House that this legislation was in conformity with the principles of Hindu law which, he claimed, had always adapted to changed circumstances, and that it in no way aimed to violate the sanctity of Hindu marriage.[32]

Marriage rules under classical Hindu law

The Parliamentary debates around the legislative enactments of the SMA and the HMA, which occupied much of the time of the House through 1954/55, provide ample evidence of the contradictory ideological and regional pressures at work in the production of a new personal law regime for independent India. Before discussing this legislation and the public discourse that it generated, however, it will be pertinent to outline the rules of marriage under the classical Hindu law—especially in so far as they concern exogamous restrictions. This is not to claim that the Dharmashastric rules have been observed in practice: they certainly have not. Nor, *strictly* speaking, are they relevant to interpretation of points of law under the HMA, which provides its own definitions of the relevant concepts.[33] All the same, it is important to recognise that the codification of Anglo-Hindu law in the latter half of the 19th century, and the subsequent enactment of a *Hindu* Law Code in post-Independence India (along with a secular and territorial marriage law), have paradoxically consolidated the legal recognition of the Dharmashastras as the authoritative source of the governing principles of family law for all Hindus.[34] It is another matter that some scholars are convinced that *genuine* Hindu law, as transmitted by the *rishis* [Hindu sages], is for all practical purposes a dead letter![35]

In short, the Hindu law books do not speak with one voice on the rules of marriage—as on any other matter.[36] There are substantive differences between the Mitakshara and Dayabhaga Schools, and between different texts and commentaries. Additionally, since the 19th century, the practice of 'Anglo-Hindu' law has generated its own body of authoritative texts and legal precedents, modified piecemeal by reformist legislation. Leaving aside the definitions of 'approved' and 'unapproved' forms of Hindu marriage, and stipulations regarding *varna* (class) and *jati* (caste) endogamy, we focus here on the rules of exogamy under the classical Hindu law. Classical Hindu law specified a very extensive range of exogamous prohibitions—'extravagant', Louis Dumont has termed them.[37] *First,* marriage was banned between kin in the patrilineal line of descent from putative *gotra* and *pravara* ancestors.[38] The *gotras,* 18 in all, are exogamous patrilineal clans whose members claim descent from eponymous Hindu sages, while the *pravara* are similarly exogamous units, subordinate to the *gotra,* to which they are complexly related.[39] Properly speaking, the *gotras* and *pravaras* are restricted to Brahmins, and only by courtesy, so to speak, extended to the second and third classes (*varna*) of the Hindu caste order.[40]

Second, marriage was prohibited between persons in what was termed a *sapinda* or 'shared body' relationship with each other. The concept of *sapinda* relationship defines graded responsibilities in ancestor worship and death rituals and, relatedly, entitlements to inheritance. In these contexts it is exclusively, or almost exclusively, agnatic (related through the male line). *However,* in the context of defining the boundaries of the exogamous group, *sapinda*-ship takes on a cognatic dimension (related through both father and mother), with just a slight prioritisation of agnatic kinship in the limit of recognition of seven degrees of relationship on the father's side *versus* only five on the mother's.[41] Unlike *gotra* and *pravara* affiliation, the relationship of shared body is universal, not restricted to Brahmins.[42] It is this *sapinda* rule that is hostile to the Dravidian practice of cross-cousin marriage.

As Thomas Trautmann and others have elaborated, numerous Dharmashastric texts expressly prohibit cross-cousin marriage. Prominent among them, and much cited in this regard, is the *Baudhayana Dharma Sutra (ca* 500-200 BC), which concedes however that mother's brother's daughter (MBD) and father's sister's daughter (FZD) marriages are among the cultural peculiarities of south India. While local custom should, in general, be taken as authoritative—and this principle has been invoked by several authorities to justify Dravidian marriage practices—*Baudhayana* himself rules that such practices are contrary to the Veda, and should be prohibited.[43] On the other hand, other jurists, notably Madhava *(ca* 1350), have argued that cross-cousin marriage is allowable *not only* on grounds of regional 'custom' practiced by 'the learned', but also for the reason that marriage in any of the four approved forms, that is, involving *kanyadana* (the symbolic 'gift' of the bride, laden with jewels, in tribute to a ritual superior), transubstantiates the bride from a *sapinda* of her father to a *sapinda* of her husband: the bride becomes, as the phrase has it, of 'one body' with her husband.[44] By this rather convoluted logic, *both* cross-cousins (MBD and FZD) are defined as non-*sapindas* and therefore marriageable—providing, of course, that the marriage is in the appropriate form. So too, logically speaking, is the elder sister's daughter (eZD),[45] marriage with the latter being another of the preferred arrangements in the region of Dravidian kinship.

Here, in sum, we have the complex legacy that confronted the law makers attempting to codify a uniform Hindu personal law for independent India: a tension between agnatic and cognatic principles of relatedness; between notions of immutable law and mutable custom; and between different and contradictory renderings of the classical law, some traditions of which found arguments to justify the distinctive practices of Dravidian kinship.

Prohibited relations under the Special Marriage Act (1954) and the Hindu Marriage Act (1955)

By 1954–55, caste endogamy was no longer a requirement for a valid Hindu marriage. Nor was the principle of *gotra* exogamy.[46] Hindu reformers had long argued that the primitive eugenic wisdom of the *asagotra* rule made no sense in modern times.[47] It might needlessly inhibit, say the marriage of a Kashmiri brahmin with a Tamil brahmin if both happened to be of the same *gotra,* though they could not conceivably be close blood relations. *However,* both the SMA and the HMA, albeit on different grounds and in different terms, laid down certain exogamous requirements for valid marriage.

Section 4(d) of the SMA specifies that a marriage may be solemnised between two persons *if, inter alia,* 'the parties are not within the degrees of prohibited relationship'. To this is appended the proviso:

> Provided that where a custom governing at least one of the parties permits of a marriage between them, such marriage may be solemnized, notwithstanding that they are within the degrees of prohibited relationship.[48]

Schedule I of the Act lists the specific kin who fall under 'prohibited degrees of relationship' from the viewpoint of the husband and wife respectively. These are (in anthropological terms) opposite sex lineal ascendants or descendants in three generations; the spouses of same sex lineal ascendants and descendants; siblings; nephews and nieces; aunts and uncles; and matrilateral and patrilateral parallel- and cross-cousins. In short, the SMA expressly prohibited, among others, the typical forms of south Indian marriage alliance (MBD, FZD and eZD marriages), which were ultimately 'saved' by 'custom' only through a 1963 amendment to the Act[49] that brought the SMA into line with the HMA in this particular regard (see below).

The HMA scheme of prohibited relationships overlaps to a large extent with that of the SMA, though conceptually speaking it tackles the question of exogamy rather differently. On the one hand, the HMA disallows marriage between persons 'within the prohibited degrees of relationship, unless the custom or usage governing each of them permits of a marriage between the two.'[50] Unlike the SMA, the HMA does not provide a Schedule listing the prohibited partners, but instead provides a sort of genealogical calculus. Perhaps this was the outcome of legislators' earlier criticism of the lists of 'prohibited relationships' in the SMA: They argued that it was an insult to intelligence to prohibit, for instance, the marriage of a man with his great grandmother; and an insult to Hindu wisdom to mindlessly copy British legislation when Hindu law had already developed a comprehensive approach to exogamy.[51] While both the SMA and the HMA prohibit marriage with lineal ascendants or descendants or their spouses (as the case may be),[52] the HMA expands this scheme to include certain other affines—'the wife of the brother or of the father's brother or mother's brother or of the grandfather or grandmother's brother of the other'.[53]

The operative provision from the viewpoint of Dravidian kinship, however, is Section 3 (g) (d) of the Act, which prohibits marriage between two persons 'if the two are brother and sister, *uncle and niece,* aunt and nephew, or *children of brother and sister* or of two brothers or of two sisters' (emphasis added). The inclusion of the children of the brother and sister in the list of prohibited relationships was apparently a change made by the Joint Committee of the two Houses of Parliament before the reintroduction of the Bill into the Lok Sabha in 1955.[54]

Secondly, and this is another point of departure from the SMA, the HMA prohibits marriage of persons who are *sapindas* of each other, *again,* 'unless a custom or usage governing each of them permits of a marriage between the two'.[55] The invocation of the concept of *sapinda*-ship, which is one of the few features that distinguish this Act as 'Hindu' law from its purported model in the British Matrimonial Causes Act, 1950,[56] unambiguously prohibits Dravidian cross-cousin and uncle-niece marriage. Though the limits *of sapinda*-ship are reduced from the classical 7/5 model to just five generations in the line of ascent through the father and three through the mother,[57] the prohibition nonetheless includes quite a broad range of agnatic *and* cognatic kin.[58] It is still needlessly comprehensive, in some opinions.[59]

In sum, then, cross-cousin and uncle–niece marriages are *doubly* prohibited in the HMA, to be saved only by 'custom' or 'usage', which must be longstanding, continuous, reasonable, and not opposed to public policy.[60] Significantly, in this case too, the allowance of 'custom' *was not originally conceded in the Hindu Code Bill,*[61] but had clearly emerged through processes of political negotiation and compromise, the precise details of which remain obscure.

'Saved' by 'custom'

It will have been obvious from the foregoing account of legal provisions and the legislative process that an intense struggle had been going on in the public domain—and no doubt even more behind the scenes—over the legitimacy of Dravidian marriage practices. In this section, we review some of the arguments for and against Dravidian marriage put forward in the course of the Parliamentary debates on the 'prohibited relationship' clauses of the SMA and the HMA.

Although the stated purposes of the two Acts were rather different, as noted, arguments on the clauses overlapped to a considerable degree; the *dramatis personae* were in many cases the same people, reiterating well-rehearsed positions; and arguments that properly speaking should have pertained to the HMA were brought up in connection with the SMA, this being the Bill that was presented first. The fact that two Hindus could choose to be married under either Act[62] further complicated matters, since legislators were acutely aware that the provisions of the one might undermine the legislative intent of the other.[63] Thus, there was constant cross-referencing between the two Bills, as well as to the anticipated provisions of the Hindu laws of succession, adoption and maintenance, still to come.

The debate on the 'prohibited degrees of relationship' was articulated primarily as a debate on the role of 'custom' and 'usage' in the legal regime of post-Independence India; an important subsidiary theme, however, was the science of eugenics. The 'saving' of 'custom'—and the reference was *especially* to Dravidian marriage practices—was a zigzag process. Allowance of custom was first an amendment proposed to the SMA, Clause 4 (d). At the time it was stoutly resisted by the government[64] and outvoted in the House, although pre-Act marriages in contravention of the clause could still be *registered* under the Act[65] (an anomaly that alert legislators did not fail to notice). Meanwhile, however, a proviso regarding 'custom' had been added to the 'prohibited relationship' clauses of the HMA and within a few months, appearing to contradict itself, the Government defended this proviso against spirited criticism and numerous amendments calling for its deletion. Finally, in 1963, the SMA was itself amended[66] to make provision for 'custom' after all, citing as justification the precedent of the HMA.[67] It was altogether a peculiar story.

One set of arguments on degrees of 'prohibited relationships' revolved around the nature of the SMA, in contradistinction to the HMA. Was the SMA to be seen as a 'special' Act, meant just for the few citizens who might seek to contract inter-religious marriages? If so, the majority of citizens would continue to marry under Hindu law, where 'custom' had a recognised role. Or was the SMA a progressive, secular and territorial law for modern times which should seek to bring ever larger numbers of citizens under its sway? If so, it would need to come to an expedient accommodation with customary practices, at least in the short run.[68] The irony of the situation was not lost on critics of the proposed SMA amendment. Love of one's own customs and usages was understandable, Hindu Mahasabha Member V.G. Deshpande conceded, but

> [y]ou are doing away with the [Hindu religious] marriage ceremonies, you are doing away with the sacred fire, you are doing away with all this sacred vow, but you are sticking to all kinds of customs which we do not know, and parading in this House that you are introducing a uniform civil law for the whole country, and that a model system of marriage is being introduced.[69]

The whole idea was 'ridiculous', he said.

Similar arguments were advanced on behalf of the HMA clause on 'prohibited relationships': if the aim of the Code was to unify, clarify and reform the Hindu law of marriage, why should deviant customs be given recognition? Pandit Thakur Das Bhargava was among the vehement critics of the introduction of a 'custom' clause into the HMA. What is the use of a Hindu law, he asked, where 'any person can marry any person and may divorce in any manner he pleases?'[70]

> In [the HMA] clause 2 [on the application of the Act] we say that it is binding on all and in the rest of the clauses we say it is not binding on all the Hindus. They can have their own customs. My submission is that we should be consistent and logical. Let us do the right thing *which will bring about solidarity among the Hindus in India*. We should have a law which will bind all people.[71]

Other parliamentarians were quite explicit in asserting that marriage practices in contravention of the *shastras* (and also, one might emphasise, of north Indian norms) should *not* be allowed under the HMA, or indeed under the SMA as well. They argued that even a secular, territorial law must endorse the principle of sacramental marriage 'that has ruled our country for at least 5,000 years ... And are you passing this legislation', asked N.C. Chatterjee in debate on the SMA, 'following India's *Swadharma,* India's tradition? ... We must keep our own culture, our *dharma,* that is, the essence of our being, our inborn nature, and we have to assimilate it and re-create our own country, our Indian society, on its old, own moorings.'[72] Just see what has happened in Western countries, he added for good measure: not the 'progress' but the 'degradation' of womenfolk.[73]

Also speaking on behalf of Hindu ideals and sentiment, Mulchand Dube reiterated Chatterjee's point:

> This [SMA] is a piece of social legislation and I take it that the object of all social legislation should be to promote unity and solidarity in the society. Now, the two parts of the Schedule mentioned in the Special Marriage Bill permit marriage between persons *which would otherwise be prohibited according to Hindu sentiment.* For instance, the children of cousins can inter-marry. *This kind of thing is repugnant to Hindu society....* [T]he persons who undertake such marriages ... would not only incur the contempt of the rest of society, but this kind of thing may create antagonism and be the cause of disruption of their society. So my submission is that the sentiments of the people who are likely to be affected thereby should receive primary consideration, and *if such a thing is incestuous or repugnant to the sentiments of Hindus,* there is no reason why this should be introduced at the present stage.[74]

Almost a decade later, U.M. Trivedi spoke in almost the same terms in opposing the 1963 SMA Amendment:

> Generally among the Hindus—leave alone the customs pertaining in some parts of South India—*it was always considered derogatory, most derogatory and most heinous, for any man to conceive of an idea of marrying his own sister*—sister in that sense includes maternal uncle's daughter, paternal uncle's daughter or aunt's daughter. To marry a sister like that was considered most abominable in North India. In North India nobody would conceive such an idea.[75]

Moreover, as many speakers pointed out, if you make an exception for 'custom' in one case, where does this end?

> Some hon. friends said that there is a custom among certain sections of the people of marrying [the] maternal uncle's daughter. If these customs are allowed, not only will one be able to marry the maternal uncle's daughter, but he would be able to marry his own sister's daughter, who is considered by some people to be one's own daughter. Not only that: there are customs prevalent among certain communities whereby one can marry the paternal uncle's daughter and sometimes also the sister of half-blood. So it would mean that all these marriages would be allowed. If you allow all these marriages, then there is no use incorporating this provision regarding prohibited degrees of relationship in the [Special Marriage] Bill.[76]

Indeed, as Tek Chand, another active north Indian participant in all these debates put it,

> Custom may be an absurd sort of custom; custom may be that of the *Vam Margis* [Tantric 'left-handed' cults] who do not recognize the

> degree of prohibited relationship. Nevertheless, they have only got to show that it is their custom, whether it is immoral or vicious, whether it is reprehensible or unacceptable to you, or whether it is intolerable. Nonetheless, it is their custom, and you jolly well have to tolerate it.[77]

However, the ultimate and clinching argument for a comprehensive schedule of 'prohibited relationships' was that of eugenics. No particular scientific authorities were cited in this regard: it was taken to be common knowledge that the universal 'horror of incest' was based on established principles of eugenic science. If 'custom' were to be allowed, medical doctor Jaisoorya said,

> [t]here will be no end to concessions to all sorts of customary laws, and the very purpose and spirit of this Bill will be lost. Do you believe that there is no such thing as eugenics, that eugenics is all bunk? In the ancient Egyptian empire, the Egyptian kings married their own sisters. There is no evidence that it was bad.[78] Where are you going to put a stop to all this? It is incestuous. Marriage with your niece is incestuous, whether you call it customary law or not; marriage with your cousin is incestuous, whether you call it customary law or not.[79]

Indeed, it was quite probable, asserted one Member early on in the debates, that consanguine marriages, such as 'are obtainable amongst the Semitic people, amongst the Arabic people, etc.', result in excessive fertility and spell 'ruin' for a country already overpopulated.[80]

For the most part, south Indians (and other advocates of the 'custom' clauses) did *not* seek to contest the eugenic argument: some of them even added their own evidence of the general ill-effects of such practices.[81] They simply argued that such marriages should be legally permitted in a 'transitional' society until such time as people could be 'educated' into *voluntarily* giving them up—an uphill task, apparently[82]—or the customs declined in the natural course.[83] A rare note of defiance on behalf of Dravidian marriage was struck by Dr Rama Rao. Speaking as a medical man, he maintained that there was no conclusive scientific evidence to substantiate the supposed harmful effects of consanguineous marriage: in any case, Parliament was not 'a scientific body deciding eugenics'.[84] 'I want to appeal to our North Indian friends', he said,

> not to have a stone curtain before their eyes but to see beyond the Vindhyas [the mountain range that is taken to divide North from South India] and understand the customs and laws of the South Indians. Most of our thinking is conditioned by things we are used to. People in South India marry their maternal uncles' daughters. That is a very common thing, but the wonderful list of prohibited relationships prohibits such

> marriages.... It is not abnormal and therefore I request my North Indian friends not to see things through their limited glasses only. Customs differ; habits differ....[85]

Bengali Brahmins eat fish; Punjabi women wear trousers—these are disgusting practices in south Indian eyes, he continued by way of illustration. 'Similarly, the thinking of our North Indian friends is conditioned by things they are accustomed to.'[86]

The struggle to prevent the outlawing of Dravidian marriage practices by the combined forces of north Indian prejudice, traditional Hindu orthodoxy and Enlightenment eugenic science was conducted over a decade or more. The upshot was a political compromise on behalf of a nation struggling for unity and stability in changing times. Few legislators actually defended Dravidian marriage practices, *except as* 'custom', and only one Member in my recall (V.G. Deshpande) referred to *shastric* endorsement of cross-cousin marriage.[87] The ultimate solution was a political one, however. This was no time to drive a wedge between north and south India, whatever one's opinions on Hindu ethics, eugenics, or other people's 'incestuous' unions. As Law Minister Pataskar put it, summing up the debate on 'prohibited relationships' in the HMA:

> I know that amongst the people in the North the prohibited degrees vary from the prohibited degrees in the South. There are customs in the South even amongst the highest [castes], the Brahmins, . . . which permit marriages between certain persons which are not allowed in the North. *It is not desirable to enter into controversy whether one is right or wrong.* It has been a subject matter of controversy in the past and it will continue to be so for some time in future also.[88]

The answer is to lay down a definitive scheme of 'prohibited relationships'—to show 'how the wind blows and what is the trend of public opinion', but to allow people to follow their own customs if they so desired:[89]

> . . . I would appeal to my hon. Friend . . . to think of the times in which there are already enough problems *and we should not add to it one of North or South.* Therefore, . . .—whatever our own ideas may be—it may be that what the hon. Member feels is more correct than what is followed by other people—it is much better to go along with the rest. . . . No one group of people living in the North or East can debate that one custom is bad. I think this should be better than exactitude in any way whatsoever.[90]

But what of the *gender* politics of 'prohibited relationships'? Both marriage Bills, the SMA and the HMA, were promoted as gestures towards women's equality;[91] both were critiqued, too, as likely to be injurious for women, particularly when it came to the liberalization of divorce. But these battles were fought for the most part over clauses on monogamy, divorce, age of marriage, maintenance and restitution of conjugal rights. The question of 'prohibited relationships' was not construed as a 'gender' issue affecting women's status one way or the other. A stray and tantalizing exception was the report by a southern legislator, Vimla Devi, of unsuccessful attempts by women's organizations to campaign against consanguineous marriage.[92]

Case law on questions of 'prohibited relationships'

The struggle for the legal recognition of Dravidian marriage practices in post-Independence India appeared to have been won by 1963 when the SMA was amended to allow breach of the 'prohibited relationships' condition on grounds of 'custom' and 'usage'. There remained a practical problem, however. 'Custom' was not recognised *ipso facto,* but *had to be established*—either by government notification (SMA) or by due legal processes (HMA). Given the litigiousness of Indians in all walks of life, one would surely have expected vigorous exploitation of the vagaries of these clauses. As it is, legal textbooks confirm that almost *all* clauses of the Hindu personal law have attracted robust case law, and clauses that bear on the validity of marriage are part of the routine armory of those claiming or contesting succession to property or seeking to avoid prosecution for bigamy or suits of maintenance, etc.[93]

'Custom' is indeed amply contested in the context of, say, Section 7 of the HMA, which specifies the ceremonies required for a valid Hindu marriage. All *other* grounds for nullity—bigamy, want of consent, impotency, mental incompetence, age of marriage, etc.—are also exploited to the full.[94] *But,* the clauses on 'prohibited relationships' have attracted hardly any case law worth looking at.[95] Much of the exemplary case law refers to judgements under Anglo-Hindu law, and though many of the latter do indeed involve south Indian cases, more recent case law is not especially focused on Dravidian kinship practices—our specific interest here—but deals with customary usage in other regions.[96]

Among the more commonly cited south Indian cases, two general points of law concerning the status and definition of 'custom' are seen to be at issue. The first concerns the density of cases required to evidence a 'custom' for the community concerned. For instance, in *K. Kamakshi vs K. Mani,*[97] a wife sought the annulment of her marriage (contesting her husband's plea for the Restitution of Conjugal Rights) on the grounds that she and her husband were within the prohibited degrees of relationship (her father and the husband's mother being brother and sister respectively), and that there was no custom in her community (identified as 'Dravida Brahmin') that allowed such a marriage.[98] The plea had been initially dismissed on the grounds that such a custom (matrilateral cross-cousin marriage, in anthropological terms) had been satisfactorily established, but on retrial it was affirmed that the grounds for asserting the existence of the 'custom' in this community were rather flimsy, to say the least:

> The sum total of the evidence [of community leaders and the learned witnesses appearing on behalf of the wife] is that there was but a single instance of a marriage [of first cousins] some time in 1918, but this was objected to by members of the community, resulting in a conference which decided that the marriage was prohibited. According to evidence on the [husband's] side, there were one or two marriages that took place in 1961 and 1965. That is the whole evidence to establish a custom permitting marriage between parties within the prohibited degrees in the community.[99]

Clearly, these stray cases were inadequate proof, for a custom needs to be sustained over 'a reasonably long time':

> Short of this, a custom cannot be the result of a process of approximation or analogy or deduction from other customs prevalent among communities or sections of the people other than that to which the parties in dispute belong.[100]
>
> A custom cannot be extended by analogy. It should be established inductively, and not by *a priori* methods. ... Evidence in this case falls very far short of establishing a custom prior to 1955 [when the HMA came into effect]. Even thereafter, only two instances have been brought to the notice of the Court, which again would be insufficient to make out a custom which would relax the condition imposed by Section V (iv).[101]

In the second case, much cited in the legal literature,[102] a property dispute between the descendants of a man of the Reddiar caste of Tirunelveli who had married his own grand-daughter (daughter's daughter) as his fourth wife, the existence of a custom of marriage between a girl and her maternal grandfather was deemed 'credible', if not widespread, in the light of five other known instances in the community concerned. All the same, the judge was explicit that:

> The requisites of a valid custom are that the same should be ancient, certain and reasonable and that [they] also should not be opposed to decency or morality. ... *A custom which is abhorrent to decency and morality, however long practiced and recognised by a particular community, can find no enforcement by a Court of Law.* We therefore feel no doubt whatever that the civilised and cultured society in which we

> live and the progressive society in which we are should not approve of an incest which would not find favour even under primitive or tribal society. *The attempt in this case is to get a judicial recognition of the propriety of a most revolting and obscene practice under the guise and pretext of usage and custom said to have the force of law.*[103]

From this, the logical next step would be legal acknowledgement that 'a man can marry his own grand-mother', was the judge's final riposte![104]

'But *everybody knows* that south Indians marry their cousins', was the explanation of one legal expert from whom I had sought to know why the case law in this area was so sparse. She presumably meant that it would normally be inexpedient for a lawyer to try and prove otherwise in the southern region (notwithstanding the judgement in *K. Kamakshi v. K. Mani,* cited above). Nonetheless, extrapolating from the ethnographic record one can imagine cases where one form of cross-cousin marriage is customarily acceptable, the other not; or cross-cousin marriage is approved but uncle-niece marriage deplored; or a marriage may be correct in one reckoning, but improper in another. All such uncertainties, one might think, would be grist to the lawyers' mill. On the other hand, a practicing lawyer construed the problem as a simple one of *locus standi:* It is unlikely, he suggested, that either party to a null marriage within the prohibited degrees would be motivated to file a nullity petition. But his answer disregards the plethora of nullity suits on *other* grounds, and the considerable utilisation of nullity clauses by heirs and other interested parties in property disputes. The puzzle remains.

Conclusion: 'prohibited relationships' or allowable custom?

South India as a region has long been known for its singular rules of marriage which, along with other related practices, appear to have had the effect of moderating the sternly patrilineal emphasis of the rules and practices of Indo-Aryan kinship. These particularities have latterly become the focus of social science attention—not alone by kinship specialists, who seem to have reached a dead-end on the issue some time ago, but by demographers, development economists, and feminists, who have taken a keen interest in the southern region's superior track-record on questions of social development and gender equity.

Yet, these same rules and practices were de-legitimised on grounds of morality and eugenic science by supposedly progressive post-Independence legislation. Ultimately, a lengthy process of political lobbying and negotiation, concluding in 1963 with the amendment to the prohibited relationships' clause of the SMA, ensured their 'saving' on grounds of 'custom'. It appears that the political class desired a 'progressive' legal regime, but ultimately *not* at the cost of driving a wedge between the Hindus of north and south India.

To keep things in proportion, the struggle to ensure the (albeit qualified) recognition of Dravidian kinship practices was a relatively minor one in the overall context of marriage law reform: as indicated, questions of monogamy, divorce, and the age of marriage were the salient points of controversy. Yet there *was,* obviously, an intense struggle going on both in public and behind the scenes, and it is rather surprising that there has been almost complete silence on the question ever since, whether in public debate or in academic discourse. Nor has the legal profession seized the opportunity to exploit the vagaries of the concept of 'custom' in this particular regard. And it appears that there is no sense of grievance over the issue, even on the part of activists of the anti-Brahmin movements which have been a powerful force on the south Indian political scene for many decades.[105]

Is this because Dravidian marriage practices are now securely 'saved' by the provision for reasonable customs and usages? Are south Indians excessively embarrassed by their usages in the face of the hegemonic ideology of Indo-Aryan kinship? Or do they just discreetly seek to avoid controversy, rather than draw further attention to south India's 'incestuous' singularity?

Whatever the answer, it remains a matter of curiosity, if not of wider public concern, that the de-legitimisation of Dravidian kinship has *not* been construed as a 'gender' issue, though the distinctive marriage practices of the Dravidian culture area appear to be at the core of the differentiation of north and south India, in family and kinship, as in a whole range of social development indicators.

Acknowledgements

I am grateful to Amita Dhanda and Archana Parashar for their encouragement and helpful suggestions. I have rehearsed these ideas in two earlier papers (Uberoi 2002; 2005).

Notes

1 The Special Marriage Act, No. 43 of 1954; The Hindu Marriage Act, No. 25 of 1955.

2 See Sivaramayya (1978); Agnes (2005). Agnes's position on this issue (2005: 117–18) is not exactly transparent. On the one hand, she deplores the implied dilution of the progressive and secular character of the SMA; on the other, she concedes that the original 'prohibited relationships' clause reflects the practices (and kinship ideology) of the 'dominant Hindu upper castes', in contradistinction to 'the customary practices of several lower castes, as well as ... Muslims, Christians, Parsis and Jews' in India.

3 Section 2, Act 32 of 1963.

4 The distinctive structure of Dravidian kinship terminologies was first highlighted by Lewis Henry Morgan (1871), one of the founding figures of the discipline

of Anthropology. On the hypothesised link between the Dravidian kinship terminologies and the practice of cross-cousin marriage, see the seminal contribution by the famous Cambridge anthropologist, W.H.R. Rivers (1907). The idea was taken up subsequently by (among others) Karve (1965; see also the excerpt in Uberoi 1993: 50–73); and—from a different theoretical perspective—by Dumont (1953, rpt 1983). On Dravidian kinship in relation to Indo-Aryan kinship, see Trautmann (1981: chap. 3; 1993: 74–90).

5 Karve (1965).

6 An important predecessor in this way of thinking was Sir Henry Sumner Maine (1822–1888), the famous author of *Ancient Law* (1961), who saw in the kinship regimes of (north) Indian communities a near approximation to the 'ancient' stage of 'patriarchy' as human society evolved from 'status' to 'contract' (Maine 1895; Uberoi 1993: 8–12).

7 This is the practice termed 'village' or 'territorial' exogamy in the ethnographic literature. Marriages and liaisons *within* the village are regarded as heinous and attract strong sanctions. See Chowdhry (1998: 339–42); Hershman (1981: 133–37); Lewis (1958: 160–61).

8 Collected in Kolenda (1987: chaps 1, 2 & 5), a book which was dedicated to the memory of Irawati Karve.

9 Kolenda's concept of 'bargaining' is somewhat different from the interpretation recently given it in the writings of feminist economists such as Agarwal (1994: chap. 2], though substantive features overlap.

10 For instance, the south has more female-favourable sex ratios, higher levels of women's education, and a greater proportion of women in salaried occupations (Kolenda 1987: chap. 5); see also Raju *et al.* (1999).

11 Dyson and Moore (1983: 42, emphasis added).

12 Regional asymmetries in sex ratios have attracted a great deal of scholarly attention on the part of both demographers and feminists. See, among others, Agnihotri (2000); Miller (1981; 1989); L. Visaria (1999); P. Visaria (1972).

13 Subsequent studies have in general endorsed Dyson and Moore's observations; for instance, Basu (1992); Das Gupta (1995); Raju *et al.* (1999).

14 Agarwal (1994).

15 Ibid., chap. 8.

16 See Drèze and Sen (1996); Jeffrey (1993).

17 Sen (2001).

18 Ibid.: 12, emphasis added.

19 Apart from the comments of Sivaramayya (1978) and Agnes (2005) and some stray remarks by the inimitable Derrett (1978: 24–27, 51–52, 61–63), the exogamic provisions of the marriage laws find no mention in standard secondary writings on the evolution of Indian family law—for instance, Menski (2001); Parashar (1992).

20 On the transformation of matriliny, see e.g., Dube (1997); Nair (1996: chap. 6); Saradamoni (1999). The gender implications of the continuance of community-specific personal law regimes in India are addressed in particular by Parashar (1992).

21 See Agarwal (1994); Derrett (1968: chap. 10); Forbes (1996); Parasher (1992); Sarkar (1976); Som (1994), among others. See also Law Minister Pataskar's introduction to the Hindu Marriage Bill, *Lok Sabha Debates* (hereafter *LSD*), 26.iv. 1955, cols 6468–70.

22 Originally introduced to legalise Brahmo marriages. Members of the reformist Brahmo Samaj, founded in the 19th century, repudiated Hindu rituals. At the same time, the form of marriage that they instituted could not be condoned as 'customary', for 'custom' by definition must be of long standing. See Biswas *LSD,* 26.iv.1954, cols 7798–99. A similar problem arose in the case of Tamil non-Brahmin marriages. See Menski (2001: 13–15).
23 This was corrected for Hindus married under the Act by an Amendment in 1976 (Article 21A, SMA).
24 Shastri, *LSD,* 16.xii.1953, col. 2319.
25 See Law Minister Biswas's introduction to the Special Marriage Bill, *LSD,* 19. v.1954, cols 7797–99; also Chakravartty, *LSD,* 16.xii.1953, col. 2317; *LSD,* 7.ix.l954, cols 1222–24; Shah, *LSD,* 19.v.1954, cols 7831–32; Chowdary *LSD,* 20.v.1954, cols 7880–82; Nehru, *LSD,* 14.ix.1954, cols 1860–62. Article 44 of the Indian Constitution states as a Directive Principle: 'The State shall endeavour to secure for the citizens a uniform civil code through the territory of India.'
26 Rao, *LSD,* 7.ix.l954, cols 1214–16.
27 Chowdary, *LSD,* 20.v.1954, cols 7881–82.
28 Chakravartty, *LSD,* 16.xii.1953, col. 2317. This point of view was also stated with eloquence by Prime Minister Nehru, *LSD,* 21.v.1954, cols 8048–54.
29 Sharma, *LSD,* 17.xii.1953, cols 2370–71.
30 See Derrett (1968: chap. 10).
31 Pataskar, *LSD,* 26.iv. 1955, cols 646S*ff.* It did not escape critics and cynics that divorce and remarriage were already allowed, often on *more* liberal grounds, by the customary law of an estimated 80 per cent of the Hindu population; and that the Act's cautious allowance of divorce made this law at once 'brahminising' for the majority, and 'liberalising' for the upper caste minority.
32 Pataskar, *LSD,* 26.iv.1955, cols 6475–502.
33 Mulla (1998: 41); Singh (1983: 18–19, 41).
34 For instance Diwan (1993); Mayne (1991); Mulla (1998). The Parliamentary debates we consider below also offer ample illustration of this point.
35 Derrett (1978).
36 For elaboration of the principles of classical Hindu law, see in particular the authoritative and pioneering work of P.V. Kane (1930–62: especially Bk II, Pt 1), and Trautmann (1981: chap. 4); Derrett (1968; 1978); Lingat (1973); Prabhu (1955:154*ff*; and others, including standard compendia of Hindu law, such as Banerjee (1915; rpt 1984: 57*ff*; Mayne (1991); Mulla (1998: vol. 1, chap 22), and more recently Diwan (1993: chaps 3&7).
37 Dumont (1983: 14–15); also Madan (1989: 91–92, 287).
38 Kane (1930–62: Bk II, Pt. 1, 482*ff*; Kapadia (1955: 19–21).
39 Trautmann (1981:239*ff*).
40 The fourth class, the Shudras, were not recognised to have *gotras,* and were allowed to be governed in matters of family life by their own customs. The Untouchables were considered to be beyond the pale of Hindu law.
41 Trautmann (1981: 246*ff*; also Dumont (1983).
42 A cognatic, *sapinda*-like concept is invoked in the so-called three- or four-*gotra* rule of marriage in north Indian kinship. This rule prohibits marriage with partners from the patrilineal descent groups, even the patronymics, of the father, the father's mother's father, the mother's father, and, possibly, the mother's mother's father.
43 See Trautmann (1981: 302–04). For further discussion see Derrett (1968: 86–87; 1978: 63); Kane (1930–62: Bk. II, Pt. 1, 458–67); Kapadia (1955: 117*ff*); Mayne (1991: 134).

44 Trautmann (1981: 291). Trautmann (1981: 438–46) also provides a useful translation of Madhava's comment on the authoritative text of the *Yajnavalkya Smrti* (1.52) that prohibits marriage with a *sapinda.*

45 On the other hand, the Dravidian taboo on marriage with the matrilateral parallel cousin might be weakened by the same logic (cf Kane, 1930–62: Bk. II, Pt. 1, 469). See Derrett's critical comments on Madhava's rationalisation of Dravidian marriage (1968: 86–87), which creates a predicament for those castes that practice marriage in the *Asura* form (marriage with 'bride price', formerly widely prevalent in south India).

46 The case for inter-caste marriages had already been won through the Hindu Marriage Disabilities Removal Act 1946, and the Hindu Marriages Validity Act 1949, which were repealed with the coming into force of the HMA (HMA, Section 30). Section 29(1) of the HMA confirms the provisions of this earlier legislation: 'A marriage solemnised between Hindus before the commencement of this Act (1955), which is otherwise valid, shall not be deemed to be invalid, or ever to have been invalid by reason only of the fact that the parties thereto belonged to the same *gotra* or *pravara* or belonged to different religions, castes or subdivisions of the same caste.' The term 'religion' in this Section refers to those religions, sects and reformist groups which are defined as 'Hindu' under Section 2(1) of the HMA: it includes Buddhists, Jains and Sikhs, but explicitly excludes Muslims, Christians, Parsis, and Jews.

47 For example Iyengar (1941: 16); Kapadia (1955: 120–21).

48 'Custom' is here defined to mean 'any rule which the State Government may, by notification in the Official Gazette, specify ... as applicable to members of that tribe, community or family.' It should be 'continuously and uniformly observed for a long time', 'not unreasonable or opposed to public policy', and, if a 'family' usage, not 'discontinued' at any point of time (SMA Section 4, 'Explanation').

49 Act 32 of 1963, Section 2 (c).

50 HMA Section 3 (g) (a) and (b).

51 See Trivedi, *LSD,* 17.xii.1953, cols 2411–12; More, *LSD,* l.ix.1954, cols 810–11. Thundered More: '.... The First Schedule is not a good thing. When you concretise certain facts you are reduced to such a ridiculousness.... If this legislation is taken up by some foreigner, he would get an impression that in India people are out to marry their grandfather's mother and therefore, the sovereign Parliament was forced to say that you cannot marry that lady. By the time he is ready to marry, she will be in her grave already' (Ibid.).

52 HMA Section 3 (g) (a) and (b).

53 HMA Section 3 (g) (c). This provision expressly disallows leviratic marriage, a common practice in many parts of India, including the northwest.

54 Pataskar, *LSD,* 26.iv1955, col. 6475. The cross-cousins (though *not* the brother's widow] were also prohibited as *sapindas.*

55 HMA Section 5 (v).

56 See Derrett (1978).

57 HMA Section 3 (f) (i) and (ii).

58 For a working out of *sapinda* relationships in the context of the HMA, see e.g., Mulla (1998: vol. 2, 29–36). That practicing lawyers find little use for this provision of the Act (Section V (v)) is surely demonstrated by the garbled, confusing, and frequently incorrect explanations of *sapinda*-ship provided in legal textbooks, including even such recognised authorities as Mulla (1998) and Diwan (1993).

59 See Kapadia (1955: 121).
60 HMA Section 3 (a).
61 See Kapadia (1955:257).
62 Originally made possible by Sir Hari Singh Gour's 1923 amendment to the SMA (1872). See Biswas's statement, *LSD*, 19.v.1954, cols 7802–04.
63 See for instance Raghavachari, *LSD*, 7.ix.l954, col. 1221; also Chakravartty *LSD*, 7.ix.1954, cols 1223–24, among many others.
64 See Biswas's statement, *LSD*, 19.v.1954, cols 7797–7811–12; also *LSD*, l.ix.1954, col. 836.
65 SMA Clause 15.
66 Many members sought to know the source of the supposed 'demand' for amendment of the Act. The only person actually named in this regard was the nationalist leader, Rajagopalachari. See Mishra, *LSD*, 28.viii.1963, col. 3268.
67 The procedure for establishing 'custom' was somewhat different, however. In the case of the amended SMA, custom was to be established by state government notification, rather than through judicial procedure, as in the case of the HMA. See Derrett's skeptical comment on the 'cumbersome' procedure of notification; writing in 1978, he had not encountered any instances of such notification (1978: 27).
68 See Das, *LSD*, 8.ix.l954, col. 1256.
69 Ibid., cols 1229-30.
70 Bhargava, *LSD*, 3.v.1955, col. 7458.
71 Ibid., cols 7458–59, emphasis added.
72 Chatterjee, *LSD*, 17.xii.1953, cols 2384–85.
73 Ibid., col. 2386-87.
74 Dube, *LSD*, 2.ix. 1954, cols 850-51, emphasis added. See also Dube's proposed amendment to the SMA First Schedule, 16.ix.1954, cols 2159–60. Dube was of the opinion that exogamous prohibitions should extend to second cousins at least.
75 Trivedi, *LSD*, 28.viii.1963, col. 3234, emphasis added.
76 Dhabhi, *LSD*, 8.ix.1954, col. 1257.
77 Chand, *LSD*, 13.ix.1954, col. 1754.
78 Presumably he was replying to a point made by Dr Rama Rao (see below] that there was no adequate scientific evidence to support the supposition of the ill effects of consanguineous marriage.
79 Jaisoorya, *LSD*, 7.ix.l954, col. 1226. Among many other references to eugenics, see e.g., Biswas, *LSD*, 19.v.1954, col. 7811; Shah, *LSD*, 19.v.1954, cols 7835–36. Eugenics is the rationalisation that many south Indians give nowadays for the discontinuance of consanguineous marriages. Some south Indians have also sought to distinguish the relatively innocuous cross-cousin marriage from the more exotic practice of uncle-niece marriage, on both eugenic and moral grounds, e.g., Iyengar (1941: 17).
80 Trivedi, *LSD*, 17.xii.1953, col. 2413. See Trivedi's similar comment almost a decade later, *LSD*, 28.viii.1963, col. 3235.
81 Vimla Devi, *LSD*, 28.viii.1963, cols 3230–34.
82 Ibid., col. 3232.
83 R. Venkataraman, *LSD*, 3.v.1955, cols 7542–43; Velayudhan, *LSD*, 7.ix.l954, cols 1235–36. Punjab Legislator Sardar Hukam Singh, however, was convinced that consanguine marriages would increase if women were given property rights under the HSA. Either that, he said, or one would see female infanticide on a large scale (*LSD*, 3.v. 1955, col. 7485).

84 Rao, *LSD,* 7.ix.l954, col. 1214.
85 Ibid., *LSD,* 7.ix. 1954, col. 1214.
86 Ibid., cols. 1214-16.
87 Deshpande, *LSD,* 7.ix.1954, cols 1227–30. Said Deshpande, who claimed to belong to a caste that practiced cross-cousin marriages: 'I would accept challenge from anybody to prove that they are against *shastras,* or against any laws of eugenics. If you read the old *nibandas* and *prabhandas,* there are very scholarly discussions on this point' (Ibid., col. 1227). Deshpande objected only to smuggling recognition of these practices into the SMA under the provision for 'custom'.
88 Pataskar, *LSD,* 3.v.1955, cols 7567–68, emphasis added.
89 Ibid.
90 Ibid., col. 7568; see similarly Mishra, *LSD,* 28.viii.1963, cols 3266–70. Though it might be assumed that the 'unity' of India in this context meant the unity of *Hindu* Indians, at least one Member argued for tolerance of Muslim (cross- and parallel-) cousin marriage, abominable as it might seem to Hindu sentiment: After all, he urged, Muslims too had 'contributed to the progress of our country and of the world' (Basu, *LSD,* 14.ix.1954, col. 1850).
91 See e.g., Chakravartty *LSD,* 16.xii.1953, cols 2317–18; *LSD,* 14.ix.1954, cols 1823–32; *LSD,* 2.v.1955, cols 7254–62; Pataskar, *LSD,* 26.iv.1955, col. 6500; More, *LSD,* 2.v 1955, cols 7392-95.
92 Vimla Devi, *LSD,* 28.viii.1963, col. 3232.
93 See Menski (2001: 35–43, and chap. 4).
94 Uberoi (1996).
95 An observation confirmed by search of the Supreme Court cases.
96 For instance, Punjab and Haryana, where Hindu law was not earlier in force. See e.g., *Shakuntala Devi v. Amar Nath,* AIR 1982 P & H, 221.
97 *Madras Law Journal Reports* (hereafter *MLJR*), 1970(2): 477–78.
98 The couple, married in 1960, had incidentally lived together for some time before the separation that induced the plea for Restitution.
99 *MLJR,* 1970(2): 477.
100 Presumably the judge, K. Veeraswami, was referring to the fact that Dravidian communities *in general* have customarily approved marriage with the mother's brother's daughter.
101 *MLJR,* 1970(2): 477.
102 *Balusami Reddiar v. Balakrishna Reddiar,* AIR 1957 Madras 97.
103 Ibid.: 99, 100, emphasis added. Quoting the British ethnographer Edgar Thurston, the judge also took the occasion to allude to some other morally questionable marital/sexual customs of the community concerned, such as the cohabitation of a woman married to a very young boy with older maternal or paternal relatives.
104 Ibid.: 99.
105 M.S.S. Pandian, personal communication.

References

Agarwal, B. 1994. *A Field of One's Own: Gender and Land Rights in South Asia.* Cambridge: Cambridge University Press.

Agnes, F. 2005. 'Law and Gender Inequality: The Politics of Women's Rights in India', in Mala Khullar (ed.), *Writing the Women's Movement: A Reader.* New Delhi: Zubaan Books, pp. 113–30.

Agnihotri, S. 2000. *Sex Ratio Patterns in the Indian Population.* New Delhi: Sage Publications.

Banerjee, G. (1915) 1984. *The Hindu Law of Marriage and Stridhana.* 4th edn. Delhi: Mittal Publications.

Basu, A. 1992. *Culture, the Status of Women and Demographic Behaviour.* Oxford: Clarendon Press.

Chowdhry, P. 1998. 'Enforcing Cultural Codes: Gender and Violence in Northern India', in Mary E. John and Janaki Nair (eds), *A Question of Silence: The Sexual Economies of Modern India.* New Delhi: Kali for Women, pp. 332–67.

Das Gupta, M. 1995. 'Life-course Perspectives on Women's Autonomy and Health Outcomes', *American Anthropologist*, vol. 97(3): 481–91.

Derrett, J.D.M. 1968. *Religion, Law and the State in India.* London: Faber & Faber.

———. 1978. *The Death of a Marriage Law: Epitaph for the Rishis.* New Delhi: Vikas Publishers.

Diwan, P. 1993. *Modern Hindu Law.* 9th edn. Allahabad: Allahabad Law Agency.

Drèze, J. and Amartya Sen. 1996. *India: Economic Development and Social Opportunity.* Pbk edn. Delhi: Oxford University Press.

Dube, L. 1997. *Women and Kinship: Comparative Perspectives on Gender in South and Southeast Asia.* New Delhi: Vistaar Publications.

Dumont, L. (1953) 1983. 'The Dravidian Kinship Terminology as an Expression of Marriage', *Man* 53, art. 54; rpt in *idem, Affinity as a Value: Marriage Alliance in South India, with Comparative Essays on Australia.* Chicago: University of Chicago Press, pp. 3–35.

———. 1983. 'The Debt to Ancestors and the Category of *Sapinda*', in Charles Malamoud (ed.), *Debt and Debtors.* New Delhi: Vikas Publishers, pp. 1–20.

Dyson, T and Mick Moore. 1983. 'On Kinship Structure, Female Autonomy and Demographic Behavior in India', *Population and Development Review*, vol. 9(1): 35–60.

Forbes, G. 1996. *Women in Modern India [The New Cambridge History of India,* vol. IV(2)]. Cambridge: Cambridge University Press.

Hershman, P. 1981. *Punjabi Kinship and Marriage.* Delhi: Hindustan.

Iyengar, S.S. 1941. 'Hindu Law Reform', *Madras Law Journal* (Golden Jubilee Number): 8–24.

Jeffrey, R. 1993. *Politics, Women and Well-being: How Kerala became a Model.* Delhi: Oxford University Press.

Kane, P.V. 1930–62. *History of Dharmasastras.* Poona: Bhandarkar Oriental Research Institute.

Kapadia, K.M. 1955. *Marriage and Family in India.* Bombay: Oxford University Press.

Karve, I. 1965. *Kinship Organization in India.* 2nd rev. edn. Bombay: Asia Publishing House.

Kolenda, P. 1987. *Regional Differences in Family Structure in India.* Jaipur: Rawat Publications.

Lewis, O. 1958. *Village Life in Northern India: Studies in a Delhi Village.* New York: Vintage Books.

Lingat, R. 1973. *The Classical Law of India.* Trans. J.D.M. Derrett. Berkeley: University of California Press.

Madan, T.N. 1989. *Family and Kinship: A Study of the Pandits of Rural Kashmir.* 2nd edn. Delhi: Oxford University Press.

Maine, H.S. (1861) 1972. *Ancient Law.* London: Everyman Edition.

———. (1871) 1895. *Village Communities in the Fast and the West.* London: John Murray.
Mayne, J.D. (1878) 1991. *Treatise on Hindu Law and Usage.* 13th rev.edn. New Delhi: Bharat Law House.
Menski, W.F. 2001. *Modern Indian Family Law.* Richmond, UK: Curzon Press.
Miller, B. 1981. *The Endangered Sex: Neglect of Female Children in Rural India.* Ithaca: Cornell University Press.
———. 1989. 'Changing Patterns of Juvenile Sex Ratios in Rural India, 1961–1971', *Economic and Political Weekly*, vol. 24(22): 1229–36.
Morgan, L.H. 1871. *Systems of Consanguinity and Affinity of the Human Family.* Washington: Smithsonian Institution.
Mulla, D. (1912) 1998. *Principles of Hindu Law.* New Delhi: Buttersworth.
Nair, J. 1996. *Women and Law in Colonial India.* New Delhi: Kali for Women.
Parashar, A. 1992. *Women and Family Law Reform in India: Uniform Civil Code and Gender Equality.* New Delhi: Sage Publications.
Prabhu, P.H. (1940) 1955. *Hindu Social Organization: A Study in Socio-psychological and Ideological Foundations.* Bombay: Popular Prakashan.
Raju S. *et al.* (comp.). 1999. *Atlas of Men and Women in India.* New Delhi: Kali for Women.
Rivers, W.H.R. 1907. 'The Marriage of Cousins in India', *Journal of the Royal Asiatic Society of Great Britain and Ireland*, pp. 611–40.
Saradamoni, K. 1999. *Matriliny Transformed: Family, Law and Ideology in Twentieth Century Travancore.* New Delhi: Sage Publications.
Sarkar, L. 1976. 'Jawaharlal Nehru and the Hindu Code Bill', in B.R. Nanda (fed.), *Indian Women from Purdah to Modernity.* New Delhi: Vikas Publishers, pp. 87–98.
Sen, A. 2001. 'Many Faces of Gender Inequality.' *Frontline,* 9 November: 4–14.
Singh, J. 1983. *Hindu Law of Marriage and Divorce.* Delhi: Pioneer Publications.
Sivaramayya, B. 1978. 'The Special Marriage Act, 1954, goes Awry', in V. Bagga (ed.), *Studies in the Hindu Marriage and Special Marriage Acts.* Bombay: N.M. Tripathi.
Som, R. 1994. 'Jawaharlal Nehru and the Hindu Code: A Victory of Symbol over Substance', *Modern Asian Studies,* vol. 28(1): 165–94.
Trautmann, T.R. 1981. *Dravidian Kinship.* Cambridge: Cambridge University Press.
Uberoi, P. fed.). 1993. *Family, Kinship and Marriage in India.* Delhi: Oxford University Press.
———. 1996. 'When is a Marriage not a Marriage? Sex, Sacrament and Contract in Hindu Marriage', in Patricia Uberoi (ed.), *Social Reform, Sexuality and the State.* New Delhi: Sage Publications, pp. 319–45.
———. 2002. 'Kinship Varieties and Political Experience: Legislating the Family in Post-Independence India', in Emiko Ochiai (ed.), *The Logic of Female Succession: Rethinking Patriarchy and Patrilinearity in Global and Historical Perspective.* Symposium Proceedings No. 19. Kyoto: International Research Center for Japanese Studies, pp. 147–76.
———. 2005. 'Legislating the Family in Post-Independence India', in Bharati Ray (ed.), *Women of India: Colonial and Postcolonial Periods.* New Delhi: Sage Publications, pp. 26–52.
Visaria, L. 1999. 'Deficit of Women in India: Magnitude, Trends, Regional Variations and Determinants', in Bharati Ray and Aparna Basu (eds), *From Independence*

Towards Freedom: Indian Women since 1947. Delhi: Oxford University Press, pp. 80–99.
Visaria, P. 1972. *The Sex Ratio of the Population of India*. Monograph No. 10. New Delhi: Registrar General, Government of India.

PART III

Plural Domains of Law and Governance

11 Conflict Resolution in Tribal Societies of Northeast India

Legal Pluralism and Indian Democracy

Nandita Haksar

'Conflict Resolution Systems in the Tribal Societies of Northeast India: Legal Pluralism and Indian Democracy' by Nandita Haksar (Melvil Pereira, Bitopi Dutta and Binita Kakati, eds, *Legal Pluralism and Indian Democracy: Tribal Conflict Resolution Systems in Northeast India*, Copyright © 2018, Routledge, Chapter 1). Reproduced by permission of Taylor & Francis Group.

I wrote on tribal laws in the 1990s but since then I have become much more aware of the political and social complexities of societies in the Northeast. While I would still argue that customary law may be useful for conflict resolution, I have had to rethink many of my assumptions, both about the tribal communities living in the Northeast and the possibilities for its application within the existing constitutional framework. This is a vast subject, so perhaps it would be best if I consider the main concepts which we need to discuss before we can establish some firm ideas about how tribal laws can be used for resolving contemporary conflicts.

Conflicts

In the context of the Northeast region of India, conflict is presumed to mean either conflict between non-state armed groups and the state or intra-community clashes. However, there are many other kinds of conflicts, and to my mind not all conflicts have a negative impact on society. Society is always changing; stagnant societies die. And these changes are brought about by conflicts. In many cases conflicts lead to violence and that, too, may not necessarily have a negative impact on society.

The sweeping condemnation of all violent conflict tends to obfuscate the complexities of the political and social causes. To the best of my knowledge the studies on conflicts in the Northeast assume that the conflicts have a negative impact on Indian democracy. While it is true that in recent years the armed groups can be rightly blamed for indiscipline, leading to poor relations with civilian populations, and extortions, in the past the challenge to the Indian state did indeed lead to greater autonomy to the region and allowed the societies to preserve their cultures, languages and ways of life.

DOI: 10.4324/9781003299561-11

I would argue that if the communities in the Northeast had not resorted to armed resistance to cultural domination they may have long been forgotten or even destroyed. However, I also believe that armed resistance without political vision is not conducive to healthy change (Haksar 2013). Broadly speaking, there are six kinds of conflicts:

1 Individuals versus the state;
2 Communities versus the state;
3 State versus the state (questions of federalism);
4 State versus corporations;
5 Individual versus the community;
6 Community versus community.

Individual versus the state

As a human rights lawyer I have mostly dealt with the first kind of conflict. This conflict is between an individual or a group of individuals whose rights have been violated by the state. In the context of the Northeast most of my cases have focused on the violation of human rights by the Indian security forces.

In those cases which involved the violation of an individual's human rights, when they had been illegally detained or tortured, the courts could be effective in providing relief. However, when the number of persons affected by the state was much greater, encompassing several villages, the legal and constitutional framework did not provide relief and left the people with no forum in which they could get their grievances redressed.

For instance, in one case in which the Assam Rifles committed large-scale human rights violations on the people living in more than 30 villages in the Senapati District of Manipur during the counterinsurgency operation in 1987, code-named Operation Bluebird, the Gauhati High Court has not yet given its judgement, after 26 long years (Haksar and Hongray 2011).

If an individual is involved in a conflict with the state on behalf of the entire community, such as the case of Irom Sharmila, then the state is unable to resolve the conflict within the legal framework.

Even in cases where the courts can protect the individual, the legal system is such that the aggrieved person has to spend a lot of time and money to get justice. The legal aid system is not effective in most parts of the country and therefore people feel increasingly alienated from the legal system.

Community versus the state

The large number of movements for self-determination within the Northeast has helped to preserve and revive many aspects of culture and history which would otherwise have been lost.

In the mobilisation of these movements, traditional institutions have often been made ample use of, with the support of the entire community. I believe that such conflicts have often led to the further democratisation of both Indian society and the Indian state. The obvious examples are the movement for inclusion of the Bodo language and the Meitei (i.e. Manipuri) language in the Eighth Schedule of the Indian Constitution. The Meiteis have not only succeeded in getting their language recognised as an official language but also revived their traditional script. The Khasis have, through their own endeavours, rescued their language from the UNESCO list of endangered languages; the Lepchas have revived their language and are continuing their struggle for its official recognition in West Bengal.

Three Northeastern languages are now included in the Eighth Schedule: Nepali, Bodo and Meiteilon. While it is true that the people had to struggle for years, sometimes decades, the constitutional framework is democratic enough to allow for accommodation of collective demands of Northeast communities.

State versus the state (and other federal states)

There have been innumerable conflicts between states in the Northeast and the central government over the sharing of political power. These involve problems related to federalism. Examples are the issue of delimitation of the constituencies or the attempt to impose a ban on eating beef in Arunachal Pradesh.

There is, perhaps, not a single Northeastern state which does not have a border dispute with a neighbouring state and often this gives rise to violent conflict, such as the conflict between Nagaland and Assam.

However, within the state, the governments have powers to redress community grievances or uphold ethnic identities. Many of these states, such as Mizoram and Assam, even have their own national songs and their languages are taught right up to post-graduate levels.

Local tribal institutions have also played an important role in promoting the communities' language and culture. However, traditional institutions do not have the finances or the skills to develop cultures, history or languages on their own without the help of state-made laws.

However, local institutions are often undermined by national institutions. For instance, the district councils under the Sixth Schedule in Meghalaya have been undermined by the Legislative Assembly. There are people who have argued that the district councils are corrupt and should be terminated, but they seldom take into account the corruption of the national political parties. There is a strong case for further strengthening the district councils and empowering them so that they may more effectively implement tribal laws.

Individuals/communities versus corporations

The conflict between transnational corporations and local communities will become sharper in the future as the region is further integrated into world markets. These conflicts are most likely to be over the terms and conditions of mining and raise questions about the impact of mining on the ecology. There have already been several protests against the reckless construction of dams in the region.

In the four kinds of conflicts mentioned earlier there is very little scope for tribal customary laws to resolve the conflict. Customary laws have not developed legal concepts or mechanisms to deal with these kinds of conflicts. Whether the laws can evolve and gain the potential to be used in this given context is another question.

This brings me to the two kinds of conflicts in which the tribal customary laws can intervene to resolve the conflicts.

Individual versus community

There are many kinds of conflicts in which individuals are pitted against their own community, which can be summarised as the following:

1 individual versus individual;
2 individual versus family;
3 individual versus traditional institution; and
4 individual versus the local insurgent group.

I think it would be safe to say that all the tribal communities have elaborate rules and regulations governing the relationships within the community and an institutional framework to enforce those rules. However, these rules have been severely undermined by the conversion of most tribes to non-indigenous organised religions.

It is also true that some communities have been able to evolve and develop their customary laws in consonance with the times while the laws in some communities have stagnated, fossilised and become irrelevant.

For instance, in the past writers observed that Nagas had an effective means of settling border disputes within the village and between villages, too, despite having no written land records. However, today disputes between neighbours over boundaries are common. Even though the sale of land is restricted by special laws, there are innumerable land disputes made more complex with the intervention of a land mafia backed by the insurgents.

I know of cases in which the insurgents have forbidden people from resorting to the courts of law and insisted that they resolve disputes in accordance with the tribal laws, and many times the insurgent group tries to implement these laws.

Women versus community

None of the tribal communities, even the so-called matrilineal ones, give men and women equal rights to land or equal rights within the family. Several women's groups outside the Northeast and some within the region have argued that since customary law does not recognise the concept of gender equality it should be done away with and customary laws should be all relegated to the dustbin of history.

The fallacy of this argument is that it is based on the assumption that state-made law incorporates principles of gender equality.

First of all the Indian Constitution does not see patriarchy as problematic, and national laws and their interpretation by judges reflect deeply patriarchal attitudes. In the few cases where the courts seem to have recognised women's rights, the decisions have been the direct result of protracted struggles by women.

Even though women, especially those who can afford expensive lawyers, do sometimes win their cases, the courts do not uphold women's rights per se. For instance, in the famous Mary Roy case, when a Syrian Christian woman filed a petition asking for equal rights to property, the court allowed it on technical grounds, not on the ground of right to equality.

Second, when the state seems apparently sympathetic to women's rights, it is because the supposed advocacy of women's rights allows it to justify or legitimise coercive state responses through the identification of the enemy in the war on terror with the repressive treatment of women and the notion of a war on women's rights. Internationally, women's rights have been used to justify the war against Afghanistan, while in the Northeast they have been used to undermine the movements for self-determination.

Of course that does not mean that the demand for gender equality must be sacrificed at the altar of nationalism or a religion; it means only that strategies and tactics must take into consideration these complexities.

In the case of the Northeast I know of several cases in which women have successfully been able to challenge the patriarchal basis of customary laws by an interpretation of customary laws in the light of women's rights. They have been successful precisely because these communities are based on consensus and inclusion.

Insurgent groups

There are many cases of local insurgent groups insisting that conflicts be settled in accordance with the tribal laws. However, in recent years these groups have displayed a rather superficial knowledge of such customary laws, and have demonstrated a penchant to manipulate the verdicts by using threat or coercion.

Community versus community

There are in the Northeast many kinds of inter-community conflicts – for example:

1. conflict between the 'indigenous' versus the non-indigenous;
2. conflict between a local community and a migrant community;
3. conflict between two communities over natural resources;
4. conflict between two communities over historical injustice.

Since almost all communities have armed groups the conflicts become ever more dangerous and the violence escalates.

Although these conflicts seem to be conflicts between two communities, the problem is that often they arise as a result of state manipulations. For instance, consider the case of the Nellie massacre. For many years it was stated that the Tiwa community was responsible for the massacre until a Japanese scholar, Makiko Kimura, exposed the role of the leaders of the Assam movement in perpetuating the conflict (Kimura 2013).

Tribal customary law is designed to deal with conflict within the community and has not been developed to deal with inter-community conflict or with conflict with the state.

Tribal laws, legal pluralism and the Indian constitution

The idea of legal pluralism is embedded in the Constitution of India in the form of the Fifth and Sixth Schedules. In many ways it was Rev. J.J.M. Nichols Roy who gave shape to the idea of having district councils under the Sixth Schedule. The district council was supposed to ensure that tribal people could preserve their customary laws. However, from the beginning the Nagas rejected it.

The other person who advocated the idea of legal pluralism with passion was Verrier Elwin, who influenced Nehru's vision for the Northeast. There was an acrimonious exchange between Verrier Elwin and G. S. Ghurye on the issue, but it was not directly on the question of legal pluralism but around the question of allowing tribal communities to live in accordance with their own values and lifestyle.

The debates around both the Sixth Schedule and legal pluralism (Elwin called it tribal jurisprudence) were deeply paternalistic. The reason why the Constitution drafters accepted the idea of the Fifth and Sixth Schedules for tribal areas was because of paternalistic concerns for 'primitive people, simple, unsophisticated and frequently, improvident' (Rao 1968).

The debates and discussions do not really go into the question of legal pluralism from the point of view of a jurist. Legal pluralism means the existence of multiple legal systems within one state. There has been a great deal of discussion on the concept outside India; unfortunately we in India have not discussed the idea of legal pluralism from a theoretical perspective.

The discipline of legal pluralism draws on several disciplines, including anthropology, law and cultural studies. The word pluralism too needs to be defined. Often it is equated with multi-culturalism. However, the two are not synonymous concepts.

In the 1970s Western scholarship developed the concept of multiculturalism in response to the challenge posed by the growing number of migrants living in Western countries. But the concept was rejected in the 1980s on the grounds that it promoted cultural relativism and did not lead to better integration – itself, of course, a heavily loaded term. Pluralism is a more acceptable term but we need to debate its meaning in our context.

In India we have really not even begun to debate how we can build the principles of pluralism into our democracy. In the context of the Northeast, the national discourse has been limited to discussing how tribal societies can be integrated into 'the mainstream'. Even when we talk about preserving unity in diversity seldom do we discuss what this means.

Tribal jurisprudence and conflict resolution

The idea of legal pluralism is attractive because tribal customary laws seem to offer an opportunity to fight against state-made laws and against state authoritarianism. Customary law, or non-state-made law, could be an instrument in the hands of those who want greater autonomy from state control, and help build a more democratic, federal structure.

Legal pluralism could help build a political pluralism, could be a way to celebrate cultural diversity and check the assimilation of communities, and could provide democratic space for tribal societies to live and develop in accordance with their values.

The question remains: how far can tribal jurisprudence offer solutions to present-day problems and can it help in conflict resolution?

Community rights versus individual rights

The difference between tribal jurisprudence and state-made law based on principles of positivist theory is that the tribal laws are designed to protect community rights while the state-made law is based on rights of individuals. In practical terms, state-made law or even international human rights standards do not recognise the rights of communities, even though Article 29 of the Universal Declaration of Human Rights does recognise that individuals can realise their rights only through the community.

Those who are critics of legal pluralism have pointed out that recognition of community-based laws does tend towards essentialising communities. It can lead to ignoring the internal diversity within the community. This is much more relevant in cases of religion-based personal laws.

The tribal laws in the Northeast are often based on the principle of 'each according to his ability, to each according to his need' rather than the principle of equality in state-made laws. The right to equality enshrined in Article 14 of the Constitution states that all persons will be treated equally under the law. The apparent objectivity and neutrality of state-made law were ridiculed by Anatole France when he wrote, 'In its majestic equality the law forbids rich and poor alike to sleep under bridges, beg in the streets or steal loaves of bread, or peeing in the streets' (1884).

Legal pluralism is a way in which India could deal with cultural diversity, and that is why the question remains of how far tribal customary laws can be used to resolve conflicts in the Northeast region of India.

Conflict resolution

I believe that the values and principles on which tribal jurisprudence in the Northeast is based are relevant to checking the reckless consumerism and negative impact of globalisation. It can be an instrument for promotion of pluralism.

However, for the effective implementation of tribal laws there needs to be effective institutions. In the past these institutions kept the tribal communities together and instilled values into their youth. Whether it was the dormitory system of the Nagas and Mizos or the ethical codes of Khasis, these were responsible for ensuring the integrity of tribal communities and ensuring that conflicts did not destroy the society.

There were elaborate laws governing war and peace. The British, in their attempt to construct the image of the Naga as a head-hunter, did not document the innumerable ways the Naga tribes had of resolving disputes even in the midst of deadly conflicts (Haksar 2011).

However, these traditional institutions were destroyed by the Christian missionaries, especially the Baptists, who practised a more fundamentalist version of Christianity. In more recent years many communities who have become Hinduised have adopted Hindu practices which are not in consonance with principles of tribal jurisprudence. I do not know what percentage of tribals have converted to Islam.

In addition, the integration of the Northeast into the global market has led to infiltration of mass culture via television, the Internet and films. This has had a ruthlessly destructive impact on the cultures of the peoples of the Northeast.

This enormous cultural loss has led tribal youth to become more and more alienated from their societies, with a large number of them migrating to cities all over India and many to places like Singapore and Dubai. There seems little chance of rescuing the tribal jurisprudence from the forces of globalisation.

Nationalism versus religion

In 2011 my husband and I drove all over the Northeast. I wanted to understand the region as a whole and see if our travels could give answers to political questions that have been troubling me and all of us in one way or the other. The one thing that struck me was that the conflicts were more and more taking on a religious tone, and this was directly linked to the loss of culture. If its distinct culture is lost the community cannot be expected to keep its traditional institutions and sense of community, which are paramount in ensuring that tribal jurisprudence remains relevant.

I apologise for ending on this rather pessimistic note, but the way forward requires political-economic analysis and a sense of the historical understanding of the law in general. In other words conflict resolution needs to be understood in the context of politics and history rather than anthropology and ethnography, on which tribal studies have been based traditionally. Theological studies often are also rooted in tribal studies, which have their roots in colonial scholarship.

Where lies the hope?

There are scholars and concerned citizens all over the Northeast who are well aware of the problems I have touched upon. They have made tremendous and heroic efforts to recover their traditional cultures and languages; they have collected their old songs and revived their dance forms. They have also made efforts to indigenise their religion and reconcile their love of their community with their faith.

Many studies have been made on the nature of tribal jurisprudence. The need of the hour is to bring together activists and scholars and think of strategies for conflict resolution within the community. There is a need to document principles of tribal jurisprudence, but I do not think we should codify tribal laws. Codification leads to the fossilisation of law and makes it impossible for law to develop, evolve and grow so that it can equip itself to deal with the complexities of modern life. But, that said, I honestly believe that tribal jurisprudence can indeed be saved. Just as languages have been revived and are now taught at the post-graduate levels in the Northeast, tribal jurisprudence too can become a live instrument for societies fighting to survive in an increasingly hostile political atmosphere.

The fight for the survival of the communities of the Northeast is vital for Indian democracy, which is threatened by the ideology of those who are now in power and who believe all cultural diversity is an obstacle to development. I believe pluralism, including legal pluralism, can be a weapon to preserve cultural diversity and political plurality. That is why I feel committed to supporting the struggles and movements of the peoples of the Northeast, because I am committed to fighting for cultural diversity, which I believe to be absolutely essential to preserve Indian democracy.

Note

This chapter was born of the keynote address of the seminar 'Conflict Resolution Systems in Tribal Societies of North East India: Legal Pluralism and Indian Democracy', held at Inspiration, Guwahati, Assam, India, on 5 and 6 June 2014, to which this entire volume owes its origins. The matter dealt with here offers a general framework, into which the case studies of the latter part of this book can be inserted and allowing for more succinct comparison between the various types of conflicts experienced in the Northeast to be made. As it served as an exceedingly useful introduction to the subsequent papers given, it is hoped that it will serve the reader as a practical introduction to the reading of the rest of this book, particularly when it comes to the differentiation of the forms of conflict in this often troubled region.

References

France, Anatole. 1894. *Le Lys Rouge [The Red Lily]*, Ch. 7. Paris: Gallimard.

Haksar, Nandita. 2011. *ABC of Naga Culture and Civilization: A Resource Book*. New Delhi: Chicken Neck.

Haksar, Nandita. 2013. *Across the Chicken Neck: Travels in Northeast India*. New Delhi: Rupa.

Haksar, Nandita and Sebastian Hongray. 2011. *The Judgement That Never Came*. New Delhi: Chicken Neck.

Kimura, Makiko. 2013. *The Nellie Massacre of 1983 Agency of Rioters*. New Delhi: SAGE.

Rao, B. Shiva (ed). 1968. *The Framing of India's Constitution*. New Delhi: The Indian Institute of Public Administration, 1968.

12 Forums for Conflict Resolution in the Jaintia Tribal Community over Land Resources

Rikil Chyrmang

'Forums for conflict resolution in the Jaintia tribal community over land resources' by Rikil Chyrmang (Melvil Pereira, Bitopi Dutta and Binita Kakati, eds, *Legal Pluralism and Indian Democracy: Tribal Conflict Resolution Systems in Northeast India*, Copyright © 2018, Routledge, Chapter 15). Reproduced by permission of Taylor & Francis Group.

The Jaintia society follows the *dorbar* (council) system, which has been customarily practised since time immemorial to attend to the people's needs. The dorbar system acts as an important forum for conflict resolution over land resources among the Jaintia. This system is modelled on the traditional self-governing institutions that work at a grass-roots level and also attend to many village problems, such as acting as an agency to facilitate the implementation of government schemes, resolving household conflict and minor crimes. Therefore, it is important to study this age-old tradition; it is a forum for conflict resolution, but also to question the role of women in the dorbar system in the present context.

The three principal tribes of Meghalaya, the Garos, Khasis and Jaintias, have continued to maintain their traditional institutions of local self-governance integrated with the local government and the Autonomous District Councils (ADCs). After the Jaintia Hills Autonomous District Council (JHADC) was set up in 1969, it served as a precedent for the rest of the state to give due recognition to the dorbar system and the Village Court headed by a village headman (*waheh chnong*), which has the power to resolve conflicts between villages at the dorbar of that particular village. Thus, traditional institutions can be an effective medium that, empowered by the District Councils, serve as a bridge between traditional societies and modern administration systems, reflecting the socio-cultural autonomy of the tribal community. In order to protect the interests of the scheduled tribes (ST) with regard to land alienation and their status as a socially deprived community, the Fifth and Sixth Schedules have been enshrined in the Constitution of India. These reflect the national recognition of the welfare and development of tribal people and respect for their local customs and traditions. Therefore, in this context, this study attempts to corroborate secondary literature with supplementary

DOI: 10.4324/9781003299561-12

information from fieldwork on a few selected cases conducted in a village in the East Jaintia Hills District via participant observation. This chapter also includes a case study of a situation in Jalaphet village where people disputed land resources, which led to violent conflicts, and how a customary law court or village court responded to such incident. A purposive sampling technique was used to select the cases during fieldwork in 2014.

This chapter is divided into nine sections, the first six of which deal with the tribe and its historical context and give an in-depth discussion of its traditional institutions. The first section provides a background to the Jaintia Hills and the tribe through a survey of previous literature. We then move on to delineate the genesis of traditional institutions chronologically from the pre-British to the British era in the two parts of the section that follows. Next, I discuss the customary law courts. This section also provides a review of the current situation and powers of the village courts. The section that follows discusses the importance of formal law courts and mainly focuses on the perspective of the judiciary. After that, there is a discussion of conflict in tribal communities and forums of conflict resolution concerning land tenure systems, and also women's participation in the forums of conflict resolution. The case study of Jalaphet village is discussed in the next section, and it is from there that the next section proceeds.

Also offered are a number of sample cases taken from fieldwork, six in total, summarised here so that the reader may have access to a few such sample cases offered as a simple narrative version of a number of incidents, the problematic nature of which the reader is invited to judge for himor herself, and serve as examples of the limitations of the tribal institutions described earlier in this chapter. Additionally, I offer a simple tabulated comparison of the advantages and disadvantages of the two systems (the traditional and the modern) that were reported by members of the tribe during fieldwork, which is given for the reference of the more casual reader, and much of this is arguably true of the traditional systems of many other tribes of the Northeast and is not wholly restricted to the Jaintia. Finally, the last section provides some analytical concluding remarks, highlighting some of the flaws in the system described earlier in the chapter that were not yet dealt with previously or brought up in the sample cases or by the respondents involved in the fieldwork study itself, and the policy implications of these significant elements.

Brief background

At the last census (2011), the total population of the undivided Jaintia Hills stood at 392,852, with 364,369 in rural areas and 28,483 in urban areas, while the decadal growth rate of its total population was 31.34%, with 32.96% in rural areas and 13.67% in urban areas between 2001 and 2011. The majority of people living in Jaintia Hills are referred to as Pnar or Synteng (which form 95% of the total population). They have no written history to corroborate their migration to the hills, but, on the other hand, their oral literature abounds with legends and folktales which describe the many facets of their lives (Mohrmen 2015). Their customs and traditions are very different from those in the rest of India, as they follow the matrilineal system of social organisation. Lamare (2005) found limited studies and written records referring to their migration to the Jaintia Hills. However, the theories propounded by many scholars stated that the Pnar or Synteng, the Wars, the Biate and the Bhois among the Jaintias are offshoots of the Mon-Khmer race of South-East Asia, and, accordingly, share similar physical features with peoples of Indo-China who had migrated to the hills through the Assam Valley and thereafter moved to the Jaintia Hills in search of food and shelter about 200 AD. (Prakash 2007; Joshi 2004). The Jaintia Hills District covers a total area of 3819 km^2. Agriculture is still the mainstay of the Jaintia economy and 80% of the population subsist upon it. The types of land are forest land, paddy land – that is land used for wet cultivation – and homestead land (Ibid.).

Before the arrival of the British, Jaintia society had already developed the traditional institutions that still govern their society. With the coming of the British and the spread of Christianity, the system underwent considerable changes in some parts of the state. However, in several Jaintia villages, traditional religious practices remained well entrenched, with members of the old faith holding on to their religious rites and ceremonies (Rymbai 2002: 32). After the British era, following the work of the Bordoloi Committee under the Sixth Schedule of the Constitution of India an Autonomous District Council (ADC) was set up to protect the way of life of the people. The Sixth Schedule provision allowed for the co-existence of traditional and modern political institutions. This is how the modern and traditional systems of conflict resolution in Jaintia Hills District came to exist today (Rani 2014).

The genesis of traditional institutions

Meghalaya has had deep-rooted traditional institutions of local governance since time immemorial and they still function today. They include the following: (1) the *nokmanship* system, which is the traditional institution of the Garos, and the leader of the Garo clan used to be designated as the *nokma* (leader); (2) *syiemship* is the distinctive traditional institution of the Khasi tribe and is the rule of a Khasi state by a leader called the *syiem* (king); and (3) finally, among the Jaintias is found the system of *dolloiship*. It is a system of judicial administration based on the principle of the social disapproval of wrongful activities and actions, with a *dolloi* (chief) acting as the administrative head of each territory. All these three popular traditional institutions of local self-government continue to work under the over-all control of their respective District Councils (Kumar 2008). Though the terms used are different, these institutions function in a similar manner and hence this particular study focused only on the Jaintia tribal community.

The pre-British Era

In ancient times, the Jaintia people created the institution of dolloiship that refers to *Ka Ri Khadar Dolloi* (The Land of 12 Tribal Chiefs) to maintain peace, fraternity and unity among its people. The villages were all clustered around a particular area and were recognised as the units of a single political entity. A number of villages in close proximity were known as an *elaka* (province). The chief of an elaka was called the dolloi and he served as its ruler. According to custom and tradition, women cannot contest for the post of dolloi nor are they allowed to cast their vote in elections (Gassah 1998). Only male members are eligible voters, and the tenure for the post is life-long. The Jaintia Hills, consisting of 12 elakas, was ruled by 12 dollois.[1]

The dolloi had the power to govern a sizeable population in an elaka. Among the dollois, the Dolloi of Nartiang was known as *U Kongsan* (pre-eminent person) because the Nartiang Elaka was the biggest and used to have the largest population. The Dolloi of Nartiang was very powerful, as he could easily raise and command the largest population. The dollois performed certain ritual functions, managed community land, maintained law and order and were also responsible for the settlement of disputes and collection of market taxes (Government of Meghalaya n.d.).

All the 12 dollois used to join hands to fight against mutual enemies. Due to the increase of the population, they needed to gain larger lands and to create new settlements. Consequently, border disputes and frequent skirmishes occurred, which ultimately led to warfare between the dollois concerned. In order to end the frequent hostilities and conflict among the people belonging to different elakas and in order to promote friendship and co-operation, the dollois unanimously appointed one person as their syiem who would rule over them and unify the 12 dollois.[2] The syiem was armed with rules and regulations framed by the subjects themselves to govern the populace. The aggregation of elakas formed the Jaintia syiemship. The Sutnga Syiemship was regarded as a mother syiemship. There is a difference between the administration of the dominant chief and the administration of the dollois of Jaintia Hills. The dollois represent the people of their respective elakas. This kind of administrative set-up is the primary administrative unit in the Jaintia Hills District (Government of Meghalaya n.d.).

The appointed syiem would rule through the help and advice of dollois. He was not an absolute monarch. The syiem had no ownership right over the land and could not levy taxes from his people, though he could collect taxes from those belonging to other kingdoms who were defeated in war. His soldiers were provided by all the 12 dollois from the people residing in their respective elakas. He could mint his own money in his name and issue it as legal tender within the kingdom. He was entitled to receive fees from the dollois and the people involved in the litigation that took place in his courts. During times of war, the duty of the syiem was to protect and defend the people and the territory of the kingdom, and lead the army in battle only when there was a great threat to the security of the kingdom. For the expansion of the kingdom, war had to be fought against neighbouring kingdoms and in such wars an appointed general would lead the army. The dollois would stay behind to look after their respective elakas. Whenever there was a dispute between one dolloi and another they had to be referred to the syiem and all concerned would abide by his ruling (Gassah 1998).

Apart from the dolloi, there was a very strong concept of belonging to a *kur* (clan). Each kur elected an official *langdoh* (priest),[3] who was young and unmarried, to manage religious affairs and discharge public duties related to land and the tax collected from the subjects (Chib 1984). The langdoh was the appellate authority for the redressal of grievances of the people in the elaka, and if the people were not satisfied with the dolloi, the layngdoh had the authority to remove the dolloi from office if he was found to be corrupt or ruling unjustly. The ancient history of the tribe is shrouded in mystery, but is invariably linked with the traditional institutions of syiem and langdoh. Thus it is not only pertinent but also interesting to know about the legends that offer a meaningful insight into the institution of the syiem. In meetings held related to village issues or conflict, the syiem would have to ask his own people (consisting of 11–12 houses called the 'village tie') for the village to debate, day and night, till they could reach on a consensus on the matter. The village tie included people from all sectors of society: men, women and children. Everybody was a part of it and it represented consensus in the tribe. All important decisions were taken by the village tie. When there was a village meeting, every adult was supposed to attend rather than go out to work.

The syiem did not possess dictatorial powers. He was a revered and respected personality of the community who, without fail, functioned as a judge during peace and a general during war. He never interfered in the internal affairs of the chiefs subordinate to him. However, it was his duty to offer them protection against external aggression and also to negotiate treaties or alliances with alien rulers. Before the arrival of the British there were 17 syiems. It was believed that the syiem of Shillong was the oldest of all and it came into existence in the concluding years of the fourteenth century. The Jaintia syiem was as powerful as that of Shillong (Chib 1984).

The British Era

In this period, the British adopted the Mughal term '*durbar*', which referred to any sort of meeting, and used it to refer to the meetings in which the Jaintia settled disputes. All rules and regulations of governance were incorporated into the durbar system. Democratic institutions like the durbar (*dorbar* in the Pnar language) and langdoh came into existence only when the tribal communities gave up their nomadic living and took to settled life.[4] During this period the village people began to use the word 'dorbar' (council) for what had previously been referred to as the 'village tie' (the informal meeting of the villagers).[5] The langdoh was concerned only with religious matters. Economic privileges were attached to the dolloi. Under the British administration, the whole of the Jaintia Hills, along with few other villages of the Khasi Hills, were grouped together under one common system of administration and they were treated as British areas and were administered directly by the British government.

It was in the year 1824 that the British started taking interest in the syiem of Jaintia Hills. When the Burmese invaded the Jaintia Hills, the Jaintia syiem sought the help of the British to repulse the attack. The British repelled the Burmese attack but assumed charge of the Jaintia defence and enforced rules and regulations on the Jaintia people. The British annexed the Jaintia Kingdom and merged it with the Khasi Kingdom to form the United Province of Khasi and Jaintia Hills. By capturing syiem after syiem, the British assumed the responsibility of defending these hill principalities against foreign aggression. Though the British took full control, the syiems were still allowed to function freely within the British-imposed framework. Later, the British merged the Jaintia *Pargana* (a group of villages or a subdivision of a district) with Sylhet Station at Jaintiapur (Chib 1984). The British collected land revenues from the people to run their administration. This tax was too heavy for the local people and they were left with no option but to wage war against the British.

The first Jaintia rebellion started when the British imposed a house tax in 1860, but the rebels were not well organised and the British effortlessly quelled the rebellion. Soon, the British imposed an income tax in addition to the house tax. There was also a plan to levy taxes on betel leaves and betel nuts. These impositions caused uproar in Jaintia society, and gave rise to a second rebellion in 1862. Jowai was besieged for over three weeks, with local officials being unable to stop the rush. The British deployed seven regiments of troops to suppress the rebellion (Prakash 2007). The leader of this rebellion was a young man named U Kiang Nongbah. He worked secretly to avoid arrest. He was a good organiser who was able to contact all the dollois without rousing any suspicion about his role. The British failed to detect his activities for quite some time, but eventually U Kiang fell into British hands and was hanged publicly on 30 December 1862, to strike terror in the hearts of the Jaintias. When he stood on the gallows, he said in a clear voice, 'If my face turns eastwards when I die on the rope, we shall be free again within 100 years. If it turns westwards we shall be enslaved forever.' His face turned eastwards and India was indeed free within a period of 100 years. It was an unequal fight as the British had far superior weapons. They succeeded in controlling the Jaintia Kingdom in 1863 and completely eliminated the syiemship in a prolonged struggle (Ibid.). Civil trials were left to the local chiefs, but from this point on criminal cases were tried by the British political agent stationed at Cherrapunjee.

Socio-political systems

As mentioned earlier, the traditional leaders of the tribe look after the administration of the syiemship, the elakas and the villages according to the tribal customs and traditions. These traditional socio-political systems are self-governing institutions and, by and large, function in a democratic manner. The dolloi has his own dorbar, as does the syiem. There are durbars at different levels, like the village dorbar, the elaka dorbar and the syiem dorbar. The power of the syiem and the dolloi was checked by the dorbars of their respective areas. The dorbars provide opportunities to people to take part in and charge of their own affairs. Therefore, consent is the basis of political authority. Historically the Jaintias have had a fairly organised three-tier system of governance, the first level of which was the syiem. The Jaintia system was divided into 12 elakas (consisting of groups of villages) under a dolloi, the second level. The next and lowest level of territorial/geographic entity was a village represented by a *rangbah shnong* constituting the third level, who was selected from among the male adults of the particular village in question. Each of these three levels had councils or dorbars. Each village was usually organised along clan lines, with a rangbah shnong concerned with basic administration and justice (Rao et al., 2011).

This old political system of governance continues to exist, except for the syiem. When the British took over the Jaintia administration, they abolished the office of the syiem. However, they retained the other two traditional institutions – that is the dolloi and rangbah shnong. The three-tiered system of administration which was in existence during the pre-British era was reduced to a two-tier system. After Independence, the formal institutions at work at the highest level called ADCs were established under the Sixth Schedule along with the existing two-tier system (Table 12.1).

Table 12.1 The integrated three-tier system of traditional institutions and local self-governance

Levels	*Before the British*	*After Independence*
1st	Syiem	ADC
2nd	Dolloi	Dolloi
3rd	Rangbah shnong	Rangbah shnong

Source: Meghalaya vision document 2011

The forums of conflict resolution begin from the lowest level – from the rangbah shnong, the head of the village courts. Disputes over land are handled by the village courts headed by the village headman, chairman, vice-chairman, secretary and executive members. Women are not allowed to hold any post. The services of the aforementioned posts are unpaid. There is no fixed tenure and changes can be made from time to time if the individual is not willing to continue in the post or if the community is critical of his performance. There is no election process to elect the village members; they are unanimously named by the consensus of the community. However, today, in some villages of Jaintia Hills, election to the post of village headman is conducted by the district council if the community or people object to the proposed headman. The dolloi was elected for life from the senior clans through an election process, in which only men are allowed to vote.

Table 12.2 The three-tier structure of organisation of the traditional institutions

Levels	*Traditional institutions*
1st	*Ka Dorbar ki Khadar Dolloi*
2nd	*Ka Dorbar Elaka*
3rd	*Ka Dorbar Shnong*

Source: Rao et al, 2011

Table 12.2 shows the three-tiered structure of the traditional institutions, which from district to the village level are (1) *Ka Dorbar ki Khaddar Dolloi* (Full District Committee of only the 12 dolloi), (2) *Ka Dorbar Elaka* (committee of the head and the village members who coordinate the affairs of a group of villages – that is a large area within an elaka comprising of several villages) and (3) *Ka Dorbar Shnong* (a village committee, which is the smallest council of people at the village level). They each meet frequently, have administrative, financial and judicial functions and discuss a variety of subjects related to their respective jurisdiction or province (Fieldwork 2014). (This information was collected in the course of fieldwork done in Jaintia Hills District of Meghalaya by the author from January to October 2014. Henceforth it will be shown as Fieldwork 2014.)

Customary law courts

In Jaintia society, most property is owned by individuals. Some common property resources (CPRs) belong to the village community and the state and some land belongs to the entire elaka. Individuals are not allowed to encroach on or use the land that belongs to the village community for any purpose without the permission of the village dorbar headed by a rangbah shnong (village headman). Some areas of the Jaintia Hills have another system called the '*patorship*'. The patorship is the system which controls and manages community land, the leader of which is called a *pator*. A pator's main role is to protect the tribal land ownership rights if there is a dispute within the tribal village or encroachment by other villages. In other words, they settle disputes of a petty nature, and primarily deal with land.

In the past, there was plenty of land available which did not actually belong to anybody. No individual had ownership rights on the land. Even though some individuals might have had claims over some portions of the land by demarcating sections of it, there are no legal documents in support of this. So there was always the chance of there being a dispute as property rights were not well defined. If two persons staked a claim to the same land, then it led to a conflict of interest if the two parties or disputants failed to settle the matter or reach a compromise. In such cases, the complainant would put the matter before the dorbar shnong (village court), the chairman, secretary, president and executive members elected by the people to debate the matter and to find a settlement. If the dispute was not settled, the matter would be referred to the dolloi to pass judgement. The dolloi's judgement was final in olden days, but at present, if the complainant is not satisfied with it, he or she can appeal to the case to the District Council Court.

In earlier times, most conflicts got resolved within the village dorbar for a fee of Rs.50 (*baibishar*). A dispute between two or more parties was referred to as '*ialehthma*' (war) when it came for public hearing in the dorbar. Ialehthma was very common after the British left because people who had acquired land had not registered it in the form of *patta* (legal documents) or landholding. In those times, most title deeds had no written records as the majority of the people were illiterate and very few had patta documents (Fieldwork 2014).

The current situation and powers of village courts

At the village level, the composition of the court reflects the traditions of the tribe for whom the district council is meant. The court consists of the traditional village headmen and functionaries. The traditional chiefs and headman are elected according to the customary practice from those who are eligible to be members of the village courts as per the District Council guidelines. The village court consists of no less than two members and no more than six members. The chief executive member (CEM) or a member of the executive committee is barred from being a member of the court. These traditional chiefs or heads function as the chairmen of the village courts and one of the members elected functions as the vice-chairman. These rules were set by the District Council for the settlement of people's disputes at a village level.

The jurisdiction of the court extends to the hearing and trial of suits and cases arising within the territorial limits of the village. The civil cases concerning immovable property fall within the jurisdiction of the village court only if its location is within the village itself. All other cases qualify only if both the parties reside in or hold land in the village. The village court can try offences of a petty nature, such as simple assault, affront and disturbances of whatever kind: drunkenness or disorderly brawling, public nuisance and simple cases of wrongful restraint.

Village courts are not permitted to try offences where the punishment is imprisonment under the Indian Penal Code (IPC), nor can they pass a sentence of imprisonment in criminal cases. They have the power to impose a fine of up to Rs.50. The Autonomous District Committee has legislative, executive and judicial powers. The administrative set-up is similar to the *Panchayati Raj* elsewhere in the country and embodies the system of rural local self-government.[6] The specific recommendation made was the establishment of a three-tier Panchayati Raj system (Laxmikanth 2013).[7] Meghalaya has continued to practise the three-tier system of traditional institutions under the ADC.[8] To assert legal claims over property, people register their land records in the district councils.

Formal law courts

The ADCs of the united Khasi-Jaintia Hills were formed in 1952 under the Sixth Schedule of the erstwhile composite Assam (Choudhury 2005). The Jaintia Hills district was carved out from the Khasi Hills district in 1967 and headquartered at Jowai. The council was created for the protection of the tribal identity, customs and rights. The ADC has three wings – namely the legislative, the executive and the judiciary. Here we are dealing only with the judicial wing.

The role of the judicial wing

The Sixth Schedule provides for the administration of justice in the Autonomous District. These provisions empower the ADC to constitute village courts or courts for the trial of suits and cases between the parties if they all belong to scheduled tribes within the autonomous areas. The ADC is empowered to appoint suitable persons to be members of village courts and the presiding officer of such courts. The ADC may also appoint officers required for the administration of laws enacted by the district councils. The governor may confer on the courts constituted by the ADC, or the officer appointed for such purposes, the power to try suits or cases arising out of any law in force in the Autonomous District. He may also confer such powers as he deems appropriate to the ADC and the courts constituted by them, under the provisions of the Code of Civil Procedure or the Code of Criminal Procedure. With the conferment of such powers, the councils, the courts, and the officers appointed shall have jurisdiction to try suits and cases. The High Court exercises jurisdiction over the suits and cases empowered under the schedule. Under the Administration of Justice Rules, three classes of courts were constituted by the district councils: (1) the village courts, (2) the subordinate district council courts and additional subordinate district council courts and (3) the district council court. The composition of these courts from the village level right up to the district level and also their powers and procedure have been prescribed in detail in these rules (KHADC n.d.).

Conflict in the tribal community and forums for its resolution

Land tenure systems and conflict

There are two types of land, the *hali* lands (irrigated paddy fields) and the high lands. These lands are further sub-divided into many different classes. The hali lands comprise the *raid* (common) lands (the former property of the syiem), service lands, village *puja* (rituals) lands, private lands and patta lands. The British abolished the office of the syiem and took over such lands to assess their revenue. The customary procedures of the Jaintia provide for the granting of these lands on lease to individuals but the occupancy rights cease if such lands are unattended for three years. The British regularised these customary procedures and issued periodic leases of these lands, often for a period of ten years. Services lands refer to the land given to the dollois, pators and other chiefs and officials as remuneration for their services to the administration of the area. The high lands are divided into private lands, unclaimed land or government wastelands.

Private lands were held by individuals and were transferred according to the will of the owner. These lands were not assessed for revenue. Patta or lease lands were allotted and settled by the British during their regime. Today, the power to allot these lands to individuals or institutions rests with the ADC with respect of the paddy fields only. Tribal property is issued from various sources, such as district councils, the syiem or village headmen who attest to the authenticity of the title deeds and their enforceability in a court of law. However, the customary notion about usage, rights and apportionment has been and is still being contextualised to modern-day developments and realities in order to facilitate credit, and other documentation and registrations under schematic and personalised needs (Government of Meghalaya 2009).

Women's participation in the forums of conflict resolution

Women are relatively better off in Meghalaya than in many other states in India as per the Gender Development Index (GDI). Despite this, one could hardly say they are empowered. Though women take an active part in economic activities, their participation in the service sector is very low (DONER and NEC 2008).

Among the Jaintias, women are empowered to take care of property as its legal custodian as well as to control the family purse, valuables and movable and immovable property. Traditionally, inherited property passes from the mother to the youngest daughter, called the '*ka khon khadduh*'. Other sisters also share the property but the youngest has a larger share because of her responsibility to stay with her parents and provide for them as per custom and traditions. No man in the uplands of the Jaintia Hills can possess landed property, unless it is self-acquired, and if a man dies and leaves behind acquired property, his heir will be his mother, if alive, to the exclusion of his wife, sons and daughters. If the wife, however, undertakes not to remarry, she will inherit half of her husband's property, which at her death will pass on to her youngest daughter. The youngest daughter who inherits the property is obliged to look after the family idols and bear all its ritual offerings out of her own pocket. If the youngest daughter changes her religion, she loses her position in the family and is succeeded by her next youngest sister, as in the case of death. As such, women enjoy a higher status and inherit their parents' property, both the ancestral and that which was acquired during their lifetime, serving as the custodian of the property and the keeper of the home and hearth; 'they inherit the lion's share of the property.' For women coming from poor or landless families, these property rights are insignificant (Joshi 2004).

Despite this, authority in its real sense is the exclusive preserve of men. Local administration is completely the domain of men (Ibid.). The social system and certain customary laws reek of gender discrimination. Hoda (2007) suggested that giving weight and recognition to various communities and social bodies by codifying their customary laws would ensure proper representation in government and semi-governmental services. The lack of reforms and efforts to revise traditional laws in relation to inheritance rights becomes a sensitive issue involving identity. On the other hand, ensuring women's decision making in the family and affairs of the village remains a challenging task (Government of Meghalaya 2009). Women do not have any role in the village dorbar. Their rights to participate in the planning process of the village administration and conflict resolution have to be ensured (Ibid.). When it comes to a dispute in the village, whoever is willing to attend and hear the judgement of the case is allowed to do so. Women can also raise their voices in the dorbar regarding the hearing of the judgment. In other conflicts also, women are allowed to participate and hear the fate of both the plaintiff and defendant. The disposal of a case is fast in the village court. After hearing from the plaintiff and defendant, the witnesses and the public at large will visit the disputed site, in the case of a land dispute, that is. Finally, the secretary will prepare a note in a register book for both the parties to sign or place their thumb impression to declare their agreement with the judgement as to who won and lost the case. The community believes that the law is equal for everybody and it should be impartial. If the first and second hearings are inconclusive, the village court can refer the case to the dolloi within its elaka. But in some cases, the judgment can be partial if the judges of the village court are not willing to comply and take action. If conflict resolution fails at the village court, the defendant can go to a civil court presided over by the district council. With the passage of time, some dispute cases are directly summoned to the civil court. The complainants expect fair justice from the civil court, but it takes a long time for the case to be tried and the disposal rate of any conflict-related matter is very slow.

The exclusion of women has a traditional link to the syiemship, where only men used to participate at the time of conflict, be it an invasion or a war against British control. Women are confined to looking after their children, household matters and religious affairs. Involvement in warfare was a source of pride for men. This continues even today. Though it is a matrilineal system where women are supposed to be the heads of the household, they do not have much power in the real sense or raise their voices in the system, such that a man spends the night with his wife and gets up in the morning and goes back to his mother. His mother prepares his food and he goes to work. Even today this system continues in most Jaintia villages. The elder daughter of the family has to find a new house and the youngest daughter stays with her mother because she inherits a great deal of the property. Sometimes, conflict arise between husband and wife because of the customary practise that the youngest daughter is entitled to inherit the property from her mother. Conflicts arise when the husband is denied the right to control or use the property by the wife.

Some of the people who were interviewed tried to explain the non-inclusion of women in the dorbar by citing their customary laws. The men felt that if a woman is treated on par with men, quarrels will ensue. The duty and responsibility of women were restricted to looking after family affairs, and men collected property and simply put it in women's names in order to maintain it. The property is given to women to look after because in the olden days the men were expected to go fight in wars and hence it was thought that women were in a better position to look after the property (Field Study 2014).

Many different kinds of conflicts occur in the villages with regard to land resources: (1) individual versus individual, (2) individual versus family, (3) individual versus village community and (4) inter-village conflict over land boundaries. Most of the conflicts over resources concern one or more of the following: *lum* (hills), *kper* (gardens), *kseh* (pine trees), *dieng* (trees), *halilum* (non-agricultural land), *hali rep* (agriculture land), *halishrah* (land that cannot be cultivated) and *kremmuiong* (rat-hole mining). The presence of coal reserves and their economic values has led to greater conflict over resources.

The dorbar system as a forum for conflict resolution:a case study from Jalaphet Village

Jalaphet is a village in the Saipung Block of the East Jaintia Hills District situated about 114 km from the state capital Shillong, and 20 km from Khliehriat, the district headquarters. Jalaphet has two parts that fall under the jurisdiction of two dollois – namely Jalaphet Bri-Sutnga, controlled by the Dolloi of Sutnga Elaka, and Jalaphet Bri-Sumer, under the Dolloi of Raliang Elaka. Jalaphet comprises nine localities; four localities belong to the Bri-Sutnga and five to the Bri-Sumer.[9] The majority of people living in the village are considered members of the scheduled tribe community (99.56%). According to the Census of 2011, the number of permanent residents was 2,945 in Jalaphet Bri-Sutnga in 492 households, and about 2,292 in Jalaphet Bri-Sumer in 371 households. Thus the total population of the whole of Jalaphet in 2011 was about 5,239. The literacy rate is just about 30%.

The majority of the people in Jalaphet village depend on agriculture for their livelihood. They mostly cultivate rice. Traditionally, wet cultivation was practised in the valleys and foothills, while shifting cultivation predominated up in the hilly terrain and around the forests. But the beginning of coal mining activities in the Jalaphet area during the early 1980s on a small scale, and extensive extraction during the late 2000s, severely affected the paddy fields, which became unfit for cultivation. As a result, people have given up agriculture and only a few households continue to practise agriculture in the unaffected places. With the presence of coal mines, land resources became very valuable to everyone. And thus it is important to conduct a case study at Jalaphet in the present contexts of how the village courts through the dorbar system settle the disputes between parties.

The dorbar system, also called the village courts or customary law courts, are at present under the purview of the District Council as the members of the dorbar in a particular village automatically become the members of the village courts recognised by the District Council.

Role and functions of the dolloi

The dolloi is the head of an elaka and functions like a king. There may be some elakas that have 50 villages, some have 40 villages, and there can be an elaka of only one village. The dolloi, during the olden days, used to be the *rajah* (king) of that area and his decision was final; he was the magistrate and below him in each village they had the village headman and the langdoh.

The langdoh covers all those villages under that elaka where there are people who are still indigenous. But the role of the headman is limited to only one particular village. In the presentday the position of the dolloi is entrusted by the District Council just to verify the land property of the people. And in case there are any conflicts or land disputes the dolloi has to report in the dorbar. The village will report to the dolloi, presenting the circumstances of the problem concerned (e.g. petty conflicts or claiming land). As soon as the dolloi gets the rice beer after two to three days the dolloi summons the second party to report to him, after which the dolloi will call a dorbar, which consists of a group of people gathering to hear the judgment of the case. The losing party is then required to pay a fine. People who don't have money have to pay a fine in kind by giving a bottle of rice beer, a rooster or a pig.

The dolloi was elected by the people in the dorbar by raising their hands (voice vote) or by a process akin to the making of a queue. If there are more than two candidates then the people will stand in the queue of that particular candidate whom they want to elect. The number of people standing in the queue for the respective candidates will then be counted. The candidate who got the highest number was elected. This system changed much later to a secret ballot system after the setting up of the District Council, and only men are allowed to vote. Money has begun to play a disturbingly prominent role in the election of dollois.

The dolloi played a role in land allotment after land became a registered private property, although the role was limited and involved only giving recommendations to the District Council that this land belongs to that person. These days the dolloi does not have land; all land is now private property. His recommendation is required to certify that a piece of land which belonged to a person was being sold to another person. The dolloi dorbar is called the elaka dorbar. From some villages they elect or nominate the headman to be the elaka member and they attend the elaka dorbar and to get information regarding how to give 'No Objection Certificates' (NOC) to any company. Apart from this they don't have any role to play nowadays. Earlier the entire dispute was settled by the dolloi and his decision used to be final. Nowadays the dolloi doesn't have many roles and much power due to the setting up of the Jaintia Hills Autonomous District Council (JHADC). The dolloi does, however, still perform a ritual function as the chief, with the langdoh in the performance of puja.

Role and functions of the customary law court or chiefs

The information gathered from the fieldwork supplied by the village headman and other members elucidates the working of the dorbar system at Jalaphet village. The headman said that a dorbar was called to elect the waheh shnong (village headman) by a show of hands. Previously, 15–18-year-olds were allowed to participate in the election, but now the minimum age has been raised to 18. Only males can become members of the dorbar system. The one who secures the majority is elected as village headman from that date and then other members like the secretary and other executive members are elected following the same procedures (Fieldwork 2014).

Traditionally the tenure of the dorbar election varied from village to village. The dorbar system has not changed much over the years. Before, the time was not fixed for the elected headman but if he is not doing much or bringing development to the village community, the populace might ask the village secretary to convene a meeting to discuss the matter. Previously to elect a headman, they looked for a person who is working hard and can have good relations with the public and is able to bear all the responsibilities required of his position. Then they have to send his name to the dolloi for recommendation and then forward it to the District Council for appointment.

Traditionally the village headman had a lot of power as far as land allotment was concerned. But, of late, this power has been abused by some, leading to the selling of land to non-residents. One of the informants said that now the power and position of the headman is limited due to the passing of the Appointment and Succession of Chief/ Headman Act back in 1959. Though the passing of the Village Administration Bills (VAB) in 2014 to codify the customary laws of the Jaintia will not put an end to the functioning of the dorbar, it should bring it within the purview of the District Council. Ahead follows a series of six case studies that may be used to demonstrate the practical functioning of the traditional institutions, the theory of which has been described earlier, and offer an insight into the nature of the dispute commonly experienced in the Jaintia Hills, and indeed, into some of the complications and limitations of the institutions.

Samples of cases

Case 1:

> *Mrs. Bon Chyrmang v. Mr. Som Chyrmang* was a dispute about the ownership rights of a paddy field. Mr Som summoned Mrs Bon to the village court and claimed that the agricultural land belonged to him. Mrs Bon said that the land belonged to her. As a compromise could not be reached, the village court conducted the trial and referred both parties to the dolloi, and finally the judgement went in favour of Mrs Bon Chyrmang. The location of the site of conflict is Hali Urmyrliang; both parties belong to the Bri-Sutnga Elaka but the area of conflict falls under Bri-Sumer under Raliang Elaka, so the Dolloi of Raliang dismissed the case in favour of Mrs Bon.
>
> (Fieldwork 2014)

Case 2:

The disputing parties were *Mrs. Ersi Chyrmang v. Mrs. Dir Chyrmang, Mrs. Kret Chyrmang and Mrs. Ïit Chyrmang*. The matter of dispute was about the ownership rights of land (dwelling land, including a road, and a boundary). Mrs Dir, Mrs Kret and Mrs Ïit summoned Mrs Ersi to the village dorbar and claimed that the land belonged to them. Mrs Ersi claimed that the land belonged to her. The complainants and defendant were not ready to compromise before the village dorbar. The village dorbar referred both parties to the dolloi, and finally the matter was settled and judgement went in favour of Mrs Ersi Chyrmang, since she had produced legal documents issued by the district council courts.

The location of the conflict was Lumsashram Bri-Sutnga, falling under the Sutnga Elaka, and so the final judgement was delivered by the Dolloi of Sutnga Elaka. The verdict was in favour of Mrs Ersi Chyrmang.

(Fieldwork 2014)

Case 3:

The disputed parties were *Mrs. Neh Bareh v. Mr. Bas Bareh*. The dispute concerned coal-mining. Mrs Neh owns agricultural land and has titled deed, and due to mining activities nearby, her land had become unfit for cultivation. Mr Bas extracts coal from his land, and through rat-hole mining reaches into the land of Mrs Neh. Mrs Neh asked Mr Bas to stop extracting coal from her land but he refused. Mrs Neh sued Mr Bas, filing a case in the District Council Court without consulting the village dorbar. Mrs Neh defended that the land belongs to her by presenting the legal documents so that she should get justice.

The location of the land is Wohwan Jalaphet Bri-Sutnga, falling under the Sutnga Elaka. Finally, the settlement was restored and the judgement went in favour of Mrs Neh. Mr Bas had to pay compensation and the District Council (civil court) disposed of the case.

(Fieldwork 2014)

Case 4:

Mr. Shil Chyrmang v. Mr. Seril Chyrmang: the matter of dispute was family property. The disputed site was at Mynthning, falling under the Sumer Patorship. Mr Shil and Mr Seril are brothers. Mr Shil is older than Mr Seril, controls the major share of the inherited properties and has extracted a huge amount of coal. He was not ready to allow his younger brother ownership of a few properties. One day, the younger brother, Mr Seril, waited silently at night for his brother. When Mr Shil was visiting his wife's home, his younger brother attacked him and Mr Shil died on the spot. The first information report (FIR) was filed at Khliehriat Police Station. The police tried to arrest Mr Seril but he fled from the village. The village dorbar of Mynthning was reluctant to help the police as they treated the subject as a family issue. The police searched for him for some time but have not followed up the case.

(Fieldwork 2014)

Case 5:

Miss. Sil Syrti v. Mr. Jrom Syrti: This dispute was concerning inheritance of property. Miss Sil and Mr Jrom were living in Urshuni, in Jalaphet village. They are siblings. According to the Jaintia tradition, the youngest daughter of the family inherits all the property. In the past, a majority of the people respected this tradition. An elder member of the family, uncle or brother, who plays a big role in managing the family assets, would transfer all the property to the youngest.

The conflict of interest started between Miss Sil and Mr Jrom as they are the youngest daughter and son of the family respectively. Mr Jrom started extracting coal by mining on the family property. He claimed he should have equal right to family property, but his sister Miss Sil was not happy with his claim and she claimed that according to tradition, she should inherit the entire property. Mr Jrom continued to extract coal, paying no heed to his sister. Miss Sil killed her brother, Mr Jrom. Many people witnessed the incident, but the village did nothing to arrest her. No police complaint was filed. The village dorbar closed the matter, stating that it was a personal issue and not their concern.

(Fieldwork 2014)

Case 6:

Mr. Liwing v. Jalaphet Village: a dispute over community land. The land is located at Kyrluh and belongs to the Jalaphet village community. Mr Liwing, from Mynthlu village, sold the land to a businessman from another village for the purpose of mining. The village headman of Jalaphet opposed the move and told Mr Liwing that the land belonged to the village community. Mr Liwing, a headman of Mynthlu village, moved forward and laid claims over the land. Though Jalaphet village repeatedly summoned him to settle the matter, he refused to appear. One day he came to Jalaphet to talk about the disputed land. He had an escort of around 6–7 policemen. The talk ended inconclusively and the villagers got angry and dragged him from the stage in front of the security guards and beat him badly along with one of his friends. The police just watched the drama. When it became dark, thousands of people dragged him about 3–4 kilometres from the village and threw him and his friend into Krem Mahin (a cave in Rysong forest), which has a depth of over 100 metres. Later, Mr Liwing's family from Mynthlu village enquired about him but the villagers told them that they taught him a lesson for what he did to the village community land. The police who escorted him came to the village repeatedly and enquired repeatedly about him but never found his dead body.

The district council court of the Jowai directed the Khliehriat Police Station to arrest the people who were involved. The police arrested six or seven people from the village. The police listed the names of the accused of Jalaphet village on a charge sheet. The villagers of Jalaphet convened a meeting and announced that one person from every household should come to Khliehriat Police Station to protest the arrests and urged that all the villagers should stand united because the case was not individual and was a problem of the village community as a whole. The household who failed to comply with the village order should be thrown out from the village with a fine of Rs.1,000. One day, thousands of villagers came to Khliehriat Police Station and protested and tried to break into the jail and release those who were arrested. But when the police retaliated, many people in the mob ran away and the police managed to arrest seven or eight persons. So altogether 15 or 16 people were put in the jail to face trial and later all were released on bail. The community land remains with the Jalaphet village and is called *sorkari* (common or public). From then onwards, any inhabitant of Jalaphet village could extract coal from the sorkari land but timber could be taken only for non-commercial purposes. The victim's family felt that they were denied justice as the civil court judgement failed to impose severe punishment on the convicted persons.

(Fieldwork 2014)

The foregoing case in particular, but the others here presented too, offers a good example of the problems facing those who would attempt to solve disputes in the Jaintia Hills. The indigenous system outlined in the first six parts of this text does not function necessarily in the idealised manner in which it was there described, and often finds itself at odds with the modern institutions, in this case with the police, who are often mistrusted and considered to be a jurisdictional imposition. This distrust manifests itself in non-cooperation (as in Case 4), or even open hostility (as in Case 6).

Thus the cases presented earlier reveal a number of problems with the traditional conflict resolution system of the Jaintia. There are times when the system breaks down into what can be described only as brutal and violent incidents of vigilante justice, which are not of course limited only to the Jaintia, but could be true of other systems which do not have a fully fledged law-enforcement capacity. Case 5, which ended in fratricide, serves as a warning of how, at times, the system as it currently stands is not necessarily able to avoid bloodshed, nor is it willing to condemn it, as to do so might limit the reconciliatory ethos of the whole system, of attempting to keep the past incident in the past, and not allow it to disturb the peace of the present or of the future. To deal with this situation would be to cause more disquiet among more people than it would be to placate the cries for justice from others.

Advantages and disadvantages of customary law courts and formal law courts: a summary

Table 12.3 Advantages and disadvantages

	Village Courts (Dorbar system and customary law)	*District Council Courts (Formal laws)*
Advantages	1) Hearing of the case proceeds very fast. 2) Before judging a dispute, the property in question is visited and properly scrutinised, with strong witnesses and village community representation. 3 It allows females to hear the case. The case can be dissolved in the village courts or at the disputed site and if both parties compromise, the case can be dissolved on its own then and there.	1) A fair trial is conducted. 2) Women are allowed to participate in hearing any disputed case, and are allowed to judge cases and serve as advocates.
Disadvantages	1) Females are not allowed to be a member of the village dorbar. 2) There exists a gender gap. In some cases, the judgment of the village dorbar can be partial. 3) The village headman is very powerful, and has influence over the decisions that are made. There is the possibility that he may exert some influence to win the thma (war), or delay the trial case in the village court. 4) The system is not free from bribery.	1) A lot of time is taken. 2) A lot of money is spent. 3) Cases may take a very long time to be dealt with.

Source: Fieldwork 2014

Concluding remarks

The ADC continues to function as a constitutional entity. It manages resources and is engaged in the codification of customary laws, particularly in the wake of the rapidly changing practices in society. However, its record of accomplishments has given rise to certain misgivings in most quarters. Through the years, the ADC has adopted a more populist outlook and this has diluted its role of protecting, promoting and preserving tribal customs, usages and traditions, as they maintain all legal documents of the people (Government of Meghalaya 2009). The purpose of the dorbar is to secure the welfare of the village community in a democratic manner. But it is observed that the village members headed by the rangbah shnong have a tendency to fall prey to bribery as they are rendering their services free of cost. There are instances where the systems of traditional institutions have misused their power when issuing of residential and no objection certificates to non-tribals. Identifying some of these loopholes of the traditional institutions, the local government proposed a bill to be introduced and for the codification some of the customary laws of the tribals: the Village Administration Bill, 2014. However, while this bill has passed for the Jaintia Hills, it is yet to pass for the Khasi Hills. Also, the traditional institutions and conflict resolution are subjected to poor auditing, a lack of monitoring, the poor maintenance of written records, the presence of uneducated members and the absence of women members in the village dorbar, all of which can be counted as significant shortcomings. In order to maintain transparency with regards to the role and functions of the village chiefs the government maintained that it would offer a sum of Rs.5,000 per month to any member of the village who is inducted to the post of a village headman. The entire village disagreed with the proposal since it would make them fall under the Right to Information Act of 2005.

The village community that elects the members should monitor activities carefully and audit the village funds from time to time with proper documentation, and there should be regular meetings to see if the village funds and various governmental schemes are implemented correctly. If this were to happen, then traditional institutions could effectively coexist with the modern trappings of governance, as they try cases very fast without incurring a lot of expenditure for the parties involved. Poor people can benefit a lot from this system of conflict resolution. Apart from the foregoing, attention must be paid to the democratisation of the functions of traditional institutions, especially with regard to gender representation in the village court. The dollois have varying levels of influence, although they are not recognized constitutionally and their demand for such recognition may be considered if these institutions are democratised and representative of all groups, instead of being exclusive entities.

In order to better recommend changes in policy, we are trying to understand the situation and see whether the kinds of policies we have followed are actually working satisfactorily. This chapter suggests that the functions of traditional institutions and ADCs are inadequate. Democratic governance is being hindered in the state as the chiefs of our traditional institutions are exerting undue influence over the people and misusing their power at the time of district council or assembly elections. Traditionally, the dolloi should be a practitioner of the traditional tribal religion, but currently he may profess another religion but should be from the same clan. Seeing as this tradition has been broken and it is possible to induct a dolloi from other religions to be the chief of an elaka, then why can't women be inducted into the village dorbar as well? The village dorbar needs to be readdressed and allow women to exercise their rights. The induction of women would balance the gender gap and go some way to achieving quality and social justice.

Notes

1 (1) Nartiang Elaka, (2) Jowai Elaka, (3) Nongbah Elaka, (4) Nongjngi Elaka, (5) Raliang Elaka, (6) Mynso Elaka, (7) Shangpung Elaka, (8) Sutnga Elaka, (9) Nongphyllut Elaka, (10) Lakadong Elaka, (11) Amwi Elaka and (12) Nongtalang Elaka.

2 The word is derived from the Khasi word '*mynsiem*', which refers to the unity of people.

3 While the Khasi spell it as lyngdoh, the Jaintia spell it langdoh.

4 A langdoh is an elected official of the clan to whom the management of affairs pertaining to traditional religion is assigned.

5 The dorbar is just like a panchayat, a grassroots-level of local self-government.

6 The Panchayati Raj has been established in all the states of India by acts of the state legislatures to build democracy at the grassroots level. It was made nationally binding through the 73rd Constitutional Amendment Act of 1992.

7 (1) The Gram Panchayat at the village level, (2) Panchayat Samiti at the block level and (3) Zilla Parishad at the district level. These tiers were originally linked though indirect election. The village Panchayat should be constituted directly of elected representatives whereas the Panchayat Samiti and Zilla Parishad should be constituted of indirectly elected members.

8 The Garo Hills Autonomous District Council seated at Tura covers the East Garo Hills Districts, the West Garo Hills District and the South Garo Hills District, as well as the more newly formed North and South-West Garo Hills Districts; the Khasi Hills Autonomous District Council seated at Shillong covers the East Khasi Hills, South-West Khasi Hills, Ri-Bhoi and the West Khasi Hills Districts; and the Jaintia Hills Autonomous District Council seated at Jowai covers the Jaintia Hills, both East and West.

9 The villages in Jalaphet Bri-Sutnga are: Pyrdung, Mooshood, Thana Mulait and Lumsashram; villages in Bri Sumer: Poh Lakba, Urshuni, Shur Shur, Lumpathoi and 7 Kilo.

References

Chib, S.S. 1984. 'Meghalaya, Caste, Tribes and Culture of India', in Shed Sethi (ed), *North-Eastern India*. New Delhi: ESS.

Choudhury, D.R. 2005. 'Autonomous District Councils and Panchayati Raj Institutions in North-East India', *Dialogue*, 7(1): 91–101.

DONER and NEC. 2008. *North Eastern Region Vision 2020*. Volume 1. New Delhi: Ministry of Development of North Eastern Region.

Gassah, L.S. 1998. *Traditional Institutions of Meghalaya: A Case Study of Dolloi and His Administration*. New Delhi: Regency.

Government of Meghalaya. n.d. West Jaintia District, http://meghalaya.gov.in/megportal/district_details/14798.

Government of Meghalaya. 2009. *Meghalaya State Development Report, 2008–09*. Shillong: Planning Department, Government of Meghalaya.

Hoda, J. 2007. *Report on the Public Hearing in Agartala: Peace, Progress and Prosperity to the Northeastern Region: Vision 2020*. New Delhi: Ministry of Development of North Eastern Region and North Eastern Council.

Joshi, H.G. 2004. *Meghalaya Past and Present*. New Delhi: Mittal.

KHADC. n.d. *The United Khasi-Jaintia Hills District (Administration of Justice) Rules, 1953* , http://khadc.nic.in/judiciary_department.htm.

Kumar, R. 2008. *Political Science XI*. New Delhi: Dorling Aindersley.

Lamare, Shobhan N. 2005. *The Jaintias: Studies in Society and Changes*. New Delhi: Regency.

Laxmikanth, M. 2013. *Indian Polity for Civil Services Examinations*. New Delhi: McGraw Hill Education (India).

Mohrmen, H.H. 2015. 'Jaintia Hills: Migration According to Clan Accounts', *The Shillong Times*, 13 April.

Prakash, V.C. 2007. *Encyclopedia of North-East India*. New Delhi: Atlantic.

Rani, A.W. 2014. 'Autonomous District Councils in Meghalaya: Fifth Wheel', *The Shillong Times*, 15 March.

Rao, G.V., Mukherjee C., Bhasin A., Barua A., Anand M., Pandey R., and R. Srinivasan. 2011. *Vision Document for The State of Meghalaya 2030*. Delhi: National Institute of Public Finance and Policy.

Rymbai, R.T. 2002. 'Culture Affinities between the Khasis and Jaintias', in P.C. Sarma (ed), *Traditional Customs and Rituals of North-East India*. Guwahati: Vivekananda Institute of Culture.

13 Pathalgadi Movement and Conflicting Ideologies of Tribal Village Governance

Anjana Singh

Introduction

On 21 February 2018, Khunti district police forces entered the Kurunga village, 51 kilometres away from the district headquarters at Khunti, and arrested the *Gram Pradhan*(Village Headman) Sagar Munda. He was charged for doing *Pathalgadi* (erection of stone slabs) on the boundary of village on which a 'misleading' interpretation of constitutional rights of *Gram Sabha*(GS)(village assembly) were inscribed, by which outsiders were prohibited from entering the village. It was declared that no central or state laws were applicable in the village. Local administration obviously deemed this act unlawful. Sagar was brought to Khunti police station and, after an interrogation, the police force numbering 35 again went to Kurunga. This time the villagers responded differently and the policemen were taken hostage by the villagers for trespassing into their area. They were however released after the District Collector and Superintendent of Police of the district gave in writing that they would not enter these areas without the permission of the GS. Sagar Munda was brought back and handed over to them the same day.[1] This was not however the solitary instance. Similar incidents had occurred in August 2017 when 300 policemen were taken hostage in Kanki village of Khunti district. These events can be interpreted as responses of the villagers to the supposed denial of the traditional as well as constitutional right of the Adivasis by the state government.

There was another aspect to the story. This was to lodge a protest against the lack of development of the region by the state. Geeta Samad, the Mukhiya (headmen) of Kurunga village, gave vent to popular frustration:

> *Gaon mein ab bhi vikas ki kiran nahi pahunchi hai. Log chahte hain ki gaon mein vikas ho. Abhi bhi gaon ke log payjal ke liye karunga nadi ke pani par nirbhar hain. Koi bimar pad jaye to Arki ya Khunti ke svasthya*

DOI: 10.4324/9781003299561-13

> *kendra jana padta hai, gaon tak pahunchne ka rasta jarjar hai Gaon ke logon ko malum hi nahi hai ki bahar ki duniya mein kya chal raha hai.*

English translation: Village has not seen the ray of development. People want that village should develop. People of Kurunga village are still dependent on Kurunga River for water. If someone gets sick then he has to be taken to either Arki or Khunti health centre. Even the approach road to the village is in a bad shape. People of village are unaware about the developments outside village (*Prabhat Khabar*, 24 February 2018).

It will be very interesting to apprehend why Pathalgadi (see Figure 13.1) should be invoked as an instrument of resurrecting the traditional form of governance? 'Pathalgadi' is a custom of Adivasis where stone slabs are erected to mark occasions of importance. The records of their pasts are enshrined in their oral tradition and cultural symbols. Pathalgadi acts as not only a parameter of tribal identity but also as something capable of addressing the aspirations and interests of the Adivasis, which the state-sponsored development schemes fail to address. In this context, it is notable that the development model adopted in India after independence had no place for socio-cultural factors because it did not have avenues for the involvement of local communities. The development model was premised on centralised rational bureaucratic planning and the implementation of industry-led development that did not suit the development requirements of the tribal and more backward regions. The overall consequence of this model was that the local communities became passive beneficiaries of the state's development policy instead of being active partners. Absence of socio-cultural factors and participative local development structures in the state's policy led to the emergence of politics over conflicting ideologies of development in which local communities resorted to agitational politics over meaningful exchange of resources with the state (Prakash 2001: 228–229).

An empiricist will be tempted to address the events as a simple conflict of ideologies that have originated since the passing of the Panchayati Raj (Extension to Scheduled Areas) Act, 1996 (PESA). But a researcher with hindsight will be tempted to argue that it had been shaped by the history of tribal rural governance as it had developed from the pre-colonial and colonial times to the introduction of the Panchayati Raj (local governance system) post-independence. Enriched by a historical and empirical understanding of the evolving system of tribal village administration, the present chapter seeks to unfold the nature and the spectrum of the conflict, the cause of discontent against the present system of governance, the polarisation of the state and people, and the recent modality of tribal protest drawing legitimacy from an official act, yet using it as a tool against the state itself. These issues will be addressed through four sections of the chapter. The first will attempt to understand the Pathalgadi movement in Jharkhand. The second will critically examine the strategy of constructing a counter narrative and the conflict between the modern and the traditional forms of governance. The third will focus on the conflict of ideologies and their manifestations and analyse the rationale behind popular protest and official policy towards it. And the last will seek to discuss the challenges it poses to the governance of the schedule areas 229).

Figure 13.1 Traditional stone slab depicting the genealogical table in the Bhandra village of Khunti

Understanding the Pathalgadi movement

Pathalgadi movement saw its emergence with the erection of a stone slab on the boundary of village Bhandra of Khunti district of Jharkhand on 9 March

2017 (*Hindustan*, Ranchi, 10 March 2018). Adivasis consider their oral tradition of *Purkha Sahitya* (ancestral literature) and cultural symbols vitally important for them, as they believe that these have been transmitted to them through succeeding generations. For Adivasis, they are embodiments of their living histories that have enclosed the question of their identity rather than creations for entertainment (Tete 2013: 12–13). In the absence of literary traditions, the Adivasi communities normally seek legitimacy from the colonial document, where their customs and traditions are recorded in various papers. They also draw support from their archaeological evidences as *sasandiri* (sepulchral stone), Pathalgadi, and such related customary symbols.

The immediate reason for the erection of the these stone slabs was the recent propaganda made by the Jharkhand government over the issue of development. The government organised a global investor's summit titled 'Momentum Jharkhand' in Ranchi on 16–17 February 2017. It aimed at making the state a hub for investments in mining and industries and a number of Memorandums of Understanding (MoUs) were signed (*Times of India*, 19 May 2017).[2] Chief Minister of Jharkhand Raghubar Das claimed that, 'MOUs worth 3 lakh crore was signed during the Momentum Jharkhand meet. Out of which, proposals worth Rs. 700 crore [7,000 million] have already been implemented on the ground'[3] (*Times of India*, 18 June 2017). Most of the investments were in the mining sector and companies as Usha Martin group, RSB group, Tata Steel Growth Shop (TGS), and others showed interest. In the wake of these announcements, Adivasis were alarmed that they would be victimised and their lands would be taken away to promote these activities.[4] The fear of land alienation mounted when it was announced by the government that the government would create conducive environment for investment in the state. The Adivasi fear of appropriation of land for the government-sponsored scheme triggered the Pathalgadi movement.

Since its inception, the popular protest gradually spread to the Ranchi, Khunti, and Saraikela districts and mineral rich and industrially viable areas as Ghatsila, Ruasol, Maubhandar, and Galudih in East Sinhbhum. In Khunti, the major areas are Ulihatu, Bhandara, Konwa, Kurunga, Kochang, and others. The stone crushers of these places supply building materials which are in great demand in the neighbouring city of Ranchi (*Hindustan*, Ranchi Live, 25 February 2018). The piece of stone slab erected on the boundary of Bhandara village mentions the provisions of the constitution namely Article 13(3)(a),[5] Article 19(5)(6),[6] Article 244(1)(b), para 5(1)[7] of the Fifth Schedule. Apparently, they were conflating Adivasi custom, symbolised by the erection of a vertical piece of stone as done in *sasandiri*, with the Fifth Schedule of the Indian constitution inscribed on it. However, in reality it was pregnant with deeper meaning. To understand its significance, I would like to quote the contents of the stone inscription and the relevant provisions of the constitution. Here, instead of a verbatim reproduction of the constitution, we notice that the words are differently presented. This change of words may be explained as a counter strategy evolved by the socially marginalised and dominated groups as against the dominant trend of the distortion of the 'historiography of class struggle … in a state-centric way' by the state and ruling class (Scott and Kerkvliet 1990: 5) (Figure 13.2).

Figure 13.2 Pathalgadi movement stone slabs erected on the boundary of the village

English translation of the declaration on the slab

1 By Article 13 (3)(a) of Constitution of India, custom or tradition is the force of law (i.e., power of constitution).

2 By Article 19(5) prohibition is imposed on entry of outsider or noncustom individuals to freely, roam, reside, stay or settle in fifth schedule district or area.

3 By the constitution of India Article 19(6) prohibition is laid on outsiders to carry trade, business and seek employment in this area.
4 Under the fifth schedule area or districts according to Article 244(1) part (b) para (5)(1) no general law of centre or state is applicable.

By Orders
Gram Sabha – Bhandra

The Pathalgadi movement appears to be a well-planned movement as conceptualised and spearheaded by Adivasi Mahasabha. Their objective is to mobilise the Adivasis on one platform around a customary practise common among many tribal communities[8] in the state (*Hindustan*, Ranchi, 14 March 2018). Contrary to this version, media reports claims that the entire programme of creating Adivasi leadership was designed in the training camps of Adivasi Mahasabha and its detail plan was prepared by Benjamin Bara who is a faculty in the Xavier Institute of Social Science (XISS), Ranchi, the leading management institute of the state(*Hindustan*, Ranchi, 14 March 2018). Apparently, since all of them are Christian by faith, the Bharatiya Janata Party, the ruling party of Jharkhand, allege that the movement is mentored and economically supported by the Church administration of the state. But Bishop Telesphore Bilung brushes aside this allegation as fanciful (*Dainik Bhaskar*, Ranchi, 5 March 2018). Adivasi Mahasabha, a political outfit, was built on the initiative of Ignace Beck, the *Chota Nagpur Unnati Samaj*, *Chota Nagpur Catholic Sabha*, and the *Hor Malto Marang Sabha* in 1938. In 1939, *Marang Gomke* (Supreme Leader) Jaipal Singh joined this party and took the leadership in its own hands. From its inception, Adivasi Mahasabha had twin objectives, the first being statehood of Jharkhand and the second being the protection of the Adivasis against the exploitation by outsiders and colonial state (Tirkey 2002: 62–73). Since the formation of the state on 15 November 2000, the party has been relegated to the background in electoral politics. Presently, its leadership is in the hands of educated Adivasis as Joseph Purty alias professor, who is a faculty in St. Joseph College, Torpa, Vijay Kujur, the Deputy General Manager in Shipping Corporation of India, Krishna Hansda, Babita Kacchap and Powell Tuti (*Dainik Bhaskar*, Ranchi, 22 February 2018; *Hindustan*, 19 March 2018, *Hindustan* 20 March 2018).

The movement has varying demands of a generic and specific nature. Adivasi Mahasabha and its leaders avow that the salient purpose of the movement is to diffuse consciousness among the Adivasis about their rights. It is crucial to know how they define the source of their rights. First, instead of drawing legitimacy from the Indian Constitution, the legal basis of rights accruing to an Indian citizen, they refer to an unspecified contract with the British. They also invoke colonial legacies such as the land revenue rule

1921, Gandhi-Irwin pact 1931, and Government of India Act 1935 (Ibid.). Leaders indulge in spreading the idea amongst the Adivasis that the SAs of Jharkhand are not a part of the government of India but that of the British Empire, which had allowed the Adivasis free existence. Through the strategy of the misrepresentation of history, they further contend that the rules framed by the constitution of India are not applicable in the SA as they have not been approved by either the Privy Council of Britain or the Parliament of Britain (Ibid.). They couple this by superimposing natural laws, explained later, which they put above state and central laws (Ibid. 12 March 2018).

After defining the source, protagonists specify their inventory of rights. The spell of demands is premised on the claim that they are the owners of Jharkhand (*Hindustan*, 8 March 2018). The following question arises: How does this ownership accrue to the Adivasis? We can draw on Asoka Sen (2018: Chap III, 76–83) to understand the basis of their argument. Territorial control is established by two processes, 'rights of occupation' and 'rights of conquest.' Here the referents are nature and British rule. Accordingly, rights of occupation are derived from the historical occupation of the unoccupied forested tracts of Jharkhand by the Munda tribe since the 6th century AD as a matter of natural right. They reinforce this claim by their imagery of a creation myth, according to which the land is *Singbonga*'s creation, and their right of occupation accrues as a divine gift. Accordingly, the Mundas became the *khuntkattidars* (clearers of primeval forest) over large swathes of Chotanagpur plateau region. The other, the right of conquest, refers to the British conquest of the tribal region of Jharkhand. The territory the British conquered devolved on them, by virtue of transfer of power referred to earlier. Since they are the real owners, GS has the right to issue currency notes, open schools, issue identity cards as *Aadhar* card and caste, income, and residential certificates. What this inventory of demands foregrounds is the prized position of the GS. This problematises the very concept of GS. This will be disentangled in the next section.

Juxtaposition of the traditional and modern forms of village governance

The protagonists of the movement juxtapose traditional and modern forms of village governance. Therefore, information empirically derived need to be replenished by an engagement with memory and history, the two principal sources for adducing an indigenous tradition. But there is a problem. Pierre Nora (1989: 8) writes, 'Memory and history, far from being synonymous, appear to be now in fundamental opposition.' In reconstructing the institutional framework of village governance, one is handicapped by paucity of information about the origin and growth of an indigenous form of self-rule. Adivasis of Jharkhand formed a pre-literate community having no written records of how the village administration functioned. Even the colonial records, which form the main source of information about the ethnic groups, fall short of our expectations. This was so because these had been written mainly by the British officials and Christian missionaries either for ethnographic or administrative use (Ranendra 2008: 12). However, we are aware that village old men had been the socially accepted custodians of Adivasi village tradition and history, which survived as a kind of social memory (Sen 2015: 27). But the reality is that the surviving memories of the customary and traditional rights of the Adivasi are not relied upon by local officials. In practise they are completely ignored when tribal villagers claim rights on the basis of their traditions. Michel Foucault (1974: 11) cautions us against the failure to preserve and honour 'the living, fragile, pulsating "history" of the pre-literate group of people.'

S. C. Roy's famous book on the Mundas published in 1912 (Roy 1970) presents a dependable and more or less detailed account of the system of village governance in Chotanagpur plateau during pre-colonial times. Understandably, his sources were the memory of the old system as related by the village old men and the author's personal observation of the institution in function. The ideology of the traditional form of village governance was laid down after the Mundas reclaimed the virgin forests of Jharkhand and founded their *hatu* (village) and later *Khuntkatti Hatu* (village of the family of original settlers) (Hallett 1917: 22–23; Roy 1970: Chapter III). The dominant idea of Adivasi polity was of pre-state village republics (Sen 2018: 83). The whole village acknowledged the chiefship of the Munda in matters temporal as well as spiritual (Tirkey 2002: 39). They grouped themselves in wider brotherhood of villages termed *Parha* or *Patti* and laid the foundation of a supra-village pre-state tribal polity headed by the Manki. The village was governed by the traditional panchayat which was composed of the Munda and the *Pahan* (religious head) among others. (Hallett 1917: 22–24; Tirkey 2002: 40–41). Originally, Adivasi settlements were autonomous and the Parha Panchayat governed their life and resources. It was observed during fieldwork that some stone slabs mentioned about the *Rurhi Pratha Prakritik Gram Sabha* (traditional natural village assembly) of the village which had issued the rules stated previously.[9] This means that the Adivasis hold that they derive their power and authority from the nature and customary social institution. But the remarkable fact is that instead of the traditional parha-panchayat, Adivasis mention the GS. This is the juxtaposition of the tradition (i.e., the former) and the modern (i.e., the latter) rather the custom and constitution. But to know why the GS became relevant for Adivasis, it is important to understand the reinvention of the institution of village governance on timeline.

The original *Parha Panchayat* system underwent several changes after the advent of the feudal rule of the Chota Nagpur rajas in the plateau region (Sen 2018: 114). The *patti* or *parha panchayat* were still there but had become subservient to the new structure (Tirkey 2002: 44). In the colonial period, whatever survived was amalgamated within the Raj administrative framework in which the villages lost their existing autonomy. But as a unit of colonial bureaucracy, it wielded the power to collect revenue, administer justice, and maintain law and order (Sen 2018: 118–123).

After independence, the state (Bihar) and the central government introduced the Panchayati Raj System to govern Indian villages, including those of the SAs. The most historic step in this direction was the passing of the separate Act for the SAs, titled PESA (Panchayats Extension to Scheduled Areas) Act by the Parliament on 24 December 1996. The PESA provides for the formation of elected GS (or panchayat at the appropriate level). The GS has been vested with the command over natural resources in the village including the minor minerals, water bodies, the minor forest produce and the power to control money lending. No mining lease can be granted without prior consultation with the GS (Sundar 2005: 4432). The act stipulates that the legislation on the Panchayats in the Fifth Schedule area shall be in conformity with the customary laws, social and religious practices, and traditional management practice of the community resources. It also makes prior consultation with the GS mandatory before any acquisition of land in the village and resettlement and rehabilitation of the project affected persons in the village.[10] On the basis of these provisions, Jharkhand passed the Jharkhand Panchayati Raj Act (JPRA) 2001. The government amended the Act three times in 2003, 2005, and 2010[11] to surmount the legal challenge and social discontent. Accordingly, Panchayat elections were held in 2010 and 2015. Thus, the Parha-Panchayat system has been relegated in the background and the GS has been constitutionally recognised as the legitimate agency of regulating and overseeing village governance in SAs.

During a recent tribal protest, through the juxtaposition of the tradition and modernity, agitators drew legitimacy from an officially created agency, yet used it as a tool against the state itself. The strategy is to deploy it as a parallel institution of village governance armed with new powers and jurisdictions which the aforementioned inventory of demands claim. The counter ideology of development detailed in the next section.

Pathalgadi movement: the conflict of ideologies

In the midst of the Pathalgadi movement my fieldwork[12] revealed that it was basically anchored on alternative ideologies of village governance[13] and development. It is shaped by their perception of the prevailing system of governance and the endemic backwardness of the region and people mainly because of its dysfunction. The main objective of the agitators was to highlight the issue of non/mal-development through the official agencies. The fulcrum of the movement was therefore to focus on the salience of development through the invented indigenous institution of rural governance. But before detailing their development-related demands, it is imperative to apprehend the Adivasi notion of development and change.

The Adivasis had their parallel discourse of development as adduced from the statement made by Sambit Topno, a Gram Pradhan (elected representative) in Ranchi on 4 April 2018 in a meeting convened by Draupadi Murmu, the Governor of Jharkhand. He averred: '*vikas ki bahari vichardhara hum par kyun thopi ja rahi hai. Sarkar Gram sabhaon se puchkar vikas kyun nahi karti hai* (Why is outsider ideology of development being imposed on us. Why doesn't government ask Gram Sabhas for the development).' This highlights that the ongoing scheme of development is extraneous and that Adiviasi's have their own notion of development which the state should adhere (*Hindustan*, Ranchi, 4 April 2018). During conversations with the villagers, I observed that they are averse to *Diku* (outsider) ideology and gave more importance to their traditional Panchayats, which are more sensitive to the ideas and aspirations of the people.

Two recent studies reveal how the concept of development has evolved over time. Adivasis imagine that the development schemes should originate at the local level as a social initiative, and that the social cost of development should be minimal (Sen 2018: 188–190). Furthermore, their voice should be heard while policies are framed and implemented at the local level. Adivasi perception has been that if the funds for the development of village are given to traditional Panchayats then real development would take place at the grass root level. If these institutions are strengthened and proper education is imparted for strengthening of these traditional institutions, then the Adivasi society would feel safe and realise that its traditions and customs are given respect by the ruling sections of the country (Sinku 2008: 128–129).

One should reason why Adivasis are opposed to the existing idea of development. The principal reason is that state-sponsored development has a strong bias towards mining, industrialisation, and urbanisation. This has rendered them victims rather than beneficiaries of development projects. Consequently, the percentage of their population is on constant decline in Jharkhand, as mining and industrialisation have attracted large number of outsiders to the state who have gained increasing control over the levers of political power and resources. The population of the Adivasis that was around 50 percent in 1901[14] came down to 26.3 percent by the 2001 Census (Corbridge 2003:156) and then to 26.2 percent according to 2011 census. This has whetted up a sense of fear that is channelled into anti-government feelings amongst Adivasis. Even during the course of the Jharkhand movement, which aimed at the creation of a separate state, the region was projected more as a cultural region than a mere political entity with a distinct identity (Adivasi), language form, cultural traits, elements of material culture, and historical development (Tirkey 2002: 243). These aspirations remained unfulfilled years after the formation of a separate state and the crisis accentuated by the problem of land alienation cited earlier.

Selective attributes like identity and self-determination have been articulated through various popular movements (Xaxa 1999), which revolve around the specificity of their landscape, against their non-development and marginalisation (Xaxa 2010; Sen 2018: Chap 10). In fact, this has been the principal reason why most of the movements in the SAs of Gujarat, Madhya Pradesh, Orissa, and others are for the safeguard of their landscape to which Adivasis are materially and morally linked. At the pan-Indian level, they worked on a more ambitious programme of building Adivasi solidarity and developed into a larger movement of the creation of Adivasi subnationalism.[15] A situation has therefore emerged which has rather posed a challenge before Adivasi society either to find a way towards re-structuring itself in accordance with the 'modern' ethos of democracy or strive to sustain the 'tradition' at the cost of its own peril. While several attributes from 'tradition' are worth preserving, changing society (and the discriminatory practices in customary system) entails the need to adopt democratic institutions (Kumar 2014: 64). A similar conflict of ideologies in the Pathalgadi movement is visible.

The key geographic locations of the Pathalgadi movement had been those where Naxalism[16] was very strong earlier, as reported by a newspaper (*Hindustan*, Ranchi, 26 Feb 2018). In fact, the entire Adivasi-dominated regions in Jharkhand saw the emergence of Maoism. Adivasis had no idea of Maoism or its basic ideology, but a favourable response to it was seemingly a way to vent their anger and protest against the failure of the state to remove their backwardness and systematic marginalisation. Adivasi disenchantment with the nationalist discourse of development is visible in the formation of what has been identified as 'Red Corridor.'[17] Gudavarthy (2013: 70) argues that the Maoist movement has, through the use of counter-violence, stalled the entry of multi-national companies and has succeeded in stopping any mining activity that involves the displacement of tribal people from proceeding ahead. In beginning with this rather condensed political question, the Maoist movement opened up spaces for political mobilisation and kept the state and capital at bay. It had questioned the legitimacy of the state in monopolising the use of violence to control, govern, and maintain order.

However, the Naxal movement began to lose its sheen slowly in tribal regions because it could not give an answer to their problems in the first place and second, instead stopping mining and industrialisation, the Naxal groups started collecting 'levy' (extortion of money) from the contractors working in the areas and nurtured their political ambitions at the cost of Adivasi sentiments. After the weakening of this movement, Adivasis therefore chose the platform of the GS and social organisations to carry out their struggle (Dungdung 2016: 183–186) for empowerment and challenging the state-sponsored policy of development. Adivasi discourse of development in this way merged into the reinvented institution of village governance symbolised by the GS.

The principal programme of the protagonists of the movement was to put restrictions on the entry of outsiders in the village without the permission of GS,[18] as the latter have been the cause and consequence of the ongoing process of development. This explicates that the protagonists consider Adivasi villages to be autonomous domains; the right of entry is restricted and to be controlled by the GS. Significantly, while choosing the source of legitimacy they deployed the provision of the constitution and not the PESA Act which alone reinforced the concept of *Gram Ganarajya* (Village Republic). But one should ask whether the constitution really accords autonomy to the Fifth Scheduled Areas and puts a blanket ban on the entry of outsiders? The digression seems to be rooted in pre-colonial past when some parts of the Adivasi homeland was *terra incognito* for the outsiders. More so, an outsider could enter and settle in the village founded by the Adivasis on the invitation of the village community headed by the Munda.

Another message is loud and clear. The movement practically seeks to assign the role of the state to the GS in the Pathalgadi villages. But this ignores the fact that drawing power from the Constitution of India and refusing to acknowledge the existence of government is contradictory. In fact, the supporters have tried to challenge the presence of the state. Weekly meetings are organised by the GS at a fixed place between 7.00 and 8.00 a.m. and those matters which have normally gone to courts and police stations since British rule are taken up here. After hearing the matter, a decision is arrived at the GS, and if a person defies its order he/she is ostracised from the village (*Dainik Bhaskar*, Ranchi, 20 February 2018). They have not only taken judicial role in their hand but GS have also appropriated the works of the administration and are issuing character certificates, caste, income, birth, and death certificates (Ibid.). The challenge to the state machinery borders on violence, as mentioned in earlier, by taking police and district officers' hostage and organising *Gheraos* (seige) of police stations (*Hindustan*, Ranchi, 14 March 2018).

In a recent essay, it has been argued (Kumar 2016) that the grassroot Adivasi movements, in their defiance of the authority of the state and subsequent assumption of the role of governance of the village, are trying to be a bargaining instrument with the state where the community intends to gain the maximum advantage. The movements signal their acceptance of the state by subscribing to an 'accepted' means of protest. Displaying their knowledge of the edifice upon which the modern state is built, they draw on the Constitution to legitimise their demands such as the implementation of laws like Schedule V, Article 244, and so on. Cultural symbols and identity issues are highlighted at the same time to bond the society, as society is, more often than not, reluctant to accept change that may be caused due to the impending effects of commodification of land.

Opposition to the state-sponsored scheme of development was the other prominent agenda. Geeta Samad's statement noted earlier articulates the popular resentment and anguish against the ongoing discourse of development. Two more recent instances are the statements of Gram Pradhans made before the Governor of Jharkhand. In one, Sameer Munda said, '*Gaon mein yojna ke naam par sirf dalali ho rahi hai* (In the name of plan only brokerage is done in the village).' In the other, Damu Munda said, '*Tribal sub plan ka paisa dusre madd mein kharch kiya jaa raha hai* (The funds for tribal sub plan is spend for other purposes).'[19] Announcements are made at the village level by GS, which refuses to take help from such government schemes as *Swachh Bharat Abhiyan* (Clean India Campaign), *Indira Awas Yojna* (Indira Housing Scheme), *Rajiv Gandhi Gram Sadak Yojna* (Rajiv Gandhi Village Road Construction Scheme), and others. Claiming the right of the management of educational institutions by the village is the other important step.[20] Villagers are dissuaded from sending their children to the government schools. Announcements are also made in the villages to abstain from the participation in national festivals and approaching government agencies. Attempts have been made to vandalise the foundation stones laid down by the government for different schemes in the village that have remained incomplete in these areas even after long years (*Prabhat Khabar*, Ranchi, 24 February 2018; *Dainik Bhaskar*, Ranchi, 24 February 2018; *Dainik Bhaskar*, 10 March 2018). Initially, only the Fifth Schedule of the Constitution and its favourable provisions for the GS used to be written on one side of the stone slabs painted in green, keeping the other side blank. Now-a-days, on the other side of the stone, the decisions of the GS are being written where voter identity cards and Aadhar cards are declared to be anti-Adivasi documents. It is declared that the Adivasis are not the citizens of India and the lease of nonAdivasi *Diku* government ended in 1969 (*Hindustan*, Ranchi, 26 February 2018).

These forms of protest definitely go beyond the urge of sub-nationalism. Challenge to the mainstream, rather Hindu mainstream, is manifest in the imposition of fines to the tune of Rs. 500 from the villagers for visiting a Durga Puja Mela. With this intention, a meeting was organised at Ulihatu (birthplace of Birsa Munda, famous leader of the Mundas who gave violent resistance to British rule) in South Arki, which was reportedly attended by thousands. The incident of 21 February 2018, cited in the introduction, has become a morale booster for the Adivasis (Ibid.). In this background, Adivasi Mahasabha's declaration to practise Pathalgadi in their respective villages has emerged as a strong wave of resentment against the state, which is absent from all aspects of people-friendly governance and omnipresent in dispossession and exploitation.

The Pathalgadi movement is not however a uniform and encompassing movement. The ideological contradictions in the movement are visible in almost every step taken by the protagonists of the movement. They dismiss the Constitution of India as an alien construct; contrarily they display that GS derives authority from the Fifth Schedule of the Constitution.[21] They arrogate the role of government and yet demand 100percent reservations for Adivasis in government employment, railways, and airways. They put restrictions on the entry of outsiders in their area and passing of even a Ramnavmi procession (Celebration of Lord Rama's birthday) from the village without the permission of GS, but they refuse to accept that their movement outside the village can be restricted on similar logic (*Hindustan*, Ranchi, 26 March 2018). This apparent contradiction is explained by Gladson Dundung, a protagonist of the movement, who bases the logical premise of this action on the argument that, as the entry of Adivasis in certain restricted areas in cities is prohibited for the safety of certain government installations, so the entry of 'outsiders' is restricted in the villages for the safety of *Jal, Jungle, Jameen* (water, forest, and land).[22]

To assume that the entire agenda of the movement is supported by all the Adivasis of the area is also a misinterpretation of facts.[23] In fact, the present nature of Pathalgadi assuming the garb of tradition is questioned by the educated and conscious Adivasi leaders and people. They are not opposed to the development schemes of the government. The Mankis and Mundas of Adivasi villages of other districts of Jharkhand except Khunti are also not in conformity with the present nature of the movement. There is nonacceptance of the demands in some villages of Khunti as well (*Hindustan*, 12 March 2018; *Hindustan*, 14 March 2018; *Dainik Bhaskar*, 27 February 2018). Presumably, the issue has flared up in a very short span of time because all the political parties are trying to take over the leadership of the Adivasis before the next Parliamentary elections. They therefore resort to interpreting history and institutions, and they seek to look at the immediate problem often overlooking the larger issue of poverty and backwardness of the region from the historical perspective.

Responses of the mainstream

The response of the mainstream to the Pathalgadi movement has been ambivalent.[24] NGOs working in these areas, and run particularly by the ideologue activists like Sanjay Bosu Mullick, have been favourable. Pathalgadi, according to Bosu Mullick, is practised only in Mundari Khuntkatti (land that was cleared by primeval settlers) villages of the Khunti district. According to him, in the entire Ranchi and Khunti districts, there are only 156 villages where the communal ownership of land prevails (*Hindustan*, Ranchi, 25 February 2018). He argues that the movement does not target outsiders per se. Rather it is directed against the entry of those outsiders who come to measure the land without the permission of the GS. Measuring land is symbolic of the government's interest in the Adivasi land for putting up projects against the will of the people.

There is yet a section of intellectuals who try to defend the movement. They believe that it is the state that is immune to both the real and perceived 'crisis of legitimacy.' In fact, the crisis of legitimacy understood in terms of democratic practice is seen as a modality, a precondition, through which state absolutism is actualised. This is somewhat akin to capitalism today, which expands in growth and development, not bereft of crisis but precisely because of crisis (Gudavarthy 2013: 71). The movements that are local, autonomous, non-violent, and open define the way we understand democracy today. All this is happening amidst the fact that Adivasi societies are heterogeneous and the entire Adivasi community does not perceive the state similarly. Their action ranges from complete alienation and armed resistance to the strategic use of non-violent methods and customary practices for accruing political benefits.

On the other hand, the newspapers, social media, and regional television, who have given wide publicity to the movement through regular reporting, are more or less critical. They criticise it for conspiring to create a parallel government in the village under the garb of tradition and misrepresentation of the Constitution. The movement, in their perception, is therefore retrograde and anti-development.[25]

The state government has completely brushed aside the professed ideology of the Adivasis and critiqued the Pathalgadi movement for blatant misrepresentation and 'mis'using of the customary laws and traditional practices of Adivasis. No wonder, therefore, has the Jharkhand government dismissed the movement as insignificant, labelled it as anti-development, and resorted to giving advertisements in dailies and billboards, declaring the acts of Pathalgadi illegal and anti-government. As the movement grew and people in the villages of Khunti joined the movement, government agencies imputed that the real motive of the leaders of the movement is more the lure of economic benefits rather than the welfare of Adivasis. In support, the state administration points to the vast stretches of land in the Pathalgadi area used for opium cultivation.[26] It is estimated that opium is cultivated in 2,700 acres of land in Jharkhand, of which 1,500 acres (i.e., almost 58 percent of total area) is in the Khunti district alone.[27] The opium produced is allegedly transported to Punjab, Chennai, Uttar Pradesh, and other parts of India. The administration argues that this has been the main reason is why the leaders are invoking tradition as a shield and propagating the idea of complete autonomy to the villages. No wonder the movement is castigated as a law and order issue. Therefore, the leaders have been charged of secession and their arrests made. In the recent past, Krishna Hansda, Vijay Kujur, Jyoti Lal Besera, and Shaktapado Hansda have been arrested and charged of treason (*Hindustan*, 19 March 2018).

The pressure of the democratic politics however forced the state government and the ruling party to soften their attitude. The Governor of Jharkhand, Draupadi Murmu, called a special meeting of the Gram Pradhans, Manki Munda, and Parha Rajas on 3 April 2018 to discuss the issues of contention in the Scheduled Areas (*Hindustan* Ranchi, 3 April 2018). She honoured them by giving shawls and *Pugries* (turban) and tried to be associated with them by saying that she herself is the daughter and granddaughter of Gram Pradhan and that she therefore understands the social set up of the Adivasis (*Hindustan*, Ranchi, 4 April 2018). However, at the same time, a caution was extended to them to situate their demands within the framework of the constitution. Clearly, the government is conscious of the sensitiveness of the issue of the governance of the Scheduled Areas, the customary rights of the Adivasis, and the perceptible difference in the ideology of development that has been reflected in the course of the movement.

Concluding remarks

Thus, it becomes clear that the Pathalgadi movement has developed as a popular form of Adivasi protest in the Scheduled Areas of Jharkhand where they have more or less lost hope of development through the state. This puts forth two claims of the villagers, the right to be governed by their historically developed distinct form of village governance and the right to be developed as per other developed regions of the country. Undoubtedly, the movement lays bare Adivasi resistance against land expropriation, displacement, and environmental degradation. The movement also underlines the need to formulate and implement a pro-Adivasi and a participatory form of development in which village mechanisms will have a decisive role. In support, historical symbols, tradition, and moments of pride are appropriated. The glorious past of Adivasi heroism and defiance of the authority is referred to create a sense of solidarity amongst the Adivasis. Interestingly, in tandem, the protagonists invoke the Indian Constitution but manipulate it to suit their activism. Clearly, the movement responds to the widespread dissensions within the Adivasi community. But its aggressive and anti-state/nation programme does not receive wide support. In the context of the present movement, the urgent need is the dispassionate reappraisal of the mode of village governance in function after the Panchayat elections so that this may become meaningful and is able to serve the people for which this is meant.

Notes

1 *Dainik Bhaskar*, Ranchi, 22 February 2018.
2 Visit, www.timesofindia.com accessed on 9 April 2018.
3 By May 2017 projects worth 30.5 crore were opened in Bokaro, Gumla and Ranchi. Textile, footwear and apparel park worth 200 crores was opened in Ranchi, Visit, www.timesofindia.com Accessed on 9 April 2018. By August 2017, 74 projects were started in the state which were expected to bring Rs. 2100 crores and generate over 10,000 jobs (*Daily Pioneer*, 5 October 2017), www.dailypioneer.com, accessed on 13 April 2018.
4 My research is based on field study conducted in Bhandra, PhutkalToli, Zillinga, Belahathi, and Kochang villages in November 2017 and February 2018. During personal interviews with the residents of the village, many villagers were refraining from providing information or interacting with the author and they viewed every outsider with suspicion. One of the respondents accused the researcher having personal agenda, i.e. spying for the government and being paid for the job. What was palpable was that the fear of land alienation that was visible in November 2017 had transformed into anger and distrust for outsiders by February 2018.
5 In this chapter, unless the context otherwise requires, 'Law' includes any ordinance, order, by law, rule, regulation, notification, custom, or usage having in the territory of India the force of law.
6 Article 19 (5) of Indian Constitution, 'Nothing in sub clause (d) and (e) of the said clause shall affect the operation of any existing law in so far as it imposes or prevent the state from making any law imposing, reasonable restrictions on the exercise of any of the rights conferred by the said sub clause either in the interest of any scheduled tribe.' Article 19 (6) says, 'Nothing in the sub clause (g) of the said clause shall affect the operation of any existing law in so far as it imposes or prevents the state from making any law imposing in the interest of the general public, reasonable restrictions on the exercise of the rights conferred by the said sub clause shall affect the operation of any existing law in so far as it relates to and prevent the state from making any law.'
7 The provision of the Fifth Schedule shall apply to the administration and control of the Scheduled Areas and Scheduled Tribes in any state other than state of Assam and Meghalaya.
8 There are 32 tribal communities that reside in the state and Pathalgadi movement is strong in Munda Khuntkatti areas of Ranchi and Khunti districts and among the Oraons.

9 Such words as *Rurhi Pratha Prakritik Panchayat* are used on stone slabs of Kochang, Belahathi, Kurunga, and other villages of Khunti. But this is missing from the stone slab of Bhandra village, the place of origin and centre of the movement, shown earlier.
10 The Provisions of the Panchayats (Extension to the Scheduled Areas) Act, 1996, No.40 of 1996 (24 December 1996).
11 Bill No. 93-F of 2010, Original. The Jharkhand Panchayat Raj (Amendment) Bill, 2010. (As Passed by the Houses of Parliament – Lok Sabha on 17 August, 2010, Rajya Sabha on 25 August, 2010).
12 My conversations, group meetings, and personal interviews were carried mostly in the affected areas of Khunti district of South Arki, namely Bhandra, Phutkal Toli, Zillinga, Belahathi, and Kochang between November 2017 and February 2018.
13 The idea of village governance is vague and although researchers and scholars are trying to study the institution of Parha Panchayat, there is no clear idea amongst the Adivasis themselves about the original form and structure of the institution.
14 Jharkhand was a part of Bihar till year 2000 and by 1900 it was part of Bengal Presidency.
15 Sati-Pati movement is a movement to create Adivasi nationalism in India. This organisation has its headquarters in Kathsavana village of Tapi district in Gujarat. It was built by Dada Kunwar Keshari Singh in 1930 and the organisations that adhere to its principles believe that it is the Government of India. Adivasi Mahasabha adheres to it and is active in Jharkhand, Gujarat, Chhattisgarh, Madhya Pradesh, and Rajasthan. The organisations that are also a part of it are 'Adivasi Pariwar Rajasthan,' 'Bhil Autonomous Council,' 'Birsa Brigade, Madhya Pradesh,' 'Sarv Adivasi Samaj, Chhattisgarh,' 'Manjhi Pargana Mahal, East Singhbhum,' and others.
16 An agrarian movement was started from a village called Naxalbari in West Bengal in 1970s.
17 The Naxal-affected states of India which are deeply forested terrain and are primarily inhabited by the Adivasis are known as *red corridor*. The red colour of the flag of Maoists is generally referred to indicate the presence of Naxals in the area.
18 Villagers were interviewed on 15 November 2017 in Bhandra and Zillinga Village; also reported in a newspaper *Dainik Bhaskar,* 10 March 2018, Ranchi.
19 *Hindustan*, 4 April 2018.
20 There are videos on the internet and news in the local and regional dailies that the Adivasis have taken their education into their own hands and teaching the basic idea of protest to their children in these school in Hindi. This blatant overlooking of the indigenous language, which is a store house of the ancestral knowledge and is deeply connected to their ethnic identity, indicates that the motive of the protagonist of the government is to create a semblance of defiance than actually intending to revive their age-old institutions.
21 The speakers of 25 February 2018 meeting of the Adivasis at Kochang village in Khunti expressed these sentiments that were repeated by many in the following days. *Dainik Bhaskar*, Ranchi, 26 February 2018.
22 Gladson Dungdung, 'Pathalgadi aur Pravesh Nisedh', http://saathijohaar.com/2018/04/08/paththargari.html, accessed on 8 April 2018.

23 *Dainik Bhaskar*, Ranchi, 15 March 2018. It was reported that to counter the present movement, a programme was organised in the native village of Jaipal Singh Munda, Takra in Khunti, which was supported by the government. In this programme the heroes of tribal movements of Jharkhand as Birsa Munda were remembered, and their contributions and sacrifices were cited to depict that the present movement negates their contribution, which helped India in gaining independence, by saying that India is not a free state.
24 Mainstream in the present context refers to the non-Adivasis residing in the state, government, media agencies, and NGOs.
25 See Newspapers of Ranchi esp., *Prabhat Khabar*, *Dainik Bhaskar*, *Hindustan*, 20 February; 22 February; 25 February; 26 February; 9 March; 10 March 2018.
26 As reported by *Dainik Bhaskar*, Ranchi on 6 March 2018, Adivasi Mahasabha and its supporters countered this attack by claiming that the illegal opium trade in the state has been practised for a decade, when Naxalism was a strong force in the area, but the movement has started in the last year. *Dainik Bhaskar*, Ranchi, 16 March 2018.
27 *Dainik Bhaskar,* Ranchi, 6 March 2018, it is estimated that almost 30 to 40 kilogram of opium is produced from an acre of land. Each kilo of opium is sold on the international market for Rs. 1,040,000.

References

Bill No. 93-F of 2010, Original. The Jharkhand Panchayat Raj (Amendment) Bill, 2010. (As Passed by the Houses of Parliament – Lok Sabha on 17 August, 2010, Rajya Sabha on 25 August, 2010).

Corbridge, S. 2003. 'The Ideology of Tribal Economy and Society: Politics in the Jharkhand 1950–1980.' In R. Dayal Munda and S. Bosu Mullick (Eds.), *The Jharkhand Movement: Indigenous People's Struggle for Autonomy in India* (pp. 131–170). Copenhagen: IWGIA Document No 108, International Work Group For Indigenous Affair.

Dungdung, G.2016. *Adivasi Aur Vanadhikar: Jharkhand Mein Van Adhikar Ka Jamini Haqueqat*. New Delhi: Prithvi Prakashan.

Foucault, M. 1974. *Archaeology of Knowledge*. London: Tavistock Publications.

Gudavarthy, A.2013, 'Democracy Against Maoism, Maoism Against Itself.' *Economic and Political Weekly*, 48(7), February 16: 69–76.

Hallett,M.G.1917.*Bihar and Orissa District Gazetteers: Ranchi.*Patna: Superintendent, Government Printing, Bihar and Orissa.

Hunter, W.W. 1975. *Annals of Rural Bengal*. New Delhi: Cosmo Publication. Interview with the villagers of Bhandra on 15 November 2017.

Interview with the villagers of Kochang on 17 February 2018. Interview with the villagers of Zillinga on 16 November 2017.

Kumar, S. 2014. 'Interrogating "Integration" in Adivasi Discourse: Customary vs. Democratic Institutions in West Singhbhum, Jharkhand.' *Journal of Adivasi and Indigenous Studies*, I(1), August. ISSN 2394–5524.

Kumar, S. 2016. *Revisiting Anti-Dispossession Resistance Movements*. Available at: www.india-seminar.com/2016/682/682_sujit_kumar.htm, accessed on 13 April 2018.

Nora, P. Spring 1989. 'Between Memory and History: Les Lieux de Memoire.' *Representations*, 26:7–25.

Prakash, A. 2001. *Jharkhand: Politics of Development and Identity*. New Delhi: Orient Longman.
The Provisions of the Panchayats (Extension to the Scheduled Areas) ACT, 1996 No. 40 of 1996 (24 December 1996).
Ranendra. 2008. 'Bhumika: Jharkhandi Itihas Ke Bare Mein.' In Ranendra and S. Pal (Eds.), *Jharkhand Encyclopaedia*, Vol. I (pp. 11–17). New Delhi: Vani Prakshan.
Roy, S.C. 1970. *The Mundas and Their Country*. Calcutta: Asia Publishing House.
Scott, J. 1990. 'Everyday Forms of Peasant Resistance.' In J.C. Scott and B.J.T. Kerkvliet (Eds.), *Everyday Forms of Peasant Resistance in South-East Asia* (pp. 5–35). London: Frank Cass.
Sen, A.K. 2015. 'Reconstructing Adivasi Village History: Problems and Possibilities.' *Journal of Adivasi and Indigenous Studies*, 3(2), August: 16–37.
Sen, A.K. 2018. *Indigeneity, Landscape and History: Adivasi Self Fashioning in India*. New York: Routledge.
Sinku, V. 2008. 'Parampara Ki Svasasi Vyavastha.' In S. Pal (Ed.), *Jharkhand Encyclopaedia*, Vol. III. New Delhi: Vani Prakashan.
Sundar, N. 2005. '"Custom" and "Democracy" in Jharkhand.' *Economic and Political Weekly*, 40(41), October8–14: 4430–4434.
Tete, V. 2013. *Adivasi Sahitya: Parampara Aur Prayojana*. Ranchi: Pyara Kerketta Foundation.
Tirkey, A. 2002. *Jharkhand Movement*. New Delhi: All India Coordinating Forum of the Adivasi/Indigenous People.
Xaxa, V. 1999. 'Transformation of Tribes in India: Terms of Discourse.' *Economic and Political Weekly*, 34(24): 1519–1524.
Xaxa, V. 2010. '"Tribes, Tradition and State", 18, The Focus: "Indigenous" India.' *The Newsletter*, No. 53, Spring.

List of newspapers

Daily Pioneer (digital edition). *Dainik Bhaskar*.
Hindustan. *Prabhat Khabar*.
Times of India (digital edition).

For Product Safety Concerns and Information please contact our EU representative GPSR@taylorandfrancis.com Taylor & Francis Verlag GmbH, Kaufingerstraße 24, 80331 München, Germany